Fearless Rust

Don't Panic!

Freek van Keulen

Fearless Rust

ISBN: 9789083574806 (paperback)
ISBN: 9789083574820 (hardcover)
ISBN: 9789083574837 (eBook)

Cover Design: Melvyn Paulino
Interior Design: Melvyn Paulino

www.rustexpertisecenter.com

Table *of* Contents

Preface

When I first started learning Rust, I was drawn in by its promise: the performance of C or C++ with the safety of a modern, high-level language. What I didn't expect was just how much it would reshape the way I think about code—how it encouraged clarity, discipline, and a deep understanding of what a program is really doing under the hood.

This book grew out of the many trainings I've given over the years, both in-company and open enrollment, to developers who were curious, skeptical, or completely new to Rust. I've seen firsthand where learners get stuck, what clicks, and which examples open the door to real understanding. My goal is to pass that clarity on to you.

Whether you're a systems programmer, a backend developer, or someone with a general programming background looking to level up, this book is meant to guide you through the essentials of Rust in a way that's structured but approachable. It starts from first principles and builds up to concepts like ownership, traits, lifetimes, and concurrency—always with the mindset of making them practical, not abstract.

Alongside this book, I run www.rustexpertisecenter.com, where you'll find additional resources:

- Training sessions for individuals and teams
- Certification
- Code review and consulting services
- And a place to share your feedback about the book

Your thoughts and experiences as a reader are extremely valuable to me. They help shape future editions and improve how we teach Rust in general. Whether you've found a typo, hit a confusing explanation, or simply want to share how the book helped you—please don't hesitate to reach out.

Thanks for reading, and enjoy the journey. Rust has a steep learning curve, but it rewards you with a powerful new way to write and reason about code.

Freek van Keulen
Rust trainer and author

Foundations

01

Variables and Types

In this chapter, we delve into the foundational concepts of **Variables** and **Types** in Rust, focusing on their declaration, usage, and the underlying principles that make Rust unique among programming languages. Rust's approach to these concepts is designed to ensure safety, performance, and reliability, distinguishing it from other languages.

In this chapter, we will cover the following topics:

- **Variables, Constants and Types**: Learn about variables, constants, types, and values in general, and how they work together in a programming language.
- **Variables in Rust**: Understand the syntax for declaring variables in Rust. Explore properties such as mutability, scope, and shadowing associated with Rust variables.
- **Constants in Rust**: Learn the differences between variables and constants in Rust, focusing on their distinct characteristics and uses.
- **Data Types in Rust**: Delve into the basics of Rust's type system, including scalar types like integers, floating points, booleans, and characters. Explore compound types like tuples and arrays, and how to use these types efficiently to handle data.

Through these topics, we'll explore how Rust's handling of variables and types contributes to its goals of efficiency, safety, and concurrency. By the end of this chapter, you should be comfortable working with Rust's type system, understanding the importance of immutability, and utilizing variables and constants to build robust programs.

Technical requirements

To follow the instructions in this chapter, you will need the following:

- A computer with either Windows, Mac, or Linux installed
- Rust 1.86.0 or newer
- An IDE or code editor (For example RustRover, IntelliJ, Visual Studio Code, or Visual Studio)
- The code for the examples and their solutions is available on GitHub at:

https://github.com/mrQuidome/Learning-Rust

Variables, Constants, and Types

In this section, we embark on a journey through the foundational elements of programming: **variables**, **constants**, and **types**. Understanding these components is crucial for any developer, as they form the backbone of coding logic and data manipulation.

Variable

A **variable** is a fundamental concept that represents a storage location in memory, which holds a value that can be changed during the execution of a program. Variables are named entities, and their names are used in the code as symbolic references to the stored values. The use of variables enables programmers to write flexible and dynamic code, as the values of variables can be modified, read, and changed as the program runs.

Constant

A **constant** is a fundamental concept that represents a storage location in memory with a fixed value that cannot be altered during the execution of a program. Unlike variables, which can be assigned new values, constants remain unchanged from their initial assignment. Defining constants is a way to improve the readability and maintainability of code, as they provide a clear, descriptive name for values that have a specific, unchanging meaning within the context of a program.

Type

A **type** is a classification that specifies the kind of value a variable or a constant can hold and the operations that can be performed on that data. Types are fundamental to understanding and organizing the data within a program, allowing the programming environment to allocate the appropriate amount of memory and to perform operations safely and efficiently.

Allowed values

A **type** defines a **domain**, which is a collection of possible values. From this domain, a specific value is chosen to be used. For instance, in Rust, the bool type encompasses just two possible values: true and false. On the other hand, the u8 type includes a domain of 256 distinct values, spanning from 0 to 255.

Allowed operations

Alongside the set of values, a type is also characterized by its interface, the set of operations or behaviors it supports. This interface defines how values of the type can be used, ensuring that all operations are consistent with the type's intended meaning. For example:

- For numeric types (such as integers and floating-point numbers), operations might include addition, subtraction, multiplication, and division.
- For `bool` types, operations typically include logical operations such as AND, OR, and NOT.
- For string types, operations might include concatenation, substring extraction, and length.
- This concludes a general description of variables, constants, and types. We now move on to how these concepts are implemented in Rust.

Variables in Rust

In Rust, variables possess distinctive characteristics that set the language apart, particularly with respect to memory safety, concurrency, and type safety. This section covers the fundamental properties of variables, though it is not exhaustive. Further properties will be explored and added to our discussion later in the book.

Declaration

A variable is declared with the let keyword:

```
let [mut] IDENTIFIER [:type] [= Expression]
```

Ch01/Examples/src/bin/example01.rs

```
let count: i32 = 12
```

The variable is named `count`, has a type of `i32`, and is initialized with the value `12`.

Numbered examples can be found on GitHub. In your IDE, you can load all the examples from a single chapter. The project is named `Chapter01/Examples`. All individual examples are located in the `bin` folder and can be run independently.

Scope

Variables are only accessible within the block they are declared in. A block is a section of code enclosed in braces `{}`. Once the block ends, the variables within that block are dropped, and their memory is freed.

Variables cannot be declared directly in the global scope. While it is possible to achieve global variable-like functionality, these methods are more complex and do not benefit from the usual guarantees provided by the Rust compiler.

Ch01/Examples/src/bin/example02.rs

```
fn main() {
    let mut x = 12;
    x = x + 2;
    {
        let y = x * 2;
        println!("y in inner scope: {}", y);
        println!("x from outer scope: {}", x);
    }
    println!("The value of x is: {}", x);
    println!("y is dropped and no longer accessible")
}
```

Within the main function, an inner scope is established, and this is perfectly permissible. Upon the conclusion of this inner scope, all its values are discarded. Following the termination of this inner scope, the `x` variable from the outer scope remains accessible.

Immutability

In Rust, **immutability** is a core principle that influences the safety and concurrency characteristics of the language. By default, all variables in Rust are immutable. This design choice enforces that once a variable is assigned a value upon initialization, its value cannot be altered. Immutability is a crucial aspect of ensuring memory safety, preventing race conditions in concurrent programming, and promoting functional programming patterns that rely on immutable data structures.

Rust enforces immutability at the compiler level. If you try to modify an immutable variable, Rust will refuse to compile the code, ensuring that immutability guarantees are upheld. This strict enforcement helps catch potential bugs and side effects early in the development process.

Ch01/Examples/src/bin/example03.rs

This does not compile:

```
let count: i32 = 12
count = 14;
```

To make a variable mutable, include the `mut` keyword in its declaration:

```
let mut count: i32 = 12
count = 14;
```

- Understanding the benefits of immutability in Rust is crucial for appreciating its design philosophy and practical advantages. Here are some key benefits of immutability:
- **Predictability**: Code is easier to reason about when you know that values don't change once they've been set. This predictability makes functions and modules more straightforward to understand, test, and maintain.
- **Concurrency**: Rust's ownership model, combined with immutability, makes concurrent programming safer and more accessible. Since immutable values can be safely shared between threads without the risk of data races, developers can write concurrent code with confidence.
- **Optimization**: The Rust compiler can perform optimizations knowing that certain values remain constant throughout their lifetime. This can lead to more efficient execution of Rust programs.

Shadowing

Shadowing in Rust is a feature that allows you to declare a new variable with the same name as a previous variable within the same scope. When you shadow a variable, the new variable takes precedence over the previous one, effectively making the original variable inaccessible and allowing you to reuse the variable name for a new value. This is particularly useful for transforming an immutable variable into another value while still keeping the variable immutable.

Shadowing is accomplished by using the let keyword to declare a new variable with the same name as an existing one. Each time you declare a variable with let, it creates a new variable. If the name matches an existing variable, it shadows the original.

Ch01/Examples/src/bin/example04.rs

```
let count: i32 = 12;
let count: f64 = 24.5;
```

In this example, a second variable is declared using the same name but with a different type, effectively rendering the first instance of `count` inaccessible.

Shadowing in Rust offers several advantages that enhance code flexibility and clarity. Here are some key benefits of using shadowing:

- **Type Transformation**: Shadowing allows the type of a variable to be changed. You can start with a variable of one type and then shadow it with another type. This is useful when you want to convert values.
- **Temporary Immutability**: It enables patterns where a variable is initially mutable for setup or calculation and then made immutable thereafter by shadowing it with an immutable binding.
- **Simplicity**: Shadowing can simplify code that needs to iteratively transform data while keeping variable names consistent and meaningful.

SHADOWING VS. MUTATION

It's important to distinguish between **shadowing** and **mutating**. Mutation changes the value of an existing variable and requires the variable to be mutable (`mut`). Shadowing, on the other hand, creates a new variable, allowing the re-use of the name. This distinction is key in Rust's approach to variable bindings and immutability.

Type Inference

Type inference in Rust is a powerful feature that allows the compiler to automatically determine the types of variables and expressions based on how they are used. This enables developers to write code that is both concise and expressive without sacrificing the safety and performance benefits that come with a strongly typed system.

```
let count = 12
```

Unlike the first `let` statement in this chapter, the type is omitted here. Since integer literals default to the `i32` type, the `i32` type is automatically inferred for the `count` variable.

Type inference is not universally applicable; for instance, specifying types is obligatory when defining functions or structs. The blend of type inference in contexts such as `let` statements, together with the requirement for explicit typing in functions and structs, contributes to code that is both elegant and maintainable.

In Rust, type suffixes are used with literals to specify their type explicitly. This is particularly useful when the type cannot be inferred from the context or when you want to ensure that a literal has a specific type. Here's how you can use type suffixes with integer and floating-point literals.

Rust provides a variety of integer types, both signed and unsigned, across different sizes, as well as two types for floating-point numbers. By appending a type suffix to an integer or floating-point literal, you explicitly define the literal's type.

Ch01/Examples/src/bin/example05.rs

```
let speed_of_light = 299_792_458i64;
let pi = 3.1415f32;
```

The first literal, 299_792_458i64, has a suffix of `i64`, making it an `i64` literal. This causes the type inference for `speed_of_light` to be `i64`, which is the default floating point type, therefore the i64 in this case is redundant. Similarly, the second literal, `3.1415f32`, has a suffix of `f32`, making it an `f32` literal and causing the type inference for `pi` to be f32 instead of the default `f64`.

The underscores in the line let speed_of_light = 299_792_458i64; are just visual separators used to make large numeric literals easier to read. In Rust, you can insert underscores in numeric literals anywhere between digits, and they have **no effect** on the actual value. It's purely for readability, similar to how we write large numbers with commas or spaces in everyday writing.

Initialization

Uninitialized variables are not allowed in Rust due to its focus on safety. Variables must be initialized before use, preventing undefined behavior common in other languages with uninitialized memory.

Initialization can be postponed to a later point, but often, it's unnecessary. This is partly because many control structures, such as `if`, also function as expressions in Rust. While there are scenarios that necessitate delayed initialization, and it is certainly possible to implement, it's generally not required in typical programming practices.

Ch01/Examples/src/bin/example06.rs

```
let value = 10;
println!("The immediate value is: {}", value);
```

In this example, the variable `value` is initialized to `10` in the same statement in which it is declared, which is the standard practice.

Ch01/Examples/src/bin/example07.rs

```
let value: i32;
if some_condition() {
    value = 10;
} else {
    value = 20;
}
println!("The delayed value is: {}", value);
```

Here, `value` is not initialized at the time of declaration; it is initialized within the if statement, both in the then and else parts.

Ch01/Examples/src/bin/example08.rs

```
let value: i32;
if some_condition() {
    value = 10;
}
println!("The delayed value is: {}", value);
```

In this case, initialization only occurs in the then part of the if statement, with no initialization in the else part. This will result in a compile error when the variable is used.

Naming

In Rust, as in many programming languages, choosing meaningful names for variables is crucial for creating readable and maintainable code. Rust adopts and encourages several naming conventions that align with its philosophy of clarity and efficiency.

Composition

Identifiers can consist of a combination of letters, digits, underscores (`_`), and hyphens (`-`), although hyphens are not allowed in regular identifiers but can appear in crate names and other contexts outside the Rust syntax proper.

Identifiers must start with a letter (either uppercase or lowercase) or an underscore. They cannot begin with a digit.

After the first character, identifiers can include any combination of letters, digits, and underscores.

Unicode Support

Rust supports Unicode identifiers, allowing the use of a wide range of characters beyond ASCII. This means you can use letters from non-English languages as identifiers, making the language more accessible to non-English speakers and allowing code to be more expressive in different languages. While Unicode characters are supported in identifiers, certain restrictions apply, excluding some Unicode characters.

Case Sensitivity

Identifiers in Rust are case-sensitive. This means that, for example, `variable`, `Variable`, and `VARIABLE` are three distinct identifiers.

Reserved Keywords

Rust has a set of reserved keywords that cannot be used as identifiers because they have special meaning in the language's syntax. Examples include `fn` for functions, `let` for variable declarations, and `struct` for defining structures. You can find the list of reserved keywords at https://doc.rust-lang.org/stable/reference/keywords.html.

If you need to use a reserved keyword as an identifier (for example, when interfacing with other languages), you can prefix the keyword with an `r#` to create a raw identifier. For example, `r#match` can be used as an identifier even though `match` is a keyword.

Convention

Rust encourages readability and consistency in its codebases through naming conventions, such as using 'snake_case' for variables. While these conventions are not strictly enforced by the compiler, adherence to them is highly recommended to maintain uniformity across Rust projects.

Building on Rust's emphasis on clarity and consistency, constants exemplify another construct that promotes readable and maintainable code.

Constants in Rust

Constants are values that are bound to a name and are immutable. Once set, their value cannot change throughout the execution of a program. Constants in Rust provide a way to use meaningful names for fixed values, enhancing the readability and maintainability of the code.

Variables are immutable by default, whereas constants are immutable by definition.

Declaration

Constants are declared using the `const` keyword, followed by an identifier, a type annotation, and the value. The type must always be provided explicitly.

```
const IDENTIFIER :type = Expression
```

The expression must be computable at compile time, often being as simple as a literal.

Scope

Constants may be declared in any scope, global or local. While the values they hold must have a 'static lifetime (meaning the data they refer to is guaranteed to live for the duration of the program), the constants themselves follow the scope in which they're defined. That is, a constant declared inside a function is only accessible within that function, even though the value it refers to may exist for the program's entire lifetime.

Naming

The naming rules for constants align with those for variables, applying universally to all identifiers in Rust. Descriptive names are, of course, encouraged. The naming convention for constants is SCREAMING_SNAKE_CASE.

Types in Rust

Rust provides a rich set of built-in types, categorized broadly into scalar and compound types. These built-in types are foundational to Rust's type system, offering versatility and safety in handling data across a wide range of applications.

In Rust, the creation of user-defined types mainly revolves around `structs`, `enums`, and `traits`. These tools empower developers to craft data types tailored to their programs' unique requirements, significantly improving code expressiveness and safety. A more detailed discussion of these types will follow later in the text.

Scalar Types

A **scalar type** is a fundamental data type that represents a single value. These types are the building blocks for more complex data structures and are typically used to store basic, indivisible values. In Rust, we have the typical scalar types: integers, floating-point numbers, booleans, and characters.

Integer

Rust provides a comprehensive set of integer types, allowing developers to choose the most appropriate size and sign for their needs, optimizing for memory usage and performance. Integer types in Rust are divided into two main categories: signed and unsigned. Each category has variants determined by their size in bits, which directly affects their range of values.

Signed Integers

Signed integers can represent both positive and negative numbers. Rust offers signed integer types with sizes of 8, 16, 32, 64, and 128 bits, named `i8`, `i16`, `i32`, `i64`, and `i128`, respectively. Additionally, there's `isize`, whose size is platform-dependent: 32 bits on 32-bit architectures and 64 bits on 64-bit architectures.

Unsigned Integers

Unsigned integers can only represent non-negative numbers (zero and positive numbers). Like signed integers, unsigned types come in sizes of 8, 16, 32, 64, and 128 bits, named `u8`, `u16`, `u32`, `u64`, and `u128`, respectively. There's also `usize`, which, similar to `isize`, is platform dependent.

Literals

In Rust, integer literals allow you to specify values of integer types in your code using different notations based on the number's base. Rust supports several kinds of integer literals:

- **Decimal literals** are straightforward and don't require a prefix. They're written as is, similar to what you're used to in most other languages.

```
let decimal = 98_222; // 98222 in decimal
```

Rust also supports the use of underscores in numeric literals for improved readability, as shown above.

- **Hexadecimal literals** are prefixed with `0x`. They're useful for representing values commonly expressed in hex, like color values or bitmasks.

```
let hex = 0xff; // 255 in decimal
```

- **Octal literals** start with `0o`. They're less commonly used but available for scenarios where octal representation is preferred.

```
let octal = 0o77; // 63 in decimal
```

- Binary literals are prefixed with `0b` and allow you to express numbers directly in binary form, which can be handy for bit-level operations.

```
let binary = 0b1111_0000; // 240 in decimal
```

- For `u8` values, Rust provides a special syntax that allows you to specify byte literals directly. Byte literals are written as a byte escape in a byte string or character.

```
let byte = b'A'; // ASCII value for 'A', which is 65
```

This notation is specifically for `u8` and is mainly used for working with byte-oriented operations, such as handling ASCII characters or binary file formats.

Type Suffixes and type Inference

Rust allows you to specify the type of an integer literal by using a type suffix. Without a suffix, Rust defaults to inferring the type based on how the literal is used in the code, defaulting to `i32` if the inference is ambiguous. By adding a type suffix, you can ensure the literal has the specific type you want.

Ch01/Examples/src/bin/example09.rs

```
let x = 42u8;
let y = 24i32;
```

The type of `x` is explicitly specified as `u8`, the type of `y` is explicitly specified as `i32`

The ability to use different bases and to clearly indicate the type of a literal at the point of declaration enhances Rust's flexibility and expressiveness in handling numbers, ensuring clarity and precision in numerical operations and representations.

Floating Point

Rust supports two primitive types for floating-point numbers, which are numbers that can have a fractional part. These types are:

- `f32`: A 32-bit floating-point type (single precision).
- `f64`: A 64-bit floating-point type (double precision).

Precision

`f32` provides approximately 6 decimal places of precision, while `f64` provides about 15 decimal places of precision. This makes `f64` more suitable for calculations requiring higher precision.

Range

`f64` has a significantly larger range than `f32`. This means it can represent both much larger and much smaller numbers.

Performance

The choice between `f32` and `f64` can also depend on the target platform's hardware. For instance, on many modern CPUs, operations with `f64` values are just as fast as those with `f32`. However, using `f32` can save memory, which might be crucial in large arrays of floating-point numbers or on systems with limited memory (such as embedded systems).

Literals

You can write floating-point literals in Rust using the standard decimal notation or scientific notation:

- Decimal notation: `3.14`, `0.1`, `.5` (equivalent to `0.5`)
- Scientific notation: `6.02e23`, `1.47e-32`

The type can be inferred from the context or explicitly specified using a suffix (`f32` or `f64`):

Ch01/Examples/src/bin/example10.rs

```
let x = 2.0;
let y: f32 = 3.0;
```

`x` is inferred to be the default type `f64`, while `y` is explicitly declared as `f32`.

Special Values

Both `f32` and `f64` types can represent a few special values:

- **Positive/negative infinity**: Created by dividing a positive or negative number by 0.0, or as a constant (`std::f32::INFINITY`, `std::f32::NEG_INFINITY`, `std::f64::INFINITY`, `std::f64::NEG_INFINITY`).
- **NaN (Not a Number)**: Represents an undefined or unrepresentable value, such as the result of `0.0 / 0.0`, or as a constant (`std::f32::NAN`, `std::f64::NAN`).

Boolean

The boolean type is represented by `bool`. It is a primitive data type that can have one of two possible values: `true` or `false`. Booleans are used to perform logical operations and control the flow of execution in Rust programs through conditionals like `if` and `while`.

The `bool` type occupies one byte of memory. Although a boolean value logically requires only a single bit, it is stored in a byte for reasons of memory alignment and performance on modern computers.

The `bool` type can be initialized using the `true` and `false` keywords.

```
let visited = true
```

Char

The `char` type represents a single character and is specified using single quotes (`''`). Unlike some other programming languages where a character is essentially a small integer (like an ASCII code), Rust's `char` type is more akin to a Unicode scalar value. This means it can represent much more than just ASCII: it encompasses a wide range of characters from virtually every writing system in the world, as well as many symbols, emojis, and even invisible control characters.

Size

A `char` in Rust is four bytes in size. This is because Rust's `char` type represents a Unicode Scalar Value, which can range from U+0000 to U+D7FF and U+E000 to U+10FFFF. The four-byte size ensures that any of these values can be represented directly.

Unicode Support

Rust's `char` type is Unicode Scalar Value compliant, adhering to the Unicode standard. This allows for the representation of characters from a multitude of languages and a variety of symbols and emojis.

Literals

Characters are defined using single quotes, e.g., `'a'`, `'1'`, or `'😀'`.

Rust supports various escape sequences within `char` literals, such as `'\n'` for newline, `'\t'` for tab, or `'\u{1F600}'` for a Unicode scalar value (in this case, the grinning face emoji).

```
let letter = 'a'
```

Casting

Casting in Rust refers to the explicit conversion of one data type into another. It's a way to transform values from one type to another, usually when there is a clear and defined way to perform this transformation, albeit potentially lossy or with limitations. Rust requires explicit casting to ensure type safety and to make the potential loss of precision or change in meaning clear to the programmer. This explicitness helps prevent accidental type conversions that could lead to unexpected behavior or errors. In contrast to other languages, casting is also required when converting from a smaller type to a larger type, such as from `i8` to `i16`.

Rust uses the `as` keyword for casting between primitive types.

Casting does not check for overflow by default. It's the programmer's responsibility to ensure that the value fits within the target type's range.

Numeric Casting

You can cast between numeric types in Rust, such as integers and floating-point numbers. For example, converting an `i32` to a `u32`, or a `u8` to an `i16`. However, these conversions can be lossy. For instance, casting from a larger integer type to a smaller one (e.g., `u32` to `u8`) might result in data loss if the original value is too large to fit in the target type.

Casting Between Integers and Floating-Points

Rust allows casting between integer and floating-point types. This can be useful for mathematical operations that require floating-point arithmetic. However, this kind of casting can also be lossy, especially when converting from floating-point to integer types, as it involves truncation of any fractional part.

Ch01/Examples/src/bin/example11.rs

```
let integer = 10;
let floating: f64 = integer as f64;
let byte: u8 = integer as u8;
```

In this example, the variable `integer` is cast from an inferred `i32` to an `f64`, and in the second statement, `integer` is cast from an `i32` to an `u8`.

Casting an integer to a floating-point number will always work, but it may lose some precision, with a significant likelihood of rounding errors in the last decimal place.

Compound Types

As we delve deeper into Rust's type system, it's essential to explore compound types that allow us to group multiple values together. This chapter focuses on tuples and arrays, two fundamental structures that enable efficient data organization and manipulation. Understanding these compound types will enhance your ability to handle complex data and implement robust, flexible solutions in your Rust programs. Let's begin by examining the characteristics, uses, and operations associated with tuples and arrays. The following text will refer to the stack and the heap, two mechanisms the compiler uses to organize memory. These concepts will be explained in more detail in Chapter 3.

Tuple

A **tuple** is a compound type that allows you to combine together a fixed number of values with potentially different types into a single compound value. Tuples are a versatile way to group together values of mixed types. They are particularly useful when you want to return multiple values from a function or when you need to pass around groups of values that logically belong together.

A tuple has the following characteristics:

- **Fixed Size**: Once declared, the size of a tuple cannot change. The number of elements in the tuple is determined when it is created.

- **Heterogeneous**: Tuples can contain elements of different types. This is in contrast to arrays, where all elements must be of the same type.
- **Stack Allocated**: By default, tuples are allocated on the stack. (All fixed-size types are allocated on the stack.)
- **Indexed**: Elements in a tuple are indexed by position, starting from 0. However, unlike arrays, you cannot use a runtime index to access elements of a tuple; you must access them using pattern matching or the `.n` syntax where `n` is the index of the element. For example .2 is the third element.

Syntax

You can define a tuple by listing its values within parentheses, separated by commas:

```
let my_tuple = (3, "hello", 4.5);
```

In this example, `my_tuple` is a tuple that contains an integer, a string slice, and a floating-point number.

Accessing Tuple Elements

You can access the elements of a tuple either by destructuring it through pattern matching or directly by their index using a period (`.`) followed by the index of the element.

Ch01/Examples/src/bin/example12.rs

```
// Destructuring
let (x, y, z) = my_tuple;
println!("x: {}, y: {}, z: {}", x, y, z);

// Direct access
let first_element = my_tuple.0;
```

Array

Array is a collection type that allows you to store multiple values of the same type in a single data structure. Arrays have a fixed length, meaning the number of elements they can hold is determined at compile time and cannot be changed during the execution of a program. This characteristic makes arrays useful for situations where you know in advance exactly how many elements you need to store and that this number will not change.

An array has the following characteristics:

- **Fixed Size**: The size of an array is part of its type, making arrays fixed-size collections. Once declared, the size cannot be changed.
- **Homogeneous Elements**: All elements in an array must be of the same type.
- **Stack Allocated**: By default, arrays are allocated on the stack, which can lead to faster access times compared to heap-allocated collections like vectors. However, this also means that very large arrays might not be suitable for stack allocation due to stack size limitations.
- **Indexed Access**: Array elements are accessed by their index, with indexing starting at 0. Rust checks array access at compile time for statically known indices and provides bounds checking at runtime for dynamically computed indices, preventing out-of-bounds access.

Syntax

An array is defined by specifying the type of its elements, followed by a semicolon, and then the number of elements it contains. The elements are enclosed in square brackets.

Ch01/Examples/src/bin/example13.rs

```
let my_array: [i32; 5] = [1, 2, 3, 4, 5];
```

Here, `my_array` is an array that can hold 5 elements of type `i32`.

Initializing Arrays

Rust provides two ways to initialize arrays:

- **Specifying All Elements**: You can explicitly specify each element of the array.
- **Repeat Expression**: For arrays that contain multiple elements of the same value, you can use a repeat expression. For example, `let zeroes = [0; 10];` creates an array of ten `0`s.

Accessing Array Elements

Elements in an array can be accessed using indexing syntax. Indices start at 0:

```
let first = my_array[0];
let second = my_array[1];
```

Attempting to access an element out of bounds will cause panic at runtime.

Arrays vs. Vectors

While arrays are useful for fixed-size collections, Rust also offers a dynamic array type called a `Vec` (vector), which can grow or shrink in size. Vectors are more flexible than arrays and are used more commonly in situations where the size of the collection might change during runtime. Vectors will be covered in more detail later in the text, where their usage and features are thoroughly explained.

Slices, and Strings in Rust

In the following section, we provide a basic explanation of slices and the two String types, giving you the essential tools to perform fundamental tasks in Rust.

Slices

In Rust, **slices** are a powerful feature that provides a way to reference a contiguous sequence of elements in a collection rather than the whole collection. Slices are especially useful when working with arrays. Here's an overview of how slices interact with arrays in Rust

- **Data structure**: A slice is a two-word object, the first word is a pointer to the data, and the second word is the length of the slice. Slices let you reference a contiguous sequence of elements in an array without taking ownership of them. This makes slices a flexible tool for functions that need to operate on a part of an array.
- **Syntax**: You can create a slice from an array by specifying a range within brackets, like `&array[start..end]`, where `start` is inclusive and `end` is exclusive. If you omit both `start` and `end`, you create a slice that includes the entire array, like `&array[..]`.

Ch01/Examples/src/bin/example14.rs

```
let fibonacci: [usize; 7]= [0, 1, 1, 2, 3, 5, 8];
let slice = &fibonacci[2..5];
println!("{:?}", slice); // prints '[1, 2, 3]'
```

The `&` symbol is used to obtain a reference, similar to its usage in C and C++. A detailed explanation will be provided in *Chapter 3*.

- **Immutability**: By default, slices are immutable. If you create a slice of an array, you cannot modify the elements through the slice unless you explicitly declare it as mutable, like `&mut array[start..end]`.

- **Type**: The type of a slice created from an array of `T` elements is `&[T]` for an immutable slice and `&mut [T]` for a mutable slice.

Examples and Use Cases

Slices are utilized extensively in various scenarios; here are a few examples:

- **String Slices**: String slices (`&str`) are a common type of slice that references a portion of a `String`. They are widely used in Rust for efficient string manipulation.
- **Passing Slices to Functions**: Slices are often used as function parameters when you want to accept any length of an array. For example, a function that operates on a slice can accept either part of an array or an entire array, enhancing its flexibility.
- **Safety and Efficiency**: Slices are safe to use because they are bound-checked at runtime. They also allow for efficient access to a sequence of elements without the overhead of copying.

Advantages over Arrays

Slices offer several advantages over arrays:

- **Flexibility**: Slices are not fixed size, unlike arrays. You can use them to dynamically reference a range of elements in arrays (or other collections like vectors), making your code more flexible.
- **Compatibility with Collections**: Slices can be used not only with arrays but also with other collections like `Vec<T>`, providing a consistent way to reference data across different types of collections.

In summary, slices offer a powerful and flexible way to work with parts of an array (or other collections) in Rust, providing both safety through runtime bounds checking and efficiency by avoiding unnecessary data copying.

String and &str

Handling text is primarily done through two types: `String` and `&str`. Understanding the difference between these two types is crucial for effectively managing text data in Rust programs. In Rust, strings are a non-trivial topic, which is why a dedicated chapter on managing strings is included later in this text.

String

`String` is a growable, heap-allocated data structure. It is the mutable string type.

Use `String` when you need to own or modify your string data.

The following are the characteristics:

- **Mutable**: You can modify a `String` by appending, removing, or altering its contents.
- **Heap Allocated**: The data of a `String` is stored on the heap, allowing it to expand as needed.

The fundamental methods for creating and modifying a String are::

- **Created from a literal**: `let mut s = String::from("hello");`
- **Modified by appending**: `s.push_str(", world!");`

&str

- `&str` is a string slice type, representing an immutable sequence of characters.

These are the characteristics:

- **Usage**: Use `&str` for borrowing a view of a string. It's often seen in function arguments where a function needs to read or inspect string data.
- **Immutable**: You cannot change the content of a `&str`.
- **Stack Allocated**: The `&str` itself is stored on the stack, though it points to data that may be located anywhere (heap, stack, or static memory).

Literals

A string literal is stored in static memory. When you assign a string literal to a variable, the variable is inferred to be a string slice that points to that literal. For example:

```
let s = "This is a string literal";
```

`String` and `&str` in Rust serve complementary roles for handling text. `String` is used when you need ownership and mutability, making it suitable for working with dynamically sized string data. `&str`, being a slice, is used for borrowing string data efficiently, ideal for read-only access. Mastering when and how to use each type is key to effective Rust programming, especially when dealing with text manipulation and processing.

Exercise preparation

At the end of each chapter, you will find exercises. To complete these exercises successfully, there are a few more concepts you need to understand, which are covered in this section. The solution to the exercises can be found in Github.

Main

In Rust, the `main` function serves as the entry point of a program. It's the first code that runs in every executable Rust program. The `main` function takes no parameters and returns nothing. Its declaration looks simply like this:

```
fn main() {
    // Your code here
}
```

Inside the `main` function, you can call other functions, perform operations, or handle input and output. If your program is designed to do something specific when it starts, the logic for that would typically be placed within or called from the `main` function. Rust programs compile into a binary executable, and when that executable is run, the commands in the `main` function are the first to execute.

println!

Using the `println!` macro allows you to output text to the console.

```
println!("Hi there");
```

The `println!` macro enables string interpolation through two methods: by printing a variable or an expression. However, defining an expression directly within the curly braces is not permitted.

```
let a = 4;
let b = 2;
println!("{a} times {b} = {}", a * b);
```

To print an array or a slice in Rust, you need to use the `:?` specifier within the curly braces for debug formatting. Here's how you do it:

```
let my_array = [1, 2, 3, 4, 5];
println!("Array contents: {:?}", my_array);
```

Summary

This chapter introduces the fundamental concepts of Variables and Types in Rust, highlighting the unique approaches Rust takes towards these essential programming constructs to ensure code safety, performance, and reliability. Through an exploration of variables and constants, data types, mutability, type inference and casting, as well as variable declaration, scope, and shadowing, the chapter lays down the groundwork for understanding how Rust manages data and memory. Additionally, it covers the critical aspects of initialization and naming conventions, which are pivotal for writing clear and maintainable code.

Key topics covered include the distinction between mutable variables and immutable constants in Rust, emphasizing the language's focus on immutability. The overview of Rust's type system includes scalar and compound types, explaining their use in efficiently managing data within a program. Insight into Rust's principle of immutability by default is provided, with guidance on explicitly declaring variables as mutable. The text covers how Rust infers the types of variables from the assigned values and the correct way to perform type casting. It also delves into the specific characteristics of variables in Rust, including their declaration, scope, and the concept of shadowing. Finally, best practices for initializing variables and recommended naming conventions to enhance code readability are discussed.

As we continue our journey through Rust, it's time to delve into another essential component of the language: expressions. Expressions play a crucial role in Rust, serving as the foundation for executing logic and manipulating data. In the next chapter, we'll unravel the intricacies of expressions, understanding how they form the building blocks for more complex operations and contribute to the language's powerful functionality. Let's embark on this next step and see how expressions enhance our Rust programming skills.

Exercises

Model answers are available on GitHub at: https://github.com/mrQuidome/Learning-Rust.git. In your IDE, you can load all the answers from a single chapter. The project is located at `Ch01/Solutions`. All individual solutions are located in the `bin` folder and can be run independently.

1. Declare a mutable variable `count` of type `i32` and initialize it with a value of 10. Write a Rust program that increases this value by 20, then prints the result.
2. Define a constant named `MAX_SCORE` of type `u32` and assign it a value of 100. Place the constant outside the main function. Write a program that prints this value.
3. Declare two variables, `is_active` of type `bool` with a value of `true`, and `temperature` of type `f32` with a value of `25.5`. Print their values.

4. Declare a variable `speed` with an initial value of `88` and let Rust infer its type. Then, print the variable's value along with its type using the `std::any::type_name_of_val()` function to verify Rust's type inference. The parameter to the function is `&speed`.

5. Create a tuple named `user` that contains a username as a string slice, an active status as a boolean, and a sign-in count as an `u64`. Destructure this tuple to print the values of its elements.

6. Initialize an array `fibonacci` of `u128`, with the first five Fibonacci numbers using explicit type annotation. Print the array.

7. Given an array `[1, 2, 3, 4, 5]`, create a slice containing the middle three elements and print it.

8. Convert a variable `distance` of type `f64` with a value of `1000.0` into an `i32`. Print the converted value.

9. Declare a variable `x` with value `5`. Shadow it with a new value of `x + x`. Print the final value of `x`. Don't use the `mut` keyword.

10. Write a Rust function that demonstrates variable shadowing within different scopes. Show how the value of a variable changes as it gets shadowed in an inner scope and then print its original and shadowed values.

02

Expressions, Control Flow, and Functions

In this chapter, we explore three core elements of Rust: expressions, control flow, and functions. Expressions form the fundamental building blocks in Rust, they are used to compute values. Control flow mechanisms, such as conditional statements and loops, allow for decision-making and repeated execution of code. Functions serve as reusable code blocks that help organize logic, take inputs, and return outputs to perform specific tasks. We will explore the following topics:

- **Expressions**: Delve into how expressions form the core building blocks of code.
- **Control Flow**: Understand the decision-making processes and loop constructs within Rust.
- **Functions**: Learn about the roles and definitions of functions in organizing and executing tasks

Mastering these concepts will help you build a strong foundation in Rust, enabling you to write well-organized, efficient code and solve programming problems effectively. Understanding these concepts not only enhances your technical proficiency but also sharpens your logical thinking and problem-solving skills.

Expressions

Expressions are fundamental to programming because they allow developers to write logic that manipulates data and makes decisions. They are used in virtually every part of a program, from simple calculations and assignments to controlling the flow of execution through decision-making structures. In this section, we delve into the key aspects of expressions.

An expression can contain literals, constants, operators, variables, or functions, which, when executed, evaluate to a single value.

Key aspects of Expressions

The following are the key aspects of expressions:

- **Composition**: Expressions can be simple, involving just a single value or variable, or they can be complex, involving multiple operators and function calls nested within one another.
- **Evaluation**: The process of computing an expression's value is known as evaluation. When an expression is evaluated, each component of the expression

contributes to the final result. The types of operations and the order in which these operations are executed are determined by the rules of the programming language.

- **Return Value**: Every expression, after being evaluated, returns a value. The type of this value depends on the elements used in the expression and the operations performed.
- **Operators**: Expressions often include operators that perform specific operations on operands. Operators can be arithmetic (like +, -, *, /), logical (like &&, ||, !), relational (like ==, !=, <, >), and others.
- **Function Calls**: Expressions can include function calls that, when evaluated, execute the function and use its return value as part of the expression.
- **Side Effects**: Some expressions do more than just evaluate to a value; they can also cause side effects. For example, an expression might assign a value to a variable, modify data, or output information to a console.

Literals and Variables in expressions

The simplest expressions return their own value. For example, the literals `5`, `3.14`, and `"Hello, world!"` are all expressions that evaluate to themselves. Similarly, if you have a variable `x`, using `x` in your code is an expression that evaluates to the value `x` holds.

```
let a = 5;
```

In this assignment statement, `5` serves as the expression that evaluates to itself. This value is subsequently assigned to the variable `a`.

```
let a = 5;
let b = a;
```

In the second line, the variable `a` is an expression that evaluates to the value it contains, which is `5`. This value is then assigned to the variable `b`.

Operators

Rust provides a variety of numerical operators that allow you to perform arithmetic, comparison, and bitwise operations. These operators work with numeric types such as integers and floating-point numbers. Below is an overview of all the numerical operators available in Rust:

The following is an overview of **arithmetic operators**:

Operator	*Description*	**Example**
+	Calculates the sum of two numbers	`5 + 3` evaluates to `8`
-	Finds the difference by subtracting the second number from the first	`5 - 3` evaluates to `2`
*	Multiplies the values of two numbers	`5 * 3` evaluates to `15`
/	Divides the first number by the second number.	`5 / 2` evaluates to `2` in integer arithmetic, and `2.5` in floating-point arithmetic.
%	Calculates the remainder when the first number is divided by the second	`5 % 2` evaluates to `1`

Table 2.1 - *Arithmetic operators*

You can see below an overview of **comparison operators**:

Operator	*Description*	**Example**
==	Compares two operands to see if they are equal	`7 == 8` evaluates to `false`
!=	Compares two operands to check if they are not equal	`7 != 8` evaluates to `true`
>	Determines if the left operand is greater than the right operand	`7 > 8` evaluates to `false`
>=	Determines if the left operand is greater than or equal to the right operand	`7 >= 8` evaluates to `false`
<	Determines if the left operand is less than the right operand	`7 < 8` evaluates to `true`
<=	Determines if the left operand is less than or equal to the right operand	`7 <= 8` evaluates to `true`

Table 2.2 - *Comparison operators*

The following is a list of logical operators, its descriptions, examples:

<table>
<tr><th>Operator</th><th>Description</th><th>Example</th></tr>
<tr><td>&&</td><td>Executes a logical AND; results in true only if both operands are true</td><td>true && false evaluates to false</td></tr>
<tr><td>||</td><td>Executes a logical OR; results in true if at least one operand is true</td><td>true || false evaluates to true</td></tr>
<tr><td>!</td><td>Executes a logical NOT; reverses the truth value of the operand</td><td>!true evaluates to false</td></tr>
</table>

Table 2.3 - *Logical operators*

Here is a list of bitwise operators:

<table>
<tr><th>Operator</th><th>Description</th><th>Example</th></tr>
<tr><td>&</td><td>Executes a bitwise AND operation on two numbers</td><td>5 & 3 evaluates to 1</td></tr>
<tr><td>|</td><td>Executes a bitwise OR operation on two numbers</td><td>5 | 3 evaluates to 7</td></tr>
<tr><td>^</td><td>Performs a binary XOR operation on two numbers Executes a bitwise XOR (exclusive OR) operation on two numbers</td><td>5 ^ 3 evaluates to 6</td></tr>
<tr><td>!</td><td>Executes a bitwise NOT operation, flipping all the bits</td><td>!252u8 evaluates to 3</td></tr>
<tr><td><<</td><td>Shifts the bits of the first operand to the left by the number of positions specified by the second operand</td><td>5 << 1 evaluates to 10</td></tr>
<tr><td>>></td><td>Shifts the bits of the first operand to the right by the number of positions specified by the second operand</td><td>5 >> 1 evaluates to 2</td></tr>
</table>

Table 2.4 - *Bitwise Operators*

Compound Assignment Operators

Rust also supports compound assignment operators, which combine an arithmetic operation with assignment. These include `+=`, `-=`, `*=`, `/=`, `%=`, `&=`, `|=`, `^=`, `<<=`, and `>>=`.

Ch02/Examples/src/bin/example01.rs

```
let mut a = 5;
a += 5;
```

`a += 5` is a shorthand for `a = a + 5`. This is particularly useful when dealing with long variable names or more complex expressions, such as specific array elements.

Operators and Type Casting

Each numerical operator has rules regarding the types of operands it can work with, and in some cases, such as division, the behavior might vary based on the types of the operands involved. Rust enforces strict type checking, so operands must be compatible with the operator being used, potentially requiring explicit type casts.

Most operators require operands of the same type, meaning that to add a `usize` to an `isize`, you must cast one of them to match the other's type, depending on the desired result type of the operation.

Ch02/Examples/src/bin/example02.rs

```
let a: usize = 10;
let b: isize = -5;
let result: isize = a as isize + b
```

The expression `a as isize` converts the type of a from `usize` to `isize` before performing the addition. This conversion is necessary because adding a `usize` to an `isize` is not defined in Rust. Rust does not generally support automatic type coercion, especially in contexts like mathematical operations. While there are a few special cases where coercion is allowed, arithmetic expressions aren't one of them. Therefore, to perform an addition, one of the operands must be explicitly converted to match the type of the other.

Precedence and Association

Operators are evaluated based on their precedence and associativity, adhering to the conventional rules taught in school, such as multiplication being performed before addition. You can alter the default order of evaluation by enclosing expressions within parentheses.

When operators of equal precedence appear consecutively in an expression, often when the same operator is used back-to-back, their evaluation order can either proceed from left to right or from right to left, based on the specific operators involved. This is known as **associativity**.

Based on the operators we have discussed, we can arrange them in the following precedence table, where operators at the top have the highest priority and are evaluated before those lower down:

Operator/Expression	*Associativity*
Unary - !	
as	left to right
* / %	left to right
+ -	left to right
<< >>	left to right
&	left to right
^	left to right
|	left to right
== != < > <= >=	left to right
&&	left to right
||	left to right
= += -= *= /= %= &= |= ^= <<= >>=	right to left

Table 2.5 - *Operator precedence and associativity*

Let's examine an example that demonstrates operator precedence:

Ch02/Examples/src/bin/example03.rs

```
let x = 15;
let y = 10;
let z = (x + y) * 3 / 2 - 5;
```

Let's break down the final statement of this example, where z evaluates to 32. First, the expression (x + y) results in 25. This value is then multiplied by 3, giving 75. Dividing 75 by 2 using integer division truncates the result to 37. Lastly, subtracting 5 from 37 gives the final value of 32.Blocks as Expressions

Blocks as Expressions

In Rust, blocks (`{}`) can be used to create scopes for variable declarations, and interestingly, they also can act as expressions. When used as an expression, a block evaluates to the last expression executed within it, ***without a semicolon***. If you add a semicolon to the last expression, the block will evaluate to `()`, (the unit type), not the value of the expression. This feature allows you to use blocks to compute values in a more structured way, encapsulating multiple steps and temporary variables.

Here's how they can be used both for basic expression evaluation and to encapsulate more complex logic within a single expression:

- **Basic Usage**: A block will return the value of the last expression in it that doesn't end with a semicolon. This allows you to execute a series of statements and return a value.

  Ch02/Examples/src/bin/example04.rs

  ```
  let x = 5;
  let y = {
      let z = x + 1;
      z + 2
  };
  println!("y: {}", y);
  ```

The block evaluates to 8 in the last line, there is no semicolon on that line! And that value is assigned to the variable y.

- **Encapsulating Logic**: Blocks allow you to encapsulate complex logic within a single expression, keeping variable scopes limited and making your code more modular and easier to follow.

Ch02/Examples/src/bin/example05.rs

```
let x = {
    let temp = 0;
    // Imagine more complex logic here
    temp + 10 // The result of the block
};
```

The variable `temp` is encapsulated in the block and is not accessible outside of it for the rest of the function.

Using blocks as expressions is a powerful aspect of Rust, allowing you to build complex expressions out of simpler ones, maintain cleaner scope control, and write more expressive conditionals. This feature, combined with Rust's strong type system and ownership model, contributes to the language's expressiveness and safety.

Control Flow

In this section, we delve deep into the fundamentals of control flow in Rust. Learning control flow is crucial for any Rust programmer aiming to master the art of directing the execution paths of their programs. Control flow mechanisms enable programmers to make decisions in their code, loop through data and perform repeated actions efficiently.

We will explore:

- **Conditional Statements**: Learn how to use if, if else, and match statements to execute different branches of code based on specific conditions.
- **Looping Constructs**: We will cover how to effectively use loop, while, and for loops to perform repetitive tasks, with detailed explanations on when and why to use each type.

By the end of this chapter, you will have a solid understanding of how to manipulate the flow of execution in Rust programs, allowing you to write more dynamic, efficient, and robust code. Whether you are building simple utilities or complex software systems, mastering control flow is an essential step in your development as a Rust programmer.

If

In Rust, the `if` statement is a fundamental control flow tool used for branching, allowing the execution of different code paths based on conditions. The `if` statement evaluates a condition which is a boolean expression (`true` or `false`) and executes a block of code if the condition evaluates to `true`. If the condition is `false`, the program skips the block associated with that `if` statement. Additionally, Rust's if can be extended with `else` and `else if` branches to provide multiple conditional pathways.

Syntax

The basic syntax of an `if` statement in Rust is as follows:

```
if condition {
    // code to execute if condition is true
}
```

Using else and else if

You can add an else block to execute code when the `if` condition is not met:

```
if condition {
    // code to execute if condition is true
} else {
    // code to execute if condition is false
}
```

For multiple conditions, you can chain `if` and `else if`:

```
if condition1 {
    // code for condition1
} else if condition2 {
    // code for condition2
} else {
    // code if none of the above conditions are met
}
```

Bringing it all together with a traffic light example:

Ch02/Examples/src/bin/example06.rs

```
let traffic_light = "green";
if traffic_light == "green" {
    println!("Go");
} else if traffic_light == "yellow" {
    println!("Slow down and prepare to stop");
```

```
} else if traffic_light == "red" {
    println!("Stop!");
}
```

Because `traffic_light` has the value of *green*, `Go` is printed to the console.

Expression-based

One of the key features of Rust's `if` statement is its use as an expression. This means that it can return a value, allowing it to be used right-hand side of an assignment or in other expressions. For this to work, all branches of the `if` expression must return a value of the same type.

Ch02/Examples/src/bin/example07.rs

```
let number = 6;
let description = if number % 2 == 0 {
    "even"
} else {
    "odd"
};
println!("The number is {}", description);
```

There is a semicolon after the `else` block, marking the end of the let statement. When using `if` without returning an expression, a semicolon is not needed.

Usage Tips

The following are some tips that will prove useful when using conditional statements:

- **Condition type**: The condition in a Rust `if` statement must always evaluate to a boolean value `true` or `false`. Unlike some languages that allow non-boolean types as conditions (like 0 or null), Rust strictly requires the condition to be a boolean.
- **Dangling else**: Rust's mandatory use of curly braces `{}` for code blocks avoids the *dangling else* problem found in some other languages, where it's unclear to which `if` an `else` belongs. This clarity is enforced by Rust's syntax rules.
- **No parentheses**: In Rust, the syntax for `if` statements is designed to be clean and concise, and one notable feature is the absence of parentheses around the condition. This design choice helps to reduce visual clutter and aligns with Rust's emphasis on readability and simplicity.

Best Practices When writing clean and efficient Rust code, following these best practices can help improve readability, maintainability, and logic flow. Here are some key guidelines to keep in mind:

- **Minimize nested if statements**: Deeply nested `if` statements can make code harder to read and maintain. Consider using match statements or breaking the code into smaller functions.
- **Use logical operators wisely**: Using `&&` (logical AND) or `||` (logical OR) in combination with `!` (logical NOT) can be challenging due to the need to carefully manage operator precedence and ensure that the conditions are grouped correctly. Try to rewrite the condition without using `!` if possible.

For complex conditions, it might be clearer to calculate the condition beforehand in a separate variable or to use match statements if you are dealing with enumeration types.

Match

Rust's `match` statement is a powerful and expressive control flow construct that allows you to compare a value against a series of patterns and execute code based on which pattern matches. It's similar to the switch statement found in many other programming languages but provides much more flexibility and power due to its pattern-matching capabilities.

While the `match` statement is often used with Rust enums, it is not limited to them. In this introduction, we'll focus on using `match` with integers. We'll discuss the use of `match` with `enum` in the chapter on structs and enums.

Basic Syntax

The following is an example of the basic syntax for `match`:

```
match value {
    pattern1 => expression1,
    pattern2 => expression2,
    pattern3 => expression3,
    // ...
    _ => default_expression,
}
```

Here's a breakdown of the basic syntax for the match statement

- `value` is the value being matched.
- `pattern` is what the value is compared against.

- `Expression` is the block of code executed if the value matches the pattern. This statement or code block is an expression, meaning that the `match` statement, like the `if` statement, can return a value. All match arms must return the same type.
- `the _ pattern` is a wildcard that matches any value not covered by previous patterns, acting as a catch-all or default case. The match statement must be exhaustive, meaning that every possible pattern must be matched. For practical purposes, when using integers, this typically requires including a default pattern to handle any values not explicitly covered by other patterns.

Ch02/Examples/src/bin/example08.rs

```
let number = 3;
let message = match number {
    1 => "uno",
    2 => "due",
    3 => "tre",
    _ => "qualcos'altro",
};
println!("message: {message}");
```

The match pattern is used as an expression, with each match arm returning the same type. The result is then assigned to the variable message. As with if, there is a semicolon after the match, marking the end of the let statement. When using match without returning an expression, a semicolon is not needed.

Do Nothing

In Rust, there are two primary ways to specify that a match arm should do nothing. This is useful when you want to handle a particular pattern but don't need to perform any action for it. The two ways are using an empty block `{}` and using the unit value `()`.

- **Empty Block**: An empty block `{}` is a straightforward way to indicate that no action should be taken for a specific pattern. This method is clear and explicit.
- **Unit Value**: The unit value `()` is the idiomatic way to indicate that a match arm should do nothing. In Rust, `()` represents an empty tuple and is used to signify a lack of meaningful value or action. More precisely, the match arm is returning the unit value, and this approach will only work if all other match arms return the unit value as well.

Ch02/Examples/src/bin/example09.rs

```
match number {
    1 => println!("uno"),
    2 => {},
    3 => println!("tre"),
    _ => ()
}
```

Ranges

Rust's `match` statement supports range patterns, which allow you to match an integer against a range of values.

The range pattern in Rust is written using two dots `..` or `..=` to specify the start and end of the range. `2..5` means from two up to, but not including, five (exclusive). `2..=5` means from two up to and including five (inclusive).

Ch02/Examples/src/bin/example10.rs

```
let age = 30;
match age {
    0..=12 => println!("Child"),
    13..=19 => println!("Teenager"),
    20..=64 => println!("Adult"),
    65..=120 => println!("Senior"),
    _ => println!("Invalid age"),
}
```

Or Pattern

You can match an integer against multiple specific values using the `|` (OR) operator.

Ch02/Examples/src/bin/example11.rs

```
let number = 2;
match number {
    1 | 2 | 3 => println!("One, two, or three"),
    4 | 5 | 6 => println!("Four, five, or six"),
    _ => println!("Some other number"),
}
```

Guards

Guards add additional conditions to patterns, providing more control over matching:

Ch02/Examples/src/bin/example12.rs

```
let number = 10;
match number {
    n if n % 2 == 0 => println!("Even"),
    n if n % 2 != 0 => println!("Odd"),
    _ => println!("Unknown"),
}
```

The match statement is a powerful feature in Rust. We've covered the basics of using match with simple types and strings. We'll revisit the match statement in more detail when we discuss structs and enums.

Loop

In Rust, a loop is a control flow construct that allows you to execute a block of code repeatedly. Unlike other looping constructs such as while or for, a loop will continue indefinitely until you explicitly break out of it using the break statement. This can be useful for creating infinite loops or loops that only terminate based on certain conditions evaluated inside the loop.

Basic Syntax

The basic syntax for a `loop` in Rust is straightforward:

Ch02/Examples/src/bin/example13.rs

```
loop {
    println!("This will print forever!");
}
```

Expression Based

You can stop a loop by using a `break` statement. Additionally, `loop` can return a value upon breaking. This is achieved by placing the value after the `break` statement, making the loop an expression that returns this value.

Ch02/Examples/src/bin/example14.rs

```
let mut count = 0;
let result = loop {
    count += 1;
    if count == 10 {
        break count * 2;
    }
};
println!("The result is: {}", result);
```

The loop will continue iterating until the `if` condition becomes `true`, at which point it will return the value `20`, which is then assigned to the variable result.

While

In Rust, the while loop is a control flow construct used to repeatedly execute a block of code as long as a specified condition evaluates to true. It provides a way to perform iteration based on a condition that is checked before each iteration of the loop. In contrast to the previous control statements, while cannot be used as an expression.

The following is an example of the basic syntax:

```
while condition {
    // Code to be executed repeatedly
}
```

Here, condition is a boolean expression that is evaluated before each iteration. If the condition is true, the loop body is executed. If the condition is `false`, the loop terminates.

Ch02/Examples/src/bin/example15.rs

```
let mut count = 1;
while count <= 5 {
    println!("Iteration: {}", count);
    count += 1;
}
```

For

In Rust, the `for` loop is a powerful and flexible control flow construct used to iterate over a range of values or the elements of a collection.

You can see the basic syntax of `for` loop here:

```
for variable in iterator {
    // Code to be executed for each element
}
```

Here, variable is a placeholder for each element in the iterator, and the loop body is executed once for each element.

Ch02/Examples/src/bin/example16.rs

```
for number in 1..=5 {
    println!("Number is: {}", number);
}
```

This is an example of a counted loop. The `for` loop iterates over each `number` in the range, assigning it to the variable number in each iteration.

Ch02/Examples/src/bin/example17.rs

```
let numbers = [1, 2, 3, 4, 5];
for number in numbers {
    println!("{number}");
}
```

This is an example of a `for` each loop that iterates over a collection, in this case, an array. The `for` loop goes through each item in the array, assigning it to the variable `number` in each iteration.

The loop is a versatile control statement, and we will discuss it further after we cover collections in more detail later in the text.

Break, Continue

The `break` statement is used to exit a loop. In a `loop` using the loop keyword, it can return a value, as discussed earlier. However, `break` can also be used to exit the loop without returning a value. Only the `loop` using the loop keyword construct can return a value with `break`; the `for` and `while` loops cannot.

The continue statement is used within loops to skip the remainder of the current iteration and proceed to the next iteration. When continue is encountered, the loop stops executing the rest of the code in the current iteration and immediately reevaluates the loop's condition to start the next iteration.

Ch02/Examples/src/bin/example18.rs

```
for number in 1..10 {
    if number % 2 == 0 {
        continue;
    }
    println!("Odd number: {}", number);
}
```

This loop iterates over the numbers from 1 to 9, printing only the odd numbers. When a number is even, the loop body terminates early, and the next iteration begins.

Labels

Loop labels are used to distinguish between multiple nested loops and control the flow of execution more precisely. They allow you to specify which loop you want to break out of or continue when using the break and continue statements. Loop labels are particularly useful in complex scenarios where you have nested loops, and you need to manage the flow of control explicitly.

A loop label is defined by a single quote (') followed by an identifier. It is placed before the loop keyword (`loop`, `while`, or `for`). When using break or continue, you refer to the loop label to specify the target loop.

The following is the basic syntax:

```
'label: loop {
    // Loop body
}
```

Here's an example of using a loop label:

Ch02/Examples/src/bin/example19.rs

```
'outer: for i in 1..=5 {
    for j in 1..=5 {
        if i == 3 && j == 3 {
            break 'outer;
        }
        println!("i: {}, j: {}", i, j);
    }
}
```

In this example, there is an inner and outer loop. Without the break, the loop body would execute 25 times in total. However, the condition specifies that when both i and j equal 3, the break statement will exit the outer loop, effectively stopping further iterations. As a result, the loop body will be executed only 13 times, and the println! statement will be executed 12 times.

Functions

Functions in Rust are fundamental building blocks that allow you to encapsulate code into reusable units. They are used to perform specific tasks, take inputs, and return outputs. Functions help in organizing code, avoiding repetition, and improving readability and maintainability.

Basic Syntax

There are two aspects to a function: *defining it* and *using it*. The syntax for defining a function is:

```
fn function_name(par1: Type1, par2: Type2) -> ReturnType {
    // Function body
}
```

Let's go through a detailed description of each element:

- fn: In Rust, fn is the keyword used to define functions.
- function_name: The function name can be any identifier you choose. It is best practice to select a name that clearly indicates the function's purpose.
- par1, par2: This specifies the values passed into the function. par1 and par2 are identifiers that typically describe the parameters. Each parameter must have a specified type, as parameter types are not inferred in a function definition. Parameters are optional.
- ReturnType: The return type is optional. However, if the function does return a value, the return type must be specified.

Using a function is straightforward. Simply call the function by its name, provide the necessary arguments (if any), and optionally, handle the return value.

Ch02/Examples/src/bin/example20.rs

```
fn square(num: i32) -> i32 {
    num * num
}
fn main() {
    let number = 5;
    let result = square(number);
```

```
    println!("The square of {number} is {result}");
}
```

In this example, the function `square` is first defined, and in the `main` function, it is called by using its name, with the return value stored in the variable `result`.

Parameters and Arguments

In programming, the terms *parameter* and *argument* are often used interchangeably, but they have distinct meanings based on their context within a function:

- **Parameters** are variables listed in the function definition. They act as placeholders for the values that will be passed into the function when it is called.
- **Arguments** are the actual values or data that you pass to the function when you call it. They are the real values that replace the parameters in the function.

Return

In Rust, returning a value from a function is optional. When a function does return a value, there are two ways to do it:

- Using the return keyword.
- As shown in the previous example, by making the last executed statement an expression without a semicolon. This is the idiomatic Rust way.

The order of function definition and usage is irrelevant in Rust; In the source file you can use a function before defining it without any issues.

To ensure your Rust code is clean, maintainable, and efficient, consider following these recommended practices when defining and organizing functions:

- Use descriptive and clear names for functions to indicate their purpose.
- Use meaningful names for parameters
- Document functions using comments, especially for public functions. Use `///` for documentation comments that can be used by tools like rustdoc.
- Keep functions short and focused on a single task. If a function becomes too long or complex, break it into smaller, more manageable pieces.
- Prefer returning values rather than modifying arguments. Use return types to indicate errors or results.

In conclusion, functions are essential in Rust for encapsulating code into reusable units, improving organization, readability, and maintainability. By defining functions with clear names and meaningful parameters, you enhance code quality and avoid repetition. Adhering to best practices such as documenting functions and keeping them focused ensures clean, testable code. Mastering functions provides a solid foundation for tackling more complex programming challenges.

Summary

This chapter delves into three foundational Rust programming concepts: expressions, control flow, and functions. Understanding these concepts is crucial for writing effective Rust programs.

Expressions are the core building blocks of code, combining values, variables, operators, and function calls to compute a value. They can be simple or complex and always return a value. Operators in Rust include arithmetic, comparison, logical, and bitwise types. Blocks can also be used as expressions, returning the value of the last expression within them.

Control flow mechanisms in Rust, such as `if`, `match`, `loop`, `while`, and `for`, direct the execution paths of programs. Conditional statements like `if`, `else`, and `else if` evaluate conditions and execute code based on the results. The `match` statement is a powerful construct that compares a value against patterns and executes corresponding code. Looping constructs, including `loop`, `while`, and `for`, allow for repeated execution of code blocks. The continue statement skips the rest of the current loop iteration, and labels help manage control flow in nested loops. The break statement, on the other hand, exits the entire loop immediately, and when used with a label, it can break out of an outer loop from within an inner one.

Functions in Rust encapsulate code into reusable units, taking inputs and returning outputs. They are defined with `fn`, optional parameters, and an optional return type. Functions can return values using the `return` keyword or the last expression. Best practices for functions include using clear names, documenting with comments, keeping them short and focused, preferring returning values over modifying arguments, and not using global variables.

Mastering these concepts will enhance your proficiency in Rust, enabling you to write more efficient, dynamic, and robust code.

In the next chapter, we will delve into the concepts of ownership and borrowing. Up until now, Rust's syntax should feel fairly familiar if you have experience with other programming languages. However, ownership and borrowing introduce unique features that set Rust apart by addressing memory safety in a distinctive way. These concepts are fundamental to understanding how Rust manages memory efficiently and safely without needing a garbage collector. We'll examine how ownership ensures each value has a single owner and how borrowing allows for references to data without transferring ownership. This deep dive will highlight Rust's approach to preventing common memory errors, such as null pointer dereferencing and data races, ultimately contributing to the robustness and reliability of your programs.

Exercises

1. Write a Rust program that evaluates the following expressions and prints the results:
   - 5 + 10
   - 3.14 * 3
   - true && false
   - 10 % 3
2. Write a Rust program that checks if a number is positive, negative, or zero using an if statement. Print "Positive", "Negative", or "Zero" based on the value.
3. Write a Rust program that uses a match statement to print the name of a day of the week based on an integer (1 to 7). If the number is outside this range, print "Invalid day".
4. Write a Rust program that uses `loop` to print numbers from 1 to 10. Use a break statement to exit the loop after printing 10.
5. Write a Rust program that iterates over an array of numbers and prints only the non-negative numbers. Use a for loop to traverse the list and the continue statement to skip any negative numbers.
6. Write a function add that takes two integers as parameters and returns their sum. In the main function, call add with different pairs of numbers and print the results.
7. Write a function `is_even` that takes an integer as a parameter and returns true if the number is even and false otherwise. In the main function, test the function with different values and print the results.
8. Write a Rust program that uses an if statement as an expression to assign a value to a variable based on a condition. For example, assign "even" or "odd" to a string variable based on whether a number is even or odd.
9. Write a Rust program that uses a block as an expression to compute and return a value. For example, compute the factorial of a number using a block.

10. Write a Rust program that demonstrates the use of compound assignment operators (+=, -=, *=, /=, %=). Perform a series of operations on a variable and print the results after each operation.

Project: Guessing Game

In this chapter, we transition from learning individual concepts and techniques to applying them in a small project. The project is designed to consolidate your understanding, provide hands-on experience, and showcase the practical application of the skills you've developed throughout the chapter.

Working on these projects will help you:

- **Integrate Knowledge:** Apply multiple concepts and techniques learned in earlier chapters to solve complex problems.
- **Develop Problem-Solving Skills:** Tackle real-world challenges that require creative and critical thinking.
- **Gain Practical Experience:** Build practical, working programs that demonstrate your proficiency and can serve as portfolio pieces.
- **Enhance Coding Practices:** Refine your coding style, improve your debugging skills, and learn how to write maintainable and efficient code.

Each project in this chapter is carefully crafted to be both challenging and rewarding, offering you the opportunity to solidify your learning and prepare for more advanced programming tasks. As you progress through these projects, you'll gain confidence in your abilities and a deeper understanding of how to use programming to create meaningful solutions.

Project Preparation

The following ingredients are needed to complete the project.

Random Numbers

Using random integer numbers in Rust typically involves the `rand` crate, which provides utilities for generating random numbers. Here's a step-by-step explanation of how to use the `rand` crate to generate random integers in Rust:

Add rand to Your Dependencies

First, you need to include the `rand` crate in your `Cargo.toml` file. This allows you to use the functionalities provided by the crate.

```
[dependencies]
rand = "0.8"
```

Import the Necessary Modules

In your Rust program, you need to import the necessary modules from the `rand` crate. The most commonly used module is `rand::Rng`, which provides methods for generating random numbers.

```
use rand::Rng;
```

Create an RNG Instance

To generate random numbers, you need to create an instance of a random number generator. The most common one is the thread-local random number generator provided by `rand::thread_rng()`.

Generate Random Numbers

You can then use methods provided by the `Rng` trait to generate random numbers. For example, to generate a random integer within a specified range, you can use the `gen_range` method.

Example

Ch02/Examples/src/bin/example21.rs

```
use rand::Rng;

fn main() {
    let mut rng = rand::thread_rng();
    let random_number: i32 = rng.gen_range(1..=100);
    println!("Random number: {}", random_number);
}
```

User Input

Getting an integer from the keyboard in Rust involves reading a line of input from the standard input (stdin) and then parsing that input into an integer type. Here's a step-by-step explanation of how to achieve this:

Import the Necessary Modules

You need to import the `std::io` module to handle input and output operations.

Read Input from the Keyboard

To read input from the keyboard, you use the `read_line` method from the `io::stdin` module. This method reads a line of input and stores it in a mutable String variable.

Parse the Input

After reading the input as a string, you need to trim any whitespace and parse the string into an integer. The parse method is used for this purpose. Since parsing can fail, you typically handle the result using pattern matching or other error handling techniques.

Ch02/Examples/src/bin/example22.rs

```
use std::io;

fn main() {
    println!("Please enter a number: ");
    let mut input = String::new();
    io::stdin().read_line(&mut input).ok();
    let input: i32 = input.trim().parse().unwrap();
    println!("You entered: {}", input);
}
```

There is a lot of magic happening in this example, which will be explained in detail later in the text. The `ok()` call essentially suppresses a compiler warning, so while it isn't strictly necessary, it's good practice to remove all compiler warnings. Additionally, we use `unwrap()` to retrieve the parsed number. However, using `unwrap()` has the consequence that if the user enters anything other than digits, the program will crash.

Guessing Game

Objective

Create a guessing game where the player attempts to guess a randomly selected number within a predefined range. The game provides feedback after each guess, indicating whether the guessed number is too high, too low, or correct. The goal is to maximize the number of tries taken by the player to guess the correct number.

Command Line Interface

The game uses a command line interface, utilizing `stdin` for input and `stdout` for output.

Number Selection

The game randomly selects a target number within a specified range (e.g., 1 to 100).

Feedback

After each guess, the game provides feedback:

- "Too high" if the guess is greater than the target number.
- "Too low" if the guess is less than the target number.
- "Correct" if the guess matches the target number.

Win Condition

The player wins by correctly guessing the target number.

Lose Condition

The game tracks the number of attempts made by the player. If the player fails to guess the correct number by the 8th attempt, they lose the game.

03

Ownership and Borrowing

As we delve deeper into Rust, we'll explore its unique approach to memory management, which distinguishes it from other programming languages. Central to this approach are the concepts of ownership and borrowing. These concepts are key to Rust's ability to ensure memory safety without a garbage collector, making your programs both efficient and secure against common issues like data races, memory leaks and, double frees. In this chapter, we'll cover the principles of ownership and borrowing, understand their rules, and see how they enable Rust to manage memory in a predictable and performant way. We will look at the following main topics:

- **Stack, Heap, and Static Memory:** Learn how the compiler manages memory allocation on the stack and heap.
- **Ownership:** Understand the rules of ownership and their implications.
- **Borrowing:** Explore the rules of borrowing and their consequences.
- **Compiler Guarantees:** Discover the guarantees provided by the Rust compiler and their importance.
- **Ownership and Borrowing Applied:** Investigate how ownership and borrowing are applled in various contexts, including functions, structs, arrays, and loops.

Gaining a grasp of these concepts will provide you with a solid foundation for effectively using Rust.

Stack, Heap, and Static Memory

Rust, like many programming languages, utilizes both the stack and the heap for memory management. Unlike C and C++, Rust automatically manages both stack and heap memory. This means there is no need for manual allocation and deallocation, which eliminates memory leaks, double free errors, and dangling pointers. Unlike Java, C#, and python, among other, with the ownership and borrowing rules, Rust has no need for a garbage collector. The end result is automatic memory management as in Java and others, and no manual deallocation as in C and C++. Let's begin by exploring how the stack operates within Rust's memory management system.

Stack

The stack is a region of memory that operates in a **last-in, first-out** (**LIFO**) manner. It is used for storing function call data, local variables, and function parameters. The stack has the following characteristics:

- **Automatic Allocation**: In Rust, variables with a fixed, known size at compile time are allocated on the stack. This includes primitive types like integers and booleans, as well as tuples and arrays of fixed size types.
- **Scope-Based Deallocation**: When a scope ends, Rust automatically cleans up the stack memory by removing the local variables that were allocated during the function's execution.

Heap

The heap is a region of memory used for dynamic allocation, where the size of the data is not known at compile time or can change during execution. Heap allocation is more flexible but generally slower than stack allocation. The heap has the following characteristics:

- **Manual Allocation**: In Rust, data is allocated on the heap using smart pointers like `Box`, `Rc`, and `Arc`. These pointers manage the heap memory and ensure that it is properly cleaned up when no longer needed. Smart pointers will be addressed later in the book.
- **Scope-Based Deallocation**: When a scope ends, Rust automatically cleans up the heap memory for **owned** values that fall out of scope.

Because deallocation in Rust is scope-based, there is no need for a garbage collector. This approach is unique to Rust. In the remaining chapter, we will discuss the rules governing this system, how Rust implements it, and the implications for your code.

Static Memory

Static memory is a region where data is stored which will not be deallocated. The main use cases for static memory are:

- **Static Variables**: In Rust, variables with the static keyword are stored in static memory. They are globally accessible and persist for the lifetime of the program. While static variables are possible to use in Rust, their use is generally discouraged, much like in many other programming languages.

- **Constant Data**: Constants (const) are also stored in static memory, and while they are immutable, they can be accessed globally.
- **String Literals**: String literals, such as “hello”, are stored in static memory and have the type &'static str. They are immutable and persist for the entire duration of the program.

Ownership

Ownership is the first central concept that enables memory safety without a garbage collector. Understanding ownership is key to mastering Rust, as it governs how memory is managed and how data is accessed, modified, and freed.

Ownership is governed by specific rules that are essential to understand and memorize. How ownership manages values is determined by Rust's copy and move semantics. But first, let's review the ownership rules:

Ownership Rules

- The three ownership rules are:
- Each value has a variable which is the owner
- There can only be one owner
- When the owner goes out of scope, the value is dropped, whether it resides on the stack or on the heap.

It's crucial to distinguish between a variable and a value in this context. According to the first rule, a variable holds a value, and the third rule states that when the variable goes out of scope, the value is dropped. Variables are simply names used by the compiler; they no longer exist when your program is running, except for debugging purposes. The compiler tracks when a variable goes out of scope and removes it accordingly, either from the stack or the heap.

It's important to note that we are specifically discussing owned values here. References, on the other hand, are managed by the borrowing rules, which we will cover in the next section.

A scope refers to the section or block of a program where a value remains valid. When the scope ends, Rust automatically cleans up the value. Typically, a value goes out of scope at the end of the block where its owning variable is declared, which occurs when the closing } of that block is reached.

The way ownership is managed varies depending on the type. Let's explore this further in the next section.

Copy vs. Move

A type in Rust can be either a move or a copy type. The semantics of an assignment depend on whether the type is Copy or Move.

When you assign a variable to another variable and the type is a copy type, a duplicate of the value is created, resulting in two separate copies of the same value in memory.

Ch03/Examples/bin/example01.rs

```
let a = 1;
let b = a;
println!("{a} {b}");
```

In this case, after the first statement, the value `1` is placed on the stack, and the variable `a` holds that value. After the second statement, another value `1` is placed on the stack, and the variable `b` holds this second `1`. Changing `a` to another value will not affect `b` and vice versa.

1. When you assign a variable to another variable and the type is a move type, the value is transferred from the first variable to the second, thereby invalidating the first variable. After the operation, there is still only one instance of the value in memory, and only the second variable is the owner. The first variable can no longer be used, enforced by Rust's ownership rules.
2. A value can be stored either on the stack or on the heap, and a type can have either move or copy semantics, depending on how it's handled. These two properties, location and, move or copy are independent of each other, so a move type can be on the heap or the stack as well as a copy type.

Ch03/Examples/bin/example02.rs

```
let a = String::from("hello");
let b = a;
println!("{a} {b}");
```

In this case, `a` is a variable of type `String`, which adheres to move semantics. Instead of making a copy of the value, ownership is transferred. The ownership of the value moves from `a` to `b`. This has two implications:

- You can no longer use `a`, resulting in a compiler error if you try, as shown in the example

- When the new owner, b, goes out of scope, the value will be dropped.

First, the value is created with a as its owner. When a is assigned to b, not only does b now hold the value, but ownership is also transferred, making a invalid. When a goes out of scope, there are no side effects since it no longer owns the value. However, when b goes out of scope, the value originally associated with a is deallocated.

Now that we've explored the ownership model, it's time to move on to references and the rules that govern them.

References and Borrowing

References are a fundamental concept in Rust, allowing you to access data without taking ownership. This is crucial for writing efficient and safe code, as it enables multiple parts of your program to read or modify data without unnecessary copying or moving.

References are independent of the copy or move semantics, meaning you can have references to copy as well as to move types.

When referencing values, you can do so in two ways: immutably or mutably. Each comes with its own set of restrictions. Let's go over them one at a time:

Immutable reference

An immutable reference allows read-only access to the value.

Ch03/Examples/bin/example03.rs

```
let a = 3;
let b = &a;
println!("{a}, {b}");
```

b has a reference to the value of a. In effect there is only one value and a as well as b are working with this single value.

You can have multiple immutable references at the same time. You have a reference from the line where the reference is created until the line where the reference is last used. This concept is called lifetime.

When you use the variable holding an immutable reference you will get automatic access to the value. You will get an automatic dereference. In the previous example a and b are both printed in the same way, a is of type i32 and, b is of type &i32. Still b is used without the * for dereference. It is allowed to do so like this:

```
println!("{}, {}", a, *b);
```

The variable b is dereferenced using the * operator before the variable name. However, this usually has the same effect as using the variable directly, so the * is often omitted when not necessary.

As an aside, when using string interpolation in Rust, you can place a variable name directly between the curly braces. However, you cannot put an expression inside the curly braces. If you need to use an expression, you must provide it as a separate argument to println!. These arguments are position-based: the first argument corresponds to the first placeholder, the second argument to the second placeholder, and so on.

Mutable Reference

A mutable reference allows read and write access to the value.

Ch03/Examples/bin/example04.rs

```
let mut a = 4;
let b = &mut a;
*b += 1;
println!("{b}");
```

In this example, b is getting a mutable reference to a. The value of a is incremented by one through the mutable reference b is holding. There are a few things to note here on how to make this work. First a must be a mut variable to get a mutable reference. Signaling to the compiler as well as to the developer that the value a is holding can be changed somewhere, and second, in the increment assignment there is no automatic dereference. The *b, is saying use the value instead of the reference itself hence doing the dereference.

This feels a little strange, when using an immutable reference you will get the automatic dereference, when using a mutable reference you will not, and have to dereference yourself. This topic will be discussed further in the book when we cover the Deref trait.

You can only have one active mutable reference to a value at any given time. However, Rust's compiler analyses the *lifetimes* of these references, how long each one is actually used, rather than just where they are declared. This means it's possible to create multiple mutable references in the same function, as long as their lifetimes do not overlap. If the compiler can determine that an earlier mutable reference is no longer used before a new one is created, it will allow it. This is a result of Rust's lifetime concept, which allow for more flexible but still safe borrowing.

This piece of code will compile:

Ch03/Examples/bin/example05.rs

```
let mut a = 5;
let b = &mut a;
let c = &mut a;
println!("{c}");
```

And this piece of code will not compile:

```
let mut a = 4;
let b = &mut a;
let c = &mut a;
println!("{b}");
```

The main difference between these two examples is that in the first example the last use of `b` is before getting the second mutable reference `c` and therefore there is no conflict. In the second example, `b` is used in the print statement, after getting the second mutable reference, in effect having an overlapping usage of two mutable references, and the compiler will complain.

As before, the lifetime of a reference spans from the moment it is created until its last use. For a mutable reference, its lifetime must never overlap with any other reference's lifetime to the same value.

Borrowing Rules

The following rules summarize having one or more reference to the same data:

- You can have multiple immutable references simultaneously.
- You can have at most one mutable reference at any given time.
- You cannot have both an immutable reference and a mutable reference at the same time.

Compiler Guarantees

Why does Rust enforce strict rules for ownership and borrowing? When learning Rust, you'll likely encounter situations where the borrow checker seems restrictive, preventing you from doing something you want. This often happens because Rust's compiler is designed to enforce certain guarantees that prevent common programming errors and ensure memory safety. These rules help prevent issues like data races, null pointer dereferencing, and memory leaks. Rust achieves this level of safety without relying on a garbage collector, which can add overhead and complexity in other languages.

The following compiler guarantees are enforced:

Memory Safety

The compiler guarantees memory safety by enforcing strict rules around ownership, borrowing, and lifetimes. This eliminates common memory-related errors such as:

- **Null Pointer Dereferencing**: Rust's type system does not allow null pointers.
- **Dangling Pointers**: Rust ensures that references cannot outlive the data they point to.
- **Buffer Overflows**: Rust's safe indexing prevents accessing out-of-bounds memory.

Data Race Freedom

The compiler guarantees that data races are impossible in safe Rust code. A data race occurs when two or more threads access the same memory location concurrently, and at least one of the accesses is a write. Rust prevents this by enforcing:

- **Exclusive Mutable Access**: Only one mutable reference to a piece of data is allowed at a time.
- **Read-Only Shared Access**: Multiple immutable references are allowed, but no mutable references can coexist with them.

No Use of Uninitialized Variables

The compiler ensures that variables are always initialized before they are used. This prevents undefined behavior that could arise from using uninitialized memory.

Move Semantics

Rust's ownership model uses move semantics to manage resource allocation and deallocation automatically. This prevents issues like:

- **Double Free Errors**: Rust ensures that each value is dropped exactly once, preventing multiple deallocations.
- **Use-After-Free Errors**: Rust prevents access to memory after it has been deallocated.

Borrow Checker

The borrow checker enforces rules on how references are used, ensuring that:

- **Lifetimes are Valid**: References do not outlive the data they point to.
- **Exclusive Mutability**: Only one mutable reference exists at a time, preventing concurrent modifications.
- Having all these compiler guarantees is a blessing on one hand as they prevent many of the classic errors that are easy to make in other languages. However, they also require you to contend with the borrow checker, which can sometimes make it more challenging to get your program to compile. This often results in more time spent during the compilation process but less time needed for debugging and testing.

Ownership and Borrowing Applied

This section will explore how ownership and borrowing are applied when using common Rust constructs such as functions, loops, and structs. Each context introduces its own considerations and nuances.

Ownership and Borrowing with Functions

When you have a function you can transfer values to and getting values from that function in three different ways:

- Give or get the value in ownership
- Give or get an immutable reference
- Give or get a mutable reference

We explore the implications of these different transfer methods, noting that the distinction between stack and heap is irrelevant in this context. Both stack and heap values follow the same rules for scope and cleanup.

Parameter with Ownership Transfer

When you transfer a value of a copy type in ownership, a copy of the value is made and passed to the function, while the original value remains valid after the function call. Once the function ends and the parameter goes out of scope, only the copied value is dropped.

Ch03/Examples/bin/example06.rs

```
fn process_copy_type(value: i32) -> i32 {
    println!("Inside function: {}", value);
    value * 2
}

fn main() {
    let x = 6;
    let y = process_copy_type(x);

    println!("Original value: {}", x);
    println!("Processed value: {}", y);
}
```

When `process_copy_type` ends, the parameter value, which is a copy, is dropped. The original variable `x` remains valid and is dropped at the end of the `main` function.

In contrast, when you transfer a value of a move type in ownership to a function, there are two key consequences. First, after the value is transferred, it is no longer accessible in the calling function. If this was a literal value, it's expected, but if it was a variable, that variable becomes invalid. Second, when the function ends and the parameter goes out of scope, the value is dropped.

Ch03/Examples/bin/example07.rs

```
fn process_move_type(value: String) -> String {
    println!("Inside function: {}", value);
    value
}

fn main() {
    let s = String::from("Hello");
    let s_processed = process_move_type(s);
    println!("Processed value: {}", s_processed);
}
```

In this case, because `String` is a move type, the variable `s` becomes invalid after calling `process_move_type`. The value is moved into the function and is passed back as a function return value.

When returning a value from a function in ownership, if the value is a copy type, a copy is sent back to the calling function, and the original value within the function is dropped. For move types, the original value and its ownership are transferred to the caller. This may involve either creating a new value within the function to transfer ownership or receiving a value as a parameter and then returning it to the caller, effectively completing a roundtrip transfer of ownership.

Parameter as Immutable Reference

When you transfer an immutable reference, it doesn't matter whether the underlying type is a copy or move type because no ownership is transferred and no copy is made. As a result, there is no cleanup required when the function ends. The original value remains accessible in the calling function, but it cannot be modified during the lifetime of the reference due to the immutable borrow. Even if the type implements `Copy`, no copy is made, which can be beneficial for performance when dealing with large types.

The following example demonstrates this idea:

Ch03/Examples/bin/example08.rs

```
fn print_value(value: &String) {
    println!("Value inside function: {}", value);
}

fn main() {
    let large_string = String::from("Hello again");

    print_value(&large_string);
    println!("Original value: {}", large_string);
}
```

Returning a Reference

Returning a reference from a function requires more careful consideration. It is not possible to return a reference to a local variable because the local variable will be dropped when it goes out of scope, which happens when the function ends. This would result in a dangling reference, violating Rust's safety guarantees, and the compiler will prevent it. Similarly, you cannot return a reference to a value that was passed in ownership to the function, as the value will be dropped when the parameter goes out of scope. The only viable option for returning a reference is to accept a reference as a parameter and then return that reference or a reference to a part of that reference.

Ch03/Examples/bin/example09.rs

```
fn valid_reference(s: &String) -> &String {
    s
}

fn main() {
    let s = String::from("Hello, world!");
    let reference = valid_reference(&s);
    println!("{}", reference);
}
```

In this example, the string s is passed in as a immutable reference and returned as a reference from the function. There is a lot more to say about this topic which will be addressed in the chapter about lifetimes.

Parameter as Mutable Reference

A mutable reference follows the same principles as an immutable reference. The key difference is that you can only have one mutable reference at a time, and you cannot have any immutable references to the same value while a mutable reference exists. Furthermore, the function can now change the value the reference is pointing to.

Ch03/Examples/bin/example10.rs

```
fn valid_mutable_reference(s: &mut String) {
    s.push_str(", world!");
}

fn main() {
    let mut s = String::from("Hello");
    println!("{}", s);
    valid_mutable_reference(&mut s);
    println!("{}", s);
}
```

In this example the reference is changed to a mutable reference, to make this work the variable must be made a mutable variable.

When trying to print `s` after calling `valid_mutable_reference` and before the print od result will give a compiler error:

Ch03/Examples/bin/example11.rs

```
fn valid_mutable_reference(s: &mut String) -> &String {
    s.push_str(", world!");
    s
}

fn main() {
    let mut s = String::from("Hello");
    println!("{}", s);
    let result = valid_mutable_reference(&mut s);
    println!("{}", s);
    println!("{}", result);
}
```

You will get a compiler error:

```
error[E0502]: cannot borrow `s` as immutable because it is also
borrowed as mutable
```

When you call `valid_mutable_reference(&mut s)`, you're creating a mutable borrow of s. This borrow is returned from the function and assigned to the variable result. As long as result is used later in the code, the mutable borrow is considered active, because Rust must assume that the reference could still be used.

Now, the issue arises when you try to access s directly again, for example, in `println!("{}", s);`, while that mutable reference (held by result) is still alive. This creates a conflict: Rust's rules state that you cannot have an active mutable borrow and an access (mutable or immutable) to the original value at the same time.

So, when you use result after trying to print s, the compiler sees this overlap in lifetimes and raises an error.

However, if you remove the `println!("{}", result);` line, or swap the order so that result is used before s is accessed again, the compiler sees that the mutable borrow ends before s is accessed, and the code compiles.

Ownership and Borrowing in Structs

Taking ownership of a part of a struct in Rust transfers the ownership of that specific field from the struct to a new owner, such as a variable or a function parameter. Once this transfer occurs, the original field inside the struct becomes inaccessible, ensuring that only one part of the program owns and can manipulate that value at any given time. This strict ownership model guarantees memory safety by preventing invalid memory access and ensuring proper resource management.

A similar principle applies to borrowing. You can borrow a single field of a struct, and this borrow does not affect access to the other fields. However, once a field has been moved or borrowed, certain restrictions apply to the entire struct. Specifically, you cannot move the whole struct or take a mutable reference to it if any of its fields are currently borrowed (immutably or mutably) or have been moved. These restrictions allow the borrow checker to enforce clear and safe access patterns, preventing conflicting accesses or unsafe mutations.

In essence, Rust treats each field of a struct as a separate entity with respect to ownership and borrowing. However, as soon as a part of the struct is moved or borrowed, Rust may limit what you can do with the struct as a whole. This ensures consistent and safe behaviour at compile time.

Let's look at an example where a single field of a struct is moved:

Ch03/Examples/bin/example12.rs

```
struct Book {
    title: String,
    author: String,
}

fn main() {
    let book = Book {
        title: String::from("Learning Rust"),
        author: String::from("Freek van Keulen"),
    };

    let moved_title = book.title;
    println!("Title: {}", moved_title);
    println!("Author: {}", book.author);
}
```

The `book.title` is moved out of the struct because `String` is a move type. As a result, `book.title` is no longer accessible, and `book_title` becomes the new owner and is accessible. Additionally, you cannot use the struct as a whole, either by moving or borrowing, after this operation.

Ownership and Borrowing in Arrays

Due to the nature of an array, there are a few restrictions on taking ownership or borrowing part of the array. This is because arrays have fixed sizes and their elements are stored contiguously in memory.

Transferring ownership

Moving a single element out of an array is not allowed. Be aware that moving is only happening when the type of the element is a move type. Because of the characteristics of an array, fixed size and contiguity, moving a single element out is prohibited. You can of course borrow a single element or a slice of elements from an array. Before delving into borrowing let's look at a few alternatives for moving a single element out.

- **Using a Vec<T>**: `Vec<T>` is a variable size array giving you the possibility to add or remove elements. This is the obvious choice. Working with `Vec<T>` will be addressed later in the book
- **Replacing with a default value**: You can take ownership of an element by replacing it with a default value if the type implements the Default trait. As with Vec<T> traits will be covered later in the book. As demonstrated in the following example:

  Ch03/Examples/bin/example13.rs

  ```
  let mut numbers = [
      String::from("one"),
      String::from("two"),
      String::from("three"),
  ];

  let taken = std::mem::replace(&mut numbers [1],
  String::default());
  println!("Taken value: {}", taken);
  println!("Array after taking an element: {:?}", numbers);
  ```

We use the `std::mem::replace` function to replace the value at index 1: `strings[1]` with the default value for String, which is an empty string: `String::default()`.

- **Swapping with a temporary variable:** Another method is to swap the element with a temporary variable and then work with that variable. As demonstrated in the following example:

  Ch03/Examples/bin/example14.rs

  ```
  let mut fruit = [
      String::from("apple"),
      String::from("banana"),
      String::from("cherry"),
  ```

```
];
let mut temp = String::from("no more fruit");
std::mem::swap(&mut fruit[1], &mut temp);
println!("Taken value: {}", temp);
println!("Array after swapping: {:?}", fruit);
```

The `std::mem::swap` function takes these two mutable references and swaps their values.

Taking an immutable borrow, slicing

It is possible to have multiple immutable borrows of single elements or slices from an array. A slice is inherently a borrow, either mutable or immutable, and represents a consecutive sequence of elements from the array. Later, when we discuss `Vec<T>`, we'll see that it's also possible to obtain slices from a `Vec<T>`. Slices from arrays and `Vec<T>` both yield the same slice type, `&[T]` for immutable slices or `&mut [T]` for mutable slices.

Here's how you can obtain a slice from an array:

Ch03/Examples/bin/example15.rs

```
let numbers = [1, 2, 3, 4, 5, 6];
let slice = &numbers[1..4];
println!("Slice: {:?}", slice);
println!("Original array: {:?}", numbers);
```

In this example, the slice is defined by the start index and the end index. The element at the end index is not included in the slice. To include the end index, you can use the = character:

```
let slice = &numbers[1..=4];
```

The type of the array is `[i32; 6]`, while the type of the slice is `&[i32]`.

To get a mutable slice, you do the following:

```
let slice = &mut numbers[1..4];
```

It's important to note that you cannot obtain more than one mutable slice from the same array in this manner even if the slices do not overlap. The following code will not compile:

Ch03/Examples/bin/example16.rs

```
let mut numbers = [1, 2, 3, 4, 5, 6];
let slice1 = &mut numbers[1..2];
let slice2 = &mut numbers[3..5];
println!("Slice: {:?}", slice1);
```

Even though the slices do not overlap, Rust's borrowing rules prevent this, resulting in the following error:

```
error[E0499]: cannot borrow `numbers` as mutable more than once
at a time
```

However, you can achieve this using the `split_at_mut` function, which divides an array into two parts at a specified index. If you need smaller slices, you can then take subslices from these split parts:

Ch03/Examples/bin/example17.rs

```
let mut numbers = [1, 2, 3, 4, 5, 6];
let (first_part, second_part) = numbers.split_at_mut(2);
let slice1 = &mut first_part[1..2];
let slice2 = &mut second_part[0..1];
println!("Slice1: {:?}", slice1);
println!("Slice2: {:?}", slice2);
```

In this code, `split_at_mut` safely divides the array into two non-overlapping mutable slices, allowing you to work with both `slice1` and `slice2` without violating the borrowing rules.

Ownership and Borrowing in Control Flow

When iterating over an array Rust moves each element out of the array when the type of the element is a move type.

Ch03/Examples/bin/example18.rs

```
let numbers = [
    String::from("one"),
    String::from("two"),
    String::from("three")];
for num in numbers {
    println!("Moved value: {}", num);
}
```

The `numbers` array is used in a way that transfers ownership of each element individually. After the loop, the array is no longer accessible. However, if the elements are of a copy type, the array remains accessible because the values are copied rather than transferred.

It is also possible to loop over the array with an immutable borrow like this:

Ch03/Examples/bin/example19.rs

```
for num in &numbers {
    println!("Immutable Borrowed value: {}", num);
}
```

Numbers is iterated over while getting an immutable borrow. The array will still be available after the loop.

Finally, the mutable borrow:

Ch03/Examples/bin/example20.rs

```
let mut numbers = [
    String::from("one"),
    String::from("two"),
    String::from("three")];
for num in &mut numbers {
    num.push('*');
}
println!("{:?}", numbers);
```

We now take a mutable borrow wit &mut on the array. Note that now the variable must be mutable as soon as you take a mutable borrow. Each element in the array gets appended with a `*` using the push function on String. And again the array will still be available after the mutable borrow.

When doing the same on a basic type the code looks slightly different:

Ch03/Examples/bin/example21.rs

```
let mut numbers = [1, 2, 3];
for num in &mut numbers {
    *num += 1;
}
println!("{:?}", numbers);
```

This feels odd again, when the element type is String and we are calling a function on string, we don't have to dereference. This is odd for a different reason though. The reason why is discussed in the chapter about structs. When the element type is a basic type we do have to dereference with a `*`.

Fighting the Borrow Checker

In this section, we'll look at examples where the borrow checker raises errors, examine the error messages, and explore how to resolve these issues. These problems can sometimes be challenging to fix, and the process is often colloquially referred to as "fighting the borrow checker." When encountering such issues, it's helpful in the long run to fully understand why the error occurs rather than opting for quick fixes, like using `clone`. By approaching borrow checker issues this way, you'll find that these problems tend to occur less frequently over time.

Here are a few examples that demonstrate how the Rust borrow checker works and the common problems that arise when borrowing is misused:

Mutable and Immutable Borrowing at the Same Time

Rust does not allow mutable and immutable references to coexist within the same scope. This is because mutable references can change the value, which would invalidate any immutable references.

Ch03/Examples/bin/example22.rs

```
fn main() {
    let x = 5;
    let r1 = &x;
    let r2 = &mut x;
    println!("r1: {}, r2: {}", r1, r2);
}
```

Produces the following error:

```
error[E0502]: cannot borrow x as mutable because it is also
borrowed as immutable
```

In this example, the lifetime of the immutable borrow starts at line 3 and lasts until line 5, while the lifetime of the mutable borrow starts at line 4 and also ends at line 5. Since these lifetimes overlap, having both an immutable and a mutable reference at the same time is not allowed. The fix in this case is simple: change the mutable reference to an immutable one by removing `mut`.

Dangling References

Rust prevents the creation of dangling references, where a reference would point to an invalid memory location after the original data is dropped.

Ch03/Examples/bin/example23.rs

```
fn main() {
    let r;
    {
        let x = 5;
        r = &x;
    }
    println!("r: {}", r);
}
```

Produces the following error:

```
error[E0597]: x does not live long enough
```

In this example, an inner scope is created where the local variable x is declared. Once the inner scope ends, x goes out of scope and its value is dropped, making any reference to x invalid afterward. There are several ways to fix this issue:

- Remove the inner scope, placing everything in the same scope.
- Declare the variable x outside the inner scope to ensure it lives longer.
- Return the value from the inner scope, transferring ownership of the value.

Double Mutable Borrow

Rust enforces strict rules for mutable references: only one mutable reference is allowed at any time. This helps prevent data races and ensures safe concurrent access.

Ch03/Examples/bin/example24.rs

```
fn main() {
    let mut s = String::from("Hello");

    let r1 = &mut s;
    let r2 = &mut s;
    println!("r1: {}, r2: {}", r1, r2);
}
```

Produces the following error:

```
error[E0499]: cannot borrow s as mutable more than once at a
time
```

This issue is similar to the first example, but now involves two mutable references instead of one, leading to a different error. To resolve this, both references can be made immutable.

Use After Move

When a variable is moved, its ownership is transferred, and the original variable can no longer be used. Rust prevents access to the original variable after it has been moved to avoid potential errors.

Ch03/Examples/bin/example25.rs

```
fn main() {
    let s1 = String::from("hello");
    let s2 = s1;
    println!("{}", s1);
}
```

Produces the following error:

```
error[E0382]: borrow of moved value: s1
```

In this case, `s1` is moved to `s2`, which makes `s1` invalid. To fix the example, you can print `s2` instead of `s1` in the final line.

Modifying While Borrowed

Modifying a value while it is borrowed immutably is prohibited. Rust ensures the data remains unchanged while it is immutably borrowed.

Ch03/Examples/bin/example26.rs

```
fn main() {
    let mut s = String::from("hello");
    let r1 = &s;
    s.push_str(", world!");
    println!("{}", r1);
}
```

Produces the following error:

```
error[E0502]: cannot borrow s as mutable because it is also
borrowed as immutable
```

In this example, the issue is less obvious because `push_str` takes a mutable borrow on `s`.While you can see this by inspecting the definition of `push_str`, it's not immediately clear when just reading the code. The name `push_str` suggests a mutable borrow, but it's not as explicit as when you pass `&mut` directly in the function call. To fix this, you can take the reference after the `push_str` operation rather than before.

Mutating an Array While Iterating Over It

This example shows the attempt to mutate an array while iterating over it, which results in a borrow checker error. The code attempts to multiply each element of the array and store the result in the first element of the array.

Ch03/Examples/bin/example27.rs

```
fn main() {
    let mut numbers = [1, 2, 3, 4, 5];
    for num in &numbers {
        numbers[0] *= *num * 2;
    }
    println!("{:?}", numbers);
}
```

Produces the following error:

```
error[E0506]: cannot assign to numbers[_] because it is
borrowed
```

The `for` loop borrows `numbers` immutably with `&numbers`. However, inside the loop, you attempt to modify the array with `numbers[0] *= *num * 2`, which requires a mutable borrow. The borrow checker flags this as an error because Rust prevents mutable and immutable borrows from overlapping in the same scope to ensure memory safety.

Changing `&numbers` to `&mut` numbers won't help as it produces another, yet similar error:

```
error[E0503]: cannot use numbers because it was mutably
borrowed
```

Let's break it down further. The `for` loop itself takes an immutable borrow of the entire array and gives an immutable borrow of each element, one at a time, to the loop body. When we loop over `&mut numbers`, the `for` loop takes a mutable borrow of the array and provides a mutable borrow of each element, represented by num, to the loop body. However, when you access `numbers[0]` inside the loop, it tries to take another mutable reference at the same time. Taking an mutable reference to a single element of an array is effectively borrowing the entire array mutably. This creates a conflict because the `for` loop is holding a mutable reference, and Rust does not allow both a mutable and immutable reference at the same time, which is why the compiler raises an error.

One solution is to iterate using indices instead of borrowing, like this:

Ch03/Examples/bin/example28.rs

```
fn main() {
    let mut numbers = [1, 2, 3, 4, 5];
    for i in 0..numbers.len() {
        numbers[0] *= numbers[i] * 2;
    }
    println!("{:?}", numbers);
}
```

These examples demonstrate how the Rust borrow checker enforces strict rules to ensure memory safety, preventing data races, dangling pointers, and other common issues in systems programming.

Summary

Rust's unique approach to memory management sets it apart from other programming languages by ensuring memory safety without the need for a garbage collector. This is achieved through the concepts of ownership and borrowing, which are fundamental to Rust's ability to prevent common issues like data races and memory leaks. These principles are crucial for writing efficient and safe Rust programs.

Rust uses both the stack and the heap for memory allocation. The stack handles fixed-size data, while the heap manages dynamic, variable-sized data. Rust automatically manages memory allocation and deallocation, preventing manual memory management errors like memory leaks and dangling pointers.

Every value in Rust has a single owner, and ownership can be transferred (moved) but not duplicated unless the type implements the `Copy` trait. When an owner goes out of scope, Rust automatically drops the owned value, ensuring proper cleanup of resources. Copy types, such as integers, are duplicated when assigned to another variable, while move types, like `String`, transfer ownership. This distinction helps Rust manage memory safely and efficiently.

Borrowing allows data to be accessed through references, enabling multiple parts of a program to use the data without taking ownership. Borrowing can be immutable or mutable, with strict rules to prevent data races and ensure safe data access. Rust's compiler enforces these rules to guarantee memory safety, preventing issues like null pointer dereferencing, dangling pointers, buffer overflows, and data races.

Ownership and borrowing principles apply in various contexts, including functions, structs, and arrays. In functions, values can be passed by ownership, immutable reference, or mutable reference, each with different implications for data safety and performance. In structs, each field is treated as a separate entity regarding ownership and borrowing, allowing for flexible data management while ensuring safety. Arrays, due to their fixed size and contiguous nature, have restrictions on moving individual elements. Instead, borrowing (both immutable and mutable) and techniques like swapping with default values or temporary variables are used.

When iterating over arrays, elements can be moved if they are of move types, or borrowed immutably or mutably. The chosen method affects whether the array remains accessible after the iteration. Rust's ownership and borrowing system is central to its design, ensuring that memory management is safe and efficient without requiring a garbage collector. By adhering to these principles, Rust programs can avoid common errors and perform well in terms of memory and speed. Understanding these concepts is crucial for mastering Rust and writing robust, high-performance code.

In the next chapter, we will explore User Defined Types (UDTs), which allow you to create your own custom data structures. We'll focus on two of the most important and widely used forms in Rust: structs, which let you group related data into a single cohesive unit, and enums, which enable you to define types that can represent different variants or states. These tools form the foundation for building complex and expressive programs in Rust.

Exercises

1. Write a function that takes an integer and a String as parameters. Explain whether the values are stored on the stack or the heap and why.
2. Given a function `take_ownership(s: String)`, explain what happens when you pass a String variable to this function. Write the code and try accessing the variable after the function call.
3. Write a function that takes an i32 as a parameter and explain why the original variable can still be used after the function call.
4. Write a function `print_length(s: &String)` that prints the length of a string. Demonstrate how to call this function without transferring ownership.
5. Write a function `append_text(s: &mut String)` that appends " World!" to a given string. Show how to call this function and ensure that the original string is modified.
6. Write code that demonstrates how you can have multiple immutable references to the same data at the same time. Explain the conditions under which this is allowed.
7. Write code to borrow a slice of an array. Show how to modify the slice.
8. Use `split_at_mut` to safely split an array into two non-overlapping mutable slices. Explain why this is necessary and what restrictions apply.
9. Write code that iterates over an array of String elements, consuming each element. Explain why the array is no longer usable after this operation.
10. Modify the previous exercise to iterate over the array with immutable references. Explain the difference in the array's usability after the iteration.

Project: Command-Line Calculator

Project Preparation

You might need one or all of the following functions to make the project

trim()

In Rust, the `trim` method is used to remove leading and trailing whitespace from a string slice `&str`. This method is particularly useful for cleaning up user input or processing data where extraneous whitespace needs to be removed.

Example

```
fn main() {
    let original = "    Hello, World!    ";
    let trimmed = original.trim();
    println!("Original: '{}'", original);
    println!("Trimmed: '{}'", trimmed);
}
```

split_whitespace()

In Rust, the `split_whitespace` method is used to split a string slice `&str` into an iterator of substrings, separated by whitespace. This method is particularly useful for parsing and processing text where words or tokens are separated by spaces, tabs, or newline characters.

Example

```
fn main() {
    let text = "Hello, world! This is Rust.";
    let words = text.split_whitespace();

    for word in words {
        println!("{}", word);
    }
}
```

Specification

Objective

Develop a command-line calculator that accepts basic arithmetic formulas as input and returns the result. The calculator should support addition, subtraction, multiplication, and division.

Features and Requirements

Input Parsing: The calculator should accept a single-line input string containing a basic arithmetic expression (e.g., "3 + 5").

- The expression should consist of two operands and one operator.
- Operands can be integers or floating-point numbers.
- Operators should include addition (`+`), subtraction (`-`), multiplication (`*`), and division (`/`).
- The program should be able to handle spaces around the numbers and operators gracefully.

Operations Supported

- **Addition:** Calculate the sum of two numbers (e.g., "3 + 5" should output 8).
- **Subtraction:** Calculate the difference between two numbers (e.g., "9 - 4" should output 5).
- **Multiplication:** Calculate the product of two numbers (e.g., "6 * 7" should output 42).
- **Division:** Calculate the quotient of two numbers (e.g., "10 / 2" should output 5). Handle division by zero by displaying an appropriate error message.

Output

Display the result of the calculation on the command line.

If the input format is incorrect, display a user-friendly error message indicating the nature of the error (e.g., "Invalid input format. Please use the format: number operator number").

For division, if the result is not an integer, output should be a floating-point number.

Error Handling

- Handle invalid input formats (e.g., missing operands or operators, non-numeric input).
- Display a clear error message for division by zero (e.g., "Error: Division by zero is undefined.").
- Prevent the program from crashing on invalid input.

User Interface

- The calculator should run in a loop, allowing the user to enter multiple expressions without restarting the program.
- Provide an option for the user to exit the program (e.g., by typing "exit" or "quit").

Extensibility

Design the program in a modular way to allow easy addition of more complex operations in the future (e.g., exponentiation, modulus, etc.).

04

Structs and Enums

Structs, short for structures, are one of the most common **User Defined Types** (**UDTs**), used to group related data together. They enable the creation of custom types by combining multiple fields, allowing developers to model complex real-world objects or abstract concepts in a concise way. In Rust, structs are not just about grouping data, they also provide functionality by allowing methods to be defined on them, making them a first-class type.

Enums, or enumerations, represent another key UDT in Rust, offering a way to define a type by specifying its possible variants. Enums are particularly powerful in Rust because they can hold data and are deeply integrated with pattern matching, a core feature of Rust's control flow and error handling mechanisms. Enums are ideal for representing data that can take on multiple distinct forms, making code more expressive and maintainable.

Both structs and enums are at the heart of Rust's ability to define and use UDTs, allowing developers to create types that go beyond the built-in primitives. This capability is essential for building complex software in a way that is both clear and manageable. While Rust is not strictly object-oriented, its use of structs, enums, and traits incorporates many object-oriented principles such as encapsulation and polymorphism.

We will cover the following main topics:

- **Structs**: Custom data types that let you group related values together in a meaningful way.
- **Enums**: Types that can represent a value which could be one of several variants, each possibly holding different types and amounts of associated data.
- **Generics**: Enable you to write flexible and reusable code by allowing types to be parameters in functions, structs, and enums.

Together, these features form the foundation for writing robust, scalable, and expressive Rust programs, empowering developers to design code that is both type-safe and adaptable to a wide range of problem domains.

Structs

The most basic elements or members of a struct are fields. A `struct` is a combination of 0 or more fields into one single container that can be handled as a unit as well as in separate parts.

Suppose we want to have a 2D point where the x and y coordinate are integers. You will do this as follows:

Ch04/Examples/src/bin/example01.rs

```
struct Point {
    x: i32,
    y: i32,
}
```

The `struct` keyword is required, and curly braces must be used when defining a struct with at least one field. Fields are separated by commas, and it's idiomatic to include a trailing comma after the last field to facilitate easy copying and pasting. It is mandatory to supply a type on each field. This can be any type so it can be a struct type as well, allowing composition.

Using the `let` keyword, we create a `Point` value. It is required to initialize all fields in the `struct`. As shown in the `println!` statement, you can access individual fields of the `struct` using dot notation.

Ch04/Examples/src/bin/example02.rs

```
fn main() {
    let p = Point {
        x: 3,
        y: 4,
    };
    println!("Point coordinates: ({}, {})", p.x, p.y);
}
```

In this example, a `Point` is created and assigned to `p`. The creation of the `Point` uses curly braces. When instantiating a struct, it's required to initialize all its fields. After the `Point` is created, the individual fields are printed, resulting in the following output:

```
Point coordinates: (3, 4)
```

To print an entire `struct` in Rust, we need to take two steps:

1. Use the `:?` formatter in the `println!` macro.
2. Add the `#[derive(Debug)]` attribute to the struct to automatically enable printing for debugging purposes.

Ch04/Examples/src/bin/example03.rs

```
#[derive(Debug)]
struct Point {
    x: i32,
    y: i32,
}

fn main() {
    let point = Point { x: 3, y: 4 };
    println!("The point is: {:?}", point);
}
```

- In this example we show the use of: `#[derive(Debug)]`: This automatically implements the `Debug` trait, allowing you to print the struct. This will be further explained in the next chapter on traits.
- `{:?}`: This is the formatter used inside `println!` to print the struct in a readable debug format.

Runing the example gives the following output:

```
The point is: Point { x: 3, y: 4 }
```

This setup makes it easy to inspect the values inside your structs during debugging.

There are two types of macros in Rust. The first type, like `println!`, is a **declarative macro**, often used for templating. These macros are expanded into Rust code by replacing the macro name and its optional parameters with the corresponding Rust code.

The second type is a **procedural macro**, which can be applied to items like structs or functions. An example of this is `#[derive(Debug)]`. Procedural macros are functions that receive the entire **abstract syntax tree** (**AST**) of the item they are applied to. This AST contains detailed information, such as the struct's name, its fields, and their types. The macro function then generates Rust code based on the AST. In the `#[derive(Debug)]` example, the macro produces Rust code that implements the `Debug trait`, which typically includes a method inside an `impl` block.

Methods

A **method** is a function defined within an `impl` block that operates on an instance of a `struct`. In this example, the `translate` method is defined for the `Point` struct and takes a reference to another `Point` as a parameter. It returns a new `Point` whose coordinates are the sum of the original point (self) and the offset point. This method encapsulates behavior related to the `Point` type, allowing for more intuitive and structured manipulation of its data.

```
impl Point {
    fn translate(&self, offset: &Point) -> Point {
        Point {
            x: self.x + offset.x,
            y: self.y + offset.y,
        }
    }
}
```

Every method that is attached to a `struct` must be put in an `impl` block. After the `impl` keyword the name of the `struct` for which you are defining the methods is specified. It is possible to have multiple methods in one `impl` block and it is also possible to have multiple `impl` blocks for the same `struct`.

Within the `impl` block, there is a method named `translate`. The first parameter, `&self`, is a reference to the instance of the `Point` struct on which the method is called. The second parameter, `offset`, is another `Point` that specifies the amount by which the original point should be translated. This method returns a new `Point` representing the translated coordinates. The notation `self.x` refers to the `x` field within the `Point` struct for the specific instance on which the method is invoked.

Ch04/Examples/src/bin/example04.rs

```
fn main() {
    let p1 = Point { x: 2, y: 3 };
    let offset = Point { x: 4, y: 5 };
    let translated_point = p1.translate(&offset);
    println!("The point is: {:?}", translated_point);
}
```

When calling the translate method `p1` is passed into the `&self` parameter, while `&offset` is passed into the `offset` parameter.

The following is the output:

```
The point is: Point { x: 6, y: 8 }
```

We will now explore various aspects of using methods in structs, focusing on the different ways to apply self and instances where self is not required.

self, &self and, &mut self

When defining a function, there are three ways to utilize the struct on which the method is called Using `self` (without &) means that ownership of the struct is transferred into the method. This implies that the struct will be dropped at the end of the method, and the value cannot be used afterward. In the context of the `translate` function, it would look like this:

Ch04/Examples/src/bin/example05.rs

```
#[derive(Debug)]
struct Point {
    x: i32,
    y: i32,
}

impl Point {
    fn translate(self, offset: &Point) -> Point {
        Point {
            x: self.x + offset.x,
            y: self.y + offset.y,
        }
    }
}

fn main() {
    let p1 = Point { x: 2, y: 3 };
    let offset = Point { x: 10, y: 12 };
    let p1 = p1.translate(&offset);
    println!("The point is: {:?}", p1);
}
```

In this example, the `translate` method takes ownership of self, which means that after the method is called, the original `p1` can no longer be used. To continue using the result of the translation, we reassign the returned `Point` to the same variable name using `let p1 = p1.translate(&offset);`. This effectively creates a new `Point` and binds it to the variable `p1`, replacing the old one. This pattern is common in Rust when working with methods that take ownership, especially when working with immutable values where in-place mutation is not possible.

Here is the output:

```
The point is: Point { x: 12, y: 15 }
```

The next example is using `&self`, meaning the point `p1` can still be used after the method is called. In that example calling `translate` on `p1` results also in a new point. In that case, we don't reassign it to the same variable but are introducing a new variable. Working this way is not strictly needed but it makes more sense to introduce a new variable here because after calling translate the value in `p1` is still valid

```
impl Point {
    fn translate(&self, offset: &Point) -> Point {
        Point {
            x: self.x + offset.x,
            y: self.y + offset.y,
        }
    }
}

fn main() {
    let p1 = Point { x: 2, y: 3 };
    let offset = Point { x: 10, y: 12 };
    let p2 = p1.translate(&offset);
    println!("The original point is: {:?}", p1);
    println!("The new point is: {:?}", p2);
}
```

Finally, we can use `&mut self`, changing the point itself. When using this strategy, it makes sense to not return a Point from the method because the Point on which the `translate` method is called is changed itself.

Ch04/Examples/src/bin/example06.rs

```
#[derive(Debug)]
struct Point {
    x: i32,
    y: i32,
}

impl Point {
    fn translate(&mut self, offset: &Point) {
        self.x += offset.x;
```

```
        self.y += offset.y;
    }
}

fn main() {
    let mut p1 = Point { x: 2, y: 3 };
    let offset = Point { x: 5, y: 7 };
    p1.translate(&offset);
    println!("The point is: {:?}", p1);
}
```

Since we are modifying `p1` directly in this case, `p1` must be declared as `mut`. The implementation of `translate` differs significantly because no new Point is created. Furthermore, there is no return value from the translate function hence there is no assignment when calling the `translate` method.

The following is the output:

```
The point is: Point { x: 7, y: 10 }
```

Associated Methods

Finally, a method defined in an `impl` block does not always require `self`, `&self`, or `&mut self` as its first parameter. A common idiomatic example in Rust is the `new` method. While it resembles a constructor from object-oriented languages, it's more accurately described as a factory method that returns a new instance of a type, such as a `Point` struct. Although it's not strictly required for such a method to be defined within an `impl` block for the same type, or even within an `impl` block at all, it is conventionally placed there for clarity and organization.

Ch04/Examples/src/bin/example07.rs

```
#[derive(Debug)]
struct Point {
    x: i32,
    y: i32,
}

impl Point {
    fn new(x: i32, y: i32) -> Point {
        Point {
            x: x,
            y: y,
        }
    }
}
```

```
fn main() {
    let mut _p1 = Point::new(2, 3);
}
```

In this case, the specification of the new method is placed within an `impl` block, and the first parameter is not a variant of `self`. When invoking an associated method, you need to reference the type name, followed by `::`, and then the method name. It's common practice to name this method `new`, which is the convention used here.

Self

Within an `impl` block, you can use `Self` (with an uppercase `S`) to refer to the type being implemented, instead of using the specific type name. In the case of `Point`, this would translate to:

Ch04/Examples/src/bin/example08.rs

```
impl Point {
    fn new(x: i32, y: i32) -> Self {
        Self {
            x: x,
            y: y,
        }
    }
}
```

Field Init Shorthand

The field `init` shorthand in Rust is a convenient syntax for initializing the fields of a struct. It allows you to directly use variables with the same name as the struct's fields without repeating the field names. This shorthand reduces boilerplate code and makes the initialization more concise and readable.

To create an instance of `Point`, you typically initialize its fields by specifying each field explicitly:

```
let x = 5;
let y = 10;
let p = Point { x: x, y: y };
```

With field `init` shorthand, you can write this more concisely if the variables `x` and `y` have the same names as the struct fields:

```
let x = 5;
```

```
let y = 10;
let p = Point { x, y };
```

In the shorthand syntax, Rust automatically infers that the variable `x` should be used to initialize the field `x` in the `Point` struct, and similarly for `y`. This shorthand can only be used when the variable names and field names are identical.

- It eliminates the need to repeat the field names, reducing redundancy in your code.
- It makes the code cleaner and more concise, making it easier to read and maintain.
- It reduces the potential for errors when assigning values, as there are fewer opportunities to mix up field and variable names.

Field `init` shorthand is a useful feature in Rust for simplifying struct initialization, particularly when dealing with structs that have many fields or when the field names match the variable names being used.

Typical use case is the new method, this will reduce to:

Ch04/Examples/src/bin/example09.rs

```
impl Point {
    fn new(x: i32, y: i32) -> Self {
        Self {
            x,
            y,
        }
    }
}
```

Ownership and Borrowing

Understanding ownership is essential when working with structs, as it dictates how data is accessed and modified. Here's a detailed explanation of how ownership works with structs:

When working with structs, the ownership and borrowing rules apply to the struct as a whole and its individual fields. We will examine each possibility individually:

- **Transferring Ownership:** When a struct instance is assigned to another variable or passed to a function, ownership is transferred (moved). After the move, the original variable can no longer be used.

  ```
  let p1 = Point::new(2, 3);
  let p2 = p1;
  ```

Even though both fields of the struct implement the `Copy` trait, the default behavior for the struct itself is `move`. This means that when you assign `p1` to `p2`, the ownership of `p1` is transferred to `p2`, and as a result, `p1` is no longer accessible after the assignment. This behavior occurs because Rust treats the struct as a single entity rather than applying the `Copy` trait to each individual field unless the entire struct explicitly implements `Copy`.

- **Partial Moves**: You can partially move fields out of a struct if the fields themselves do not implement `Copy`.

Ch04/Examples/src/bin/example10.rs

```
#[derive(Debug)]
struct Container {
    a: String,
    b: String,
}

fn main() {
    let c1 = Container {
        a: String::from("Hello"),
        b: String::from("Rust")
    };
    let _a_string = c1.a;

    println!("{}", c1.b);
}
```

After the last statement in this example `c1.a` is no longer accessible. `c1.b` can still be used. When part of a struct is moved, the remaining struct can no longer be used as a whole.

- **Immutable Borrowing:** You can borrow a struct immutably, allowing multiple reads but no writes.

Ch04/Examples/src/bin/example11.rs

```
fn print_point(point: &Point) {
    println!("Point is at ({}, {})", point.x, point.y);
}

fn main() {
    let p = Point { x: 5, y: 10 };
    print_point(&p);
}
```

In this example, the `println`! macro is taking two immutable borrows from fields of the struct. When you borrow a field of a struct, you are effectively borrowing the entire struct. Both borrows are immutable and happening simultaneously, this is allowed under Rust's borrowing rules.

- **Mutable Borrowing:** Mutable borrowing allows modifying the borrowed data but ensures no other references exist during the mutation.

Ch04/Examples/src/bin/example12.rs

```
fn move_point(point: &mut Point, dx: i32, dy: i32) {
    point.x += dx;
    point.y += dy;
}

fn main() {
    let mut p = Point { x: 5, y: 10 };
    move_point(&mut p, 3, 4);
}
```

When you take a mutable borrow of a field, you're actually borrowing the entire struct mutably. Rust's borrowing rules prevent having two mutable borrows at the same time. In this example, `point.x += dx;` takes a mutable borrow, and the next line, `point.y += dy;`, takes another mutable borrow on the same struct. Since these borrows occur sequentially, not simultaneously, the borrowing rules are upheld.

Copy Instead of Move

When you want a struct to exhibit copy behavior instead of move at the struct level, you can mark the struct with the `Copy` and `Clone`. The full explanation on this marking and the related traits is deferred to the next chapter on traits. For now, you can look at this as an annotation.

```
#[derive(Copy, Clone)]
struct Point {
    x: i32,
    y: i32,
}
```

Adding the `Copy` trait in the first line changes the struct's behavior from Move to Copy semantics. The `Clone` trait is required to provide a default implementation for cloning the struct's value. A restriction is that every field type in the struct must also implement `Copy`, and therefore, `Clone` as well.

Struct Update Syntax

The struct update syntax in Rust is a convenient feature that allows you to create a new struct instance by copying most of the fields from an existing instance while specifying new values for some fields. This is particularly useful when you want to create a new instance that is similar to an existing one but with some modifications.

The struct update syntax uses the `..` syntax to copy remaining fields from an existing instance. Here's a detailed breakdown:

- **Specify New Values**: You first specify the new values for the fields you want to change.
- **Use .. to Copy the Rest**: After specifying the new values, you use `..` followed by the name of the existing instance from which you want to copy the remaining fields.

Ch04/Examples/src/bin/example13.rs

```
#[derive(Debug)]
struct Point {
    x: i32,
    y: i32,
    z: i32,
}

fn main() {
    let p1 = Point { x: 1, y: 2, z: 3 };
    println!("p1: {:?}", p1);

    let p2 = Point { x: 10, ..p1 };
    println!("p2: {:?}", p2);
}
```

In this example a variable p1 of type Point is created. It's initialized with the values `x = 1`, `y = 2`, and `z = 3`. A second variable `p2` of type Point is created. The x field of `p2` is set to `10`, but the `..p1` syntax means that the remaining fields (y and z) are copied from `p1`. Resulting in the following output:

```
p1: Point { x: 1, y: 2, z: 3 }
p2: Point { x: 10, y: 2, z: 3 }
```

- **Ownership and Copying:** The fields being copied must implement the `Copy` trait if they are being taken from `p1` because the original instance `p1` might still be used after the update. If the fields do not implement `Copy` and the original instance is no longer used, Rust will move the fields instead of copying them otherwise this will result in a compile error.

- **Immutable Fields:** If `p1` were mutable and `p2` were mutable, any changes to `p2` would not affect `p1` because a new instance is created, and the fields are either copied or moved.
- **Partial Struct Update:** The struct update syntax only allows you to change certain fields, not add new ones or remove existing ones. The struct's type and layout must remain consistent.

References and Self Referential Structs

For now, we'll only use owned types in our structs, meaning we won't include reference fields. This is because working with reference fields requires additional considerations, such as lifetimes, which we'll cover later in the book. It's also possible to have a field that is the same type as the struct itself, creating a self-referential struct. However, this requires more advanced techniques, like using smart pointers, which we'll also explore later.

Tuple Structs

Tuple structs in Rust are a form of struct that behaves like a tuple but has a name associated with it, providing more clarity and type safety compared to using plain tuples. Tuple structs are useful when you want to group multiple values together without naming each field but still want to give the grouping a distinct type.

A tuple struct is defined similarly to a regular struct but without field names. Instead, it consists of a name and a list of types, just like a tuple. The fields in a tuple struct are accessed using positional indices, starting from 0.

Here's the basic syntax for defining a tuple struct:

```
struct TupleStructName(Type1, Type2, Type3, ...);
```

Consider a tuple struct representing a 3D point:

```
struct Point3D(i32, i32, i32);
```

This tuple struct, `Point3D`, groups three `i32` values. You can create instances of `Point3D` and access its fields using positional indices.

To create an instance of a tuple struct, you use its name followed by the values for each field in parentheses:

```
let point = Point3D(1, 2, 3);
```

This creates a `Point3D` instance with the fields set to 1, 2, and 3, respectively.

Fields in a tuple struct are accessed using a dot (`.`) followed by the index of the field:

```
let x = point.0;
let y = point.1;
let z = point.2;
```

In this example, `point.0` accesses the first field of the `Point3D` tuple struct, `point.1` accesses the second field, and `point.2` accesses the third field.

Tuple structs are particularly useful in the following scenarios:

- **Newtype Pattern:** When you want to create a new type that wraps an existing type, providing type safety and possibly new behavior. For example:

  ```
  struct Inches(i32);
  let length = Inches(10);
  ```

Here, `Inches` is a new type that wraps an `i32`, making it distinct from other `i32` values.

- **Simplifying Complex Data Structures:** When you need to group multiple values together without the overhead of naming each field, especially in cases where the fields are conceptually similar or closely related.

Tuple structs in Rust provide a useful middle ground between plain tuples and regular structs. They offer the conciseness of tuples with the added benefit of a distinct type name, making your code more type-safe and expressive. By choosing tuple structs, you can encapsulate and organize data in a way that is both efficient and clear, depending on the needs of your application.

Field-less Structs

Field-less structs, also known as **unit-like structs** or **unit structs**, are a special type of struct in Rust that do not have any fields. These structs are defined without specifying any data, and they are typically used for purposes other than holding data, such as type-level programming, creating distinct types, or implementing specific traits.

A field-less struct is defined similarly to a regular struct but without any fields in the following ways:

```
struct StructName;
```

```
struct StructName{}
struct StructName();
```

Here, `StructName` is the name of the field-less struct, and it does not contain any data fields inside the curly braces or parentheses. For example:

```
struct Unit;
```

In this example, `Unit` is a field-less struct with no data fields.

Field-less structs can be instantiated without any arguments:

```
let u = Unit;
```

Because they have no fields, there is no need to provide data during instantiation.

The following use cases have been identified for field-less structs:

- **Type-Safe Flags or Markers:** Field-less structs can be used to create distinct types that act as flags or markers, making the code more type-safe and self-documenting. For example, in a state machine, different states can be represented using different field-less structs.
- **Zero-Sized Types:** Field-less structs are considered **zero-sized types** (**ZSTs**) in Rust, meaning they occupy no memory. This property is useful when the struct is used only for type-level distinction or tagging, without the need to store any data.
- **Trait Implementation:** Sometimes, you might want to implement a trait for a type that doesn't need to store data. Field-less structs provide a way to do this.
- **Unit-Like Struct Instances:** Field-less structs can also be used to create unit-like struct instances, similar to the unit type `()`. This is particularly useful in cases where the presence of a type is required, but the data itself is not important.

When comparing with other structs we observe the following:

- **Regular Structs:** Unlike regular structs, field-less structs do not store any data. Regular structs are used to group related data together, whereas field-less structs serve as types with specific meanings or purposes.
- **Tuple Structs:** Tuple structs have unnamed fields and can store data, while field-less structs do not have fields at all.

Field-less structs in Rust are a versatile feature used for a variety of purposes beyond data storage. They are primarily used for type-level programming, acting as markers, flags, or phantom types. By understanding and leveraging field-less structs, you can create more expressive and type-safe Rust code, especially in scenarios where the existence of a type conveys important information without the need for associated data.

Generics with Structs

Generics in Rust allow you to write flexible and reusable code by defining data types or functions that can operate on many different types while ensuring type safety. When used with structs, generics enable the creation of data structures that can store or operate on values of any type, provided certain constraints are met. Here's a detailed explanation of how to use generics with structs in Rust:

Defining a Struct with Generics

To define a struct with generics, you use angle brackets < > after the struct name, specifying one or more generic type parameters. These parameters act as placeholders for the types that will be used when an instance of the struct is created.

```
struct StructName<T> {
    field: T,
}
```

In this example, `T` is a generic type parameter, and `field` is a field of type `T`.

Consider a simple example of a generic `Point` struct that can hold coordinates of any type:

```
struct Point<T> {
    x: T,
    y: T,
}
```

Here, `Point` is defined with a generic type `T`, allowing `x` and `y` to be of any type `T`.

Creating Instances of Generic Structs

When creating an instance of a generic struct, you must specify the concrete type for the generic parameters. Rust can often infer these types based on the values you provide.

```
let int_point = Point { x: 5, y: 10 };
let float_point = Point { x: 1.5, y: 4.2 };
```

In this example, `int_point` is a `Point` with `i32` coordinates, and `float_point` is a `Point` with `f64` coordinates. Rust infers the types from the values provided.

Multiple Generic Parameters

You can use multiple generic parameters in a struct, each with its own constraints.

```
struct Pair<T, U> {
    first: T,
    second: U,
}
let pair = Pair { first: "Hello", second: 123 };
```

Here, `Pair` is a generic struct with two type parameters, `T` and `U`, allowing each field to be of a different type.

Generic Methods and Implementations

You can define methods on generic structs and also implement traits for them. When defining methods, additional generic parameters must be specified if they are not directly tied to the struct's definition. Here is a basic example:

Ch04/Examples/src/bin/example14.rs

```
impl<T> Point<T> {
    fn new(x: T, y: T) -> Self {
        Point { x, y }
    }
}
```

This implementation provides a `new` method for `Point` that works with any type `T`. There is much more to discuss about writing generic functions or methods, which will be covered in the next chapter on traits.

Enums

Enums, short for **enumerations**, are a powerful feature in Rust that allow you to define a type by enumerating its possible variants. Unlike enums in some other languages that are limited to being simple collections of constants, Rust's enums are more expressive and can hold different types and amounts of associated data for each variant. This makes enums in Rust versatile tools for representing a wide range of concepts.

Basic Enums

An enum in Rust is defined using the `enum` keyword, followed by the enum's name and a list of variants. Each variant can optionally hold data, and different variants can hold different types and amounts of data.

```
enum EnumName {
    Variant1,
    Variant2,
    Variant3,
}
```

Here, `EnumName` is the name of the enum, and `Variant1`, `Variant2`, and `Variant3` are its variants. Variants are typically written in CamelCase.

Ch04/Examples/src/bin/example15.rs

```
enum Direction {
    North,
    South,
    East,
    West,
}
```

In this example, `Direction` is an enum with four variants: `North`, `South`, `East`, and `West`.

Creating a value from an enum:

```
let current_direction = Direction::South;
```

The `South` value is selected from the `Direction` enum and assigned to the `current_direction` variable.

Enums with Data

Rust enums can hold additional data. Each variant can have different types and amounts of associated data, making them similar to tagged unions or algebraic data types in other languages.

Ch04/Examples/src/bin/example16.rs

```
enum Message {
    Quit,
    Move { x: i32, y: i32 },
```

```
    Write(String),
    ChangeColor(i32, i32, i32),
}
```

Here:

- `Quit` has no associated data.
- `Move` includes an anonymous struct with two `i32` fields, `x` and `y`.
- `Write` includes a `String`.
- `ChangeColor` includes three `i32` values as a tuple representing RGB color components.

To create an instance of the enum from example 17, specify the enum name, followed by the variant and any associated data.

```
let m1 = Message::Quit;
let m2 = Message::Move { x: 10, y: 20 };
let m3 = Message::Write(String::from("Hello"));
let m4 = Message::ChangeColor(255, 0, 0);
```

Using Enums

When it comes to working with enums, Rust offers several powerful tools for handling comparisons, particularly suited for working with different enum variants. We begin by exploring direct comparison techniques, where enums are compared using equality operators. From there, we move on to more advanced approaches like `match`, which allows for exhaustive pattern matching across all possible enum variants, and `if let`, a shorthand for handling specific cases without requiring a full `match` expression. Each of these tools provides flexibility in how enum variants are compared and processed.

Direct comparison

In Rust, comparing values of an `enum` type, such as a traffic light's state, often requires implementing the `PartialEq` trait. By default, Rust enums don't automatically support equality checks, so adding `PartialEq` enables the comparison of enum variants. For example, in a traffic control system, the `TrafficLight` enum can have variants like `Red`, `Yellow`, and `Green`. To check if the current traffic light is red, you need to compare the current state (`TrafficLight::Red`) with the stored state in the system. By deriving `PartialEq`, this comparison becomes straightforward using the == operator. The easiest way to do this is deriving it just like Debug

Ch04/Examples/src/bin/example17.rs

```
#[derive(Debug, PartialEq)]
enum TrafficLight {
    Red,
    Yellow,
    Green,
}

fn main() {
    let traffic_light = TrafficLight::Red;

    if traffic_light == TrafficLight::Red {
        println!("The light is red. Please stop.");
    }
}
```

In this example, comparison between enum values is made possible by deriving `PartialEq` in the first line. Without this derive (or manually implementing the trait), such comparisons would not be allowed.

Match

Enums are typically used with pattern matching, which allows you to execute code based on which variant of the enum you have. Rust's `match` expression is a powerful control flow construct for this purpose.

Ch04/Examples/src/bin/example18.rs

```
match msg {
    Message::Quit => println!("The Quit variant has no data."),
    Message::Move { x, y } => println!("Move to: {}, y: {}", x,
y),
    Message::Write(text) => println!("Text message: {}", text),
    Message::ChangeColor(r, g, b) => {
            println!("Change color to r: {}, g: {}, b: {}", r,
g, b)
    }
}
```

In this example:

- `Message::Quit`: This branch matches if msg holds the `Quit` variant. The code `println!("The Quit variant has no data.");` is executed, indicating that the `Quit` variant does not carry any data.
- `Message::Move { x, y }`: This branch matches if msg holds the `Move` variant. The `{ x, y }` part destructures the data inside the `Move` variant, assigning the values to the local variables `x` and `y`. The `println!("Move to: {}, y:`

`{}", x, y);` statement prints the `x` and `y` coordinates, showing where the movement should occur.

- `Message::Write(text)`: This branch matches if msg holds the `Write` variant. The text part destructures the String inside the `Write` variant, assigning it to the local variable `text`. The `println!("Text message: {}", text); statement` prints the content of the text message.
- `Message::ChangeColor(r, g, b)`: This branch matches if msg holds the `ChangeColor` variant. The `(r, g, b)` part destructures the three `i32` values inside the `ChangeColor` variant, assigning them to the local variables r, g, and b. The `println!("Change color to r: {}, g: {}, b: {}", r, g, b);` statement prints the RGB values, indicating the new color.

If let

The `if let` syntax in Rust is a convenient way to work with enums when you are only interested in a single pattern. It provides a concise way to match a specific pattern and execute code if the pattern matches, without needing to use a full `match` statement.

Based on the previous `Message` enum example, `if let` can be used to handle a specific variant of the enum. For instance, if you're only interested in handling the `Message::Write` variant and want to ignore the others, you can use `if let`.

Ch04/Examples/src/bin/example19.rs

```
fn main() {
    let msg = Message::Write(String::from("Hello, world!"));
    if let Message::Write(text) = msg {
        println!("Text message: {}", text);
    } else {
        println!("Not a Write message.");
    }
}
```

Let's take a closer look:

- **Setting the value:** The `Message` enum has four variants: `Quit`, `Move`, `Write`, and `ChangeColor`. Each variant can optionally hold different data. In this example, `msg` is set to the `Write` variant of the enum with `Hello, world!` as payload.
- **Using `if let`**: The syntax `if let Message::Write(text) = msg` checks if `msg` matches the `Message::Write` variant. If `msg` is a `Write` variant, the pattern `Message::Write(text)` extracts the associated `String` value and

assigns it to the variable `text`. The code block following the `if let` runs if the pattern matches, in this case printing the content of the `text` message.

- **Else Block**: Optionally, you can include an `else` block to handle cases where the pattern does not match. In this example, the `else` block prints `Not a Write message.` if `msg` is not a `Write` variant.

Here are the key points:

- **Simplicity and Readability:** `if let` provides a simpler and more readable way to handle specific cases, especially when you're only interested in one specific variant or condition. It avoids the need to handle all possible variants, as required by `match`.
- **Optional else Block:** While `if let` focuses on a single pattern, you can use an `else` block to manage other cases if needed.
- **Single Pattern Matching:** It is ideal for scenarios where you only need to deal with one case and ignore the rest.

`if let` is a useful feature in Rust for pattern matching when you are only concerned with one variant of an enum or one specific condition. It enhances code clarity and reduces the verbosity compared to a full `match` statement, making it a preferred choice for simple conditional checks and extractions.

Advantages of Enums:

- **Type Safety:** Enums provide a way to define a type that can only take on a set of predefined variants, ensuring that only valid values are used.
- **Expressiveness:** With the ability to attach data to each variant, enums can represent complex states or choices in a type-safe manner.
- **Pattern Matching:** Rust's pattern matching capabilities allow for concise and expressive handling of different enum variants.
- **Enums in Structs and Functions:** Enums can be used as fields in structs or as parameters and return types in functions, further enhancing their versatility.

Basic enums in Rust are a versatile and powerful feature that allows developers to define types with a fixed number of variants. By optionally attaching data to each variant, enums can represent a wide range of complex data structures and states. The combination of enums and pattern matching in Rust provides a powerful way to write safe, clear, and concise code for handling different types of data.

Common Enums

Enums can also be combined with generics. This technique is demonstrated with the help of two enums from the standard library. Arguably, the most frequently used enums in Rust are `Result` and `Option`. Both are commonly employed to handle communication from functions, though they can be used in other contexts as well. The `Result` enum is utilized when a function might return an error, such as an I/O error. The `Option` enum is used when it is acceptable for a function to return no value. In this section, we will describe both enums and their basic usage patterns.

Option

Option is defined as:

```
enum Option<T> {
    None,
    Some(T),
}
```

The `Option` enum uses a generic type parameter `T`. This means that `Option` can hold a value of any type. The actual type to be used is specified when creating an instance of `Option`.

`Option<T>` has two variants:

- `None`: Indicates the absence of a value.
- `Some(T)`: Contains a value of type T.

Suppose we want a function that loops through a slice in search of a specific value. It is perfectly valid that the search may find nothing. This scenario is a typical example for using an `Option`. Because Rust does not support null pointers, using `Option` is the preferred way to handle such cases.

Ch04/Examples/src/bin/example20.rs

```
fn find_value(slice: &[i32], target: i32) -> Option<usize> {
    for i in 0..slice.len() {
        if slice[i] == target {
            return Some(i);
        }
    }
    None
}

fn main() {
    let numbers = [1, 2, 3, 4, 5];
```

```
    match find_value(&numbers, 3) {
        Some(index) => println!("Found at index {}.", index),
        None => println!(" not found in the slice."),
    }

    match find_value(&numbers, 6) {
        Some(index) => println!("Found at index {}.", index),
        None => println!("not found in the slice."),
    }
}
```

The code defines a function `find_value` that takes a slice of integers and a target integer as arguments. It searches through the slice to find the target value. The function returns an `Option<usize>` that has a value of `Some(index)` if the target is found at a particular index, or `None` if the value is not found.

Result

Result is defined as:

```
enum Result<T, E> {
    Ok(T),
    Err(E),
}
```

The `Result` enum uses two generic type parameters: `T` and `E`.

- `T`: Represents the type of the value that is returned when the operation is successful.
- `E`: Represents the type of the error that is returned when the operation fails.

`Result<T, E>` has two variants:

- `Ok(T)`: Indicates a successful operation and contains a value of type T.
- `Err(E)`: Indicates a failed operation and contains an error of type E.

NOTE

Rust does not support an exception handling mechanism like Java or Python. Instead, using the Result enum for error handling is the preferred approach.

Imagine we want to create a function that calculates the square root of a number. If the input is greater than or equal to zero, the function should return the square root. However, if the input is negative, the function should return an error. Here's how we can implement this logic in the function:

Ch04/Examples/src/bin/example21.rs

```
#[derive(Debug)]
enum SqrtError {
    NegativeNumber,
}

fn calculate_sqrt(number: f64) -> Result<f64, SqrtError> {
    if number < 0.0 {
        Err(SqrtError::NegativeNumber)
    } else {
        Ok(number.sqrt())
    }
}

fn main() {
    let numbers = vec![4.0, -3.0, 9.0, -1.0];

    for number in numbers {
        match calculate_sqrt(number) {
            Ok(sqrt) => println!("The square root of {} is
{}.", number, sqrt),
            Err(e) => println!("Error: {:?} for number {}", e,
number),
        }
    }
}
```

We define a custom error enum `SqrtError` with a variant `NegativeNumber`, indicating the input is negative. The `calculate_sqrt` function takes a `f64` as input and returns a `Result<f64, SqrtError>`. It checks if the number is negative, returning `Err(SqrtError::NegativeNumber)` if true. Otherwise, it computes the square root using the `sqrt` method and returns `Ok(sqrt_value)`.

Summary

In this chapter, we explored two crucial components of Rust's data representation: Structs and Enums. These constructs allow Rust developers to model complex data in an efficient and structured manner, while adhering to the language's emphasis on safety and performance.

Structs are a fundamental data type used to group related data together by combining multiple fields into a single entity. They help organize and represent complex data structures, modeling both real-world objects and abstract concepts. Structs can contain fields and methods, and although Rust is not a purely object-oriented language, it incorporates many object-oriented principles such as encapsulation and polymorphism. Fields within structs are individual pieces of data that can be accessed using dot notation, and each field must have a specified type. Methods, defined in `impl` blocks, allow struct instances to perform actions or calculations. These methods can use `self`, `&self`, or `&mut self`, indicating different levels of ownership and mutability. Additionally, associated methods, those without `self`, are often used for constructing new struct instances. Structs can also be combined with generic types, enhancing flexibility and reducing code duplication while maintaining type safety.

Enums, or enumerations, define a type by listing its possible variants, each of which can hold different types and amounts of associated data. This makes enums highly versatile for representing various states or choices. Rust's enums are more powerful than in many languages, as they can hold additional data, allowing for more complex data structures. Pattern matching with the `match` statement enables precise handling of different enum variants, while the `if let` syntax offers a simpler way to match a specific variant without needing a full `match` block. Two commonly used enums in Rust are `Option`, which represents an optional value (`Some` for a value and `None` for the absence of it), and `Result`, which is used for error handling, indicating success with `Ok` or failure with `Err`.

In summary, Rust's structs and enums provide versatile, powerful tools for structuring and managing data. They allow developers to clearly and concisely represent complex data structures and states, while leveraging the strong typing and pattern matching features that make Rust an efficient and safe programming language.

Building on the foundation of structs and enums, the next step in mastering Rust's type system is understanding traits. Traits define shared behavior in a way that is both flexible and type-safe, allowing different types to implement the same interface. They enable polymorphism without the need for inheritance, making them central to Rust's approach to code reuse and abstraction. In the next chapter, we will dive into how traits work, how to define and implement them, and how they interact with generics to create expressive and reusable code patterns.

Exercises

1. Define a Person struct with fields name (String) and age (i32). Create an instance of Person and print the fields as well as the complete struct with debug formatting.
2. Define a Rectangle struct with fields width and height. Implement a method area that calculates the area of the rectangle.
3. Define a tuple struct Color that stores three values: red, green, and blue. Create an instance. Print the fields with the help of the index.
4. Define an Enum called TrafficLight with variants Red, Yellow, and Green. Write a function that takes a TrafficLight and prints the state.
5. Define an Enum called Shape with variants Circle(f64) and Rectangle(f64, f64) to represent geometric shapes. Write a function to calculate the area for each variant.
6. Create a struct Point3D with fields x, y, and z. Write a constructor using field init shorthand to initialize Point instances.
7. Define an enum Message with variants Text(String), Move { x: i32, y: i32 }, and Quit. Implement a function that prints the contents of the Message based on its variant.
8. Define a struct Counter that holds a value count and has methods to increment the count. Use self, &self, and &mut self in different methods to demonstrate ownership and borrowing.
9. Define a generic struct Pair that holds two values of potentially different types. Then, implement a few methods for the struct to manipulate and access its data. These methods should demonstrate the use of generics, ownership, and borrowing.
10. Define a Book struct with fields title, author, and pages. Implement a method is_long that checks if the book has more than 300 pages. Demonstrate the use of the is_long method and struct update syntax to create a new Book with an updated title, keeping other fields the same.

Project: Library Management System

You are tasked with building a simple library management system that allows users to interact with a collection of books. The system should enable users to perform common library operations such as borrowing, returning, and viewing books, with additional features such as filtering books by genre.

The system should meet the following requirements:

Book Structure

- Each book has attributes: title, author, genre, number of pages, and status (available, borrowed, or reserved).

Library Structure

- The library holds a predefined collection of books. Keep a fixed number of books in an array.
- Borrow a book by its title, provided it is available.
- Return a book they have borrowed, making it available again.
- View all available books in the library.
- View books by genre (e.g., Fiction, NonFiction, Science, History, Fantasy).

Operations

- When borrowing a book, the system should update its status to `borrowed` and provide a message indicating the book has been successfully borrowed, or notify if the book is not available.
- When returning a book, the system should mark the book as `available` and confirm the return.
- The system should list all books currently available in the library.
- Users should be able to filter and list books by genre.

When you use an array for the collection, after initialization of the library it is not possible to add or remove books.

Sample Book Collection

- *Starlight Chronicles: Voyage Beyond the Edge of Time* by Dr. Celeste Orion (Science Fiction, 384 pages).
- *The Hobbit* by J.R.R. Tolkien (Fantasy, 310 pages).
- *A Brief History of Time* by Stephen Hawking (Science, 256 pages).

Functionality

- Implement the ability to search for a book by title when borrowing or returning.
- Display details such as title, author, genre, and status when listing books.
- Ensure the system handles cases where a book is not found or is unavailable for borrowing.

Create the required structures (`Book`, `Library`, `Genre`, `BookStatus`) and methods to fulfill these operations and interactions.

05

Traits

Traits are a fundamental feature in Rust that enable polymorphism, code reuse, and abstraction, making them an essential concept for any Rust programmer to master. At their core, traits define shared behavior for different types, allowing you to write code that can operate on multiple types in a generic and reusable way. This chapter will introduce the concept of traits in Rust, explore how they work, and demonstrate how they can be used to create flexible and modular code.

Rust's approach to traits is similar to interfaces in languages like Java or abstract base classes in C++, but with some key differences that align with Rust's focus on safety, performance, and flexibility. Unlike interfaces and abstract classes, Rust traits are implemented at compile time, ensuring zero-cost abstractions with no runtime overhead. This makes traits an incredibly powerful tool for defining common behavior and interfaces across a variety of types, without sacrificing performance or type safety.

In this chapter, we will cover the following topics:

- **Basics of Traits:** Learn what traits are in Rust, how to define and implement them, and how to use default implementations to provide common behavior for multiple types.
- **Common Traits in Rust:** Explore commonly used traits like Debug, Display, Clone, Copy, Eq, and PartialEq, and how they simplify standard operations and comparisons.
- **Advanced Trait Features:** Understand advanced features such as trait bounds, generics, associated types, and the Sized and ?Sized traits, which enhance flexibility and type management.
- **Trait Objects and Dynamic Dispatch:** Discover trait objects and dynamic dispatch, allowing for runtime flexibility, and learn about object safety and its importance in using traits effectively.
- **Super traits:** Learn about trait inheritance to build upon existing traits and create more powerful and reusable abstractions.

By the end of this chapter, you'll have a solid understanding of how traits empower you to write expressive, efficient, and idiomatic Rust code. Whether you're coming from C++'s world of virtual functions and abstract base classes or just getting started with generics, traits will become a cornerstone of your Rust programming toolkit.

Basics of Traits

In this section, we will explore the basics of traits in Rust, including what they are, how to define and implement them, and how to use default method implementations to provide common behavior.

Definition and Purpose of Traits in Rust

In Rust, a trait is a collection of methods defined for an unknown type. Traits can be implemented by any type that wants to provide the behavior or functionality defined by the trait. Essentially, a trait is like a contract that a type must adhere to, specifying what methods it must implement.

Traits allow you to define shared behavior across different types without knowing what those types are in advance. By defining a set of methods in a trait, you can ensure that any type implementing that trait will have those methods available. This enables polymorphism, where the same code can operate on different types in a generic way, provided they all implement the same trait.

For example, consider a trait called `Animal` that defines a behavior for making a sound:

Ch05/Examples/src/bin/example01.rs

```
trait Animal {
    fn make_sound(&self);
}
```

Any type that implements the `Animal` trait must provide an implementation for the `make_sound` method. This allows you to write code that can work with any type implementing `Animal`, regardless of what that type actually is as shown in the following example.

Ch05/Examples/src/bin/example02.rs

```
struct Dog;

impl Animal for Dog {
    fn make_sound(&self) {
        println!("Bark!");
    }
}
```

```
struct Cat;

impl Animal for Cat {
    fn make_sound(&self) {
        println!("Meow!");
    }
}
```

In this example, both `Dog` and `Cat` implement the `Animal` trait, allowing them to be used interchangeably.

Defining and Implementing Traits

To define a trait in Rust, you use the `trait` keyword followed by the trait's name and a block containing method signatures. A method signature in a trait does not include a method body. Instead, it specifies what methods a type must implement to fulfill the trait. Here's the basic syntax for defining a trait:

```
trait TraitName {
    fn method_name(&self);
}
```

Let's define a simple trait named `Printable` that requires a method `print`:

```
trait Printable {
    fn print(&self);
}
```

This `Printable` trait specifies that any type implementing it must provide a `print` method.

To implement a trait for a specific type, you use the `impl` keyword followed by the trait name for the type you want to implement it for. Inside the `impl` block, you provide the actual method implementations required by the trait:

Ch05/Examples/src/bin/example03.rs

```
struct Document {
    content: String,
}

impl Printable for Document {
    fn print(&self) {
        println!("Document content: {}", self.content);
    }
}
```

```
struct Image {
    data: Vec<u8>,
}

impl Printable for Image {
    fn print(&self) {
        println!("Image with {} bytes", self.data.len());
    }
}
```

In this example, both `Document` and `Image` implement the `Printable` trait. This means they both have a `print` method that can be called.

Default Implementations in Traits

Traits in Rust can also provide default method implementations. This allows you to define a method in the trait itself, which types can use without having to provide their own implementation. Default methods can be overridden if a type needs to provide a different behavior.

To provide a default implementation, you simply define the method in the trait with a body:

```
trait Describable {
    fn describe(&self) -> String {
        String::from("An object")
    }
}
```

In this example, the `Describable` trait has a method `describe` with a default implementation that returns a generic description.

A type implementing a trait with default methods can override those methods by providing its own implementation. If a type does not override a default method, it uses the default implementation provided by the trait.

Ch05/Examples/src/bin/example04.rs

```
struct Book {
    title: String,
}

impl Describable for Book {
    fn describe(&self) -> String {
        format!("A book titled '{}'", self.title)
```

```
    }
}

struct Author;

impl Describable for Author {
    // Uses the default implementation of describe
}
```

In this example, `Book` provides its own implementation of the `describe` method, while `Author` uses the default implementation.

Traits in Rust are a powerful mechanism for defining shared behavior across different types. By understanding how to define, implement, and use traits effectively, you can write more modular, reusable, and flexible code. This chapter covered the basics of traits, including how to define and implement them, as well as how to use default methods to provide common behavior. With this knowledge, you can start leveraging traits to create more powerful abstractions and cleaner code in Rust.

Common Traits in Rust

Traits in Rust define shared behavior for different types, and the standard library provides several commonly used traits that make everyday tasks more convenient and idiomatic. In this section, we'll explore some of these core traits, `Debug`, `Display` and `Clone`, `Copy` and `From`. Understanding these traits is crucial for writing effective Rust code, as they enable fundamental functionality like output formatting and data duplication.

Debug and Display

In Rust, the formatting traits `Debug` and `Display` play an essential role in controlling how types are presented when printed to the console for example. Each trait serves a different purpose: `Debug` is geared towards developers by providing detailed and unambiguous information about a type's internal state, while `Display` focuses on presenting user-friendly, aesthetically pleasing output. Understanding and implementing both traits can help in making custom types more flexible and readable for both debugging and user-facing output. Below is a deeper look at how each trait works, along with an example of how to implement both `Debug` and `Display` for a custom struct.

Debug

The `Debug` trait is used for developer-facing output, providing a way to format a type in a manner that is useful for debugging. When a type implements `Debug`, it allows instances of that type to be formatted using the `{:?}` and `{:#?}` placeholders in the `println!` macro and other formatting functions. The `Debug` output is designed to be unambiguous and is often used to provide detailed information about the internal state of a type. Adding # after the colon will format the output in a more readable, multi-line style instead of displaying everything on a single line.

To implement the `Debug` trait for a custom type, you need to use the `#[derive(Debug)]` attribute on the struct or manually implement the trait, providing a definition for the `fmt` method, which specifies how to format the type. In this case, you will typically rely on the derive.

Display

The `Display` trait is used for user-facing output, providing a way to format a type in a manner that is more readable and suitable for end-users. Unlike `Debug`, which is focused on providing detailed information for developers, `Display` is intended for producing output that is human-readable and aesthetically pleasing. Types that implement `Display` can be formatted using the `{}` placeholder in the `println!` macro.

To implement the `Display` trait for a custom type, you need to manually implement the trait and provide a definition for the `fmt` method, which specifies how to format the type in a user-friendly way.

In the function header `fmt(&self, f: &mut std::fmt::Formatter<'_>) -> fmt::Result`, the fmt parameter represents the formatting logic for how a type should be displayed when using the Display or Debug traits in Rust. Here's a breakdown of its components:

The `fmt` parameters are as follows:

- `&self:` A immutable reference to the type where this trait is implemented for
- `f: &mut fmt::Formatter<'_>`:
  - This is a mutable reference to a `fmt::Formatter` instance, which provides the tools needed to format and write the output for a given type.
  - The Formatter manages how the output should be structured, including options for width, alignment, and other formatting configurations.

- The '_ indicates a lifetime parameter, which is borrowed for the duration of the formatting process (you don't need to specify the lifetime in most cases). Lifetime parameters will be discussed at the end of the book.

`fmt` is utilized in the following manner:

- The `f` parameter is passed to the `write!` macro, which writes the formatted output to the given Formatter. This macro is used to construct and write the formatted string inside the `fmt` method.
- The `write!` macro accepts the `f` reference and the format string (in this case, `Point({}, {})`), followed by the values you want to insert into the placeholders `(self.x and self.y)`.
- Note that the `write!` macro functions similarly to the `println!` macro, with the key difference being that `write!` requires a formatter as its first parameter.

Let's look at an example where we implement both `Debug` and `Display` for a custom struct:

Ch05/Examples/src/bin/example05.rs

```
#[derive(Debug)]
struct Point {
    x: i32,
    y: i32,
}

impl std::fmt::Display for Point {
    fn fmt(&self, f: &mut std::fmt::Formatter<'_>) ->
std::fmt::Result {
        write!(f, "Point({}, {})", self.x, self.y)
    }
}

fn main() {
    let point = Point { x: 10, y: 20 };

    println!("Debug: {:?}", point);
    println!("Debug#: {:#?}", point);
    println!("Display: {}", point);
}
```

In this example:

- We define a struct `Point` with fields `x` and `y`.

- We derive the `Debug` trait, allowing the struct to be formatted using `{:?}` and `{:#?}`.
- We manually implement the `Display` trait to provide a custom, user-friendly output format using the `{}` placeholder.

Giving the following output:

```
Debug: Point { x: 10, y: 20 }
Debug#: Point {
    x: 10,
    y: 20,
}
Display: Point(10, 20)
```

The first `println!` produces the standard debug output in a single line. The second one presents a pretty-printed version spread across multiple lines, while the last one uses the display formatting as defined in the trait implementation.

Clone and Copy

The `Clone` and `Copy` traits in Rust are used for duplicating values, they are closely related but serve different purposes.

Copy

The `Copy` trait is used for types that support a bitwise (shallow) copy, meaning that the type's data can be duplicated simply by copying the bits on the stack. This is a very fast operation because it involves no heap allocation or complex logic. Types that implement `Copy` must have a fixed size and cannot own heap-allocated memory. Common `Copy` types include simple scalar types like integers and floats, as well as types composed entirely of `Copy` types. To implement `Copy` for a custom type, you can either use the `#[derive(Copy, Clone)]` attribute or manually implement it. The derive approach is the idiomatic and preferred method in Rust. As we covered in chapter 4 on structs and enums, a struct in Rust has move semantics by default. The `Copy` trait is a marker trait, meaning it doesn't require any functions to be implemented; it's essentially an empty trait. By implementing the `Copy` trait for a struct, you change its semantics from move to copy. (This means that, for example, in an assignment, the value is copied rather than transferring ownership.)

For a type to implement the `Copy` trait, it must meet several criteria:

- The type must have a fixed size known at compile time.
- The type must not implement the `Drop` trait, which is used for types that need to run custom logic when they go out of scope.

- All of the type's fields must also implement `Copy`.
- The `Clone` trait must be implemented when you implement the `Copy` trait.

The requirement to implement the `Clone` trait when you implement the `Copy` trait is enforced with trait inheritance which we'll cover in more detail later in this chapter. Essentially, this means that types must explicitly implement the `Clone` trait to allow cloning, and Rust's type system ensures this through its trait system. On the other hand, the restriction against implementing `Drop` on types that also implement `Copy` is an internal compiler rule. This is built directly into the language to prevent memory management conflicts, ensuring safe and efficient handling of resources.

Clone

In Rust, the `#[derive(Clone)]` attribute automatically generates a Clone implementation for a struct or enum. This means Rust will automatically create a method that allows instances of your type to be explicitly cloned by calling `.clone()`. The behavior of the auto-generated `Clone` method depends on the types of the fields in the struct or enum. If the fields themselves are Clone, Rust will generate code that calls `clone()` on each of them.

We will explore the different aspects of cloning:

Shallow Copy vs. Deep Copy

- **Shallow Copy**: A shallow copy creates a new instance of a type, but it only duplicates the references or pointers to the underlying data, rather than the data itself. In Rust, shallow copies happen automatically for **Copy types**, which are types stored on the stack and can be trivially duplicated without concern for ownership.
- **Deep Copy**: A deep copy duplicates both the values of the object and any heap-allocated or external resources it may contain. When Clone is derived for types that involve heap allocation (e.g., String, Vec), it ensures that the data on the heap is also duplicated, not just the reference to the heap memory. This prevents two objects from sharing the same heap memory, which could lead to data corruption or memory issues.

Copy vs. Move in Relation to Clone

- **Copy Types**: Rust allows types that are simple and have a fixed size (like integers, booleans, or types entirely on the stack) to implement the `Copy` trait. For Copy types, copying is trivial and happens automatically when they are assigned or passed to functions. If you derive Clone for a Copy type, the generated `.clone()` method will effectively be a shallow copy because the data can be copied by simply duplicating the bits on the stack. No heap allocation or resource management is involved.

Ch05/Examples/src/bin/example06.rs

```
#[derive(Copy, Clone)]
struct Point {
    x: i32,
    y: i32,
}
fn main() {
    let point1 = Point { x: 10, y: 20 };
    let point2 = point1;

    println!("Point1: {:?}", point1);
    println!("Point2: {:?}", point2);

    let point3 = point1.clone();
    println!("Point3: {:?}", point3);
}
```

In this case, assigning `point2` to `point1` and calling `clone()` on `point1` both perform a shallow copy because the struct implements `Copy`.

- **Move Types**: In contrast, move types are types that can manage resources (such as heap-allocated memory) and when they do cannot be trivially copied. When a move type (e.g., `String`, `Vec`) is assigned to another variable or passed to a function, ownership is transferred, and the original variable becomes invalid. To create a duplicate of the data without transferring ownership, the `Clone` trait is required. When `Clone` is derived for move types, Rust generates a deep copy, duplicating the heap-allocated data or resources.

Strictly speaking, you don't have to implement the `Clone` trait when working with a move type; you could simply define a `clone` method as a regular function. However, deriving the `Clone` trait is the simpler and more conventional approach, as shown in the following example.

Ch05/Examples/src/bin/example07.rs

```
#[derive(Clone)]
struct MyStruct {
    data: String,
}

fn main() {
```

```
    let s1 = MyStruct {
        data: String::from("Hello"),
    };
    // let s2 = s1;
    let s2 = s1.clone();
    println!("s1: {}", s1.data);
    println!("s2: {}", s2.data);
}
```

In this example, assigning `s1` to `s2` (in comment) transfers ownership because the struct follows move semantics. Since `String` is not `Copy`, the struct cannot implement `Copy`. If you want to duplicate the struct rather than move it, you need to call `clone()` in the code, which performs a deep copy, as shown in the next line.

You can write your own implementation of `Clone`, but in most cases, deriving it will handle the necessary shallow or deep copy, depending on the struct or enum's definition.

From

The `From` trait in Rust provides a simple and consistent way to convert one type into another. It is part of Rust's standard library and allows for easy, lossless conversions between types. Conceptually, the `From` trait defines how to transform a value of one type into another type in a well-defined manner. The key concepts are:

Lossless Conversion: The `From` trait is typically used when the conversion between types is safe and lossless, meaning no data is discarded or transformed in unexpected ways.

Simple Conversion: Implementing the `From` trait allows you to write conversions in a clean, readable manner, avoiding manual transformations. Once implemented, the `from()` method can be used to convert between types.

Automatic Integration with Into: When you implement the `From` trait for a type, Rust automatically provides the `Into` trait implementation for free. This means that you can either use `.from()` or `.into()` to convert between types.

Suppose we have a `Point2D` type that we want to convert into a `Point3D` type. The conversion will keep the `x` and `y` values the same and set `z` to 0. We can implement the `From` trait on `Point3D` for `Point2D`, which provides the associated `from()` method for `Point3D` and the `into()` method on a `Point2D` instance, both of which take ownership of the `Point2D` value.

Here is the From implementation:

Ch05/Examples/src/bin/example08.rs

```
#[derive(Debug, Copy, Clone)]
struct Point2D {
    x: i32,
    y: i32,
}

#[derive(Debug, Copy, Clone)]
struct Point3D {
    x: i32,
    y: i32,
    z: i32,
}

impl From<Point2D> for Point3D {
    fn from(point: Point2D) -> Self {
        Point3D { x: point.x, y: point.y, z: 0 }
    }
}

fn main() {
    let point2d = Point2D { x: 5, y: 10 };

    let point3d = Point3D::from(point2d);
    println!("{:?}", point3d);

    let point3d: Point3D = point2d.into();
    println!("{:?}", point3d);
```

In this example, note that the From trait is implemented for Point3D, which is the type we want to convert to. The generic type for the From trait is Point2D, which represents the type we are converting from. This allows you to implement the From trait on Point3D for different types. The implementation provides us with a from function, which is an associated method on Point3D that takes a Point2D parameter, and it also enables the into function, which is called on a Point2D instance.

This wraps up the first set of common traits used in Rust. Before diving into a few more, we need to cover some other topics, starting with operator overloading.

Operator Overloading

In Rust, operator overloading allows you to define custom behavior for operators when applied to your custom types. This is done by implementing specific traits that correspond to the operators you want to overload. For example, to overload the + operator, you need to implement the `Add` trait for your type. Similarly, for the equality operators == and `!=`, you can derive a default implementation of the related traits `PartialEq` and `Eq` or implement these yourself.

We demonstrate operator overloading by implementing the `Add` trait and deriving the `PartialEq` and `Eq` traits.

Add

To illustrate operator overloading for the + operator, let's create a simple 2D `Point` struct and implement the `Add` trait for it. This will enable us to use the + operator to add two `Point` instances together. Pay close attention to the definition of the trait parameters in the `add` function. Both parameters are defined with ownership, meaning that if the type is a copy type, both operands are copied. However, if the type is a move type, ownership of both operands is transferred, and both values are dropped after the addition is completed.

Ch05/Examples/src/bin/example09.rs

```
#[derive(Debug)]
struct Point {
    x: i32,
    y: i32,
}

impl std::ops::Add for Point {
    type Output = Point;

    fn add(self, other: Point) -> Point {
        Point {
            x: self.x + other.x,
            y: self.y + other.y,
        }
    }
}

fn main() {
    let p1 = Point { x: 2, y: 3 };
    let p2 = Point { x: 5, y: 7 };
```

```
    let p3 = p1 + p2;

    println!("{:?}", p3);
}
```

Lets break it down:

- **Struct Definition**: We define a `Point` struct with two fields, `x` and `y`, both of type `i32`.
- **Trait Implementation**: We implement the `Add` trait for `Point`. This requires defining the `Output` type (which is the result type of the addition) and the `add` method. The `add` method takes ownership of `self` and another `Point` instance (`other`), adds their respective `x` and `y` values, and returns a new `Point` instance.
- **Using the + Operator**: With the `Add` trait implemented, we can now use the `+` operator to add two `Point` instances, which results in a new `Point` where each coordinate is the sum of the corresponding coordinates of the two points.

Eq and PartialEq

In addition to custom trait implementations, Rust allows you to derive some traits automatically, including `PartialEq` and `Eq`. These traits enable the use of the `==` and `!=` operators to compare instances of your type for equality or inequality.

Ch05/Examples/src/bin/example10.rs

```
#[derive(Debug, PartialEq, Eq)]
struct Point {
    x: i32,
    y: i32,
}

fn main() {
    let p1 = Point { x: 2, y: 3 };
    let p2 = Point { x: 2, y: 3 };
    let p3 = Point { x: 5, y: 7 };

    println!("p1 == p2: {}", p1 == p2);
    println!("p1 != p3: {}", p1 != p3);
}
```

In this example getting operator overloading working for `==`and `!=` is as simple as deriving `PartialEq` and `Eq`.

Operator overloading in Rust is a powerful feature that allows you to define custom behavior for operators by implementing the corresponding traits. In this section, we implemented the `Add` trait for a 2D `Point` type to overload the `+` operator, and we derived the `PartialEq` and `Eq` traits to automatically enable the `==` and `!=` operators for comparing points. By leveraging these traits, you can make your custom types more expressive and intuitive to use, just like Rust's built-in types.

In the next section, we will explore trait bounds, which ensure that generic functions are type-safe at compile time.

Trait Bounds

Rust's type system and its use of generics and traits provide powerful abstractions that make code reusable and flexible without sacrificing performance. This section explores trait bounds and generics, key features of Rust that enable writing concise and efficient code.

Generics enable you to write flexible and reusable functions and types that can work with various data types. We have already discussed generic types, where a type is parameterized by a generic type. Now, we will look into using generics in functions. To achieve this, we need to use trait bounds, which provide additional flexibility. Trait bounds, similar to Haskell type classes, allow for polymorphism by enabling a single implementation to operate on different types, thus avoiding code duplication while maintaining type safety.

Introducing Trait Bounds

Trait bounds specify that a generic type must implement certain traits, imposing constraints that enable specific functionalities. They ensure that a type has the required methods and behaviors to be used in generic functions or types. In other words, trait bounds restrict a generic type to those that implement the necessary traits, guaranteeing that the type will exhibit the expected behavior. In Rust, trait bounds are applied using the `:` symbol after the generic type in a function signature or type definition. Here's an example:

Ch05/Examples/src/bin/example11.rs

```
fn largest<T: PartialOrd>(x: T, y: T) -> T {
    if x > y {
        x
    } else {
        y
```

```
    }
}

fn main() {
    let num = largest(10, 20);
    let char = largest('a', 'b');

    println!("Largest number: {}", num);
    println!("Largest char: {}", char);
}
```

In this example the function `largest` is generic over `T`, which means it can accept any type `T` as long as it implements the `PartialOrd` trait (for ordering comparisons).

The function is called with integers and characters, demonstrating its flexibility to work with different types.

Combining Trait Bounds

Sometimes, a generic type must satisfy multiple trait bounds. Rust allows combining multiple trait bounds using the + operator. You can require a generic type to implement multiple traits by listing them with +.

Ch05/Examples/src/bin/example12.rs

```
fn display_and_clone<T: std::fmt::Display + Clone>(value: T) {
    println!("{}", value);
    let _copy = value.clone();
}

fn main() {
    let s = String::from("Hello, world!");

    display_and_clone(s);
}
```

The function `display_and_clone` requires that the generic type `T` implement both the `Display` and `Clone` traits. This ensures that `T` can be printed and cloned. The function is called with a `String`, which implements both `Display` and `Clone`.

Where

For readability and to handle complex trait bounds, Rust provides a `where` clause, allowing you to specify trait bounds outside the function signature.

The where clauses come after the function signature, providing a clear way to list trait bounds.

Ch05/Examples/src/bin/example13.rs

```
fn complex_function<T, U>(t: T, u: U)
where
    T: std::fmt::Debug + Clone,
    U: std::fmt::Display + PartialEq,
{
    println!("{:?}", t);
    let _clone = t.clone();
    if u == u {
        println!("{}", u);
    }
}

fn main() {
    let num = 42;
    let text = "Hello";

    complex_function(num, text);
}
```

The complex_function uses a where clause to specify that T must implement Debug and Clone, and U must implement Display and PartialEq. T must implement the Debug trait because :? is used on it, and it must also implement the Clone trait since clone() is called on T. Similarly, U must implement the Display trait to allow it to be printed using {}, and it must implement PartialEq because the == operator is used for comparison. The function is called with an integer and a string slice, which satisfy the required trait bounds.

Impl as shorthand

In Rust, impl can be used as a shorthand for specifying a trait bound in a function parameter. This feature simplifies the syntax when you want to require that a function parameter implements a certain trait, making the function more concise and readable.

When defining a function that accepts a parameter with a trait bound, you typically specify the generic type with explicit trait bounds. For example:

```
fn print_value<T: std::fmt::Display>(value: T) {
    println!("{}", value);
}
```

This is an example with a regular trait bound where:

- The function `print_value` takes one argument, `value`, of generic type `T`.
- The type `T` is constrained by the `std::fmt::Display` trait, which means that `value` must implement the `Display` trait.

To simplify this syntax, Rust allows you to use `impl` as a shorthand. The function above can be rewritten using `impl`:

```
fn print_value(value: impl std::fmt::Display) {
    println!("{}", value);
}
```

In this rewritten version:

- The parameter `value` is directly specified as `impl std::fmt::Display`.
- This means "any type that implements the `Display` trait," effectively applying the same constraint as before without needing to explicitly declare a generic parameter.

The impl shorthand gives us the following benefits:

- **Conciseness**: Using `impl Trait` reduces boilerplate code by eliminating the need to declare and use generic type parameters explicitly when only one trait is involved. This makes function signatures shorter and easier to read.
- **Simplicity**: For simple cases where you only need a single trait bound, using `impl Trait` provides a straightforward way to express trait requirements without introducing additional syntax.
- **Readability**: It improves code readability by directly showing the trait bound next to the parameter, making it immediately clear what capabilities the parameter must have.

If a function parameter needs to satisfy multiple trait bounds, you can combine them using the + operator like this:

Ch05/Examples/src/bin/example14.rs

```
fn print_and_clone(value: impl std::fmt::Display + Clone) {
    println!("{}", value);
    let _ = value.clone();
}
```

You can use `impl` with multiple parameters, each with its own trait bounds like this:

Ch05/Examples/src/bin/example15.rs

```
fn compare_and_display(a: impl std::fmt::Debug, b: impl
std::fmt::Display) {
    println!("{:?}", a);
    println!("{}", b);
}

fn main() {
    compare_and_display((1, 2), 3);
}
```

In this example, `a` has a trait bound on `Debug`, while `b` has a trait bound on `Display`. This allows us to assign a value to `a` that only implements `Debug`. For instance, we can provide a tuple, which implements `Debug` but not `Display`, demonstrating the flexibility of having different trait bounds for `a` and `b`.

When Not to Use impl Shorthand?

While the `impl` shorthand is useful for simplifying function signatures, there are situations where the traditional generic syntax is more appropriate:

- **Complex Trait Bounds**: When a function requires more complex trait using explicit generics with the `where` clause can improve clarity.
- **Multiple Uses of the Same Generic Type**: If you need to use the same generic type in multiple places within a function signature, using explicit generics ensures consistency and avoids repetition.
- **Associated Types and Type Aliases**: When working with associated types or type aliases, explicit generics are often required to fully express the relationships between types. Associated types are discussed a little bit further in this chapter.

In summary, using `impl` is a powerful shorthand for simple trait-bound parameters, making function signatures shorter and more readable. However, in cases requiring more advanced type constraints or multiple references to the same type, the traditional generic syntax may be more suitable.

Sized and ?Sized

In Rust, understanding the `Sized` trait and its counterpart, `?Sized`, is crucial for working effectively with different types, especially when dealing with dynamically sized types. The `Sized` trait plays a foundational role in Rust's type system, influencing how types are handled in terms of memory layout and function calls. Both `Sized` and `?Sized` are marker traits that do not contain any functions. Instead, the compiler uses these traits to make decisions about whether a type's size is known at compile time.

Sized

The `Sized` trait in Rust represents types with a known size at compile time. This knowledge allows Rust to allocate memory for these types and manage them efficiently. The Size trait has the following characteristics:

- **Automatically Implemented**: The `Sized` trait is automatically implemented for types with a statically known size. Common types such as integers, floating-point numbers, structs, and arrays (with fixed size) are all `Sized`.
- **Default Assumption**: In Rust, generic type parameters are **assumed** to be `Sized` by default. This assumption means functions, structs, and enums with generic parameters implicitly expect the types to have a known size.
- **Memory Management**: Knowing the size of types at compile time is essential for efficient memory management and safe pointer arithmetic. The compiler can allocate memory on the stack or heap appropriately and optimize code execution based on the size of the data.
- **Function Signatures**: Function signatures rely on the `Sized` trait to define input parameters and return types. Functions typically work with `Sized` types to ensure that they can safely pass, return, and manipulate values.

?Sized

While most types in Rust are `Sized`, there are some cases where types do not have a known size at compile time. These types are known as **dynamically sized types** (**DSTs**) or unsized types. Examples include:

- **Slices**: `[T]` is a dynamically sized type representing a sequence of elements of type `T`. A slice does not have a fixed size because it could represent any number of elements.
- **Trait Objects**: `dyn Trait` is a dynamically sized type representing an object that implements a particular trait. The size of a trait object is not known at compile time because different types can implement the same trait, each with potentially different sizes. Trait objects are explained later in this chapter.
- **Strings**: `String` is a dynamically sized type representing a sequence of characters. Like slices, the size of a string is not known at compile time.

- To handle dynamically sized types, Rust provides the `?Sized` trait bound. This bound indicates that a type may or may not be `Sized`, allowing for more flexibility when working with such types. The `?Sized` trait has the following characteristics:
- **Opt-Out of Sized Requirement**: By using `?Sized`, you indicate that a type parameter does not have to be `Sized`. This opt-out is essential for functions and data structures that need to handle both sized and unsized types.
- **Trait Bounds**: `?Sized` is typically used in trait bounds to relax the requirement for a type to be sized. For example, `T: ?Sized` means that `T` can be either sized or unsized.

In the following example we demonstrate a case where you can use ?Sized to make it work. The following code will not compile:

Ch05/Examples/src/bin/example16.rs

```
fn print_value<T: std::fmt::Debug>(value: &T) {
    println!("{:?}", value);
}

fn main() {
    let arr: &[i32] = &[1, 2, 3];
    print_value(arr);
}
```

The function `print_value` accepts a generic parameter of type `T`, which by default implements `Sized` but not `?Sized`. Attempting to pass `arr` to the function results in the following error:

```
error[E0277]: the size for values of type `[i32]` cannot be
known at compilation time
```

There are two ways to get this to compile: either pass a reference to the function, like `&arr` instead of `arr` directly, or add the `?Sized` trait bound to the parameter as follows:

```
fn print_value<T: ?Sized + std::fmt::Debug>(value: &T)
```

This concludes the section on trait bounds, we are now moving on to the next topic which is how to work with a function which is generic in the return type.

Generic Return Types

When using a generic type as a return type in a Rust function, several important details and constraints must be considered. Unlike parameters, where using generics is straightforward, returning a generic type has additional implications regarding the nature of the returned value, its lifetime, and its compatibility with trait bounds.

Basics

A function in Rust can return a value of a generic type by specifying the generic parameter in the function signature. This approach allows the function to return any type that meets the criteria defined by the generic parameter. For example:

Ch05/Examples/src/bin/example17.rs

```
fn identity<T>(x: T) -> T {
    x
}
```

The function `identity` takes a single parameter `x` of any type `T` and returns a value of the same type `T`. The type `T` is generic, meaning that `identity` can accept and return any type, such as `i32`, `String`, or custom types.

Using Trait Bounds with Generic Return Types

If you want to return a generic type that must satisfy certain trait bounds, you can specify those bounds using `impl Trait`, put the trait bound after the declaration of T or the `where` clause syntax. Here is an example using basic trait bounding:

```
fn clone_and_return<T: Clone>(x: T) -> T {
    x.clone()
}
```

The function `clone_and_return` takes a parameter `x` of type `T` that must implement `Clone`. The function returns a cloned value of `x`, which is also of type `T`. The trait bound `T: Clone` ensures that any type used with this function must have `Clone` implemented.

Constraints on Generic Return Types

When using generics as return types, several constraints and rules apply:

- **Concrete Types Must Be Known at Compile Time**: The Rust compiler must be able to determine the exact type being returned at compile time. This is why using `impl Trait` is often beneficial for abstracting away concrete types while still ensuring that the return type implements a specific trait.
- **Consistency of Return Types**: A function must return the same type for all possible execution paths. You cannot return different types from a function with the same generic or `impl Trait` return type.

For instance, the following code example fails to compile:

```
fn maybe_return_string(condition: bool) -> impl
std::fmt::Display {
        if condition {
            "Hello"
        } else {
            42
        }
    }
```

This function would not compile because it attempts to return both a `&str` and an `i32`, which are different types despite both implementing `Display`.

Common Patterns for Returning Generic Types

We can recognize several common patterns for utilizing generic return types. For example:

- **Returning Complex Data Structures**: Generic return types are often used when functions return collections or data structures that are parameterized by some type.

  Ch05/Examples/src/bin/example18.rs

```
fn make_vector<T>(item: T) -> Vec<T> {
    vec![item]
}
```

- **Returning impl Trait for Abstractions**: Using `impl Trait` in the return type is a powerful way to return an abstract type without exposing the concrete type, making the code more flexible and easier to refactor. This pattern is common when returning iterators, closures, or any other types where the specific implementation should be hidden.

Ch05/Examples/src/bin/example19.rs

```
fn get_name() -> impl std::fmt::Display {
    "Alice"
}
```

Using generics as return types in Rust functions provides flexibility and reusability. By leveraging trait bounds, `impl Trait` syntax, and lifetime annotations, you can create functions that work with a wide range of types while maintaining safety and performance. However, it's essential to follow Rust's strict rules about type consistency, ownership, and lifetimes to ensure that your functions are both correct and efficient.

Turbofish

The **turbofish** (`::<>`) is a syntax in Rust used to explicitly specify type parameters for generic functions, methods, or other associated items. While Rust's compiler often infers types automatically, there are situations where you need to use the turbofish to explicitly define the types you want to use. This is particularly useful when a function has a generic return type, causing the type inference mechanism to fail. While you can specify the type explicitly for a variable, this isn't always feasible, especially when using method chaining.

Here are the main scenarios when you need to use the turbofish:

Type Inference is Ambiguous

If Rust's type inference cannot determine the type of a generic parameter unambiguously from the context, you must use the turbofish to specify the type explicitly. In this case, using the turbofish is not strictly necessary, as you can also specify the type for the variable directly.

```
let v = "42".parse::<i32>().unwrap();
```

In this example:

- The `parse` method is generic and can return any type that implements the `FromStr` trait.
- Since `parse` does not know which type to parse into from the context, the turbofish `::<i32>` is used to explicitly specify that the string should be parsed as an `i32`.

`parse()` returns a `Result`, and using `unwrap()` extracts the payload in an unchecked way. More details on `unwrap()` can be found in Chapter 7 on error handling.

Calling Associated Functions on Generic Types

When you call an associated function (usually a static method) of a type that is generic, and Rust cannot infer the generic type from the arguments, you need to use the turbofish. Again, in this case, using the turbofish is not strictly necessary, as you can also specify the type for the variable directly.

```
let mut vec = Vec::<i32>::new();
```

In this example:

- `Vec::new` is an associated function that creates a new vector.
- Without any arguments to infer the type from, Rust cannot determine what kind of `Vec` to create.
- The turbofish `::<i32>` explicitly tells Rust to create a `Vec<i32>`.

Chaining Method Calls on Generic Functions

When chaining method calls, if the first method is generic and does not provide enough context for Rust to infer the type, you might need to use the turbofish.

```
let sum: i32 = vec![1, 2, 3].iter().sum::<i32>();
```

In this example:

- `iter` returns an iterator over `&i32`.
- `sum` is a generic method that needs to know the type it is summing into.
- Using `::<i32>` specifies that the result of the sum should be an `i32`.

Using Generic Structs or Enums Without Type Inference

When creating an instance of a generic struct or enum without providing enough context for Rust to infer the type, the turbofish is necessary. In this case, providing sufficient context can also be achieved by using a typed literal.

```
struct Point<T> {
    x: T,
    y: T,
}

let p: Point<f128> = Point { x: 0.0, y: 0.0 };
```

If you initialize `Point` without specifying the type for `T`, Rust would not know what type `Point` is supposed to hold. However, if the context doesn't provide enough information for Rust to infer the type, you might need to use the turbofish.

```
let p = Point::<f64> { x: 0.0, y: 0.0 };
```

The turbofish is a useful syntax in Rust for specifying generic types explicitly when type inference does not provide enough information for the compiler to decide. It ensures that you can always precisely control how your generics are used, making your code clearer and more type-safe in scenarios where the compiler cannot infer types automatically. While in most cases there are alternative ways to provide enough context to the compiler, there are times when using the turbofish is the only way to ensure your program compiles.

Associated Types

Associated types are a powerful feature in Rust that provide a way to define types that are associated with a particular trait. This feature allows you to create more flexible and expressive trait definitions, simplifying the use of generic programming by reducing the number of parameters and improving readability.

In this section, we will explore what associated types are, how they work, and when to use them effectively. We will also look at examples that illustrate their usage in real-world scenarios.

Syntax

An associated type is a form of a type alias used within a trait definition. Instead of specifying a type parameter every time a trait is used, an associated type lets you declare a placeholder type within the trait. Implementations of the trait then specify the concrete type to be used for the associated type.

```
trait TraitName {
    type AssociatedType;
}
```

Here, `AssociatedType` is an associated type for the `TraitName` trait. When a type implements `TraitName`, it must also specify what `AssociatedType` should be. The previous discussion on operator overloading emphasizes the use of an associated type in the `Add` trait. This associated type, `Output`, defines the result of the addition operation, providing flexibility in specifying the return type, which is often, but not necessarily, the same as the operand types.

```
pub trait Add<Rhs = Self> {
    type Output;
```

```
    fn add(self, rhs: Rhs) -> Self::Output;
}
```

Associated Types vs. Generic Type Parameters

While associated types and generic type parameters can sometimes be used interchangeably, there are scenarios where one is more suitable than the other.

- **Associated Types**: Best when there is a strong relationship between the trait and the types. They provide a clear, consistent way to specify types that are closely associated with a trait's functionality.
- **Generic Type Parameters**: More flexible and can be useful when the trait needs to work with multiple types independently. Use generics when you want to allow more variability in the types being used.

Using Generic Parameters:

```
trait Graph<T, U> {
    fn nodes(&self) -> Vec<T>;
    fn edges(&self) -> Vec<U>;
}
```

Using associated types:

```
trait Graph {
    type Node;
    type Edge;

    fn nodes(&self) -> Vec<Self::Node>;
    fn edges(&self) -> Vec<Self::Edge>;
}
```

The associated type version is simpler and more focused, especially when `Node` and `Edge` are inherently part of the trait's concept. The main distinction is the moment the type is specified. When you use an associated type, the type is chosen when implementing the trait. When you use a generic type the type is chosen when using the function.

Why

Associated types provide several benefits:

- **Simplifying Trait Definitions**: By using associated types, you can avoid having to specify multiple generic type parameters. This makes the trait definitions more straightforward and easier to understand.

- **Reducing Boilerplate Code**: Associated types reduce the need for verbose syntax. Instead of specifying generic parameters and their constraints in multiple places, associated types allow you to define these once within the trait.
- **Enhanced Readability**: Traits that use associated types are often easier to read and work with because they reduce the complexity of the type signatures.
- **More Natural Abstractions**: Associated types allow you to define abstractions more naturally. For example, when defining a collection trait, you can use an associated type to specify the item type of the collection, making the trait more intuitive.

Let's consider a simple trait `Graph` that represents a graph structure. The graph has nodes, and each node is connected to other nodes by edges. Instead of specifying a generic parameter for the node and edge types, we use associated types.

Ch05/Examples/src/bin/example20.rs

```
trait Graph {
    type Node;
    type Edge;

    fn nodes(&self) -> Vec<Self::Node>;
    fn edges(&self) -> Vec<Self::Edge>;
}
```

In this example:

- `Node` and `Edge` are associated types of the `Graph` trait.
- Any type that implements `Graph` must specify what types `Node` and `Edge` are.

Implementing the Trait:

```
struct SimpleGraph;

impl Graph for w {
    type Node = i32;
    type Edge = (i32, i32);

    fn nodes(&self) -> Vec<Self::Node> {
        vec![1, 2, 3]
    }

    fn edges(&self) -> Vec<Self::Edge> {
        vec![(1, 2), (2, 3)]
    }
}
```

In this `SimpleGraph` implementation:

- `Node` is defined as `i32`.
- `Edge` is defined as a tuple of `i32` values.

This implementation of `Graph` can now be used without needing to specify the types of nodes and edges repeatedly.

Best Practices and Considerations

Here are some best practices and considerations while using associated types:

- **Use Associated Types for Natural Abstractions**: When there's a clear connection between a trait and a type, associated types make the trait easier to use and understand.
- **Prefer Generic Parameters for Flexibility**: If the trait needs to work with multiple independent types or if the types may vary significantly between implementations, generic parameters might be more suitable.
- **Combine Associated Types with Default Methods**: Provide default method implementations when possible to reduce the amount of boilerplate required from implementers.
- **Be Mindful of Trait Object Limitations**: When using associated types, traits cannot always be used as trait objects (`dyn Trait`) due to potential ambiguity about what type should be used for the associated types. Use them when compile-time checks and monomorphization are more important than dynamic dispatch. Dynamic dispatch will be explained in the following paragraph.

Trait Objects and Dynamic Dispatch

In Rust, traits provide a powerful way to define shared behavior across different types. However, there are times when you need to work with multiple types that implement a trait without knowing their exact types at compile time. This is where trait objects and dynamic dispatch come into play. In this section, we will explore trait objects, the difference between static and dynamic dispatch, and the concept of object safety.

Trait Objects

A trait object is a way to achieve dynamic polymorphism in Rust. Unlike generics, which work with any type that implements a trait and are determined at compile time, trait objects allow you to work with any type that implements a trait at runtime. This is particularly useful when you want to write functions or data structures that can operate on values of different types that share common behavior.

Trait objects enable **dynamic dispatch**, where the method to be called is determined at runtime based on the actual type of the object. This allows for more flexible code, especially in cases where you don't know all the possible types at compile time or when you need to store or pass around different types that implement the same trait.

To create a trait object in Rust, you use the `dyn` keyword followed by the trait name. The `dyn` keyword makes it explicit that you are working with a trait object, which enables dynamic dispatch.

```
fn print_description(item: &dyn Describe) {
    println!("{}", item.describe());
}
```

In this example:

- `&dyn Describe` is a reference to a trait object that implements the `Describe` trait.
- The function `print_description` can accept any type that implements the `Describe` trait, but it doesn't need to know the exact type at compile time.

Let's consider a scenario where you want to create a list of different shapes, each with its own way of calculating the area.

Ch05/Examples/src/bin/example21.rs

```
trait Shape {
    fn area(&self) -> f64;
}

struct Circle {
    radius: f64,
}

impl Shape for Circle {
    fn area(&self) -> f64 {
        std::f64::consts::PI * self.radius * self.radius
    }
```

```
}

struct Rectangle {
    width: f64,
    height: f64,
}

impl Shape for Rectangle {
    fn area(&self) -> f64 {
        self.width * self.height
    }
}

fn print_area(shape: &dyn Shape) {
    println!("Area: {}", shape.area());
}

fn main() {
    let circle = Circle { radius: 5.0 };
    let rectangle = Rectangle { width: 3.0, height: 4.0 };

    let shapes: Vec<&dyn Shape> = vec![&circle, &rectangle];

    for shape in shapes {
        print_area(shape);
    }
}
```

In this example:

- We define a `Shape` trait with a method `area`.
- We then implement `Shape` for `Circle` and `Rectangle`.
- The function `print_area` takes a reference to a `dyn Shape`, allowing it to handle any type that implements `Shape`.
- The `main` function demonstrates how to store different types in a `Vec` of `&dyn Shape` and call their `area` methods dynamically at runtime.

Static vs. Dynamic Dispatch

We will take an in-depth look at the differences and benefits of static and dynamic dispatch:

Static Dispatch

- In static dispatch, the compiler determines the exact method to call at compile time based on the concrete type.

- This is how generics typically work in Rust. The compiler generates separate code for each type used with a generic function or struct.
- The primary advantage of static dispatch is its speed, as method calls are resolved at compile time, eliminating any runtime overhead.

Dynamic Dispatch

- In dynamic dispatch, the exact method to call is determined at runtime, based on the type of the object.
- This is achieved through trait objects (`dyn Trait`). The method resolution involves a lookup in a vtable (a table of function pointers), introducing some runtime overhead.
- The primary advantage of Dynamic dispatch is it allows for greater flexibility and polymorphism, enabling you to work with multiple types that implement the same trait without knowing their exact types at compile time.
- Dynamic dispatch comes with a performance cost compared to static dispatch. The primary overhead is the runtime cost of looking up the method in the vtable and the potential for cache misses due to the indirect function calls. However, this overhead is generally small and acceptable in many cases where the flexibility of dynamic dispatch is more valuable than the slight performance hit.
- Let's compare both methods with an example:

```
fn print_area<T: Shape>(shape: &T) {
    println!("Area: {}", shape.area());
}
```

In this case:

- The function `print_area` is generic over any type `T` that implements the `Shape` trait.
- The exact type and method call are resolved at compile time, resulting in a direct function call without any runtime overhead.

```
fn print_area_dyn(shape: &dyn Shape) {
    println!("Area: {}", shape.area());
}
```

Here:

- The function `print_area_dyn` uses a trait object (`&dyn Shape`), which introduces dynamic dispatch.

- The method call `shape.area()` is resolved at runtime, incurring a slight performance cost due to the vtable lookup.

While static dispatch is faster, dynamic dispatch is necessary when you need to store or pass around different types that implement the same trait but are not known until runtime.

Object Safety

Not all traits can be used to create trait objects. For a trait to be used as a trait object (e.g., `dyn Trait`), it must be **object-safe**. Object safety ensures that the methods of a trait can be called through a trait object, where the specific type implementing the trait is not known at compile time. Object safety means:

- **No Self in Method Signatures**: The trait does not have any methods that require `Self` (the implementing type) as a parameter in a way that the compiler cannot resolve. For example, a method signature like `fn new() -> Self` is not object-safe because the return type depends on the concrete type implementing the trait.
- **No Generic Methods**: The trait does not contain any methods that are generic over types other than `Self`. For instance, a method signature like `fn do_something<T>(&self, value: T)` is not object-safe.

Trait Inheritance

In Rust, traits provide a way to define shared behavior across multiple types. Sometimes, you might want to create more complex behaviors by combining multiple traits or building on top of existing ones. This is where **trait inheritance** and **supertraits** come into play. Trait inheritance allows one trait to inherit the methods and associated types of another trait, enabling more structured and reusable code.

A supertrait is a trait that must be implemented for another trait to be considered fully implemented. In other words, when a trait inherits from a supertrait, it implicitly requires that any type implementing the derived trait must also implement the supertrait.

Supertraits enable trait composition by allowing a trait to build upon the functionality of another trait. This form of inheritance is different from object-oriented inheritance, as it doesn't involve inheriting fields or state but rather the required behavior (methods and associated types).

To define a supertrait, you declare a trait with another trait as a requirement using the `:` syntax. This syntax indicates that the new trait depends on the methods and functionality provided by the supertrait.

```
trait SuperTrait {
    fn super_method(&self);
}

trait SubTrait: SuperTrait {
    fn sub_method(&self);
}
```

In this example:

- `SuperTrait` is a trait with a single method `super_method`.
- `SubTrait` is defined as a trait that inherits from `SuperTrait`. Any type implementing `SubTrait` must also implement `SuperTrait` and provide a definition for `super_method`.

The rules for trait inheritance are:

- **Traits Can Only Inherit Other Traits**: A trait can inherit from multiple other traits, but it can only inherit from traits, not concrete types or structures.
- **Implementation Requirements**: When a type implements a trait that inherits from a supertrait, it must implement all methods from both the trait and its supertrait(s).

Let's consider a scenario where you have a `Draw` trait for rendering shapes and a `Colored` trait for coloring objects. You can create a `ColoredShape` trait that inherits from both `Draw` and `Colored`:

Ch05/Examples/src/bin/example22.rs

```
trait Draw {
    fn draw(&self);
}

trait Colored {
    fn color(&self) -> String;
}

trait ColoredShape: Draw + Colored {
    fn describe(&self) {
        println!("This shape is {} and can be drawn.", self.
color());
    }
```

```
}

struct Circle;

impl Draw for Circle {
    fn draw(&self) {
        println!("Drawing a circle.");
    }
}

impl Colored for Circle {
    fn color(&self) -> String {
        String::from("red")
    }
}

impl ColoredShape for Circle {}

fn main() {
    let circle = Circle;
    circle.draw();
    println!("Color: {}", circle.color());
    circle.describe();
}
```

In this example:

- Draw and Colored are two independent traits.
- ColoredShape is a trait that inherits from both Draw and Colored.
- The Circle struct implements all three traits, inheriting the behavior of both Draw and Colored and adding functionality through the ColoredShape trait.

Summary

Traits are a fundamental feature in Rust, enabling polymorphism, code reuse, and abstraction, making them essential for any Rust programmer. At their core, traits define shared behavior across different types, allowing developers to write generic and reusable code that can operate on various types. This chapter explores how Rust uses traits to create flexible, modular programs while maintaining type safety and performance.

In Rust, traits serve a role similar to interfaces in languages like Java or abstract base classes in C++. However, traits in Rust are implemented at compile time, ensuring zero-cost abstractions without runtime overhead. This makes them a powerful tool for defining common behavior across different types.

Throughout the chapter, we begin by discussing the basics of traits, what they are, how to define and implement them, and how to use default method implementations to share behavior across multiple types. We then explore common traits provided by Rust, such as `Debug`, `Display`, `Clone`, `Copy`, `PartialEq`, and `Eq`, which simplify everyday tasks like output formatting and comparisons.

The chapter also covers more advanced features of traits, including how to work with trait bounds, generics, and associated types to write flexible, reusable code. Rust's `Sized` and `?Sized` traits are explained to provide a better understanding of memory management and handling types of unknown size at compile time.

Dynamic dispatch through trait objects (`dyn Trait`) is introduced, showing how Rust allows you to work with multiple types implementing the same trait at runtime. The concept of object safety is explained, which ensures that a trait can be used in dynamic dispatch scenarios.

Finally, the chapter touches on trait inheritance, explaining how supertraits allow one trait to build upon another, creating powerful abstractions by combining multiple traits into a cohesive structure.

In the next chapter, we will cover the next key components of Rust fundamentals: Modules, Crates, and Testing.

Exercises

1. Define a trait named Identifiable with a single method id that returns an i32. Implement this trait for a struct User with an id field.
2. Create a struct Person with fields name and age. Implement two traits, Named and Aged, for Person. The Named trait should have a method name that returns the name, and the Aged trait should have a method age that returns the age.
3. Create a trait Describable with a default method describe that returns a generic description "This is an item". Implement this trait for a struct Book and override the describe method to return "This is a book".
4. Create a struct Point with fields x and y. Derive the Debug, Clone, and PartialEq traits for this struct and demonstrate their use by creating instances of Point, printing them, cloning them, and comparing them.
5. Implement the Add trait for a struct Point3D that represents a point in 3D space. This should allow you to use the + operator to add two Vector instances together.

6. Create a function largest that takes a slice of any type that implements the PartialOrd trait and returns the largest element.
7. Write a function print_value that accepts any argument that implements the Display trait and prints it.
8. Define a trait Container that has an associated type Item and a method contains that checks if a given Item is in the container. Implement this trait for a struct BoxContainer that holds a single value of generic type T.
9. Create two traits Shape and Colored. Make Colored a supertrait of Shape by requiring that any type implementing Colored also implements Shape. Implement both traits for a struct Square.
10. Define a trait Drawable with a method draw. Create two structs Circle and Square and implement Drawable for both. Write a function draw_shapes that takes a slice of trait objects and calls draw on each one.

Project: Payment Processing System

In this project, you'll create a payment processing system that supports CreditCard, PayPal, and Bitcoin. Using Rust's trait system, you'll define a common `PaymentMethod` trait for handling different payment types. The system will validate and process payments dynamically, allowing easy addition of new methods in the future. You'll also handle invalid details and error scenarios, providing a flexible and robust payment solution.

Project Preparation

Strings are covered in *Chapter 8*, but for this project, you'll need to be familiar with a few additional string functions to work effectively.

len()

To determine the length of a string, you can use the `len()` function. However, keep in mind that this function returns the byte length of the string, which only corresponds to the character count when dealing with ASCII characters. For strings containing multi-byte characters (like those in Unicode), the result may differ from the actual number of characters.

Example

```
fn main() {
    let s = "len() test".to_string();
```

```
    println!("{}", s.len());
}
```

contains()

The `contains` function checks if a specific character is present in the string and returns `true` if found, or `false` if not.

Example

```
fn main() {
    let s = "len() test".to_string();
    println!("{}", s.contains('('));
}
```

Specification

Develop a system that processes payments using various methods: CreditCard, Paypal, and Bitcoin. The system will define a common trait, `PaymentMethod`, which includes the methods `process_payment()` and `validate_details()`. Each payment type will implement this trait, and the system must be capable of handling different payment methods dynamically using *trait objects*.

Context

The payment processing system serves as the backend for a web shop. It includes three structs, each representing a different payment method. During checkout, the user provides payment details, which are then collected and used to populate the respective payment struct. Once the struct is created, the details must be validated and the payment processed accordingly.

Objective

- Utilize *trait objects* to manage multiple implementations of the `PaymentMethod` trait.
- Ensure that the system is flexible, allowing easy addition of new payment methods in the future.

Trait Definition

- Define a trait `PaymentMethod` that encapsulates common behaviors for all payment types. It will contain the following methods:
- `process_payment`
- `fn validate_details`

CreditCard

fields:

- `number: String`
- `expiry_date: String`
- `cvv: String`

Methods:

- Implement `process_payment()` to simulate credit card processing (e.g. print a message to the console that the payment is processed). Handle a negative amount as an error situation.
- Implement `validate_details()` to check if the card number is exactly 16 characters long, if the expiry date is exactly 5 characters long and if the ccv is exactly 3 characters long.

Paypal

Fields:

- email: String
- password: String

Methods:

Implement `process_payment()` to simulate Paypal transaction. Handle a negative amount as an error situation.

Implement `validate_details()` to check if the email and password are valid. The email contains a `@` and a `.` and is at least 5 characters long. The password is at least 1 character long.

Bitcoin

Fields:

- wallet_address: String

Methods:

- process_payment: Simulate processing a Bitcoin transaction.
- validate_details: Validate the wallet address, ensuring it is between 26 and 35 characters in length.

Payment Handling

Create a function `handle_payment` that takes a payment method as a trait object and processes the payment.

Parameters:

- payment_method: The payment method to be processed.
- Amount: f64: The amount to be processed.

Functionality:

- First, call validate_details() to ensure the payment method's details are valid.
- If the details are valid, call process_payment() to complete the transaction.
- Return the result of the transaction as a Result<(), String>

Test

In the main() function, test all payment methods with both valid and invalid transaction details:

- CreditCard: Test with both valid and invalid credit card numbers.
- Paypal: Test with both valid and invalid emails.
- Bitcoin: Test with both valid and invalid wallet addresses.

06

Modules, Crates, and Testing

This chapter explores the key aspects of organizing and maintaining code in Rust through modules, crates, and testing. Modules allow developers to break their codebase into logical pieces, improving readability and enabling better code reuse. Through encapsulation and namespace management, modules ensure that functionality is well-structured and accessible where needed.

Next, crates (Rust's primary units of compilation and code packaging) are introduced. Crates enable the modularization of projects into reusable packages and libraries, making dependency management easier with the help of Cargo, Rust's package manager.

Finally, testing is covered, a critical practice for ensuring code behaves as expected. Rust's built-in testing framework simplifies writing and executing both unit and integration tests, helping developers catch bugs early and ensure stability when making changes. Together, these topics provide essential tools for writing clean, maintainable, and reliable Rust programs.

This chapter will cover the following topics:

- **Modules**: Modules allow for better organization, code reuse, and encapsulation, grouping related functions, types, and constants together.
- **Encapsulation and Visibility**: Modules control visibility determining which items are accessible outside the module.
- **Inline and File-Based Modules**: Modules can be defined directly within a file or spread across multiple files, improving code organization in larger projects.
- **Paths**: Both absolute and relative paths are used to access items within modules, providing flexibility in navigating Rust's module hierarchy.
- **Crates**: Crates are the fundamental unit of code packaging, either as executables (binary crates) or reusable libraries (library crates).
- **Cargo for Dependency Management**: Cargo, Rust's package manager, handles external crates and ensures smooth versioning, fetching, and integration of dependencies.
- **Versioning**: Crates use semantic versioning to ensure compatibility and maintain stability when updating or modifying dependencies.
- **Testing**: Rust includes built-in testing enabling developers to write unit and integration tests directly in the code.
- **Running and Interpreting Tests**: Using `cargo test`, developers can run tests, filter results, and interpret output, ensuring that their code is functioning as expected.

By mastering these concepts, you will be well-equipped to structure your Rust projects effectively, manage dependencies with confidence, and ensure the reliability of your code through robust testing practices.

Modules

In Rust, modules are the primary mechanism for organizing and managing code. Modules allow you to break your codebase into smaller, more manageable pieces, enabling better readability, easier debugging, and code reuse. A module is a logical grouping of related functions, types, constants, and traits. They help structure large codebases into distinct sections with clearly defined responsibilities.

Modules Introduced

Modules serve several important purposes:

- **Encapsulation**: They provide a way to group related functionality together while controlling what is visible to other parts of the program. This helps in enforcing boundaries and restricting access to internal implementation details.
- **Code Organization**: By dividing code into multiple modules, developers can maintain a cleaner, more navigable codebase. Modules encourage modular design, where functionality is broken down into smaller, self-contained pieces.
- **Namespace Management**: Rust modules create namespaces, which means you can have functions or types with the same name in different modules without causing conflicts. You can refer to these items using their module path, such as `module_name::function_name`.
- **Reusability**: Modules allow functionality to be reused in multiple places without duplicating code. You can import and reuse items from other modules as needed.

In Rust, modules are defined with the `mod` keyword. A module can either be defined inline, within a file, or in the case of submodules, spread across multiple files in a directory structure. By organizing your code into modules, you can make it easier to maintain and scale, especially for larger projects.

There are two main types of modules in Rust:

- **Inline Modules**: These modules are declared and defined within the same file.
- **File-Based Modules**: These modules are placed in separate files and brought together within the main codebase.

Each module can contain:

- **Functions**, that define the behavior within the module.
- **Types**, (structs, enums) used within the module or exposed outside.
- **Constants**, used within or across modules.
- **Traits**, that define shared behavior for types within the module.

Defining Modules

In Rust, modules are defined using the `mod` keyword. This section explores how to define modules, work with submodules, understand paths and visibility, and use the `pub` keyword to control access to various parts of the code. To define a module, you simply use the `mod` keyword followed by the `module_name`.

Here's a simple example of defining an inline module:

Ch06/Examples/example01

```
mod math {
    pub fn add(a: i32, b: i32) -> i32 {
        internal_add(a, b)
    }

    fn internal_add(a: i32, b: i32) -> i32 {
        a + b
    }
}

fn main() {
    println!("The sum is: {}", math::add(5, 3));
}
```

In this example, a module called `math` is defined using `mod math`. The `add` function is marked as `pub`, making it accessible from outside the module. The `internal_add` function is private by default, as it lacks the `pub` keyword. In the `main` function, the `add` function is called using its fully qualified name: `math::add(5, 3)`.

Rust supports nested modules, allowing you to create submodules within existing modules. This hierarchical structure enables deeper organization, where you can logically separate various functionalities into different levels of modules.

Let's look at an example of nested modules:

Ch06/Examples/example02

```
mod library {
```

```
    pub mod books {
        pub fn add_book() {
            println!("A new book has been added.");
        }

        fn remove_book() {
            println!("A book has been removed.");
        }
    }

    pub mod users {
        pub fn add_user() {
            println!("A new user has been added.");
        }
    }
}

fn main() {
    library::books::add_book();
    library::users::add_user();
}
```

In this example, the `library` module contains two submodules: `books` and `users`. Functions within each submodule can be accessed using their full paths, such as `library::books::add_book()`. The `add_book` and `add_user` functions are `pub`, making them accessible outside their respective submodules, but the `remove_book` function is private to its module. Note that the library module is not marked as `pub`. Since it's defined within the main module, it is accessible within its own namespace without the need for the `pub` keyword. However, submodules must be marked as `pub` for their items to be accessible outside of the submodule.

Visibility Rules

In Rust, all items (such as functions, types, and constants) within a module are private by default. To make a module or its contents accessible outside its own scope, you must explicitly mark them as `pub` (public). The visibility rules work as follows:

- Modules can access there own private items
- Submodules can access private (non-`pub`) items from their parent module
- Parent modules cannot access private items from their submodules unless those items are marked as `pub`

This creates a hierarchical visibility structure, where submodules can look up and access items from parent modules, but parent modules cannot look down into submodules unless explicitly allowed.

The `pub` keyword is crucial for controlling visibility in Rust modules. When applied to an item, it makes that item accessible outside its current module. You can use `pub` in the following contexts:

- **Functions**: Making a function `pub` allows it to be called from outside the module.
- **Structs**: Making a struct `pub` enables other modules to use the struct itself, but the individual fields of the struct remain private unless they are also marked `pub`.
- **Enums**: Making an enum `pub` allows other modules to use the enum and all of its variants, as enum variants are automatically `pub` when the enum itself is made public.
- **Modules**: Making a module `pub` allows its contents to be accessed from other modules, but individual items within the module still need to be explicitly marked as `pub` if you want them to be accessible.

Let's examine the use of `pub` in a slightly more complex case:

Ch06/Examples/example03

```
mod store {
    pub struct Book {
        pub title: String,
        pub price: f64,
        pages: u32,
    }

    impl Book {
        pub fn new(title: String, price: f64, pages: u32) ->
Self {
            Self { title, price, pages }
        }
    }
}

fn main() {
    let my_book = store::Book::new(
        String::from("Rust Programming"),
        29.99, 300);

    println!("{} {}", my_book.title, my_book.price);
}
```

In this example, the `Book` struct is made public (`pub`), so it can be used outside the `store` module. However, not all fields are accessible. The `title` and `price` fields are marked `pub`, meaning they can be accessed from outside the module. The `pages` field is private, so it cannot be accessed from outside the `store` module, even though the struct itself is public. The `new` function is public, allowing you to create a `Book` instance from outside the module, although you cannot access it directly it can still initialize the private `pages` field internally.

By carefully using the `pub` keyword, you can control which parts of your code are accessible from other modules, maintaining encapsulation and avoiding accidental misuse of internal logic.

Module Files and Directories

In Rust, modules can be defined inline, within a single separate file or spread across multiple files in a directory structure. This flexibility allows you to organize code in a way that best fits the size and complexity of your project.

Inline modules

In the previous examples, we defined the module directly within the same file where we used it. This is done by placing the module's content immediately after the `mod` keyword, encapsulating all functions, types, and other items inside the module. This inline module definition is the simplest approach, making it ideal for small projects or when the module's content is minimal. Inline modules are also commonly used for placing unit tests, as we will see later in the chapter.

However, as your project grows or your modules become more complex, it becomes more practical to separate each module into its own file. This improves code organization and readability, especially in larger projects.

Single file modules

By moving the module into a separate file, you can keep the main file concise and focused on the broader structure of the program. To do this, you import the module in the main file using the `mod` keyword, but instead of including the module's body directly, Rust will look for a corresponding file with the same name as the module.

For example, if you declare a module like this in `main.rs`:

```
mod math;
fn main() {
    println!("{}", math::add(2, 3));
}
```

Rust will expect to find a `math.rs` file in the same directory as `main.rs`. Inside `math.rs`, you can then define the contents of the `math` module, like so:

```
pub fn add(a: i32, b: i32) -> i32 {
    a + b
}
```

A FEW NOTES

The `mod` keyword isn't needed inside a module file. Placing code in a separate file automatically makes it a module. However, this setup doesn't align well with the `bin` folder, which is used for organizing multiple binaries. Each file in the `bin` folder acts as its own entry point, overriding the default module behavior. When a project contains a single entry point and multiple modules, they should be conventionally placed together in the `src` folder.

When a single-file module contains submodules, those submodules must be placed inline or in a directory with the same name as the module. For example, if you have a module named `person` with two submodules, `client` and `employee`, the files `client.rs` and `employee.rs` must be placed inside a directory called `person`.

Directory-based modules

For more complex modules that need to include submodules, Rust allows you to organize them into directories. A directory-based module has a `mod.rs` file within a folder. This file acts as the root of the module, with submodules placed as separate files within the same directory. Consider the following file structure

```
src/
├── main.rs
└── store/
    └── mod.rs
```

The `store` directory functions as a module because it contains a `mod.rs` file. You could place all the code for the `store` module into this `mod.rs` file. The main file still imports the module using `mod store;`. The key difference here is that the module is now housed in a directory with a `mod.rs` file instead of being in a single file named after the module itself.

Let's take it a step further by adding submodules, resulting in the following structure:

```
src/
├── main.rs
└── store/
    ├── mod.rs
    ├── book.rs
    └── inventory.rs
```

Here, `book` and `inventory` are submodules of store. To make this work you have to add those modules into `mod.rs` as follows:

```
pub mod book;
mod inventory;
```

Here the submodule book is pub therefore it is available as a submodule for main and the submodule inventory is not public and therefore not visible for main.

Obviously it is possible to have multiple directory-based submodules side by side into a single project. By organizing code this way, each module has its own clear scope, making it easier to navigate and maintain large projects.

Now that we have a clear understanding of how to organize your codebase into modules and distribute them across multiple files, let's explore how to reduce repetitive typing when using items from a module. Currently, we need to fully qualify each item with the module name every time we use it. This brings us to the `use` keyword, but before we dive into that, let's first explore the concept of paths.

Paths

There are four types of paths used to access items in modules:

- **Absolute Paths**: These paths start from the crate root (**crate**) and specify the full hierarchy of modules to the desired item. Example: `crate::library::books::add_book()`.
- **Relative Paths (Child Modules)**: These paths start from the current module and navigate to child modules or items within the current module. Example: `books::add_book()` when inside the `library` module.
- **Relative Paths (Parent Modules)**: These paths use **`super`** to navigate to parent modules. Example: `super::add_book()` when moving up one level in the module hierarchy.
- **Relative Paths (Current Module)**: These paths use **self** to explicitly refer to items within the current module. This makes it clear that the item resides in

the current module and is not being accessed from a parent or child module. Example: `self::add_book()` accesses the `add_book` function defined in the same module.

We can apply these path options to access elements from various modules. Now, let's dive into the `use` keyword.

Use

The `use` keyword doesn't import code; instead, it brings elements from another module into the current module's scope. (The actual *importing* is handled by the `mod` keyword.) This allows you to avoid fully qualifying the path every time you access an item. For instance, rather than writing `crate::module::submodule::Item` repeatedly, you can bring `Item` into scope with `use` and reference it directly.

Using a single item

The syntax for the `use` keyword involves providing the path to the item or module you want to bring into scope, followed by a semicolon, explicitly including the item itself in the path.

```
use crate::module::submodule::Item;
```

After this, item can be referenced directly in your code.

Using multiple items

To import all items from a module, you can use the glob operator `*`. However, this is typically discouraged for large modules, as it can lead to namespace pollution and make the code less readable. For example:

```
use crate::library::books::*;
```

In this case, all the items from the `books` module are brought into the current module's namespace.

Renaming

Sometimes you might want to bring an item into scope but avoid naming conflicts or improve clarity. You can rename an imported item using the as keyword. As shown in the following example:

```
use library::books::add_book as addNewBook;
```

In this case, the item `add_book` is now referenced as `addNewBook`.

Grouping syntax

When importing multiple items from the same module, you can group them into a single `use` statement, as shown in the following example:

```
use crate::library::{
    books::{add_book, remove_book},
    magazines::Magazine,
};
```

This `use` statement imports multiple items from different submodules of the `library` module in one go, making them directly accessible in the current scope. Here's a breakdown:

- `crate::library::` refers to the root `library` module from the crate's root.
- Inside `library`, two submodules are accessed:
- `books::{add_book, remove_book}`: This imports the `add_book` and `remove_book` functions from the `books` submodule.
- `magazines::Magazine`: This imports the `Magazine` struct from the `magazines` submodule.

Reexporting

You can combine `pub` with `use` to re-export items, making them accessible outside the current module. Essentially, `pub use` brings items from submodules into the module's own namespace. This approach is particularly helpful for organizing and simplifying access to module contents. For example, placing the following line in `mod.rs`:

```
pub use book::test_book;
```

It makes `test_book` available directly under `store` rather than requiring access through `store::book`.

Scope

Typically, `use` statements are placed at the top of your module, but this isn't strictly required. You can specify a `use` statement within any scope. Each scope has its own namespace, and the `use` statement imports the identifier into the namespace of the specific scope where it's declared.

To wrap up, we've covered how Rust's module system helps organize, encapsulate, and structure your codebase. By leveraging modules, you can logically group related functionality, control visibility, and make your code easier to maintain and extend. Whether you use inline modules, file-based modules, or directory-based modules, Rust provides flexible mechanisms to organize even the largest projects. Additionally, by utilizing the `use` keyword, you can simplify references to items in other modules and avoid repeated qualifications, streamlining your code further.

The next step in understanding Rust's code organization involves crates. Crates represent the next level of organization in Rust, allowing you to package and share your code as libraries or applications. In the following section, we will dive into crates, how they differ from modules, and how they serve as the building blocks of Rust projects and libraries.

Crates

In Rust, a crate is the fundamental unit of compilation and code packaging. It is the building block of Rust projects and can be thought of as a package of code that encapsulates related functionality. Crates play a critical role in structuring your Rust project, making it easier to manage, scale, and share your code.

Crate Basics

At a high level, crates serve two key purposes:

- **Compilation Unit**: Every Rust project is treated as a crate, and the Rust compiler compiles crates as a whole.
- **Code Packaging**: Crates allow you to package your code into reusable modules or libraries that can be shared with other projects or developers.

Binary vs. Library Crates

There are two main types of crates in Rust: **binary crates** and **library crates**.

Binary crates compile into executables that can be run directly. They define one or more entry points through one or more `main` functions, and are used to build command-line tools, servers, or any other standalone applications. By default, Cargo treats a Rust project containing a main.rs file as a binary crate.

Library crates, on the other hand, do not produce executables. Instead, they define reusable functionality that can be imported and used by other projects. Library crates do not contain a `main` function but instead expose useful functions, types, or modules through the `pub` keyword, making them accessible to other crates. By default, Cargo treats a Rust project containing a lib.rs file as a library crate.

Although it's not commonly done this way, you can combine both a binary and a library into a single crate. The same rules apply: you can have multiple binaries, but only one library within the crate.

Managing Dependencies and Functionality

Crates are also the primary way Rust manages dependencies. A Rust project can include multiple external crates (dependencies) in its codebase, thanks to Cargo, Rust's package manager and build system. Cargo uses the `Cargo.toml` file to specify the dependencies (crates) your project needs, as well as versions and any additional configurations.

By modularizing code into crates, Rust enables clear separation of concerns. Each crate can focus on a specific area of functionality, making it easier to manage, maintain, and share code across projects. You can include as many crates as needed in your project, and Cargo handles fetching, compiling, and linking them automatically.

In summary, crates in Rust help organize your codebase into reusable, manageable units, whether you are building a full-fledged executable (binary crate) or a reusable set of utilities (library crate). They also simplify dependency management, enabling you to leverage the vast ecosystem of open-source crates to build more robust applications.

There are specific rules and distinctions that govern binary and library crates, based on their structure, purpose, and configuration. Here are the key rules and guidelines for each:

Binary crate rules

- **Main Entry Point**: A binary crate **must have** at least one entry point, which is the `main` function. This function serves as the starting point for execution when the compiled program is run.
- **Produces Executables**: Binary crates compile into executables, meaning they generate a file (such as a `.exe`, depending on your operating system) that you can run directly.
- **Single Binary Crate Per Package by Default**: A Rust project can produce multiple binaries by organizing them in the `src/bin` directory or specifying them in `Cargo.toml`. By default, the `src/main.rs` file serves as the entry point for the primary binary crate in the package.
- **Binary Crates Do Not Export Items**: Since binary crates are meant to be executable programs, they do not expose functions, structs, or other items for

other crates to use. They use functionality from libraries, but typically do not export any themselves.

Library crate rules

- **No Main Function**: Library crates do not have a `main` function. Instead, they provide reusable code, which other crates (both binary and library crates) can use.
- **Reusable Functions and Types**: Library crates define functions, types, constants, traits and, modules that are meant to be reused across different projects. You can make these accessible by marking them `pub` (public).
- **lib.rs File**: A library crate is defined by having a `src/lib.rs` file, which serves as the root of the library. This file typically contains the module structure and the public API for the library.
- **Multiple Library Crates**: A single package can only have one library, defined by `src/lib.rs`. Unlike binary crates, which can have multiple binaries, a Rust crate can only include one library.
- **Exporting Code**: The primary purpose of a library crate is to export functionality that can be used by other crates. Any item you want to make available outside the crate needs to be marked with the `pub` keyword, making it part of the crate's public API.

Here is the summary of the comparison:

Feature	Binary Crate	Library Crate
Entry Point	Must have a `main` function	No `main` function
Output	Produces an executable	Produces reusable code
File Name	`src/main.rs` or `src/bin/*.rs`	`src/lib.rs`
Multiple Instances	Can have multiple binaries	Can have only one library
Exporting Functionality	Doesn't export items	Exports reusable functions, structs, etc.

Table 6.1 - *Comparison of Binary and Library crates*

External Crates

In Rust, crates are the primary way to manage code, but projects often require external crates to avoid reinventing the wheel. Cargo, Rust's package manager and build system, simplifies the process of adding and managing these external crates. In this section, we'll explore how to add dependencies, manage versions, and use your own local crates.

Adding Dependencies via Cargo.toml

To include an external crate in your project, you must declare it in the `Cargo.toml` file. This file serves as the configuration for your package, including metadata and dependencies.

For example, to add the popular `serde` crate for serialization and deserialization, you add the following lines under `[dependencies]`:

```
[dependencies]
serde = "1.0.210"
```

This tells Cargo to download and use version `1.0.210` of the `serde` crate. Dependencies are fetched from the central Rust crate registry, `crates.io`.

`crates.io` is the official package registry for Rust, where developers can discover, publish, and share Rust libraries and tools, known as **crates**. It serves as a central repository where developers can upload their open-source Rust projects, making them available for others to use as dependencies in their own projects. Crates.io supports versioning, ensuring compatibility and stability across different versions of a crate, and is tightly integrated with Rust's build tool, Cargo, to simplify dependency management, updates, and publishing of crates.

Versioning and Updating Dependencies

In Rust, crate versions are managed using **semantic versioning** (**semver**), a system that ensures compatibility between versions and helps manage dependencies efficiently. In `Cargo.toml`, you can specify versions in a flexible way to allow updates without breaking changes, while maintaining control over how versions are resolved.

Exact Versions

You can specify an exact version by omitting any symbols and specifying three version numbers:

```
serde = "1.2.3"
```

This will lock the dependency to exactly version `1.2.3` and prevent any updates unless manually modified. This provides the most stability but limits flexibility in receiving important patches or improvements.

Caret (^)

The caret (`^`) is the default symbol used when no symbol is specified and you use less than three version numbers. It allows updates to any version that is backward-compatible according to semver rules. For example:

```
serde = "^1.2.3"
```

or

```
serde = "1.2"
```

This permits updating `serde` to any version from `1.2.3` up to but not including `2.0.0`. In semantic versioning, changes in the minor or patch versions (e.g., `1.2.4` or `1.3.0`) should be backward-compatible, so Cargo will fetch those updates, but it will block updates to a new major version (`2.0.0`), which may introduce breaking changes.

Tildc (~)

The tilde (`~`) allows you to restrict updates to a specific minor version. For example:

```
serde = "~1.2.3"
```

This allows updating `serde` to patch versions only within the `1.2.x` range, such as `1.2.4` or `1.2.5`, but it will not allow updates to `1.3.0` or beyond. This is useful when you want to restrict updates to bug fixes or small improvements without risking new features that may alter behavior.

Wildcard (*)

You can also use wildcard characters (`*`) to specify more flexible ranges:

- `serde = "1.2.*"` allows updates to any patch version within `1.2.x`, like `1.2.3`, `1.2.4`, etc.
- `serde = "1.*"` allows updates to any minor or patch version within `1.x.x`, like `1.2.3`, `1.3.0`, but not `2.0.0`.

Pre-release Versions

If you specify a version with a pre-release tag, like `1.0.0-beta`, Cargo will only match pre-release versions explicitly. It won't automatically update to stable versions unless specified.

Updating Dependencies

To update your dependencies to the latest compatible versions allowed by the version constraints, you can run:

```
cargo update
```

This will update the dependencies listed in `Cargo.lock` (the file that locks dependencies to specific versions) to the latest versions that fit the constraints defined in `Cargo.toml`.

By carefully choosing these version specifiers, you can balance flexibility with stability, ensuring that your project benefits from bug fixes and minor updates without unexpectedly introducing breaking changes.

Using an external crate

A crate is accessed using its name and behaves like a regular module under that name. For example, let's demonstrate this with the `regex` crate.

First, you need to add the `regex` crate as a dependency in your `Cargo.toml` file:

```
[dependencies]
regex = "1.10"
```

This will get the latest version smaller than 2 in the project, but at least `1.10`.

After adding the crate, you can now use it in your code. Here's a simple example that demonstrates pattern matching in a string using regular expressions.

Ch06/Examples/example04

```
use regex::Regex;

fn main() {
    let re = Regex::new(r"\d+").unwrap();
    let text = "The house number is 118.";
    println!("Found match: {:?}", re.find(text));
}
```

In this example, the `regex` crate is used to enable pattern matching in text using regular expressions. Here's how the crate is integrated:

1. `use regex::Regex;` This line imports the `Regex` struct from the `regex` crate. The `Regex` struct provides the functionality to work with regular expressions. By adding `regex = "version"` as a dependency in your `Cargo.toml` file, you can use this crate to perform complex text pattern matching.
2. `Regex::new(r"\d+").unwrap();` This uses the `Regex::new()` method from the `regex` crate to compile a regular expression. Without the `regex` crate, you wouldn't be able to create and use regular expressions easily in Rust.

Overall, this code searches for a sequence of digits (`\d+`) in the string and prints out the first match it finds.

Using a local crate

To include your own local package as a dependency in a Rust project, you can reference it in your project's `Cargo.toml` file using a file path. This is useful for developing and testing multiple crates locally without needing to publish them on `crates.io`. Here's how to do it:

1. **Structure Your Project**: Ensure that the local package you want to include has its own directory and contains its own `Cargo.toml` file.
2. **Modify Cargo.toml**: In your main project's `Cargo.toml` file, under the [dependencies] section, specify the path to the local package.

   ```
   [dependencies]
   my_local_crate = { path = "../path/to/my_local_crate" }
   ```

3. Replace `"../path/to/my_local_crate"` with the relative or absolute path to your local package directory.

For example If you have the following structure:

```
/my_project
    /Cargo.toml
    /src/main.rs
/my_local_crate
    /Cargo.toml
    /src/lib.rs
```

You would add the following line in `my_project/Cargo.toml`:

```
[dependencies]
```

```
my_local_crate = { path = "../my_local_crate" }
```

Once the dependency is added, you can use it in your project like any other crate:

Ch06/Examples/example05/runner

```
use my_local_crate::some_function;

fn main() {
    some_function();
}
```

This setup allows you to develop and test multiple crates locally, streamlining collaboration between multiple projects or libraries before publishing them.

The Standard Library

Rust's standard library (`std`) is a core crate of every Rust program, providing essential utilities, data structures, and functions that allow developers to write efficient and expressive code without importing external crates. The `std` crate is automatically included in all Rust programs, and it serves as a foundational building block for most Rust applications.

The Rust standard library (`std`) offers a wide range of common functionalities, such as:

- **Memory Management**: Provides tools for working with heap memory through data structures like `Box`, `Vec`, and `String`.
- **I/O Operations**: Includes utilities for handling input/output, such as reading from files, writing to the console, and managing streams via `std::io`.
- **Concurrency**: Tools for concurrent programming, like threads and channels, are available through `std::thread` and `std::sync`.
- **Error Handling**: Includes types like `Result` and `Option`, which are foundational for Rust's approach to error handling and null safety.
- **Collections**: Standard data structures like `Vec`, `HashMap`, and `HashSet` are part of `std::collections`.

Because `std` is automatically available in every Rust program, you do not need to manually import it. However, the library is modular, so you can use specific parts of it as needed.

Rust's `std` library is organized into modules, which group related functionality. To use specific parts of the standard library, you can import them directly into your code. For instance, if you need to use a hashmap, you would do something like this:

Ch06/Examples/example06

```
use std::collections::HashMap;

fn main() {
    let mut scores = HashMap::new();
    scores.insert(String::from("Alice"), 50);
    scores.insert(String::from("Bob"), 40);
    println!("{:?}", scores);
}
```

The `HashMap` will be covered in more detail in *Chapter 9* on Collections. For this example, how you `use` the `HashMap` is key. It's part of the standard library and therefore imported by default, it's not made available in the namespace automatically so you need to do that with a `use` statement or fully qualify it each time you `use HashMap`.

The Prelude

The Rust prelude is a small collection of items from the standard library that are automatically imported into the namespace of every Rust module. This feature simplifies the development process by reducing the need to manually use commonly used types, functions, and traits. Without the prelude, you would need to include many more `use` statements for basic functionalities, making the code more verbose.

Key Features of the Rust Prelude

Here are the key features of prelude:

- **Automatic Import**: The prelude is automatically included in every Rust program, so you don't need to explicitly import it. This ensures that essential functionality is always available without extra boilerplate.
- **Common Traits**: Traits like `Clone` and `Copy` are part of the prelude. These traits provide common behavior for types (like copying, printing, and comparing) and are crucial for basic operations in Rust.
- **Standard Types**: Some commonly used types, such as `Box`, `Option` and `Result` are part of the prelude. These types are foundational to Rust programming, especially for handling memory, collections, and error management.

- **Basic Functions**: Standard library functions like `drop`, which is used to explicitly drop a value, are included in the prelude.

Some of the most notable items in the prelude include.

Traits

- `Copy`, `Clone`: For duplicating values.
- `Debug`: For formatting types for debugging.
- `Default`: For default values of types.
- `Drop`: For custom behavior when types go out of scope.
- `Iterator`: For iterating over collections.
- `ToString`: For converting types to a string.

Types

- `Option`: For optional values (i.e., a value or `None`).
- `Result`: For error handling, encapsulating success (`Ok`) or failure (`Err`).
- `Vec`: A growable, heap-allocated array.
- `String`: A growable string.
- `Box`: A heap-allocated smart pointer.

Crates are the foundation of Rust's compilation and code management system. They allow developers to break their code into reusable, modular units that can be easily shared across projects or with the wider Rust ecosystem. Whether you're building an executable (binary crate) or a reusable library (library crate), crates provide a clear structure and make it easy to manage dependencies and functionality using Cargo. Crates also facilitate code reuse and enable you to tap into a vast ecosystem of open-source libraries, simplifying development and encouraging modular design.

Now that we've covered the basics of organizing code with crates and managing dependencies through Cargo, it's time to explore another crucial aspect of software development: testing. Rust includes robust testing tools that help ensure your code behaves as expected. In the next section, we'll dive into how to write and run tests in Rust, covering everything from basic unit tests to integration tests and more.

Testing

Testing is a critical aspect of software development that ensures your code functions as intended and remains maintainable over time. Writing tests helps identify bugs early, prevents regressions when making changes, and provides confidence that your application behaves correctly in different scenarios. In the context of a growing project, testing becomes even more important as it allows you to refactor or add new features without fear of breaking existing functionality.

The Importance of Testing

Before we dive into Testing in Rust, it's important to highlight why testing is critical in software development. Testing is not just a process to catch bugs, but a fundamental practice that ensures your code is robust, reliable, and maintainable. Here are several key reasons why testing should be a priority in any development project:

- **Error Prevention**: Writing tests helps catch errors and bugs during the development process before they make it to production. Early detection of issues saves time and reduces the cost of debugging.
- **Code Refactoring**: As your codebase evolves, refactoring is necessary to improve design or performance. Tests provide a safety net, ensuring that behavior remains consistent when making changes.
- **Documentation**: Tests serve as a form of living documentation. When you look at well-written tests, you get a clear sense of how the code is intended to behave, making it easier for others (or your future self) to understand and use the code.
- **Confidence in Code Changes**: As your project grows, making changes or adding features can be risky. Tests help ensure that your new code integrates well with existing code and doesn't introduce new bugs.
- **Long-Term Maintainability**: Without tests, it becomes harder to maintain a codebase over time, as it can be difficult to tell whether a change will break other parts of the system. Tests provide a foundation for maintainability and stability.

Rust has a built-in testing framework that simplifies writing and running tests, making it easy to incorporate testing into your development workflow. Some key features include:

- **Test Annotations**: Rust's framework uses the #[test] attribute to mark functions as tests. These functions are then automatically executed when you run your test suite.

- **Assertions**: The framework provides several assertion macros, such as `assert!`, `assert_eq!`, and `assert_ne!`, to verify expected outcomes in tests.
- **Integration with Cargo**: Testing is deeply integrated with Cargo, Rust's package manager and build system. Running tests is as simple as executing cargo test, which compiles and runs all your test cases.
- **Unit Tests**: Small tests that focus on individual functions or components, conventionally placed directly in the same file as the code they test.
- **Integration Tests**: Larger tests that focus on the interaction between different parts of your codebase. These are placed in a dedicated `tests` directory.

Rust's testing framework is designed to be simple and flexible, encouraging developers to adopt testing as a standard part of their coding process.

In the next section, we will explore Unit Testing in Rust, focusing on how to write effective unit tests and run them as part of your development cycle.

Writing Tests

In Rust, the testing framework is built into the language, making it easy to write unit tests, organize them, and assert different outcomes. Let's explore the basics of writing tests, structuring them in a project, and the key macros used for asserting outcomes.

Unit tests are written using the `#[test]` attribute, which marks functions as test functions. The test runner will automatically find and execute these functions when you run `cargo test`. Each test function should validate a specific behavior or condition in your code. Here's an example of a simple unit test:

Ch06/Examples/example07

```
#[cfg(test)]
mod tests {
    #[test]
    fn addition_works() {
        assert_eq!(2 + 2, 4);
    }
}
```

Typically, tests are organized within a dedicated test module. In this case, the module is named `tests`. A test module can contain multiple test functions, allowing you to group related tests in one place. Let's go through the code step by step:

`#[cfg(test)]`:

- The `#[cfg(test)]` attribute is a conditional compilation attribute. It tells the Rust compiler to include the code block only when running tests.
- When you run `cargo test`, Rust knows to compile and execute the code within `#[cfg(test)]` blocks. When running `cargo build` or `cargo run`, this code will be ignored, ensuring that the test code does not interfere with production code.

`mod tests {...}`:

This defines a module named tests. The module encapsulates the test functions, organizing all your test cases in one place. By convention, test-related code is grouped inside a mod tests block, but you can use different names if needed.

`#[test]`:

- The `#[test]` attribute marks a function as a test case. When you run cargo test, the Rust testing framework will automatically discover and run all functions marked with `#[test]`.
- Each `#[test]` function should contain assertions (like `assert_eq!`, `assert!`, etc.) to check that the code behaves as expected.

`fn addition_works()`:

- This is a simple test function that checks whether the expression 2 + 2 equals 4.
- The `assert_eq!` macro compares the two values. If they are equal, the test passes; if not, the test fails, and Rust will show an error with the expected and actual values.

Structuring Tests

Rust provides a flexible way to organize tests in your project. Tests can be written inline within the same file as your production code, or they can be placed in a separate test directory for more comprehensive testing. Here's how to structure tests:

- **Inline Unit Tests**: Inline tests are written directly in the file they are testing, usually within a `#[cfg(test)]` module. They are primarily used for unit testing.
- **Integration Tests**: For larger projects or more complex tests, you can place tests in a dedicated `tests/` directory. These integration tests ensure that your modules work together correctly.

For example, the `integration_tests.rs` file in the `tests/` directory can contain multiple tests that validate the behavior of the application as a whole. Using the same example as before you can find an example in:

Ch06/Examples/example08

```
#[test]
fn addition_works() {
    assert_eq!(2 + 2, 4);
}

#[test]
fn subtraction_works() {
    assert_eq!(6 - 4, 2);
}
```

In this example, the tests are placed in a separate test file within the `tests` directory. There's no need to use the `mod` keyword, nor is there a requirement for the `#[cfg(test)]` attribute. All files in the `tests` directory are automatically compiled and executed only when you run `cargo test`.

Asserting Outcomes

Rust provides several powerful macros to assert test outcomes:

- **assert!**: Asserts that a condition is true. If the condition is false, the test will fail.

  ```
  assert!(4 > 2);
  ```

- **assert_eq!**: Asserts that two values are equal. If the values are not equal, the test will fail and display the expected and actual values.

  ```
  assert_eq!(3 + 3, 6);
  ```

- **assert_ne!**: Asserts that two values are not equal. If the values are equal, the test will fail.

  ```
  assert_ne!(4 + 4, 10);
  ```

These macros help ensure that your code behaves as expected, making it easier to detect bugs and prevent regressions in future code changes.

You can enhance the usefulness of test failures by adding custom error messages to `assert!` statements. This allows you to provide more context when a test fails, making debugging easier.

```
assert!(condition, "Custom error message: {}", value);
```

Here, the custom message can include placeholders (like {}) that are filled with values at runtime, using the same syntax as Rust's println! macro. When the assertion fails, this message will be printed along with the failure, giving more insight into what went wrong.

For example:

```
let x = 5;
let y = 10;
assert!(x == y, "Expected x to equal y, but got x = {} and y =
{}", x, y);
```

If x and y are not equal, the output will be:

```
thread 'main' panicked at src/main.rs:2:5
Expected x to equal y, but got x = 5 and y = 10', src/main.
rs:2:5
```

This custom message provides valuable information to help identify the cause of the failure.

Running Tests

Testing in Rust is made simple through the use of cargo, Rust's package manager and build system. cargo test is the primary command used to run tests, and it provides a variety of options to run, manage, and filter your tests. In this section, we'll explore how to run tests, manage outputs, and interpret results.

Run all tests

To run all the tests in your project, simply execute:

```
cargo test
```

This command compiles your project in test mode and executes all the test functions defined in your code. By default, it runs all tests from every module that contains #[test] annotated functions, including those in both the main source code and any tests module.

After running the tests, cargo will show how many tests were executed and whether they passed or failed. For each failed test, it will display the error message or assertion that caused the failure.

Running Specific Tests

You can target specific tests or filter the tests you run using several options:

- **Filter by partial name**: You can also run tests by matching part of the test function's name:

```
cargo test some_partial_name
```

This will run all tests whose names contain `some_partial_name`. Note that you can only run a specific test function if its name is not a part of any other test function's name.

- **Exclude output for successful tests**: By default, `cargo test` will show output for both successful and failed tests. To see only the output of failed tests, use:

```
cargo test -- --nocapture
```

This is especially useful for large test suites where you want to focus on errors.

- **Ignoring Tests**: If there are tests you don't want to run by default (e.g., long-running tests), you can mark them with the `#[ignore]` attribute:

```
#[test]
#[ignore]
fn long_running_test() {
    // test code here
}
```

To run ignored tests, you can use:

```
cargo test -- --ignored
```

This allows you to manage long or special-case tests separately from your main test suite.

Interpreting Test Results and Failures

When all tests pass, `cargo test` will output a summary like:

```
running 3 tests
test module::test_name_1 ... ok
test module::test_name_2 ... ok
test module::test_name_3 ... ok

test result: ok. 3 passed; 0 failed; 0 ignored; 0 measured; 0
filtered out; finished in 0.00s
```

This summary shows the total number of tests executed and how many passed, failed, were ignored, or filtered.

If a test fails, `cargo` will report which test failed and display the assertion or panic message that caused the failure:

```
running 1 test
test tests::addition_works ... FAILED
failures:
---- tests::addition_works stdout ----
thread 'tests::addition_works' panicked at src/main.rs:9:9:
assertion `left == right` failed
  left: 4
 right: 5
note: run with `RUST_BACKTRACE=1` environment variable to
display a backtrace
failures:
    tests::addition_works
test result: FAILED. 0 passed; 1 failed; 0 ignored; 0 measured;
0 filtered out; finished in 0.00s
error: test failed, to rerun pass `--bin example07`
```

This information helps you pinpoint exactly where and why a test failed, making it easier to debug.

`cargo test` is a powerful tool for managing tests in Rust. Whether you're running the full suite or focusing on specific tests, it gives you flexibility to filter and interpret results easily. Understanding how to interpret test results and manage test outputs ensures your code remains robust and maintainable.

The output presentation differs significantly between running tests in an IDE and using `cargo test`. In an IDE, test results are often displayed in a more user-friendly and visually structured format, with color coding, collapsible sections for individual test cases, and icons indicating success or failure. This allows for quick navigation to failed tests, viewing detailed logs, and even directly interacting with failed assertions by jumping to the relevant lines in the code. In contrast, `cargo test` outputs results as plain text in the terminal, with test statuses (pass/fail) listed sequentially. While `cargo test` supports colored text to differentiate between successes and failures, it lacks the interactive features and rich visual formatting provided by an IDE, requiring users to manually scroll through the output to find details about failed tests.

Error handling in Tests

Testing error handling in Rust is essential, as it ensures that your code behaves correctly when things go wrong. Since Rust emphasizes safety, many functions return types like `Result` or `Option`, which need to be properly handled in tests. This section will guide you on how to test functions that return `Result` or `Option`, and provide best practices for managing errors during testing.

Testing Functions that Return Result or Option

When writing tests for functions that return `Result` or `Option`, you need to ensure that both the success and failure cases are covered. You can use pattern matching or methods like `unwrap()` to handle `Result` and `Option` types in tests.

Handling Result in Tests

Functions that return Result indicate either success (`Ok`) or failure (`Err`). When testing these functions, you want to verify both scenarios. Consider the following function that needs to be tested:

Ch06/Examples/example09

```
fn divide(a: i32, b: i32) -> Result<i32, String> {
    if b == 0 {
        Err("Cannot divide by zero".to_string())
    } else {
        Ok(a / b)
    }
}
```

And here is the corresponding test code:

```
#[cfg(test)]
mod tests {
    use super::*;

    #[test]
    fn test_divide_success() {
        let result = divide(10, 2);
        assert_eq!(result.unwrap(), 5);
    }

    #[test]
    fn test_divide_failure() {
        let result = divide(10, 0);
        assert!(result.is_err());
    }
```

```
}
```

In the `test_divide_success` function, `unwrap()` is used to retrieve the `Ok` value from the `Result`, while `test_divide_failure` uses `is_err()` to check if the function returns an error.

Handling Option in Tests

Functions that return `Option` can either contain a value (`Some`) or no value (`None`). Tests for `Option` types can check for both cases. Consider the following function that needs to be tested:

Ch06/Examples/example10

```
fn find_item(items: Vec<i32>, target: i32) -> Option<i32> {
    for item in items {
        if item == target {
            return Some(item);
        }
    }
    None
}
```

And here is the corresponding test code:

```
#[cfg(test)]
mod tests {
    use super::*;

    #[test]
    fn test_find_item_some() {
        let items = vec![1, 2, 3, 4];
        assert_eq!(find_item(items, 3), Some(3));
    }

    #[test]
    fn test_find_item_none() {
        let items = vec![1, 2, 3, 4];
        assert_eq!(find_item(items, 5), None);
    }
}
```

In this example, `assert_eq!` is used to directly compare the `Option` returned by the `find_item` function with either `Some` or `None`.

Testing panic!

If your code uses `panic!` in some scenarios, Rust provides the `should_panic` attribute for tests:

```
#[test]
#[should_panic(expected = "division by zero")]
fn test_panic() {
    divide(10, 0).unwrap();
}
```

This ensures that your code panics with the expected message, making it useful for testing edge cases where a panic is the correct behavior. When a panic occurs during a test marked with `#[should_panic]`, the test is considered successful and continues running, unlike in a regular program where a panic causes the program to fail and stop execution.

Summary

In this chapter we explored how Rust utilizes modules, crates, and testing to organize, structure, and ensure the quality of code. Modules in Rust allow developers to break down large codebases into smaller, manageable pieces by logically grouping related functions, types, constants, and traits. This chapter discusses the importance of modules for encapsulation, code organization, and namespace management, while emphasizing how they promote code reuse across projects. Modules can be defined inline or spread across multiple files, with visibility controlled through the `pub` keyword, ensuring proper access restrictions.

The chapter introduces the concept of paths, explaining how both absolute and relative paths are used to access items within modules. It also covers the use keyword, which simplifies code by importing items into the current scope. Furthermore, the chapter delves into Rust's hierarchical module system, exploring how nested modules are structured and how visibility rules work across parent and submodules.

The discussion transitions into crates, which serve as Rust's primary compilation and packaging unit. Crates can be either binary or library crates, each with specific rules governing their structure and use. Crates allow for better management of dependencies through Cargo, Rust's package manager. Cargo ensures smooth integration of external libraries from crates.io and allows projects to manage versions and update dependencies efficiently. Crates provide modularity, enabling developers to share and reuse code across projects.

Finally, the chapter focuses on testing, which is a critical aspect of maintaining robust and reliable code. Rust's built-in testing framework makes it easy to write and execute both unit and integration tests. The framework provides annotations like `#[test]` and assertion macros (`assert!`, `assert_eq!`, and `assert_ne!`) to ensure that the code behaves as expected. The chapter also discusses running tests, interpreting results, and writing tests for functions that return `Result` or `Option`. Testing not only helps catch bugs early but also provides confidence when refactoring code or adding new features.

By covering these key topics, modules, crates, and testing, this chapter provides a solid foundation for organizing and maintaining Rust projects efficiently, with a strong emphasis on code quality and reuse.

Next, we'll cover error handling in Rust. Using `Result` and `Option` types, Rust ensures safe, clear management of errors without crashing. You'll learn how to handle errors effectively, use the `?` operator for simplicity, and create custom error types for more precise control.

Exercises

The model answers for this chapter are organized differently. Each solution will be contained in its own separate project, rather than having one project with multiple binaries in `src\bin\`.

1. Define a simple inline module called math with a function factorial(n: u32) -> u128 that returns the factorial of a number (n! = n * (n-1) * ... * 1). Call the factorial function from the main function and print the result for n = 5.

2. Create a module `greetings` with a public function `say_hello()` and a private function `whisper_hello()`. Call `say_hello` from the main function and try to call `whisper_hello()` to see the visibility rules in action.

3. Create a module school with two submodules, students and classes. Each submodule should have one public function (`add_student` and `add_class`). Call these functions from the main function, using the full path to access the nested modules.

4. Move the code from Exercise 2 into separate files. Place `school`, `students`, and `classes` in their respective files (`school.rs`, `students.rs`, `classes.rs`), student. Modify `main.rs` to use these file-based modules and call the functions as before.

5. Refactor the project from Exercise 4. Use the `use` keyword in `main.rs` to avoid fully qualifying the module paths every time a function from `books` or `users` is called. Refactor the file-based solution to a directory-based solution, by moving the `school.rs` to the school folder in the file `mod.rs`

6. Add the external crate `chrono` to your project. Write a simple program that gets the current date and time, formats it, and displays it in a human-readable format.

7. Create a new Rust library crate (`my_utils`) with a simple function `greet(name: &str) -> String` that returns a greeting message. Add this local crate as a dependency in another project and use the `greet` function.

8. Write unit tests as inline tests for the `greet` function from Exercise 7. Use `assert_eq!` or `assert!` macro to verify the correctness of your function.

9. Create an integration test for the library crate `my_utils` that tests multiple functions from the library. Place the integration tests in the `tests/` directory, following Rust's integration testing conventions.

10. Make a libaray named `solution10` and create a function `fibonacci(n: i32) -> Result<u64, String>` that calculates the Fibonacci number for a given index n. If n is a non-negative integer, return the Fibonacci number at index n wrapped in `Ok`. If n is negative, return an error message wrapped in `Err`. Write tests to ensure that both the success (`Ok`) and failure (`Err`) cases are handled correctly.

Project: Geometric Shapes

The Geometric Shapes library is a versatile tool for working with different geometric shapes such as circles, squares, and rectangles. It provides simple and efficient methods to calculate key properties like area and perimeter, making it ideal for applications that require geometric computations.

By organizing the code into distinct modules, the library ensures that the logic for each shape is well-encapsulated, promoting clean code and easy reusability. Additionally, the library is thoroughly tested using unit tests to ensure the accuracy and reliability of all calculations.

The library's structure includes:

- A Shapes module, containing submodules for specific shapes like Circle, Square, and Rectangle.

- Comprehensive unit tests to verify the correctness of the library's functionality.

Library API

The public API provides access to the following functionality:

- **Shapes**: Structs and methods for working with different shapes:
- `Circle::new(radius: f64)`: Creates a new circle.
- `Square::new(side: f64)`: Creates a new square.
- `Rectangle::new(width: f64, height: f64)`: Creates a new rectangle.
- **Trait Shape**: Implements the following methods for all shapes:
- `area()`: Calculates and returns the area of the shape.
- `perimeter()`: Calculates and returns the perimeter of the shape.

Implementation Guidelines:

- The `Shape` trait is defined within the Shapes module.
- Each geometric shape (`Circle`, `Square`, `Rectangle`) is implemented as a submodule within the `Shapes` module.
- Each shape implements the `Shape` trait.
- Organize the library using a directory-based module structure for clarity and maintainability.
- Write unit tests for each shape, ensuring full code coverage. Tests should reside within their respective Shape submodules.
- Use the library in another project to demonstrate it's working

Stdlib

07

Error Handling

In software development, errors are an inevitable part of the process. Whether they result from user input, external data sources, network failures, or bugs in the code, effectively handling errors is crucial for building robust and reliable applications. Proper error handling ensures that a program can gracefully recover from unexpected conditions, provide meaningful feedback to users, and maintain data integrity.

Rust takes a unique approach to error handling that sets it apart from other languages like C++ or Java. Instead of relying on exceptions, which can lead to unpredictable program flow and hidden bugs, Rust emphasizes safety, explicitness, and reliability. Rust's error handling model encourages developers to think critically about potential errors and handle them in a controlled and deliberate manner at compile time.

In this chapter, we'll explore Rust's approach to error handling, its underlying principles, and how they shape the language. By the end, you'll know how to handle errors effectively, making your code safer, more predictable, and easier to maintain.

Topics handled in this chapter are:

- **Rust's Explicit Error Handling**: Rust requires explicit error management using types like `Result` and `Option`, avoiding exceptions.
- **Panic**: The `panic!` macro handles critical errors, causing the program to terminate and unwind the stack.
- **Option and Result:** `Option` handles cases where a value might be absent. `Result` provides structured error handling..
- **Pattern Matching**: Use match expressions to explicitly handle all possible outcomes in `Result` and `Option`.
- **Unwrap, expect and ok**: These methods offer quick access to values but can lead to panics if misused. We look at safer alternatives like `unwrap_or`
- **The ? Operator**: The `?` operator simplifies error handling by automatically propagating errors.
- **Custom Error Types**: Custom error types offer more context and clarity for domain-specific errors.
- **Trait-Based Error Handling**: Use trait objects like `Box<dyn Error>` for handling multiple error types flexibly.

Mastering Rust's approach to error handling will not only make your programs more reliable, but will also sharpen your skills as a developer, empowering you to write code that is safer, clearer, and more resilient than ever before.

Understanding Errors in Rust

Error handling in Rust is unique and quite different from other languages. Rust's emphasizes on handling as much as possible at compile time has led to the notable decision of run-time errors always halting the program. To achieve this, Rust enforces the handling of the `Option` and `Result` types. We'll first explore Rust's general approach to error handling, followed by how Rust deals with runtime errors, known as panics. Finally, we'll examine the key types used for handling errors: `Option` and `Result`.

Rust's Approach

Rust is designed with a strong emphasis on safety and explicit error handling. Unlike many other programming languages that use exceptions to handle errors, Rust takes a different approach that aligns with its core principles of safety and control. It's error handling strategy requires developers to explicitly manage the errors types `Result` and `Option`. This design choice forces programmers to handle errors in a clear and predictable manner, ensuring that all possible error conditions are considered during the development process.

In traditional exception-based languages such as C++ or Java, errors are often handled through exceptions that can be thrown and caught at various points in the code. While this approach can simplify error handling by allowing errors to propagate up the call stack automatically, it can also lead to unexpected program flow and hidden bugs. If exceptions are not properly managed, they can cause the program to terminate unexpectedly or leave it in an inconsistent state, making debugging and maintenance more challenging. Rust's approach to runtime errors is to halt the program whenever one occurs.

Rust's way of error handling offers several advantages over exception-based models. One of the key benefits is the use of compile-time checks. In Rust, the compiler enforces that all errors must be accounted for, either by handling them directly or by explicitly propagating them to the caller. This strict requirement eliminates many classes of bugs that arise from unhandled exceptions, making Rust code more reliable and predictable.

Additionally, Rust's explicit error management makes code easier to understand and maintain. Since errors are treated as values, they must be dealt with consciously, rather than being hidden away in a separate exception-handling mechanism. This leads to code that is not only safer but also more transparent, as it clearly communicates the developer's intent when handling different error scenarios.

Rust's error handling is focused on two types: `Option`, which is used to handle situations where a value might be missing, and `Result`, which is designed for managing and communicating errors.

Panic

In Rust, a program can encounter a runtime error known as a **panic**, which is similar to unhandled exceptions in other languages but handled differently. When a panic occurs, it means the program has encountered an unrecoverable error, and as a result, it will terminate execution immediately. Unlike some languages that allow exceptions to be caught and handled, Rust's panic is a signal that something has gone fundamentally wrong, and the program cannot continue safely.

A panic typically leads to a **stack unwinding** process, where the program cleans up by rolling back through the stack and releasing resources until the program halts. This behaviour makes panics something to be avoided in most cases, as they lead to a complete program failure with no chance of recovery.

For example, the following statement, which tries to parse a string into an `i32`, fails because the string contains a letter. Using `unwrap` forces the program to extract the parsed value from the `Err`, which causes a panic since the value isn't present:

```
let i:i32 = "12a".parse().unwrap();
```

A detailed explanation of how this works will be provided later in the chapter. For now, we'll focus on the fact that the program encounters a panic, causing it to halt, unwind the stack, and display the following runtime error:

```
thread 'main' panicked at src\bin\example01a.rs:2:31:
called `Result::unwrap()` on an `Err` value: ParseIntError {
kind: InvalidDigit }
```

Therefore, it's important to prevent panics as much as possible, ensuring that your code handles potential issues gracefully, using Rust's robust error-handling tools like `Result` and `Option`. However, in certain situations, such as prototyping or when the failure of the program is acceptable, panics can be used intentionally.

These are cases where the program is designed to stop if a critical condition is not met, and continuing would lead to unpredictable or unsafe behavior.

In summary, while Rust's panic mechanism is a powerful tool, it should be used cautiously, only in situations where failure is either unavoidable or desirable for the logic of the application.

panic!

The `panic!` macro in Rust is used to handle unrecoverable errors, signaling that something has gone fundamentally wrong, and the program cannot continue executing safely. When `panic!` is invoked, it causes the program to immediately terminate by unwinding the stack (cleaning up memory) or by aborting, depending on the configuration. It's typically used in scenarios where the program cannot reasonably recover from an error.

The `panic!` macro works similarly to the `println!` macro. It can accept zero or more parameters, with the first being the message displayed when the panic occurs. This message can include optional placeholders for string interpolation to incorporate additional values.

For example, look at the following code:

```
let n = -3;
if n < 0 {
    panic!("n should be at least zero it is {}", n);
}
```

It will result in a panic with the message:

```
n should be at least zero it is -3
```

Option<T>

In Rust, the `Option` type is used to represent a value that may or may not be present. It is an enum that encapsulates an optional value, making it a powerful tool for dealing with situations where data might be missing or undefined. The `Option` enum is defined as:

```
enum Option<T> {
    Some(T),
    None,
}
```

The `Option<T>` enum has two variants:

- `Some(T)`: This variant is used when a value is present. It wraps and stores a value of type `T`, indicating that the operation was successful or that the data is available.
- `None`: This variant is used when no value is present. It signifies the absence of data, meaning that the operation did not yield a result or that the value is not available.

The `Option` type is particularly useful in scenarios where a value might not always be present. For example, consider a function that searches for an item in a collection. If the item is found, the function can return `Some(T)` with the found item. If the item is not found, the function returns `None` to indicate the absence of a result.

Ch07/Examples/bin/example01.rs

```
fn find_item(items: &[i32], target: i32) -> Option<i32> {
    for &item in items {
        if item == target {
            return Some(item);
        }
    }
    None
}

fn main() {
    let numbers = [1, 2, 3, 4, 5];

    match find_item(&numbers, 3) {
        Some(number) => println!("Found: {}", number),
        None => println!("Item not found"),
    }

    match find_item(&numbers, 6) {
        Some(number) => println!("Found: {}", number),
        None => println!("Item not found"),
    }
}
```

In this example, the `find_item` function searches through an array of integers for a specified target value. If it finds the target, it returns `Some(item)`. If the target is not found, it returns `None`. The `main` function then uses pattern matching to handle both cases, demonstrating how `Option` enables explicit handling of the presence or absence of a value.

`Option` provides a clear and explicit way to manage cases where data might be missing, avoiding the pitfalls of null references found in other programming languages. By forcing the programmer to explicitly handle the `Some` and `None` cases, Rust ensures that all potential states are accounted for, leading to more robust and error-free code.

Here are common use cases for Option:

`Option` is commonly used in situations where an operation could fail for various reasons. Some typical use cases include:

Optional return values: Functions that may or may not return a value use Option. For example, looking up an item in a collection might return Some(item) if found, or None if not.

Optional Struct Fields: Some fields in a struct may not always have a value, so they can be represented using Option.

Result<T>

The `Result` type in Rust is an enum used to represent the outcome of operations that can succeed or fail. It is one of the core components of Rust's error handling strategy, providing a structured way to manage and propagate errors. The `Result` type is defined as:

```
enum Result<T, E> {
    Ok(T),
    Err(E),
}
```

The `Result<T, E>` enum has two variants:

- **Ok(T)**: This variant indicates that the operation was successful. It contains a value of type `T`, which represents the result of the successful operation.
- **Err(E)**: This variant indicates that the operation failed. It contains an error value of type `E`, which provides information about the failure.

By using `Result`, Rust enables developers to explicitly handle both the success and failure cases of an operation, ensuring that errors are managed in a controlled and predictable manner. This contrasts with languages that use exceptions for error handling, where errors can be less predictable and harder to manage.

`Result` is commonly used in situations where an operation could fail for various reasons. Some typical use cases include:

- **File I/O Operations**: Reading from or writing to a file can fail for many reasons, such as the file not existing or lacking necessary permissions. A function performing a file I/O operation will often return a Result to indicate success or failure.
- **Network Requests**: Making requests over a network can result in various errors, such as connectivity issues or timeouts. Functions that perform network requests frequently return a Result to handle these potential errors.
- **Parsing Input**: Converting a string into a number or other type might fail if the input is invalid. Parsing functions often return a Result to account for both valid and invalid input cases.
- **External Command Execution**: Running an external command or script may fail due to various reasons such as incorrect command syntax or missing dependencies. A function handling external command execution will use Result to indicate success or failure.

Consider the following example of a function that performs a division operation and returns a `Result`:

Ch07/Examples/bin/example02.rs

```
fn divide(numerator: f64, denominator: f64) -> Result<f64,
String> {
    if denominator == 0.0 {
        Err(String::from("Cannot divide by zero"))
    } else {
        Ok(numerator / denominator)
    }
}

fn main() {
    match divide(10.0, 2.0) {
        Ok(result) => println!("Result: {}", result),
        Err(e) => println!("Error: {}", e),
    }

    match divide(10.0, 0.0) {
        Ok(result) => println!("Result: {}", result),
        Err(e) => println!("Error: {}", e),
    }
}
```

In this example, the `divide` function takes two floating-point numbers as input: `numerator` and `denominator`. It returns a `Result<f64, String>`, indicating either a successful division (`Ok(f64)`) or an error (`Err(String)`). If the `denominator` is zero, the function returns an `Err` with an appropriate error message. Otherwise, it returns `Ok` with the result of the division.

The `main` function then demonstrates how to handle the `Result` returned by `divide`. Using pattern matching, it differentiates between the `Ok` and `Err` variants, providing appropriate handling for each case.

This example illustrates the explicit and safe error handling that Rust's `Result` type encourages. By requiring developers to consider both success and failure scenarios, Rust helps ensure that errors are managed predictably and effectively.

This wraps up the first section on the basics of error handling. Next, we'll explore various ways to work with Result and Option once they are returned from a function in your code. In the next section, we will dive into the Option and Result types and explore the different methods for handling them.

Simple Error Handling

Result and Option types can be managed explicitly through pattern matching with match or if let, allowing you to account for all possible outcomes. Alternatively, Rust provides shortcuts like unwrap and expect for quick access, though these can panic if used improperly. Methods like unwrap_or and unwrap_or_else offer safer ways to handle missing or error values by supplying defaults Let's look at them one by one.

Match

The most explicit way to handle a `Result` or `Option` is through a `match` expression, which lets you handle every possible outcome. For `Result`, you match against the `Ok` variant (representing success) and the `Err` variant (representing an error). For `Option`, you match against the `Some` (containing a value) and `None` (no value).

In the case of `Option`, working with the previous example:

Ch07/Examples/bin/example01.rs

```
match find_item(&numbers, 3) {
    Some(number) => println!("Found: {}", number),
    None => println!("Item not found"),
}
```

In this case:

- If the item is found, the `Some` variant is matched and the result printed
- If the item is not found, the `None` variant is matched and the result is printed

Similarly for `Result`, working with the previous example:

Ch07/Examples/bin/example02.rs

```
match divide(10.0, 2.0) {
    Ok(result) => println!("Result: {}", result),
    Err(e) => println!("Error: {}", e),
}
```

In this case:

- If the division is successful, the `Ok` variant is matched and the result is printed.
- If the division fails (division by zero), the `Err` variant is matched, and the error message is printed.

Let's look at a more practical scenario where we need to open a file and handle potential errors:

Ch07/Examples/bin/example03.rs

```
use std::fs::File;
use std::io::ErrorKind;

fn main() {
    let file_path = "example.txt";
    let file_result = File::open(file_path);

    match file_result {
        Ok(_) => println!("File opened successfully: {:?}",
file_path),
        Err(ref error) if error.kind() == ErrorKind::NotFound
=> {
            println!("File not found, creating a new file...");
            match File::create("example.txt") {
                Ok(_) => println!("File created successfully."),
                Err(e) => println!("Failed to create the file:
{:?}", e),
            }
        }
        Err(error) => println!("Failed to open the file: {:?}",
error),
    }
}
```

In this example:

- We first attempt to open a file.
- If the file is found (`Ok`), we print a success message.
- If the file is not found (`Err` with `ErrorKind::NotFound`), we attempt to create it.
- If there's any other error, we print the error message.

If let

The `if let` syntax is a convenient way to handle pattern matching for simple cases, particularly when working with enums like `Option` and `Result`. It allows for more concise code compared to a full match statement when you're only interested in handling one particular pattern and ignoring the other. Here is an example in combination with Option:

Ch07/Examples/bin/example04.rs

```
fn main() {
    let option = Some(12);

    if let Some(value) = option {
        println!("The value is: {}", value);
    }
}
```

In this example, the `if let Some(value) = option` syntax checks if the option is `Some` and binds the inner value to `value`.

Use if let when you're only interested in handling a single pattern and you want to ignore the other, if let is perfect for concise and readable code. It's also useful when the logic is short and simple. Use match if you need to handle both patterns, it's better to use match. This provides a clear, exhaustive way to cover both cases.

Unwrap, expect and, ok

While pattern matching is thorough, Rust provides shortcuts for cases where you are confident about the outcome.

Unwrap

One of these is the unwrap() method. It allows you to extract the value inside a `Result` or `Option` without explicitly handling the error case.

- For `Result`, calling `unwrap()` on an `Ok` variant returns the value inside.

- For `Option`, calling `unwrap()` on a `Some` variant returns the value inside.

However, if the `unwrap()` method encounters an `Err` or `None`, it causes the program to **panic** and crash.

Example using `unwrap()`:

Ch07/Examples/bin/example05.rs

```
fn main() {
    let number: Option<i32> = Some(5);
    println!("The number is: {}", number.unwrap());

    let result: Result<&str, &str> = Ok("Success!");
    println!("Result: {}", result.unwrap());
}
```

In this case, `unwrap()` works fine because both `Option` and `Result` contain valid values (`Some` and `Ok`, respectively). However, using `unwrap()` recklessly can lead to panics if the value is `None` or `Err`.

Expect

The `expect()` method works similarly to `unwrap()`, but it allows you to provide a custom error message if the program panics. This is much more informative than the default panic message and helps with debugging by making the error easier to trace.

Example using `expect()`:

Ch07/Examples/bin/example06.rs

```
fn main() {
    let config_file = std::fs::File::open("config.txt")
        .expect("Failed to open the configuration file");
    println!("Config file opened: {:?}", config_file);
}
```

If the file is not found, the program will panic, but it will print the custom error message `Failed to open the configuration file` instead of the generic panic message provided by `unwrap()`.

Ok

Another method often used for handling `Result` is the `ok()` method. This method converts a `Result<T, E>` into an `Option<T>`, discarding any error information in the process. It's useful when you're only concerned about whether or not a value exists, and you don't need to handle the error case explicitly.

For `Result`, calling `ok()` on an `Ok` variant returns `Some` with the value inside.

If the `Result` contains an `Err`, `ok()` will return `None`.

This method is helpful in situations where you don't care about the exact error and just need to know if the operation succeeded.

Example using `ok()`:

Ch07/Examples/bin/example07.rs

```
fn main() {
    let success_result: Result<i32, &str> = Ok(10);
    let failure_result: Result<i32, &str> = Err("Error!");

    let success_option: Option<i32> = success_result.ok();
    let failure_option: Option<i32> = failure_result.ok();

    println!("Success as Option: {:?}", success_option);
    println!("Failure as Option: {:?}", failure_option);
}
```

In this example, `ok()` transforms the `Ok` variant of `Result` into `Some(10)`, while the `Err` variant is converted into `None`. This method allows you to extract the success value as an `Option` while discarding the error.

When to Use expect(), unwrap(), or ok()

Use `expect()` when you are confident an operation should succeed, but you want to provide a meaningful error message in case it fails. This is particularly useful for critical operations, such as file handling or mandatory inputs, where failure should be clearly communicated. In contrast, `unwrap()` is a convenient shortcut that panics with a generic error if the operation fails, it should only be used when it's absolutely clear it won't panic.

While `ok()` converts a `Result` into an `Option`, discarding the error, it should be used when the specific error details aren't important. However, over-reliance on methods like `unwrap()`, `expect()` or `ok()` can lead to panics if the values aren't what you expect, and excessive use of these can make your code fragile.

In summary, `unwrap()`, `expect()` and `ok()` can be helpful in specific cases but should be used cautiously. For more complex or critical applications, safer and more explicit error-handling strategies are preferable. Instead, consider safer alternatives like pattern matching or the `unwrap_or` family.

Unwrap_or...

The `unwrap_or` family of functions in Rust provides a safe way to handle `Option` and `Result` when they may contain `None` or `Err` values. Instead of panicking, these methods allow you to supply a default value or compute an alternative when the `Option` is `None` or the `Result` is `Err`.

unwrap_or

For both `Option` and `Result`, this returns the value if it's `Some` or `Ok`. If it's `None` or `Err`, it returns the provided `default_value`, for example:

```
let opt: Option<i32> = None;
let result = opt.unwrap_or(10);
```

In this case, result will be 10 after the `unwrap_or`.

unwrap_or_else

This is similar to `unwrap_or`, but instead of providing a fixed value, you supply a function or closure that computes the default when the `Option` is `None` or the `Result` is `Err`, for example:

```
let opt: Option<i32> = None;
let result = opt.unwrap_or_else(|| 10);
```

In this example, `unwrap_or_else` takes a function, and here it's provided as a closure. Closures will be covered in detail in *Chapter 11* on functional programming. For now, you can think of the parameter to `unwrap_or_else` as an anonymous function. The `||` captures the function's parameter list (which is empty in this case), and `10` is the function body. As with any function, if the last expression is written without a semicolon, that value is returned. So, the result will be `10`.

unwrap_or_default

For types that implement the default trait, this returns the value if it's `Some` or `Ok`. Otherwise, it returns the type's default value.

```
let opt: Option<i32> = None;
let result = opt.unwrap_or_default();
```

In this case, result will be `0`, because the default value of a `i32` is `0`.

In summary, handling `Result` and `Option` types can be done explicitly using pattern matching, where all possible outcomes are accounted for. This is the most comprehensive approach, ensuring that both success and failure cases are handled. Alternatively, shortcuts like `unwrap()` and `expect()` provide quicker access to values, but should be used cautiously as they can cause panics if the value is `None` or `Err`. Safer methods like `unwrap_or()` and `unwrap_or_else()` offer a way to supply default values without panicking when errors occur. For simpler logic, `if let` can also be used to streamline pattern matching.

Advanced Error Handling

In Rust, advanced error handling allows you to write efficient and expressive code that manages various error scenarios. This section explores techniques such as using the `?` operator to propagate errors and handling multiple error types with trait objects like `Box<dyn Error>`. Additionally, combinators such as `and`, `or`, `map`, and `and_then` provide functional ways to chain and transform `Result` and `Option` values. These methods offer powerful tools to simplify error handling while maintaining robust and concise code.

Combinators

Rust offers several functional methods to transform and combine `Result` and `Option` types, allowing you to write concise and expressive code for chaining operations and handling errors. These methods include:

- `and()`: Chains two `Result` or `Option` values, returning the second one if the first is Ok/Some.
- `or()`: Chains two values, returning the first `Ok/Some` or the second `Err/None`.
- `map()`: Transforms the `Ok/Some` value by applying a function to it, leaving `Err/None` unchanged.
- `and_then()`: Similar to map(), but used when the transformation function returns another Result or Option.
- `or_else()`: The `or_else()` method allows you to provide a fallback function that returns an alternative `Option` or `Result` if the original is `None` or `Err`.
- `filter`: The `filter()` method on `Option` in Rust allows you to conditionally retain the `Some` value based on a predicate, returning `None` if the predicate is false.

and

Let's take a closer look with the help of an example:

Ch07/Examples/bin/example08.rs

```
fn main() {
    let first_ok: Result<i32, &str> = Ok(10);
    let second_ok: Result<i32, &str> = Ok(20);

    let first_err: Result<i32, &str> = Err("first error");
    let second_err: Result<i32, &str> = Err("second error");

    println!("ok - ok: {:?}", first_ok.and(second_ok));
    println!("ok - err: {:?}", first_ok.and(second_err));
    println!("err - ok: {:?}", first_err.and(second_ok));
    println!("err - err: {:?}", first_err.and(second_err));
}
```

In this example, we combine two result values in all possible combinations with the `and()`, giving the following output:

```
ok - ok: Ok(20)
ok - err: Err("second error")
err - ok: Err("first error")
err - err: Err("first error")
```

If both results are `Ok`, the last value is returned. If either one is an `Err`, the last error is returned or think of it like a logical "and": if both are `Ok` (`true`), you'll receive the last value. If either one is an `Err`(`false`), you'll get the first `Err`.

or

Now, let's apply the same analysis to `or()` with the same result variables as the previous example:

Ch07/Examples/bin/example09.rs

```
println!("ok - ok: {:?}", first_ok.or(second_ok));
println!("ok - err: {:?}", first_ok.or(second_err));
println!("err - ok: {:?}", first_err.or(second_ok));
println!("err - err: {:?}", first_err.or(second_err));
```

In this example, we combine two result values in alle possible combinations with the `or()`, giving the following output:

```
ok - ok: Ok(10)
ok - err: Ok(10)
err - ok: Ok(20)
err - err: Err("second error")
```

If at least one result is `Ok`, you'll get the first value. If both are `Err`, you'll get the second `Err`. Think of it like a logical "or": if at least one of the two is `Ok` (true), you receive the first value, but if both are `Err` (false), you get an the last `Err`.

map

The `map()` transforms a `Result` or `Option` by applying a function to the success case (`Ok`/`Some`), while leaving the error (`Err`/`None`) unchanged, for example:

```
let value: Result<i32, &str> = Ok(10);
let mapped = value.map(|x| x * 2);
println!("{:?}", mapped);
```

In this example, `mapped` is assigned the value `Ok(20)`. Here, a closure is used again. This anonymous function accepts one parameter, `x`, which represents the payload of `Ok()`. The value is then multiplied by 2 within the closure's body and returned.

and_then

The `and_then` function in Rust is available for both `Option` and `Result` types, allowing you to chain computations based on the value inside. It accepts a closure or function, which is applied only if the value is `Some` (for `Option`) or `Ok` (for `Result`). The closure must take exactly one parameter of the same type as the contained value. If the value is `None` or `Err`, the closure is not called, and the original `None` or `Err` is returned. For example:

Ch07/Examples/bin/example10.rs

```
fn is_even(num: i32) -> Result<i32, String> {
    if num % 2 == 0 {
        Ok(num)
    } else {
        Err("Not even",to_string())
    }
}

fn main() {
    let value: Result<i32, String > = Ok(4);
    let result = value.and_then(is_even);
    println!("{:?}", result);
}
```

If the value had been an `Err`, it would have been returned immediately, but since the value is `4`, the `is_even` function is called. The `is_even` function either returns the value, as it does in this case, or it returns an `Err` if the value is not even. This approach enables chaining of operations where each step has the potential to fail.

or_else

The `or_else` function in Rust is used with `Option` and `Result` types to provide a fallback action when the original value is `None` or `Err`. Instead of simply returning a default value like `or`, `or_else` accepts a closure or function that can dynamically compute and return another `Option` or `Result`. This makes it more flexible, especially in cases where the fallback requires some logic or computation.

Here is an example:

Ch07/Examples/bin/example11.rs

```
fn main() {
    let some_number = Some(10);
    let none_number: Option<i32> = None;

    let result1 = some_number.or_else(|| Some(20));
    let result2 = none_number.or_else(|| Some(20));

    println!("Result 1: {:?}", result1);
    println!("Result 2: {:?}", result2);

    let result3 = none_number.or_else(|| None);
    println!("Result 3: {:?}", result3);
}
```

In this code, the `or_else` method is used to provide an alternative value if the original `Option` is `None`. If the `Option` is `Some(value)`, it returns the value without running the closure. If the `Option` is `None`, the closure is executed, and its result is returned. In the first case, `or_else` doesn't modify `Some(10)`, so the result is `Some(10)`. In the second case, since the original is `None`, the closure runs and returns `Some(20)`. In the third case, the closure returns `None`, so the result stays `None`.

filter

In Rust, the filter method on an `Option` allows you to conditionally retain the value inside an `Option` based on a predicate (a closure or function that returns a boolean). If the predicate evaluates to `true`, the `Option` remains unchanged (i.e., still `Some(value)`). If the predicate evaluates to `false`, the `Option` is transformed into `None`. Note that `filter` is not a method provided directly for `Result`.

Ch07/Examples/bin/example12.rs

```
fn main() {
    let some_number = Some(10);
    let none_number: Option<i32> = None;

    let even_number = some_number.filter(|&n| n % 2 == 0);
    let odd_number = some_number.filter(|&n| n % 2 != 0);

    println!("Even number: {:?}", even_number);
    println!("Odd number: {:?}", odd_number);

    let filtered_none = none_number.filter(|&n| n % 2 == 0);
    println!("Filtered None: {:?}", filtered_none);
}
```

In this code, the `filter` method is used to conditionally retain values inside an `Option`. The `filter` method applies a predicate (a condition) to the value inside `Some`. If the condition is true, the value is kept as `Some`; if false, the result becomes `None`.

For `some_number`, which is `Some(10)`, the first `filter` checks if the number is even. Since 10 is even, the result is `Some(10)`. The second `filter` checks if the number is odd. Since 10 is not odd, the result becomes `None`.

For `none_number`, which is `None`, the `filter` method doesn't apply any checks because there's no value to filter. It simply remains `None`, and the final result is `None`.

Combined example

Here's an example combining some of the previous functions for a series of operations that either succeed or fail:

Ch07/Examples/bin/example13.rs

```
fn check_positive(x: i32) -> Result<i32, String> {
    if x > 0 { Ok(x) } else { Err("Not positive".to_string()) }
}

fn is_even(num: i32) -> Result<i32, String> {
    if num % 2 == 0 { Ok(num) } else { Err("Not even".to_
string()) }
}

fn main() {
    let value = Ok(10)
        .and_then(check_positive)
```

```
        .and_then(is_even)
        .map(|x| x * 2)
        .or(Err("Some check failed"));

    println!("{:?}", value);
}
```

We see that the chain of computations begins with `Ok(10)`, which represents a successful result wrapped in a `Result<i32, String>`. This initial value (`Ok(10)`) will be passed through a series of functions that may succeed or fail.

The first `and_then` applies the `check_positive` function to the value inside the `Result`. If the value is positive (Ok with a value greater than 0), `check_positive` will return `Ok(value)`. If not, it will return `Err("Not positive".to_string())`. Since `10` is positive, the result remains `Ok(10)` and the chain continues.

The second `and_then` applies the `is_even` function to the value. If the number is even, `is_even` returns `Ok(value)`. If it's odd, it returns `Err("Not even".to_string())`. In this case, `10` is even, so the result remains `Ok(10)` and the chain moves forward.

The `map` function is applied to transform the inner value if it is `Ok`. The closure multiplies the value by 2. Since the current value is `Ok(10)`, the transformation results in `Ok(20)`.

Handling Errors with `or(Err("Some check failed"))`. The or function is used as a fallback in case any of the previous operations return an `Err`. If an error occurred at any step, the chain would immediately return `Err("Some check failed")`. Since the current value is `Ok(20)`, `Ok(20)` is returned and printed.

In the next section, we are going to look into the `?` operator. The `?` operator offers a concise way to propagate errors in functions that return `Result`. It automatically returns an error if one occurs, eliminating the need for manual `match` expressions.

The ? Operator

The `?` operator is a shorthand in Rust that allows you to propagate errors without the need for verbose pattern matching. It simplifies code by automatically returning a `Result` or `Option` from the current function if an error occurs, making error handling more concise and readable.

When used, the `?` operator attempts to unwrap a `Result` or `Option`. If the value is `Ok` or `Some`, it continues execution. If it's `Err` or `None`, it returns the error or `None` from the current function.

Detailed Explanation of How the ? Operator

The `?` operator is syntactic sugar for an early return. When applied to a `Result` or `Option`, it effectively performs the following steps:

1. It checks if the value is `Ok` or `Some`. If so, it proceeds to the next operation.
2. If the value is `Err` or `None`, it immediately returns the error (or `None`) from the current function, propagating it upwards.

Here's an example of manual error handling and how the `?` operator simplifies it:

Ch07/Examples/bin/example14.rs

```
fn read_file(path: &str) -> Result<String, std::io::Error> {
    let mut file = match File::open(path) {
        Ok(f) => f,
        Err(e) => return Err(e),
    };
    let mut contents = String::new();
    match file.read_to_string(&mut contents) {
        Ok(_) => Ok(contents),
        Err(e) => Err(e),
    }
}
```

In this example, we attempt to open a file and read its contents into a `String`. Both of these I/O operations can fail and need proper error handling. If there's an issue with opening the file, we return early, passing the error back to the caller. If the file is successfully opened, we proceed to read from it. If everything goes well, the `String` is returned inside `Ok`; otherwise, the error is propagated. This pattern is common, but handling it with two match statements can result in verbose code. The `?` operator simplifies this by significantly reducing boilerplate, as shown in the next example:

Ch07/Examples/bin/example15.rs

```
fn read_file(path: &str) -> Result<String, std::io::Error> {
    let mut file = File::open(path)?;
    let mut contents = String::new();
    file.read_to_string(&mut contents)?;
    Ok(contents)
}
```

By using `?`, you eliminate the need to manually `match` each error and return it, streamlining the function while keeping the same functionality.

When using the `?` operator in Rust, all errors returned by functions in a chain must either be of the same type or a compatible type. The `?` operator automatically attempts to convert the error into the expected type using the `From` trait. If the conversion is not possible, because the `From` trait for that specific conversion is not implemented, the compiler will produce an error.

To overcome this limitation and allow functions to return different, incompatible error types, Rust offers the Box<dyn Error> type.

Box<dyn Error>

Sometimes, functions can encounter different kinds of errors (e.g., I/O errors, parsing errors, or custom errors). Instead of restricting your function to return one specific error type, you can use a trait object (Box<dyn Error>) to handle multiple error types in a flexible manner. This allows you to return any error that implements the `std::error::Error` trait.

`Box` will be covered in detail in *Chapter 12* on smart pointers. For now, it's enough to understand that `Box` is a smart pointer that stores data on the heap instead of the stack. This indirection allows handling different types in a more generic and flexible way.

Trait objects like Box<dyn std::error::Error> are used to abstract over different types of errors. The `Error` trait from the standard library is implemented by most error types (e.g., I/O errors, custom application errors). By boxing the error, you can return any type of error, as long as it implements `std::error::Error`.

Here's an example where a function handles both an I/O error and a parsing error, and returns a Box<dyn Error>:

Ch07/Examples/bin/example16.rs

```
use std::error::Error;
use std::fs::File;
use std::io::{self, Read};
use std::num::ParseIntError;

fn read_and_parse_file(path: &str) -> Result<i32, Box<dyn
Error>> {
    let mut file = File::open(path)?;  // I/O error
    let mut contents = String::new();
    file.read_to_string(&mut contents)?;  // I/O error
```

```
    let num: i32 = contents.trim().parse()?;  // Parsing error
    Ok(num)
}

fn main() -> Result<(), Box<dyn Error>> {
    match read_and_parse_file("data.txt") {
        Ok(n) => println!("Parsed number: {}", n),
        Err(e) => println!("An error occurred: {}", e),
    }
    Ok(())
}
```

In this example:

The function returns a boxed error, allowing it to handle both I/O and parsing errors.

The caller can match on the result and deal with the error in a unified manner.

- The `?` operator automatically converts the error type because the necessary `From` trait is implemented in the standard library.

These advanced techniques help you handle complex error situations in Rust with elegance and flexibility, making your code more maintainable and less error-prone.

As we move forward, it's important to understand how custom error handling can enhance both the clarity and functionality of your Rust applications. In the next section, we will explore how to define and use custom error types, giving you the ability to provide more specific, context-aware errors, improve debugging, and integrate seamlessly with Rust's error-handling ecosystem.

Custom Error Types

Rust provides powerful mechanisms for error handling using types like Result, Option, and trait-based error handling via `std::error::Error`. While Rust's standard error types are highly effective, creating custom error types gives you the ability to provide more meaningful, context-specific information in your application's errors. This section explores why custom error types are useful, how to define them, and how to implement the `std::error::Error` trait for better integration with Rust's error-handling ecosystem.

Why Custom Error Types

Custom error types are essential for providing specific and detailed error messages that add valuable context to the problem that occurred. When you create custom error types, you can:

- **Capture domain-specific error scenarios**: Instead of using generic error types, custom error types allow you to handle application-specific errors that align with your domain (e.g., network errors, parsing errors, etc.).
- **Improve debugging**: By encoding more information in your errors, you make debugging easier. Developers can immediately understand the nature of the error and where it originated.
- **Provide richer error information**: You can include relevant details such as the function that failed, the file that couldn't be opened, or other contextual data, making it easier to diagnose problems in production.

Readability

Custom error types help separate error-handling logic from business logic, which improves both readability and maintainability of code. They allow you to clearly differentiate between different kinds of failures, such as I/O errors, parsing errors, or application-specific issues. This makes your code more expressive and easier to understand, especially in larger projects.

For example, consider the difference between using a standard `Result<T, String>` type and a custom error type, first using the standard Result type:

Ch07/Examples/bin/example17.rs

```
fn process_file(file_name: &str) -> Result<(), String> {
    if file_name.is_empty() {
        return Err(String::from("Filename cannot be empty"));
    }
    // More logic here...
    Ok(())
}
```

And with a custom error type:

Ch07/Examples/bin/example18.rs

```
#[derive(Debug)]
enum FileError {
```

```
    EmptyFilename,
    NotFound(String),
    ParseError,
}

fn process_file(file_name: &str) -> Result<(), FileError> {
    if file_name.is_empty() {
        return Err(FileError::EmptyFilename);
    }
    // More logic here...
    Ok(())
}
```

In this second example, the use of FileError makes the possible error scenarios much clearer and easier to interpret.

Defining

In Rust, the most common way to define custom error types is by using an enum, where each variant of the enum represents a different kind of error. This is highly flexible because each variant can hold additional data relevant to that specific error type.

Here's a step-by-step guide to defining custom error types:

1. **Define the enum for your error types**. Each variant represents a different error scenario.

2. **Add relevant data to the error variants**, if needed. You can include strings, numbers, or other types to provide more context for the error.

3. **Use your custom error type** in the Result<T, E> type for your functions.

The std::error::Error Trait

The `std::error::Error` trait is the standard interface for error types in Rust. Implementing this trait allows your custom error types to integrate seamlessly with Rust's ecosystem, enabling better error handling and interoperability with other libraries.

The `Error` trait has one primary method: `source()`, which returns an optional reference to the underlying error that caused the current one, if any (used for error chaining). By default, this method returns `None`, but it can be overridden to provide more detailed information about the underlying cause of the error.

In most cases, implementing the `Error` trait is done alongside implementing the `Display` trait. Since `Display` is a supertrait of `Error`, it must be implemented when you implement `Error`.

Here is an example:

Ch07/Examples/bin/example19.rs

```
use std::fmt;

#[derive(Debug)]
enum FileError {
    NotFound(String),
    PermissionDenied(String),
    ParseError,
}

impl fmt::Display for FileError {
    fn fmt(&self, f: &mut fmt::Formatter<'_>) -> fmt::Result {
        match self {
            FileError::NotFound(file) => write!(f, "File not
            found: {}", file),
            FileError::PermissionDenied(file) => write!(f,
           "Permission denied for file: {}", file),
            FileError::ParseError => write!(f, "Failed to parse
file"),
        }
    }
}

impl std::error::Error for FileError {}

fn main() {
    let error = FileError::NotFound("config.toml".to_string());
    println!("{}", error);
}
```

Here:

- `Display` defines how the error should be formatted as a string.
- `Error` is implemented without any additional methods since we don't need to chain any underlying causes.

With both Display and Error implemented, you can easily print and propagate custom errors throughout your application, ensuring meaningful messages and seamless integration with the Rust error-handling system.

By creating custom error types and implementing the `std::error::Error` trait, you can write more expressive and maintainable Rust code. This allows you to give more context when errors occur, making your application easier to debug and work with in production environments.

Summary

Error handling is an essential aspect of building robust and reliable applications, as errors inevitably occur due to factors such as user input, external data sources, or bugs in the code. In Rust, error handling is approached differently from other languages like C++ or Java, emphasizing safety, explicitness, and reliability. Rather than using exceptions, Rust encourages developers to handle errors explicitly with types like `Result` and `Option`, ensuring all possible errors are considered and managed predictably. This chapter explored the foundational principles behind Rust's error handling, covering how to manage both recoverable and unrecoverable errors through types like Option and `Result` and tools such as the `panic!` macro. Through pattern matching and various utility methods, Rust makes handling both success and failure conditions easy while maintaining clarity and safety.

In addition, the `?` operator simplifies error propagation by reducing boilerplate, while trait objects such as `Box<dyn Error>` offer flexibility when handling multiple error types. Creating custom error types is another advanced technique that enhances code clarity and debugging. By defining specific error types, developers can capture domain-specific issues and provide richer context in error messages. Custom error types are commonly defined using enums, and by implementing the `std::error::Error` and `std::fmt::Display` traits, they can be seamlessly integrated with Rust's error-handling ecosystem. Overall, Rust's approach ensures that error management is an integral and explicit part of the development process, making code more predictable, maintainable, and reliable.

With a solid foundation in error handling, we're ready to tackle another essential part of Rust: strings. Although strings might seem straightforward at first, Rust's approach introduces unique challenges and concepts that can easily trip up newcomers. In the following chapter, we'll break down how strings work in Rust and clear up the confusion, one step at a time.

Exercises

1. Write a function `square_root(n: f64) -> Result<f64, String>` that calculates the square root of a given number. If the number is negative, return an error message in `Err`. Otherwise, return the result wrapped in `Ok`. In the `main` function, handle both success and error cases using pattern matching.

2. Write a function `find_even(items: &[i32]) -> Option<i32>` that searches for the first even number in a list of integers. If an even number is found, return `Some(number)`, otherwise return `None`. Use pattern matching in the main function to handle both cases and print the result.

3. Modify the previous `square_root` function to propagate the error using the `?` operator. Then, create a new function `safe_square_root(n: f64) -> Result<f64, String>` that calls `square_root` and propagates any errors using the `?` operator. Make sure to handle the error in main.

4. Create a custom error type `MathError` using an enum with variants `DivisionByZero`, `NegativeLogarithm`, `NegativeSquareRoot` and `UnsupportedOperation`. Write a function `perform_math_operation(a: f64, b: f64, operation: &str) -> Result<f64, MathError>` that simulates mathematical operations and returns different errors based on the operation and input values. Use pattern matching to handle each variant in the main function.

5. Write a program that attempts to read a number from a string using `.parse::<i32>()`. Use `.unwrap()` to extract the result, and then to the same again using `.expect()` to provide a meaningful error message if parsing fails.

6. Write a function `is_positive(n: i32) -> Result<i32, String>` that returns an error if the number is negative. Then, create a second function `is_even(n: i32) -> Result<i32, String>`. Chain these two functions using `.and_then()` to verify that a number is both positive and even, returning an appropriate error message otherwise.

7. Write a function `get_positive_number(input: &str) -> i32` that Attempts to parse the input string into an integer (`i32`). If the string is successfully parsed but the number is negative, return a default value of 0. If the string cannot be parsed at all, also return the default value of 0. Call `get_positive_number` with various inputs and print the results.

8. Write a function `get_valid_age(input: Option<i32>) -> Option<i32>` that checks if the given `Option<i32>` contains a valid age (a positive integer). If the input is None or the age is not valid (i.e., less than or equal to 0), return a default age of 18 using the `.or_else()` method. In the main function, call `get_valid_age` with various inputs and print the results.

9. Write a function `fetch_and_parse_data(api_data: &str) -> Result<i32, Box<dyn std::error::Error>>`. This function should simulate fetching data from an API, and then attempt to parse the response into an integer. Handle both missing data errors and parsing errors using `Box<dyn Error>`. Use the `?` operator to propagate errors.

10. Write a function `factorial(n: i128) -> Result<i128, String>` that recursively calculates the factorial of a non-negative integer n. Return an error wrapped in `Err` if n is negative. Additionally, check for potential overflow, and return an error if it occurs. If no error occurs, return the factorial result wrapped in `Ok`. In the main function, handle both success and error cases using pattern matching.

Project: Math Quiz Game

The Math Quiz Game is a command-line program where the player solves randomly generated arithmetic problems involving addition (+), subtraction (-), multiplication (*), and division (/). The player's score increases as they correctly answer problems. The game handles invalid inputs gracefully by showing error messages, prompting the player to try again, and preventing the program from crashing. The game consists of four rounds, one for each operator, and concludes after all rounds are completed.

Features:

- **Random Arithmetic Problems**:

The game generates random math problems using basic arithmetic operations: addition, subtraction, multiplication, and division.

The difficulty of the problems increases as the player's score for each round rises.

The first problem of each round is always "1 + 1" or equivalent for simplicity.

- **User Input**:

The player is prompted to enter an answer for each problem.

If the input is correct, the player receives feedback and their score is updated.

If the input is incorrect, the player is notified, and the game moves to the next round.

If the player enters invalid input (non-numeric characters), they are prompted to try again.

- **Error Handling**:

The game uses Result to handle input parsing and errors. If the input is not a valid number (e.g., alphabetic characters or symbols), the program displays an error message and allows the player to retry.

The game gracefully handles errors without crashing, ensuring a smooth user experience.

- **Scoring System**:

The player's score is tracked throughout the game. The score for each question is the sum of the operands.

After each question, the player is informed of their current score for that round.

For division problems, the score is the sum of the divisor and the quotient (i.e., b + c).

- **Game Loop**:

The game consists of 4 rounds, each round focused on a different operator: addition (+), subtraction (-), multiplication (*), and division (/).

Each round has a maximum of 10 questions.

If the player provides an incorrect answer, the round ends and the game moves to the next round.

The game continues until all rounds are completed or the player chooses to exit by typing "exit".

At the end of the game, the final score is displayed.

Random Problem Generation:

For each question, two numbers (a and b) are randomly generated. For division problems, the divisor (b) and the quotient (c) are generated first, and then the dividend (a = b * c) is calculated.

The difficulty of the problems increases with the player's score in the current round. The maximum integer value for operands is determined by the player's score, e.g., if the score is 17, the operands will be between 1 and 17 (inclusive).

The first question of each round is always "1 + 1" (or an equivalent easy problem for the operator) to ease the player into the round.

Scoring:

For addition, subtraction, and multiplication problems, the score is the sum of the two operands (a + b).

For division problems, the score is the sum of the divisor (b) and the quotient (c).

Input Parsing and Error Handling:

The player's input is validated using Rust's Result type.

If the input cannot be parsed into a valid number, the game displays an error message and prompts the player to enter the answer again.

Non-numeric or invalid input (e.g., alphabetic characters) is handled gracefully, and the game continues without crashing.

The player can also choose to quit the game at any time by typing "exit".

08

Strings

Strings are a fundamental part of programming, representing sequences of characters that are often used for text processing, communication, and data manipulation. In Rust, string handling is both powerful and efficient, reflecting the language's emphasis on safety, performance, and control over memory.

Rust's approach to strings involves two primary types: `String` and `&str`. Understanding these types and how they interact with Rust's ownership and borrowing system is crucial for effective string manipulation in the language. This chapter provides an introduction to these types, explores their characteristics, and highlights how they fit into the broader context of Rust's design principles.

This chapter will cover the following topics:

- **String Types**: Rust primarily uses `String` for growable, heap-allocated strings and `&str` for borrowed, immutable string slices, both essential for managing text in Rust.
- **Unicode Handling**: Rust handles strings using UTF-8 encoding, making it essential to understand Unicode concepts like code points and graphemes for accurate string manipulation.
- **Creating Strings**: Strings can be created through methods like `new`, `from`, `to_string`, and `to_owned`.
- **Slicing Strings**: Slicing strings requires careful consideration of UTF-8 boundaries to avoid panics, with methods like `char_indices` and get ensuring safe slicing.
- **String Inspection**: Functions like `len`, `is_empty`, `contains`, and `find` allow developers to inspect and retrieve information about strings efficiently.
- **Modifying Strings**: Methods like `push`, `push_str`, and `replace_range` allow in-place or new-value modification of `String`, but not `&str`.
- **Parsing Strings**: The `parse` method converts strings into various types like integers or floats, with custom parsing available through the `FromStr` trait.
- **Formatting Strings** The `format`! macro creates formatted strings using placeholders, providing flexible and customizable text generation based on the implementation of the `Display` and `Debug` traits.
- **Performance Considerations**: Efficient memory management, avoiding excessive cloning, and using pre-allocation (`with_capacity`) help optimize string operations.

Rust uses Unicode for character encoding, but unlike some other languages, it doesn't hide the complexities of Unicode. As a result, it's important to understand the implications of working with Unicode in Rust. We'll begin this chapter by exploring what Unicode is and how it impacts development in Rust.

Unicode

Unicode is a comprehensive character encoding standard that aims to provide a unique number for every character across different languages and systems, ensuring consistency and compatibility in text representation. Developed and maintained by the Unicode Consortium, Unicode has become the most widely used character encoding standard in the world.

The Unicode standard encompasses more than just encoding; it defines properties for characters, such as case mappings and sorting orders, and provides guidelines for the handling of text, including directionality (left-to-right or right-to-left), normalization, and collation. Below are some of the key components of Unicode's functionality: /

- **Mappings**: This refers to the process of converting characters from one form to another, such as changing lowercase letters to uppercase or normalizing text to a standard form for consistency.
- **Sorting Order**: Purely based on the numeric Unicode code points of characters. It is consistent and fixed across all languages but may not align with linguistic or cultural expectations.
- **Collation**: Collation is the process of ordering strings of text according to the linguistic rules of a particular locale. It ensures that text is sorted and compared in a way that aligns with cultural expectations, taking into account variations like accents and case sensitivity.
- **Normalization**: Normalization converts text to a standard form to ensure that different representations of the same character or sequence are treated as identical. This is important for text comparison, searching, and data storage, ensuring consistency and accuracy in text processing.

Not all of these concepts are supported by Rust's standard library. For example, in cases like normalization and grapheme cluster handling, you will need to use an external crate. These topics will be introduced briefly without going into full detail.

Code Points

A **code point** is a unique numerical value assigned to each character in the Unicode standard. These code points are used to represent characters from a wide range of writing systems, symbols, and other textual elements. Each code point corresponds to a specific character, and together they provide a way to encode and standardize the representation of text across different systems and platforms.

In Unicode, code points are often written in the format `U+XXXX`, where `XXXX` is a hexadecimal number. Code points are 32-bit values. For example:

The code point for the letter "A" is `U+0041`.

The code point for the symbol "©" (copyright) is `U+00A9`.

The code point for the emoji "😊" is `U+1F60A`.

Characters, graphemes, and code points

What we as humans interpret as a character is not always equivalent to a single code point. While they often correspond, there are exceptions. For instance, the character "é" can be represented by a single code point or by combining an "e" with an acute accent (´), which together form one grapheme. In other words, what we as humans consider a character is actually a grapheme, which can be encoded using one or more Unicode code points.

This also implies that there are multiple ways to encode the same grapheme, which can in turn lead to different visualizations of the semantically the same grapheme.

Code points and encoding

The Unicode standard specifies the code points but does not dictate how these are represented in memory or transmitted over networks. This is where character encodings like UTF-8, UTF-16, and UTF-32 come into play:

- **UTF-8**: A variable-width encoding that uses one to four bytes per Unicode code point. It is backward-compatible with ASCII and can represent any Unicode character.
- **UTF-16**: A variable-width encoding that uses one or two 16-bit code units. It uses surrogate pairs for characters with the higher numbers.
- **UTF-32**: A fixed-width encoding that uses four bytes per character, directly mapping each code point to a 32-bit integer.

ASCII is a Subset of Unicode. The first 128 characters of Unicode (code points `U+0000` to `U+007F`) are identical to the ASCII character set. This means that any valid ASCII text is also valid in Unicode. Unicode was designed with backward compatibility in mind, so ASCII characters can be seamlessly represented in Unicode without any conversion issues. For example, the letter "A" is represented as `U+0041` in Unicode, which corresponds to the same `65` decimal value in ASCII.

Character Categories and Properties

Each Unicode code point is associated with a specific character and its properties. These properties include:

- **General Category:** Describes the type of character, such as letter, digit, punctuation, symbol, or separator.
- **Script:** Indicates the writing system or script to which the character belongs, such as Latin, Cyrillic, Arabic, or Han.
- **Combining Class:** Used for characters that modify the preceding base character, such as diacritics.
- **Bidirectional Class:** Important for text that mixes right-to-left and left-to-right scripts, such as mixing English with Arabic.

In this section, we explored Unicode, the global standard for representing and encoding text from various languages and systems. We covered essential concepts such as code points, graphemes, and different Unicode encodings like UTF-8, UTF-16, and UTF-32. Understanding these concepts is crucial when working with text in Rust because the language handles text encoding explicitly. Rust's Unicode support ensures compatibility across platforms while giving developers the tools to manage complex text operations, such as normalization and collation.

Next, we will move on to Rust's string types, `String` and `&str`, which are integral for text manipulation in the language. We'll explore how these types interact with Rust's ownership model, memory management, and borrowing system. Understanding these string types, as well as Rust's careful handling of Unicode, will allow you to efficiently and safely work with text in Rust.

String Types in Rust

Rust provides several string types, with the main ones being `String` and `&str`. However, when interacting with C libraries for example, these types are not sufficient, and you'll need to use other string types for compatibility like `OsString` and `CString`. In this chapter, we will focus exclusively on `String` and &`str`.

A string consists of a list of characters. A character in Rust is a single Unicode code point, not a grapheme. This means that a character can represent a portion of a grapheme. The notion of graphemes is not build into standard rust. If you need to use graphemes for your application you have to use an external library like `unicode-segmentation`. In this chapter, when we refer to a character, we actually mean a Unicode code point, not a human-perceived character, which is a grapheme. Most of the time, there is no distinction between the two.

A `char` (the basic type) is always 4 bytes in size. Combining characters into String Rust uses the UTF-8 encoding scheme. This implies that looping over characters is not the same as looping over the bytes. In UTF-8 a Unicode code point can be between 1 and 4 bytes. Rust strings are therefore optimized for memory usage.

String

The `String` type is a commonly used data structure for managing dynamic, growable, and mutable strings of UTF-8 encoded text. It is an owned type, meaning it has full control over the memory in which it stores its data. Here are the key characteristics of the `String` type:

- **Owned Type:** `String` owns the data it contains, meaning it is responsible for managing the memory associated with that data. When a `String` instance goes out of scope, its memory is automatically deallocated.
- **Heap Allocation:** `String` allocates its contents solely on the heap. This allows `String` to dynamically resize and grow as needed.
- **Mutable:** `String` is mutable, allowing its contents to be modified after creation. You can add, remove, or change characters within a `String`. This mutability makes `String` a suitable type when the text content needs to change dynamically.
- **UTF-8 Encoded:** `String` stores its data as a sequence of UTF-8 encoded bytes, which allows it to represent any Unicode character. This encoding is efficient and widely supported, ensuring compatibility with many systems and protocols.

The `String` type in Rust is a versatile and powerful tool for managing dynamic, mutable text data. Its design integrates seamlessly with Rust's ownership and memory safety features, providing both flexibility and security.

&str

`&str` (pronounced *string slice*) is a fundamental data type used to represent a sequence of Unicode scalar values, usually as a view or reference to a portion of a string. Here are the key characteristics of `&str`:

- **Borrowed Type:** `&str` is a borrowed reference to string data. It does not own the data it points to, meaning the underlying data must remain valid for the lifetime of the `&str` reference. Which is managed by the borrowing system.
- **Immutable:** `&str` is an immutable reference to a sequence of characters. Once a string slice is created, you cannot modify its content. This immutability ensures that string slices can be safely shared across multiple parts of a program without concern for concurrent modifications.
- **Memory Efficiency:** `&str` does not allocate new memory for its contents. It is a reference to a portion of an existing string or string literal, making it efficient in terms of both memory usage and performance. This is particularly useful for large strings where creating new owned copies would be costly.
- **Static Lifetime:** A string literal has a `'static` lifetime, meaning it is embedded in the program's binary and exists for the entire duration of the program. For example, `let s: &str = "Hello";` where "Hello" is a string literal with a static lifetime. (Lifetimes will be discussed in chapter 14)
- **Dynamic Lifetime:** A `&str` can also have a dynamic lifetime, determined by the scope of the data it references. For example, a `&str` referencing a portion of a `String` will have a lifetime tied to that `String`'s scope.
- **String Slices:** `&str` can represent a full string or a substring by using slicing. For example, `"hello world"[0..5]` is a slice of the string literal "`hello world`", containing only "`hello`".
- **Boundary Checks:** Rust ensures that slicing respects code points boundaries, avoiding the creation of invalid `&str` references that would split multibyte code points.

In summary, `&str` is an efficient, immutable, borrowed reference to a sequence of UTF-8 encoded characters, providing a wide range of methods for working with textual data in Rust. It is a core part of Rust's string handling capabilities, offering both flexibility and safety.

Using Strings

When explaining collections, such as strings, it is helpful to organize the functions according to the **Create, Read, Update, Delete** (**CRUD**) concept. This approach aids in understanding the collection more clearly. CRUD can be applied both to the collection as a whole and to its contents. In this chapter, we follow the CRUD structure to present the information effectively.

It's important to note upfront that functions that modify strings are limited to `String`, as such operations cannot be performed on `&str` due to its immutability. This is because `&str` is an immutable reference to a `String`, and a `&mut str` is not allowed. Functions that only read from a string, without modifying it, typically work on `&str`. The distinction between these two types can be confusing when first learning Rust.

There are many more functions available for working with strings than what we will cover in this chapter. These often include left and right variants, limits on the number of results returned, and specialized versions for ASCII or whitespace handling, among others. I strongly recommend consulting the official documentation if you need to perform an operation on a string that isn't directly addressed by the functions below. There's no need to reinvent the wheel.

Let's start with string creation.

Creating Strings

There are multiple ways to create a `String`. You can create an empty string using `String::new`, or create a string from another source, with the most common case being converting a `&str` into a `String`. This conversion can be done using `String::from`, `str::to_string`, or `str::to_owned`. All three methods offer similar performance, so the choice between them typically comes down to personal preference or specific scenarios that might require one over the others.

String::new

`String::new` is a function used to create a new, empty `String`. `String::new` initializes a `String` with no content. It is often used when you need to create a mutable `String` that will be filled with data later. The `String` created by `String::new` has a length of 0. The created `String` can be modified (characters can be added, removed, or changed) because `String` is a mutable type.

`String` is stored on the heap, allowing it to grow dynamically as more data is added. For example:

Ch08/Examples/bin/example01.rs

```
fn main() {
    let mut s = String::new();
    println!("Length: {}", s.len());

    s.push_str("Hello, Rust!");
    println!("Content: {}", s);
    println!("Length: {}", s.len());
}
```

In this example, we create an empty `String` named `s` using `String::new()`. The length of `s` is initially 0, indicating that it contains no characters. We then add some text to `s` using the `push_str` method. After adding content, the length of `s` increases to reflect the number of characters stored, and the string is no longer empty.

`String::new` is particularly useful when you need a mutable string that will be populated or manipulated over time, such as building strings dynamically in a loop or from user input.

String::from

The primary purpose of `String::from` is to convert a string slice (`&str`), which is an immutable view of a string, into a `String`, which is an owned, growable, and mutable UTF-8 encoded string. `String::from` takes a `&str` as an argument and returns a `String` containing the same data. Here is the syntax:

```
let my_string = String::from("Ciao");
```

When you call `String::from` with a `&str`, it creates a new `String` by allocating enough memory on the heap to store a copy of the string slice's contents. The function then copies the data from the slice into the newly allocated memory, resulting in a `String` that owns its data.

`String::from` is generally efficient because it directly creates a `String` with the necessary capacity for the contents. However, like all allocations, it has some overhead because it involves allocating memory on the heap and copying data.

`String::from` is commonly used when you have a string literal or a string slice and need to convert it to a `String`. This is often necessary when you need a mutable string or when ownership of the string data is required.

Here's an example that demonstrates the use of `String::from`:

Ch08/Examples/bin/example02.rs

```
fn main() {
    let slice = "This is a nice sentence";
    let my_string = String::from(slice);
    println!("{}", my_string);
}
```

In this example `slice` is a string slice (`&str`), which is a borrowed, immutable view of a string. `String::from(slice)` creates a new `String` copying the data from the string slice `slice`.

`str::to_string` and `str::to_owned` are two other methods that can be used to convert a string slice (`&str`) into an owned String. While these methods have slight differences in intent and implementation pathways, they all achieve the same result. Let's explore `to_string` and `to_owned` in detail:

str::to_string

`str::to_string` is a method provided by the `ToString` trait, which is implemented for the `str` type. It creates a `String` by allocating memory on the heap and copying the contents of the string slice (`&str`) into the newly allocated memory.

The method is called on a `&str` instance:

```
let s = " Hola".to_string();
```

`str::to_string` internally calls the `ToString` trait's `to_string` method, which in turn calls `String::from` under the hood. It is a convenient and idiomatic way to convert a `&str` to a String, especially in contexts where method chaining is preferred for readability and style. It's commonly used when the conversion to String is needed during inline operations, such as when formatting strings or when working with methods that produce string slices.

Here's an example:

Ch07/Examples/bin/example03.rs

```
fn main() {
    let s = "Hola".to_string();
    println!("{}", s);
}
```

Here the string slice Hola is making a copy as an owned String.

str::to_owned

str::to_owned is a method provided by the ToOwned trait, which creates an owned version of any borrowed data. For str, it converts the string slice into an owned String.

The method is called on a &str instance:

```
let s = "Hello, Rust!".to_owned();
```

str::to_owned allocates memory on the heap and copies the contents of the &str to create a new String.

It is more general-purpose than to_string because to_owned is implemented for many other types that can have an owned version, not just strings. This makes it versatile when working with different types that implement the ToOwned trait.

str::to_owned is often used when you need an owned copy of borrowed data, particularly in contexts where the ToOwned trait is used generically. It can be preferred when working with a variety of types that implement ToOwned, as it is a more uniform way to get owned versions across different types.

Ch08/Examples/bin/example04.rs

```
fn main() {
    let s = "Bonjour".to_owned();
    println!("{}", s);
}
```

Again, a String is constructed from a string slice but now by using to_owned.

All three methods of converting a &str into a String are based on trait implementations. In this specific case, these different traits (ToString, ToOwned, and From<&str>) perform the same task, converting a string slice into an owned String. When working with &str directly, there is no functional difference between these methods. However, when dealing with generic types, you might prefer one method over the others based on the constraints or capabilities of the types involved in your code.

Creating string slices

At its core, a `String` in Rust is essentially a collection of bytes, specifically a `Vec<u8>`. When you slice a `String` using the standard slicing syntax, you get a `&str` (a string slice) instead of a `&[u8]` (a byte slice). For example:

```
let slice = &s[0..3];
```

Results in slice being a `&str`, not `&[u8]`. It's important to note, however, that when slicing, the start and end indices must align with valid Unicode code point boundaries. If they do not, the program will panic at runtime. As a result, this slicing method is only guaranteed to be safe if the data consists solely of ASCII characters, as ASCII characters are single-byte and therefore always aligned with valid boundaries.

Slicing a string in Rust can be done safely by ensuring that the start and end indices are on valid UTF-8 character boundaries, especially when dealing with non-ASCII characters that may consist of multiple bytes. Here are some methods and practices for slicing strings safely:

char_indices

The `char_indices()` method returns an iterator of pairs, where each pair consists of the byte index and the character at that index. This can be used to determine valid slice boundaries. In the following example, "こんにちは" (konnichiwa) is a typical Japanese greeting used to say "hello" or "good afternoon."

Ch08/Examples/bin/example05.rs

```
fn main() {
    let s = "こんにちは";
    let start = s.char_indices().nth(2).map(|(i, _)| i).unwrap_
    or(s.len());
    let end = s.char_indices().nth(5).map(|(i, _)| i).unwrap_
    or(s.len());
    let slice = &s[start..end];
    println!("{}", slice); // Outputs: "にちは" (a valid
    substring)
}
```

In this example, `char_indices()` provides valid starting indices for each character, ensuring that slicing doesn't occur within a multi-byte character. The methods `nth(2)` and `nth(5)` are used to safely obtain the byte indices of the third and sixth characters, respectively. Each call to `nth()` returns an `Option<(usize, char)>`, where `usize` is the starting index of the nth character, and `char` is the character itself. The `map()` function is used to extract the index, while `unwrap_or` provides the end of the string as the index when the requested character is out of bounds.

get

The `get()` method can be used to safely extract slices from a `String` or `&str`. This method returns an `Option<&str>`, which is `Some(&str)` if the slice is valid and `None` otherwise.

Ch07/Examples/bin/example06.rs

```
fn main() {
    let s = "Hello, world!";
    if let Some(slice) = s.get(7..12) {
        println!("{}", slice);
    } else {
        println!("Invalid slice");
    }
}
```

In this example, `get(7..12)` safely attempts to extract a slice from indices 7 to 12. If these indices are not on valid UTF-8 boundaries or are out of bounds, it returns `None` instead of panicking.

Inspecting strings

Most functions for reading (parts of) a `String` also work on `&str`. This is useful because, in many cases, it doesn't matter whether you're working with a `String` or a `&str`. These functions are generally defined on `&str`, which is compatible with `&String`. A `&String` is simply a reference to a `String`, much like `&str` is a reference to a string slice. A deeper explanation of how this works will be covered in *Chapter 12* on smart pointers. In the following text, `string` will be used in lowercase to refer to either a &`String` or a `&str`.

len

The `len()` function returns the length of the string in bytes, not the number of characters. For example:

```
let hello = "こんにちは".to_string();
println!("{}", hello.len());
```

This will output 15, even though there are only 5 characters. To get the actual number of characters, you can use:

```
println!("{}", hello.chars().count());
```

This will correctly output 5 as the number of characters.

is_empty

The `is_empty()` function returns a boolean indicating whether the string is empty or not. For example:

```
println!("{}", "".is_empty());
```

This will print true.

contains

The `contains(&str)` function checks if a given substring or pattern exists within a string, returning true if the substring is found and false otherwise. For example:

```
let text = " Once upon a time";
println!("{}", text.contains("time"));
```

This example prints true.

find

The `find()` function searches for a given substring or pattern within a string and returns an `Option<usize>` representing the starting index of the first occurrence of the substring. If the substring is not found, it returns `None`. For example:

```
let text = " I can't believe I forgot the book in the
bookcase!";
println!("{:?}", text.find("book"));
println!("{:?}", text.find("bookcase?"));
```

The first `println!` prints Some(30) and the second `println!` prints `None`.

trim

The `trim()` function returns a string slice with all leading and trailing whitespace removed. It does not modify the original String but returns a new view (slice) of the string, excluding the whitespace at the start and end.

```
let s = String::from("   Hello, world!   ");
let trimmed = s.trim();
println!("Original: '{}', Trimmed: '{}'", s, trimmed);
```

This will output:

```
Original: '   Hello, world!   ', Trimmed: 'Hello, world!'
```

In this example, trim removes the spaces at the beginning and end, but leaves the inner content unchanged.

Functions returning an iterator

Iterators are commonly used in string manipulation functions like `chars()`, `split()`, and `matches()` to allow you to iterate over components of the string efficiently. In all these functions, iterators provide a lazy and efficient way to process the string, allowing you to avoid unnecessary allocations and intermediate data structures while working with its components. Iterators are discussed in detail in *Chapter 11* on functional programming.

> **NOTE**
>
> The parameter `pat` in `find()` is a generic type `P` constrained by the `Pattern` trait, which is implemented by several types. For string-like types, it performs a substring search, while the function variant allows for arbitrary character selection based on custom logic.

chars

The `chars()` function returns an iterator over the characters of a string slice. Each element produced by this iterator is a char, which represents a Unicode scalar value. This function allows you to iterate through a string one character at a time, including multi-byte characters, as Rust's strings are UTF-8 encoded.

Here's a basic example:

```
let text = "hello";
for c in text.chars() {
```

```
    println!("{}", c);
}
```

This code will print every characters on a new line.

matches

The matches function returns an iterator over the substrings of a string slice that match a specified pattern. The pattern can be a string slice, a single character, or a more complex pattern like a regular expression, depending on the implementation. Each item produced by the iterator is a substring that matches the given pattern. For example:

```
let haystack = "banana";
let needles = haystack.matches("an");
for needle in needles {
    println!("{}", needle);
}
```

In this case, matches iterates over the string and finds all occurrences of the substring “an”. The function doesn’t modify the original string; it just finds the matching substrings. Similar to find, the pat parameter is a generic type constrained by the Pattern trait, with the same characteristics.

Note: `find` and `matches` are simple string matching functions. To use regular expressions, you’ll need the external `regex` crate.

split

`split()` is a method that splits a string slice into substrings based on a specified delimiter, which can be a character, string, or pattern. It returns an iterator over the substrings between the delimiter occurrences. Empty substrings between consecutive delimiters are included in the result. For example:

```
let text = "apple,banana,pear";
let parts = text.split(',');
for part in parts {
    println!("{}", part);
}
```

This will output the following:

```
apple
banana
pear
```

The split method doesn't modify the original string and operates on string slices, making it efficient and versatile.

Changing Strings

Modifying strings is done on the `String` type, not on `&str` as mentioned earlier. Some update functions operate on `&mut String`, allowing the mutable String to be changed directly in place. Other functions accept a `&String` and return a new `String` value. Always make sure you know exactly what type is being passed into a function and what the return type will be. This applies to every function in Rust.

push

`push()` is a function in Rust that appends a single character (char) to the end of a `String`. It modifies the original `String` in place by adding exactly one char to it.

```
let mut s = String::from("Hello");
s.push('!');
println!("{}", s);
```

In this case, the `push` function is used to append the character `!` to the String s resulting in `hello!`.

push_str

The `push_str()` function appends a string slice to the end of a String. It modifies the original `String` in place, extending its content by adding the provided string slice. Here's an example:

```
let mut s = String::from("New");
s.push_str(" York");
println!("{}", s);
```

This will output `New York`. In this example, the `push_str` method appends `York` to the original string `New`.

replace_range

The `replace_range` function allows you to replace a specific range of characters in the string with a new string or character sequence. The range must be specified as a byte range, and it replaces the part of the string within that range with the provided replacement. The parameters are:

- `range`: A range of bytes (e.g., `0..4`), where the start and end define the portion of the string to be replaced.
- `new_string`: The string or character sequence that will replace the specified range.

The key points are:

- **Range is byte-based**: Since Rust strings are UTF-8 encoded, character boundaries might not align with byte boundaries for multi-byte characters. You must ensure that the range you provide corresponds to valid UTF-8 character boundaries; otherwise, the operation will panic.
- **Modifies the original string**: The `replace_range` method directly modifies the string in place, changing its content.
- **String size changes**: The new string can have a different length than the original portion being replaced.

Here's an example:

```
let mut s = String::from("Hello, John!");
s.replace_range(7..11, "Marie");
println!("{}", s);
```

In this example, the string "`Hello, John`" is initially created. The `replace_range(7..11, "Marie")` call replaces the portion of the string from the 7th to the 12th byte (which corresponds to "`John`") with "`Marie`". The result is "`Hello, Marie!`".

> **NOTE**
>
> The following three functions, `replace`, `join`, and `repeat`, operate on a string slice and produce a new `String`. While these functions may seem like mutation operations, they are actually string creation functions, as they leave the original string slice unchanged.

replace

The `replace()` function in Rust returns a new `String` where all occurrences of a specified substring or pattern are replaced with another substring. The original string remains unchanged. Here's an example:

```
let s = String::from("good morning");
let replaced = s.replace("morning", "evening");
```

```
println!("{}", replaced);
```

This will output:

```
good evening
```

In this example, "`morning`" is replaced with "`evening`", resulting in the new string "`good evening`". All instances of the pattern are replaced, not just the first one.

join

The `join` function in Rust is used to concatenate elements of an iterable (such as a slice or vector) into a single String, with a specified separator between each element.

```
let words = ["are", "you", "there", "?"];
let sentence = words.join(" ");
println!("{}", sentence);
```

This will output:

```
Are you there ?
```

In this example, the `join` method takes each element of the `words` array and joins them into a single string, with a space " " as the separator between each word. It takes an iterable (e.g., slices, vectors) of string slices and joins them into one String. You can specify any separator between the elements, such as spaces, commas, or even no separator at all, in which case you use an empty string to concatenate the elements without spaces.

repeat

The `repeat()` function in Rust returns a new String that is a repeated concatenation of the original string. You provide a number as an argument to specify how many times the string should be repeated. The original string remains unchanged. Here's an example:

```
let s = String::from("abc");
let repeated = s.repeat(3);
println!("{}", repeated);
```

This will output:

```
abcabcabc
```

In this example, the string “abc” is repeated three times, resulting in “abcabcabc”. Upon closer inspection, `repeat` is a string creation function. It operates on a string slice and, using `n`, generates a new `String`. It does not change an existing `String`.

This concludes the basic introduction to a subset of string functions available in Rust. As mentioned earlier, the standard library offers many more string functions, along with additional ones provided by external crates. Now, we will move on to a separate section covering parsing and formatting, which are specialized string operations that deserve special attention due to their unique roles and use cases.

Parsing and formatting

A separate section on parsing and formatting is essential because these processes are fundamental but opposite in nature. Parsing involves interpreting and converting input data (often strings) into structured forms, such as numbers, dates, or objects, for internal processing. Formatting, on the other hand, is about converting data from internal structures into a human-readable or specific output format (e.g., displaying a date or creating structured output for a report).

Each process involves different strategies, rules, and error handling techniques, which justifies a distinct focus on each.

Parsing

Rust provides various ways to parse strings efficiently, with built-in methods for common conversions, and customizable parsing mechanisms for more complex cases. The standard way to parse strings is by using the parse method, but you can also leverage other libraries or write custom parsing logic.

The basics

The parse method is the most common way to convert a string into another type. It works with any type that implements the `FromStr` trait, which includes basic types like integers, floating-point numbers, and many others.

The basic syntax for using parse is:

```
let num: Result<i32, ParseIntError> = "42".parse();
```

This example converts the string “42” into an `i32`. If the string cannot be parsed into the target type, it results in an error, which you can handle using Rust’s error-handling mechanisms.

Since string parsing can fail (e.g., when attempting to parse non-numeric characters into a number), the parse method returns a Result type. You can handle parsing errors using methods like `unwrap`, `expect`, or by matching on the `Result`. As shown in the following example:

Ch08/Examples/bin/example07.rs

```
fn main() {
    let input = "abc";
    match input.parse::<i32>() {
        Ok(num) => println!("Parsed number: {}", num),
        Err(e) => println!("Error parsing: {}", e),
    }
}
```

In this example, attempting to parse “abc” into an integer will fail, and the error will be printed.

The parse method works with a variety of types, such as:

- **Integers**: (`i32`, `i64`, `u32`, etc.):
- **Floating-Point Numbers**: (`f32`, `f64`):
- **Booleans**: (`bool`):
- **Custom Types**: You can also parse strings into custom types by implementing the `FromStr` trait for those types (explained further below).

The parse method uses generic type inference, so you need to either specify the type you want to parse into or allow Rust to infer it from the context. If you’re parsing into a custom type or one that Rust can’t infer, you can specify the target type using the “turbofish” syntax (`::<Type>`).

```
let num = "42".parse::<i32>().unwrap();
```

Here, `::<i32>` explicitly tells Rust to parse the string into an `i32` type.

When parsing strings, keep in mind that extra whitespace will often cause parsing to fail, depending on the type you’re parsing into. You can use the trim method to remove leading and trailing whitespace before parsing.

Custom Parsing

The parse method is based on the `FromStr` trait, which defines how types can be constructed from a string. Most built-in types implement `FromStr`, but for custom types, you can implement the trait yourself.

Example of implementing `FromStr` for a custom type:

Ch08/Examples/bin/example08.rs

```
use std::str::FromStr;
use std::num::ParseIntError;

#[derive(Debug)]
struct Point {
    x: i32,
    y: i32,
}

impl FromStr for Point {
    type Err = ParseIntError;

    fn from_str(s: &str) -> Result<Self, Self::Err> {
        let mut coords = s.split(',');
        let x = coords.next().unwrap().trim().parse()?;
        let y = coords.next().unwrap().trim().parse()?;
        Ok(Point { x, y })
    }
}

fn main() {
    let input = "10, 20";
    match Point::from_str(input) {
        Ok(point) => println!("Parsed point: {:?}", point),
        Err(e) => println!("Failed to parse point: {}", e),
    }
}
```

In this example, the custom Point struct can now be parsed from a comma-separated string like "10, 20". Note: This function is not completely panic-safe. Making it fully safe would require additional code, which is beyond the scope of this example.

Parsing use cases

Parsing is an essential part of many applications, as it enables the conversion of strings into various data types based on the input format. Different use cases call for different parsing methods. For example, parsing command-line arguments involves converting string arguments into appropriate types like integers or floats. Similarly, when working with structured strings, such as comma-separated values, splitting and then parsing each component is a common approach. For more complex patterns, such as dates or custom data structures, using **regular expressions** (**regex**) can be a powerful tool to extract and parse specific portions of a string.

Proper error handling ensures that parsing failures are gracefully managed, which is key to building robust applications. We are going to look at a few different use cases of parsing, demonstrating various techniques to handle string data effectively.

Parsing from Command-Line Arguments

When parsing command-line arguments, they are usually obtained as strings and need to be parsed into appropriate types. For example:

Ch08/Examples/bin/example09.rs

```
use std::env;
fn main() {
    let args = env::args();
    for arg in args.skip(1) {
        let parsed_arg: i32 = arg.parse().unwrap();
        println!("Parsed argument: {}", parsed_arg);
    }
}
```

Here, all command-line arguments are parsed into `i32` values. The `skip(1)` method is used to ignore the first command-line argument, which is the program name. Keep in mind, this example isn't production-ready, as it lacks error handling for invalid input.

When testing this in an IDE, you'll need to provide command-line arguments. In RustRover, you can do this by editing the run configuration and appending the parameters in the command field like this:

```
run --package Examples --bin example09 -- 1234
```

This command instructs Cargo to run a binary named example09, which is defined in the package called Examples. The --package flag is used to specify which crate to run the binary from. This is particularly important in workspaces that contain multiple packages. The --bin flag selects a specific binary target within that package; in this case, example09 refers to a file like src/bin/example09.rs.

Everything that appears after the double dash (--) is passed directly to the binary itself, rather than being interpreted as a Cargo option. Here, the number 1234 is passed as a command-line argument to the program. Inside the example09 binary, you can access this argument using the `std::env::args` function, which returns an iterator over the arguments given to the program. The first element is always the name of the executable, and the following elements are the actual arguments.

Using split for Parsing

Sometimes you need to break a string into multiple parts before parsing each part. You can use the split method to split a string into an iterator and then parse each piece separately as follows:

Ch08/Examples/bin/example10.rs

```
fn main() {
    let input = "12, 34, 56";
    for number in input.split(", ") {
        let number = number.parse::<u8>().unwrap();
        println!("number: {}", number);
    }
}
```

This example splits the string by ", " and then parses each segment into an i32, printing each result. Typically, this would be done in an idiomatic, functional style, which we'll delve deeper into in *Chapter 11* when we explore functional programming concepts.

In the next section, we will focus on the other way around, formatting.

Formatting

In Rust, the `format!` macro is used to create formatted strings. It is analogous to the `println!` and `print!` macros but differs in that it returns a string instead of printing to the console. This is useful when you need to generate strings with specific formatting without immediately displaying them, for example, when concatenating data or constructing complex text to be used later in a program.

The basics

The `format!` macro works similarly to `println!`, but instead of outputting the string to the terminal, it returns a String that you can store, manipulate, or pass to other functions. Look at the following example:

Ch08/Examples/bin/example11.rs

```
fn main() {
    let name = "Alice";
    let age = 30;
    let formatted_string = format!("{} is {} years old.", name,
age);
    println!("{}", formatted_string);
```

```
}
```

It prints:

```
Alice is 30 years old.
```

In this example, `format!` takes a string literal with two placeholders `{}`, and substitutes the values of name and age into those placeholders. The result is a string `Alice is 30 years old.` which is stored in the variable `formatted_string`.

Placeholder syntax

The general syntax of `format!` involves placing curly braces `{}` in the string, where values are interpolated. The values to be formatted are supplied after the string literal as additional arguments. See the following example:

```
let s = format!("{} + {} = {}", 2, 3, 5);
```

It generates:

```
2 + 3 = 5
```

/The values are assigned in the order of the arguments: the first value, 2, is placed in the first placeholder, 3 goes into the second placeholder, and finally, 5 is placed in the last one.

Placeholder Types

There are three types of placeholders in string formatting: implicit, positional and named, placeholders.

- **Implicit Placeholders: In the previous example, we began with the implicit version, which is usually the first method you choose. The primary limitation is that each argument can only be used in one placeholder.**
- **Positional Placeholders**: You can explicitly specify which value are inserted into a placeholder using positional arguments. The index starts at 0. See the following example:

  ```
  let s = format!("{1} is {0} years old.", 30, "Alice");
  ```

It generates:

```
Alice is 30 years old.
```

In this example, the last argument is placed in the first placeholder, and the first argument is inserted into the last placeholder. It's also possible to use a single argument in multiple placeholders.

- **Named Placeholders:** You can also use named placeholders to improve the readability of the formatting. Let's consider the following example:

```
let name = "Alice";
let age = 30;
let s = format!("{name} is {age} years old.", name = name,
age = age);
```

It generates:

```
"Alice is 30 years old."
```

This `format!` can be written more concisely. When the named argument and the variable name are the same, you don't need to specify the parameters, similar to the field init shorthand in structs, like this:

```
let s = format!("{name} is {age} years old);
```

Now that we've explored various options for placing values in placeholders, we'll move on to formatting those values.

Formatting Specifiers

The curly braces `{}` can be customized to format the values in different ways, similar to formatting options in other languages. You can specify formatting parameters such as width, precision, alignment, and more within the braces.You can control how the values are displayed using format specifiers inside the curly braces. Format specifiers follow the `{}` in the form `{:<specifier>}`, where `:<specifier>` controls alignment, padding, precision, etc.

Width and AlignmentWidth and alignment in string formatting work together to control the size of the output and how values are positioned within that space.

Width, You can specify the minimum number of characters to display for a value. For example, if you want a value to occupy at least 5 characters in width, you would specify it like this: `{:5}`. If the value is shorter than 5 characters, it will be left aligned for string values and right aligned for numeric values.

Alignment:

- **Left alignment**: This is the default behavior when you specify a width. For example, `{:<5}` and `{:5}` will both left-align the text and add padding to the right if necessary.
- **Right alignment**: You can right-align the text by using `{:>5}`. This will pad the text with spaces on the left to meet the specified width.
- **Center alignment**: You can center-align the text with `{:^5}`, which will pad the text with spaces equally on both sides (any remainder will pad more on the right).

These formatting options are helpful for organizing outputs into columns or creating structured data displays, ensuring consistent alignment across lines. Let's see the following example:

```
let s = format!("{:5}", "foo");
let s_left = format!("{:<5}", "foo");
let s_right = format!("{:>5}", "foo");
let s_center = format!("{:^5}", "foo");
```

It generates:

```
"foo  "
"foo  "
"  foo"
" foo "
```

Padding

Padding is often used with alignment to fill the space with a specific character. Let's consider the following example:

```
let padded = format!("{:0>5}", "foo");
let padded_left = format!("{:*>5}", "foo");
```

It generates:

```
"00foo"
"**foo"
```

In both cases, the string has a width of 3 characters, while the specified width is 5 characters, resulting in extra space that is, by default, filled with spaces. Choosing a padding character like `0` or `*` will replace the spaces with the selected character.
Floating-point Precision

You can specify the number of decimal places, width, and alignment for precise formatting.

- **Precision**: You can control the number of decimal places by specifying the precision in the format string, like "{:.2}", which will format the number with two decimal places.
- **Width and Precision**: You can combine width and precision with floating-point formatting, such as "{:8.2}", which ensures a minimum width of 8 characters and 2 decimal places, padding with spaces as needed.
- Let's see the following example:

```
let formatted = format!("{:.2}", 3.141592);
```

It generates:

```
"3.14"
```

/Limiting the number of decimal places to two.

Custom Types and Formatting

Rust allows you to define custom types and control how they are formatted by implementing the `Display` or `Debug` traits.

Display Trait

If you want to use `{}` to format a custom type, you need to implement the `Display` trait. Look at the following example:

Ch08/Examples/bin/example12.rs

```
use std::fmt;

struct Point {
    x: i32,
    y: i32,
}

impl fmt::Display for Point {
    fn fmt(&self, f: &mut fmt::Formatter) -> fmt::Result {
        write!(f, "({}, {})", self.x, self.y)
    }
}

fn main() {
    let p = Point { x: 10, y: 20 };
    println!("The point is: {}", p);
}
```

It prints:

```
The point is: (10, 20)
```

Debug Trait

If you want to format a custom type using the `{:?}` specifier (used for debugging), you need to implement the `Debug` trait. See the following example:

Ch08/Examples/bin/example13.rs

```
#[derive(Debug)]
struct Point {
    x: i32,
    y: i32,
}

fn main() {
    let p = Point { x: 10, y: 20 };
    let s = format!("{:?}", p);
    println!("Debug format: {:}", s);
}
```

It prints:

```
Debug format: Point { x: 10, y: 20 }
```

Adding an extra # to the debug specifier enables pretty-printing of the struct, like this:

```
let s = format!("{:#?}", p);
```

It will generate the following result:

```
Debug format: Point {
    x: 10,
    y: 20,
}
```

Notice that the `format!` macro includes the additional #, while `println!` does not. The `format!` is formatting a struct, producing a pretty-printed string. On the other hand, `println!` is printing the string as is. If you mistakenly use `:#?` when printing the string, like this:

```
println!("Debug format: {:#?}", s);
```

It will print the following:

```
Debug format: "Point {\n    x: 10,\n    y: 20,\n}"
```

In this case, using # or not doesn't make a difference, you'll get the same result. When printing a string in Debug mode, the string is enclosed in double quotes, and newline characters are displayed as `\n`.

In the previous example, the `Debug` trait is implemented using the procedural macro `#[derive(Debug)]`. However, you can also manually implement the `Debug` trait, following a pattern similar to how the `Display` trait is implemented.

Combining specifiers

You can combine all the above in a single specifier. The order is important. The formal specification of the format specifiers is:

```
[[fill]align][sign]['#']['0'][width]['.' precision]type
fill := character
align := '<' | '^' | '>'
sign := '+' | '-'
width := count
precision := count | '*'
type := '' | '?' | 'x?' | 'X?' | identifier
```

We haven't covered every detail, but we've gone over the most commonly used ones. For the full specification, you can refer to the official documentation at https://doc.rust-lang.org/std/fmt/.

Performance and Efficiency

The `format!` macro dynamically allocates memory to return a String. This means that it is less efficient than directly using `println!` or `write!` for outputting strings, especially if you don't need to store the result for later use. For performance-critical applications, it's recommended to avoid unnecessary memory allocations.

The `format!` macro is highly flexible and powerful, enabling complex string construction and formatting in Rust. By leveraging its options for customizing output and formatting various data types, you can create clear and maintainable formatted output in your Rust programs.

Performance Considerations

In Rust, strings are an essential part of programming, but due to their dynamic nature and the way memory is managed, handling them efficiently is crucial to writing performant code. This section delves into how Rust manages string memory, highlights common pitfalls when working with strings, and offers guidelines on choosing between `String` and `&str`.

Memory Management

Memory management for `String` involves both allocation and deallocation, which happens automatically via Rust's ownership and borrowing system. Understanding how memory works for strings can help avoid inefficiencies.

Heap Allocation and Deallocation

A `String` is dynamically allocated on the heap. Rust ensures automatic memory deallocation when the string goes out of scope, preventing memory leaks. However, frequent allocations, such as in cases of string concatenation, can lead to performance issues if not managed well.

Efficient Memory Management Strategies

Here are some strategies to help with efficient memory management:

- **Pre-allocation**: When you know the size of the string in advance, using methods like `String::with_capacity` can prevent frequent reallocations and improve performance.

```
let mut s = String::with_capacity(50);
```

This ensures that enough memory is allocated upfront, avoiding reallocations as the string grows.

- **Avoiding Repeated Allocation**: Repeatedly appending to a string or copying data unnecessarily can degrade performance. Use efficient concatenation techniques or pre-allocate space.

Common Pitfalls

Handling strings efficiently can be tricky, especially for those new to Rust. Here are some common mistakes and how to avoid them:

- **Incorrect Slicing**: Rust strings are encoded in UTF-8, so indexing into a string via slicing must respect character boundaries. Direct indexing can lead to panics if not done correctly.

```
let s = "hello";
let first_letter = &s[0..1];
```

When dealing with non-ASCII characters, use methods like `.chars()` to avoid panics.

- **Overuse of clone**: Cloning a String is a costly operation as it involves copying all the data from one string to another. Often, cloning can be avoided by borrowing string slices (`&str`) instead of creating new owned strings.

```
let s1 = String::from("hello");
let s2 = s1.clone();
let s3 = &s1;
```

- **Excessive Use of Dynamic Strings**: Allocating and growing a String dynamically can be costly. If possible, prefer static string slices (`&str`) when the content is known at compile time.

Here is an example with preallocation:

Ch08/Examples/bin/example14.rs

```
fn main() {
    let mut inefficient = String::new();
    for _ in 0..5 {
        inefficient.push_str("hello ");
    }
    println!("Inefficient String: {}", inefficient);

    let mut efficient = String::with_capacity(30);
    for _ in 0..5 {
        efficient.push_str("hello ");
    }
    println!("Efficient String: {}", efficient);
}
```

The first print is inefficient because the String needs to reallocate space multiple times as it grows. In the second case, sufficient space is allocated upfront, preventing the need for reallocation.

String or &str

Choosing the right type for string manipulation is key to writing efficient Rust code. The difference between `String` and `&str` often comes down to ownership and mutability.

Use `String` when you need a mutable, heap-allocated string that can grow. Use `&str` when the string data is immutable, borrowed, or part of a larger structure. `&str` is ideal for function parameters, as it avoids unnecessary allocation and allows flexibility by referencing both string literals and `String` objects.

By carefully choosing between `String` and `&str`, and using slices instead of cloning or copying, you can write string-handling code in Rust that is both memory-efficient and fast. Always aim to avoid unnecessary allocations and prefer borrowing when possible to keep performance optimized.

Summary

In Rust, strings are an essential part of text processing and data manipulation. Rust provides two main string types: `String`, a mutable, heap-allocated, growable type, and `&str`, an immutable, borrowed string slice. Understanding how these types work within Rust's ownership and borrowing system is crucial for safe and efficient string handling. Rust uses UTF-8 encoding for strings, allowing for compatibility with any Unicode character, but developers need to manage Unicode complexities, such as graphemes and code points.

The process of creating strings can be done through methods like `String::new`, `String::from`, and `str::to_string`, all of which achieve the same task. These methods are possible due to the implementation of specific traits. When working with concrete types, it usually doesn't matter which one you use. However, when dealing with generic types, a specific choice might be required.

Slicing strings must be performed carefully to respect UTF-8 character boundaries, using methods like `char_indices` to avoid panics.

String operations like inspection (`len`, `is_empty`, `contains`, `find`) are typically performed on string slices, whereas modification operations (`push`, `push_str`, `replace`) are primarily limited to the `String` type due to its mutability. Parsing strings into other types is done using the `parse` method, while the `format!` macro is used to generate formatted strings efficiently.

Performance in string manipulation can be optimized by using pre-allocation (`with_capacity`) to minimize reallocation, avoiding excessive cloning, and leveraging string slices when possible. Choosing between `String` and `&str` is crucial for memory efficiency and performance, with `&str` preferred for static or borrowed text, and String for dynamic, modifiable content.

Rust's approach to strings combines performance and memory safety, ensuring developers have precise control over text data while maintaining efficiency in string handling.

In the next chapter, we will explore additional collection types in Rust's standard library, such as Vec<T> and HashMap<T>.

Exercises

1. Create an empty `String` using `String::new()` and append the text `Learning about String and string slices` to it. Print the result.
2. Create a `String` from the slice `Nice to meet you`. Check the length of the string in bytes and whether it contains the substring `you`. Print the results.
3. Given the string "`こんにちは, World!`" (UTF-8 encoded), extract the substring `World!` with slicing and print it. Print the length in bytes as well as the number of characters of the original string.
4. Create a `String` with the text `Hi there`. Append an exclamation mark using `push()` and then replace `Hi there` with `Hello`. Print the final result. Print the length in bytes as well as the capacity after each step, observe the result.
5. Write a function that takes a name and age as arguments and returns a formatted string, e.g., "Alice is 30 years old.". Use the `format!` macro.
6. Write a function that takes a `&str` and attempts to parse it into an integer. If parsing succeeds, return the number. If it fails, return a default value (e.g., 0).
7. Write a loop that appends a single character to an initially empty `String`. Within the loop, print both the length and capacity of the string, and observe how the capacity changes as the string grows. Afterward, create a string with an initial capacity of 33 and repeat the process, observing how pre-allocating capacity affects the string's behavior.
8. Write a function that takes a comma-separated string (e.g., "apple,banana,pear") and returns a single string where the elements are joined with a space, e.g., "apple banana pear". You may use string splitting and joining utilities, but do

not use the replace function. Focus on using appropriate string manipulation methods to achieve the desired transformation.

9. Write a function that takes a UTF-8 string and prints each character individually on a new line. The function should also print the total number of characters as well as the number of bytes.

10. Write a function that safely slices a string at character boundaries using `char_indices` to extract the substring starting from the second Unicode character and ending at the fifth character. Print the result.

Project: Hangman

The goal of this project is to create a command-line version of the classic word-guessing game Hangman. In this game, the player attempts to guess a hidden word by suggesting letters within a limited number of attempts. The game tracks correct and incorrect guesses, revealing parts of the word as the player makes correct guesses, and drawing a hangman graphic when wrong guesses are made.

```
  +---+
  |   |
  O   |
 /|\  |
 / \  |
      |
=========
```

Game Flow

- The game will randomly select a word from a predefined list of words at the start of each game.
- The player guesses a single letter at a time.
- If the guessed letter is in the word, the game will reveal the positions of that letter in the word.
- If the guessed letter is not in the word, it counts as a wrong attempt. The player is allowed a limited number of incorrect guesses (e.g., 6).
- The game ends when the player either guesses the word correctly or reaches the maximum number of incorrect guesses.
- At the end of the game, offer the player the option to restart and play again with a new word.

Features

Display the word as underscores (_) for each unguessed letter. For example, for the word "hello", the display might start as _ _ _ _ _.

Track and display the letters the player has already guessed.

- Display the number of incorrect guesses remaining. Each incorrect guess reduces this counter by 1.
- Instead of just showing the remaining attempts, create a visual ASCII representation of the hangman figure that changes as incorrect guesses are made.

Victory/Defeat Condition

- The player wins if they guess the word before running out of attempts.
- The player loses if they run out of attempts before guessing the word.

Input Handling

The program will prompt the user to enter a letter. Input validation should ensure that the input is a single letter and that it hasn't been guessed before.

If a player enters an invalid input (e.g., multiple letters, non-alphabetic characters), the game should notify the player and prompt for a valid guess.

A list of words should be predefined. The program should select one word at random at the start of each game.

Continuously display the current state of the word, guessed letters, and remaining attempts after each guess.

Modules and Structure

The project should be divided into logical modules or functions:

- **Main Game Loop**: Contains the main game logic, running until the game ends (either through victory or defeat).
- **Word Selection**: A function that selects a random word from a predefined list.
- **Input Handling**: A function to manage user input, ensuring valid guesses.
- **Game Display**: A function to display the current state of the word, guessed letters, and the hangman picture
- **Win/Loss Check**: A function to determine if the game has been won or lost, and to display the appropriate message.

09

Collections

Rust's standard library provides a powerful and flexible set of collection types that are designed to efficiently store, manipulate, and organize data. Collections are fundamental to many programming tasks, as they allow developers to handle dynamic sets of data, whether it's managing lists of items, mapping keys to values, or storing unique values. Rust's collections are built with a strong focus on performance, safety, and flexibility, leveraging Rust's ownership system to provide safe and efficient memory management.

In this chapter, we will explore the collection types provided by Rust, these are:

- **Vec**: A dynamically-sized array type for storing elements in a contiguous block of memory. Vectors are ideal for managing ordered lists where the number of elements can change.
- **VecDeque**: A double-ended queue that allows fast insertion and removal of elements from both ends. Useful for queue and stack-like operations where items need to be added or removed from both sides efficiently.
- **HashMap**: A key-value data structure that allows fast lookups based on hashed keys. Perfect for when you need efficient access and storage by unique keys.
- **BTreeMap**: A key-value data structure that stores keys in sorted order, making it useful for ordered traversal and range queries.
- **HashSet**: A collection that stores unique values without duplicates, with fast lookup times, using hashing for efficient retrieval.
- **BTreeSet**: Similar to HashSet, but keeps elements in sorted order, useful when you need to maintain the order of unique values.
- **BinaryHeap**: A priority queue implemented as a binary heap. It allows quick access to the largest (or smallest) element, making it ideal for tasks such as scheduling or any scenario where elements need to be processed in a priority-based order.
- **LinkedList**: A doubly linked list. While not as commonly used due to its performance trade-offs compared to `Vec`, it's helpful when you need efficient insertions or deletions at arbitrary positions in a list.

Each collection type in Rust is uniquely suited to different use cases, offering various trade-offs between performance, memory usage, and ease of use. In this chapter, we will focus in detail on two of the most commonly used collections: `Vec` and `HashMap`, as these are fundamental tools for managing dynamic data. We'll thoroughly explore their features, use cases, and effective manipulation techniques. For other collection types, such as `VecDeque`, `BTreeMap`, `BTreeSet`, `HashSet`, `BinaryHeap` and `LinkedList`, we will provide an overview to introduce their key characteristics and intended use cases, given the scope of this book. By the end of this chapter, you will have a thorough understanding of how to use `Vec` and `HashMap` in detail, as well as an overview of Rust's other collection types. You will be equipped to effectively select the right collection for your needs.

Aspects of collections

When working with collections in any programming language, including Rust, several key aspects must be considered to ensure optimal use of resources and performance. These aspects guide how developers approach the usage of various collection types based on their specific needs. This section provides a conceptual understanding of the core principles that underlie the collections in Rust.

Memory

Memory usage is a key aspect of collections, particularly in performance-critical or resource-constrained environments. The design of a collection can greatly affect how memory is allocated, managed, and reclaimed. / Here's a breakdown of the key factors affecting memory usage in collections:

- **Dynamic vs. Static Sizing**: All these collections allow dynamic resizing, meaning they can grow or shrink as elements are added or removed. While this makes them flexible, it also involves memory reallocations, which can be expensive. Pre-allocating memory (setting an initial capacity) can mitigate this, but at the cost of using extra memory upfront.
- **Contiguous vs. Fragmented Memory**: Collections can either store data in contiguous blocks of memory (as in arrays or vectors) or in fragmented blocks linked together (as in linked lists). Contiguous memory collections generally offer better cache performance and are faster for random access, while fragmented memory collections excel in scenarios where frequent insertions and deletions in arbitrary positions are required.
- **Overhead**: Each collection comes with its own memory overhead, often in the form of additional metadata or pointers needed to maintain structure (like trees, hash tables, or linked lists). It's important to be mindful of this overhead when working with large datasets.

Internal Behavior of Collections

To make the most effective use of collections, it's helpful to understand their internal behavior. While these details may not be immediately visible when using high-level APIs, knowing how collections are structured and operate behind the scenes can guide developers in selecting the right collection type for each scenario. When examining the internal behavior, we consider the following aspects:

- **Linear Structures**: Collections like arrays and vectors store elements in a linear, contiguous block of memory. This makes them efficient for sequential access but may result in slower performance for operations like inserting or deleting elements in the middle, as the entire collection might need to be shifted.
- **Hierarchical Structures**: Collections such as trees or heaps organize data hierarchically. These structures support more complex operations, such as sorted access or priority-based retrieval, but may require additional memory and computational overhead to maintain their structure.
- **Hashing Mechanisms**: Some collections rely on hashing algorithms to distribute data across an internal table. This allows for fast lookup times but can involve additional memory usage to handle collisions (when two different elements share the same hash).
- **Resizing and Reallocation**: The collections discussed in this chapter automatically resize as elements are added. This process involves allocating new memory, copying over the existing data, and releasing the old memory. While this provides flexibility, it comes at the cost of performance spikes during resizing, which can be mitigated by choosing an appropriate initial size for the collection.

Performance

Performance is a critical factor when selecting or designing a collection. It impacts how efficiently data can be added, retrieved, updated, or deleted. The performance characteristics of collections typically vary based on the operations you perform on them, such as inserting elements, accessing elements by index or key, or removing elements.

- **Time Complexity**: Different operations on collections, such as inserting, deleting, or accessing data, have varying time complexities (often expressed in Big-O notation). For example, some collections provide constant-time access for retrieving elements, while others may require logarithmic or linear time depending on the data structure used.

- **Insertion vs. Lookup**: Some collections are optimized for fast insertions and deletions, while others are designed for fast lookups and retrievals. Understanding which operations are most frequent in your use case helps guide the selection of the most suitable collection.
- **Ordered vs. Unordered**: The performance of operations in collections is also influenced by whether the collection maintains the order of elements. For example, collections that enforce sorted order typically have slower insertion and deletion times compared to unordered collections, which prioritize quick access over ordering.

Function Description Ordering

When describing a collection, the CRUD acronym, Create, Read, Update, Delete, is followed for managing elements and the collection itself as well as managing the collection as a whole. CRUD helps categorize the basic operations performed on collections. Understanding how a collection handles these operations is key to its use. Creating a collection involves initializing and populating it, either incrementally or with a predefined structure for performance. Reading refers to accessing elements, with efficiency varying based on the collection's structure. Updating involves modifying or replacing elements, with some collections supporting direct updates while others require re-insertion. Deleting refers to removing items, and efficiency in this operation depends on how the collection manages memory and structure.

When working with collections in Rust, understanding these conceptual aspects, performance, memory usage, and internal behavior, is essential to making informed decisions about which collection to use. Rust's collections are designed to offer both flexibility and safety, but choosing the right collection for the job requires an awareness of the trade-offs involved. Whether prioritizing speed, memory efficiency, or ease of manipulation, each collection type is built to solve different kinds of data management challenges effectively.

This concludes the conceptual overview of the key concepts necessary to understand Rust's standard library collections. This chapter won't cover every detail of each collection, we will focus on the most commonly used two: `Vec` and `HashMap`. Their functions will be discussed in CRUD order, along with performance considerations and implementation details to help you grasp the internal behavior of these collections. Other collections will be covered at a higher level, providing enough insight for you to choose the right collection for your specific needs.

The internal workings of `Vec`, such as memory management and dynamic resizing, directly influence how its functions perform. With this foundation, we can now explore the methods Vec provides, like new, push, and insert.

Vec

The `Vec` (vector) in Rust is implemented as a growable, heap-allocated array. It offers dynamic resizing and efficient access by managing its own memory. Here are the key implementation details of `Vec`:

- **Contiguous Memory**: `Vec` stores elements in contiguous blocks of memory on the heap, which allows for fast random access to elements via indexing. This layout is similar to an array, but `Vec` can dynamically grow or shrink.
- **Capacity vs. Length**: A `Vec` has both a length (the number of elements currently in the vector) and a capacity (the amount of allocated memory). The capacity is usually greater than the length to minimize the number of memory reallocations when the `Vec` grows.
- **Amortized Growth**: When the `Vec` runs out of capacity, it reallocates memory by growing the capacity, typically by doubling it. This resizing is done in such a way that the cost of reallocations is amortized over multiple operations, meaning that while resizing is expensive, it happens infrequently enough that the average insertion is still efficient.
- **Reallocation**: When the `Vec` grows, it allocates a new block of memory, copies over the existing elements, and deallocates the old memory.
- **Drop Trait**: When a `Vec` goes out of scope, Rust automatically deallocates its memory via the Drop trait. This ensures that memory is safely reclaimed without the need for manual memory management.
- **Bounds Checking**: `Vec` automatically checks that you don't access out-of-bounds elements. If you try to access an index that is out of range, Rust will panic preventing undefined behavior.
- **Type Inference**: In Rust, when you create a `Vec<T>`, the type `T` can often be inferred by the compiler based on how the vector is used. For example, if you push an `i32` into a `Vec`, Rust will infer that `T` is `i32`. However, if there isn't enough context for Rust to infer the type, you may need to explicitly specify the type, such as `Vec<i32>`, to clarify what kind of values the `Vec` will store. This allows for flexibility while maintaining type safety.

The `Vec` in Rust is designed to provide a flexible, growable array while maintaining performance and safety through efficient memory management and the ownership system. Its implementation ensures that dynamic resizing is handled in an amortized way, and it combines fast access with automatic memory management.

Here's an overview of the various methods for working with `Vec`, covering creation, element addition, reading, updating, and deletion.

Collection creation

In Rust, there are several ways to create a `Vec` (vector), each tailored to different use cases. The time complexity for all vector creation functions is `O(n)`, where `n` is the number of elements initially inserted, regardless of the allocated capacity. Even if the vector pre-allocates more capacity than the number of elements inserted (to avoid future reallocations), the time complexity for creating the `Vec` only depends on the number of elements actually inserted, not on the allocated capacity. Allocating memory itself (without initializing the elements) is typically `O(1)`, but filling that memory with elements makes the complexity `O(n)`. It's worth noting that while you need to create a vector to use it, memory freeing happens automatically through Rust's ownership model. When the vector goes out of scope, Rust automatically deallocates both the `Vec` and its owned contents, ensuring efficient memory management without the need for manual cleanup. Below are all the common methods to create a `Vec`:

new

This method creates an empty vector with no elements and zero capacity. It's the most basic way to create a Vec when you don't know the size upfront.

For example:

```
let v: Vec<i32> = Vec::new();
```

This creates an empty `Vec v` that can store integers (`i32`). No memory is pre-allocated, and the `Vec`'s length and capacity are both 0. The `Vec` will dynamically allocate memory as elements are added.

with_capacity

`with_capacity` creates an empty vector but with a specified initial capacity. This is useful when you know in advance the number of elements that will be inserted, as it avoids multiple reallocations. For example:

```
let v: Vec<u64> = Vec::with_capacity(10);
```

This creates an empty `Vec` that can store integers (`u64`). It pre-allocates enough memory for 10 elements, but the `Vec`'s length is initially 0. This allows you to add up to 10 elements without reallocating memory.

vec![] Macro

The `vec![]` macro is a shorthand to create a vector with initial elements. It is widely used due to its simplicity and ability to infer types from the initial values. For example:

```
let v = vec![1, 2, 3];
```

This creates a new `Vec` in Rust using the `vec!` macro, which is a convenient way to initialize a `Vec` with predefined elements. In this case, the `Vec v` is initialized with three integers: 1, 2, and 3. Rust automatically infers that the type of the vector is `Vec<i32>` because the elements provided are integers. The `vec!` macro simplifies `Vec` creation, avoiding the need to call `Vec::new()` and manually pushing elements.

vec![value; count]

This variation of the `vec![]` macro creates a vector with a specified number of repeated elements. All elements are initialized to the same value. For example:

```
let v = vec![0; 5];
```

This creates a `Vec` with 5 elements, all initialized to the value `0`. The `vec!` macro is used here with a shorthand syntax where the first argument (`0`) is the value to be repeated, and the second argument (`5`) specifies the number of times the value should be repeated. This results in a Vec `v` with the value `[0, 0, 0, 0, 0]`, and Rust infers the type as `Vec<i32>` based on the value provided.

from([T; N]) or from(slice)

This method converts an array or slice into a `Vec`. It copies the contents of the array or slice into the newly created vector. For example:

```
let arr = [1, 2, 3];
let v = Vec::from(arr);
```

In this example, an array [1, 2, 3] is defined and then converted into a `Vec` using `Vec::from(arr)`. This transforms the fixed-size array into a growable vector.

collect

You can create a `Vec` from an iterator using the `.collect()` method. This is a more functional approach to vector creation, often used with iterators, maps, filters, or other iterator methods.For example;

```
let v: Vec<i32> = (0..5).collect();
```

This creates a `Vec v` containing the integers from 0 to 4. The range `0..5` generates an iterator that yields the numbers 0, 1, 2, 3, 4, and the `collect()` method is used to gather these values into a `Vec<i32>`. The type annotation `Vec<i32>` explicitly specifies that the collected values should be stored in a vector of 32-bit integers. The result is a `Vec v` with the contents `[0, 1, 2, 3, 4]`.

Element creation

Now that we've covered the various ways to create a vector, it's important to understand how to modify and grow it dynamically. Vec provides several functions to add elements to an existing vector, each with varying time complexities and use cases. Whether you need to append elements at the end, insert them at a specific position, or combine multiple vectors, Vec offers methods to achieve these tasks. Let's take a look at the most common ways to add elements to a vector and how they perform.

push

The `push` function in Rust adds an element to the end of a vector. The time complexity of this operation is amortized O(1), meaning that in most cases, adding an element takes constant time. However, if the vector needs to reallocate memory when its capacity is full, the operation takes O(n), but the average time per insertion remains constant.

```
let mut v = vec![1, 2, 3];
v.push(4);
```

After the push operation, the vector contains [1, 2, 3, 4]. This method is preferred for adding new elements to the vector because it is the fastest.

insert

The `insert` function in Rust adds an element at a specified index in the vector, shifting all subsequent elements one position to the right. The time complexity of this operation is `O(n)`, where n is the number of elements after the insertion point.

This is because all elements following the inserted element need to be moved to new positions, which makes the operation slower as the vector grows.

```
let mut v = vec![1, 2, 4];
v.insert(2, 3);
```

After the insert operation, the vector contains `[1, 2, 3, 4]`.

append

The `append` function moves all elements from another vector into the current vector, leaving the original vector empty. The time complexity of this operation is `O(m)`, where `m` is the number of elements being appended, as it involves moving the elements but not reallocating them individually.

```
let mut v1 = vec![1, 2];
let mut v2 = vec![3, 4];
v1.append(&mut v2);
```

In this example, the `append` function moves all elements from `v2` into `v1`, combining the contents of both vectors. If the elements in the vector implement the `Copy` trait (such as integers), the elements are copied rather than moved, but `v2` is still cleared afterward. If the elements are not `Copy` types, such as more complex objects, the elements are physically moved from `v2` to `v1`. In both cases, `v2` is left empty after the operation.

extend

The `extend` function in Rust appends elements from an iterator to the end of a vector, increasing its length by the number of elements in the iterator. The time complexity of this operation is `O(m)`, where m is the number of elements being added from the iterator.

```
let mut v = vec![1, 2];
v.extend([3, 4]);
```

After running this example `v` contains `[1, 2, 3, 4]`. Note that this example works because Rust automatically converts arrays (and other collections) into iterators when passed to functions like extend, which expect an iterator. In Rust, types that implement the IntoIterator trait can be passed to functions that expect an iterator. Arrays implement the IntoIterator trait, meaning that when you pass an array like [3, 4] to the extend method, Rust implicitly converts it into an iterator.

element read

After creating a vector and populating it with elements, the next step is learning how to read those elements efficiently. There are several methods available for accessing and reading elements in a vector, each with its own behavior and use cases. Whether you want to retrieve a single element by index, create a slice of elements, or safely handle out-of-bound cases. These techniques ensure that you can work with vector data effectively. Let's explore the different ways to read from a vector and understand how each approach works.

Indexing

When reading an element from a `Vec` using indexing (`vec[index]`), Rust first checks if the index is within the valid range, and it will panic if it's out of bounds. For copy types, the value is copied when accessed, but for move types, direct access through indexing won't compile. Instead, you need to borrow the value with an immutable reference. This operation remains very efficient (O(1)) as it directly accesses memory after the bounds check.

Here is an example with a copy type:

```
let v = vec![10, 20, 30];
let element = v[1];
```

In this case, the value is copied, so taking an immutable borrow is optional.

Here is an example with a move type:

```
let v = vec!["no move".to_string()];
let element = &v[0];
```

In this case, the value is a move type, so taking an immutable borrow is mandatory.

Slicing

When creating a slice from a Vec using slicing (`&vec[start..end]`), Rust first checks if the start and end indices are within the valid range, and it will panic if they are out of bounds. Slicing always returns a reference to a section of the vector, so there's no distinction between copy or move types. The slice is an immutable reference to part of the vector, allowing you to read multiple elements without transferring ownership. This operation is efficient (O(1)) because it accesses the original vector directly, without copying or moving any elements. For example:

```
let v = vec![10, 20, 30];
let slice = &v[0..2];
```

After execution `slice` contains `&[10, 20]`. `slice` is an immutable reference to part of the vector, so no ownership is transferred, regardless of the type of elements in the vector.

get

When accessing an element from a Vec using the get function (`vec.get(3)`), Rust checks if the index is within the valid range. Instead of panicking if the index is out of bounds, get returns an `Option<&T>`, where `Some(&T)` contains the reference to the element if the index is valid, and None is returned if the index is out of bounds. This approach provides safe access to elements without risking a runtime panic.

For example:

```
let v = vec![10, 20, 30];
if let Some(element) = v.get(1) {
    println!("{}", element);
}
```

In this case, the value is accessed through an immutable reference, which works for both copy and move types without transferring ownership or risking errors.

last and first

When accessing the last element of a `Vec` using the last function (`vec.last()`), Rust returns an `Option<&T>`, where `Some(&T)` contains an immutable reference to the last element if the vector is not empty, and `None` is returned if the `Vec` is empty. This method allows safe access to the last element without causing a runtime panic. Like with other access methods, last is efficient (O(1)) because it directly accesses the element in memory.

There is also a first function (`vec.first()`) that works similarly, providing access to the first element of the vector with the same safe handling of empty vectors. For example:

```
let v = vec![10, 20, 30];
if let Some(element) = v.last() {
    println!("{}", element);
}
```

In this case, the value is accessed as an immutable reference, making it work seamlessly for both copy and move types.

element update

After understanding how to read elements from a vector, it's essential to know how to modify those elements effectively. Vec offers several methods to update the contents of a vector, from changing individual values at specific indexes to replacing entire sections with new elements. Let's explore these different ways to modify a vector's elements, each with its own performance considerations and use cases.

Indexing

When changing values in a `Vec` using indexing (`vec[index]`), the language allows direct access to modify elements at a specific index. It checks if the index is within the valid range, and if it is, you can update the value at that index by assigning a new one. If the index is out of bounds, it will trigger a panic.

For types that implement the `Copy` trait (like `i32`), you can directly replace the value with another, and the original value is simply overwritten. For non-`Copy` types (like `String`), you are also allowed to move or replace the value at the given index, transferring ownership of the new value to the vector while the old value is dropped.

The operation of updating an element via indexing is efficient, with a time complexity of O(1), because it involves direct access to memory and doesn't require shifting any elements. For example:

```
let mut v = vec![1, 2, 3];
v[1] = 5;
```

In this case, the value at index 1 is directly modified, and the vector now holds the new value. This works for both copy and move types.

Slicing

Mutable slicing allows you to borrow a portion of a `Vec` as a mutable reference, enabling you to modify the elements within that slice. The syntax is similar to immutable slicing, but with a `&mut` reference. This provides write access to the elements in the slice. The size of the vector and the slice remains unchanged during the borrowing period. Unlike immutable slices, which provide read-only access, mutable slices let you modify the elements in place. However, while a mutable slice exists, Rust ensures that no other references (mutable or immutable) to the same vector or its elements are allowed, enforcing exclusive access to the total vector.

In a mutable slice, you can change the values of the elements within the range, but you cannot alter the length of the slice or the vector. This allows for efficient, in-place modification without reallocating or copying the data in the vector.

For example, consider a vector of integers where a mutable slice is created to modify a subset of the elements:

```
let mut v = vec![1, 2, 3, 4, 5];
let slice: &mut [i32] = &mut v[1..4];
slice[0] = 10;
slice[2] = 30;
```

In this example, a mutable slice of `v` from index 1 to 3 is created, allowing modifications to the elements in that range. The slice allows the first element of the slice (the second element in the original vector) to be changed to 10 and the third element (`v[3]`) to be changed to 30. Resulting in `[1, 10, 3, 30, 5]`.

get_mut

`get_mut` is similar to `get`. When accessing an element from a `Vec` using the `get_mut` function (`vec.get_mut(index)`), it checks if the index is within the valid range. Instead of panicking if the index is out of bounds, `get_mut` returns an `Option<&mut T>`, where `Some(&mut T)` contains a mutable reference to the element if the index is valid, and `None` is returned if the index is out of bounds. For example:

```
let mut v = vec![10, 20, 30];
if let Some(element) = v.get_mut(1) {
    *element += 5;
}
```

In this case, `v.get_mut(1)` returns a mutable reference to the element at index 1. This allows you to modify the value in place, without transferring ownership. As with `get`, `get_mut` is safe for both copy and move types, but it allows direct mutation of the data. Note that modifying the value requires explicit dereferencing, unlike when using an immutable reference, where dereferencing happens implicitly.

fill

When using the `fill` function on a `Vec` (`vec.fill(value)`), the function replaces every element in the vector with the specified value. It does not change the size of the vector but overwrites all existing elements, providing a simple way to update all values in place. The operation is O(n). Foe example:

```
let mut v = vec![10, 20, 30];
v.fill(0);
```

In this case, each element of the `v` is replaced with the value 0. This function works for both copy and move types. For move types, the original elements are dropped and replaced with new values, while the vector retains its original size. Note that for move types, the value supplied to `fill` is cloned for each item in the vector.

splice

The `splice` function allows you to replace a range of elements in a `Vec` with elements from an iterator. This operation both removes the specified range from the vector and inserts new elements in its place, modifying the vector in place. The removed elements are returned as an iterator, allowing you to collect or discard them as needed. The vector is resized accordingly, depending on the number of elements inserted. The time complexity of the splice function is `O(m + n)`, where `m` is the number of elements being removed from the vector, and *n* is the number of elements being inserted.For example:

```
let mut v = vec![1, 2, 3, 4, 5];
let removed: Vec<_> = v.splice(1..4, vec![10, 11].into_iter()).
collect();
```

In this case, the elements in the range from index 1 to 3 (`[2, 3, 4]`) are removed and replaced by the values 10 and 11. The splice method adjusts the size of the vector accordingly, removing three elements and adding two, while returning the removed elements as an iterator.

element delete

Now that we've covered how to update elements within a vector, the next step is understanding how to remove elements from a vector. There are several functions available for this purpose, each suited to different scenarios depending on whether you want to remove elements by their index, by value, or clear the entire vector. Let's explore these deletion methods and how they impact the structure and performance of the vector.

pop

The `pop` function in a Vec removes and returns the last element of the vector. It provides a simple way to shrink the vector by one element. If the vector is empty, pop returns `None`, and if it contains elements, it returns `Some(value)`, where value is the last element. This method reduces the length of the vector by one but does not affect its capacity.

The time complexity of pop is O(1). This is because removing the last element does not require shifting any other elements in the vector. For example:

```
let mut v = vec![10, 20, 30];
let last = v.pop();
```

In this case, pop removes the element 30 from v, and v is now left with [10, 20]. The pop function returns Some(30), indicating that the last element was successfully removed.

If pop is called on an empty vector, it returns None:

```
let mut v: Vec<i32> = vec![];
let last = v.pop();
```

In this case, since the vector is empty, pop returns None, and the vector remains unchanged. This makes pop a safe and efficient way to remove elements from the end of a vector without causing any runtime errors.

remove

The remove function in a Vec allows you to remove a specific element at a given index, returning the removed element while shifting all subsequent elements to fill the gap. This reduces the length of the vector but does not change its capacity. After the element is removed, the vector remains contiguous, maintaining its structure. The function ensures that the vector's order is preserved, though it requires shifting elements, which affects performance.

The time complexity of remove is O(n), where n is the number of elements after the removed index. This is because those elements need to be shifted left by one position.

Consider the following example:

```
let mut v = vec![1, 2, 3, 4, 5];
let removed_element = v.remove(2);
```

In this example, the element at index 2 (3) is removed, and the elements after it are shifted left. The removed element is returned and stored in removed_element. The vector is now [1, 2, 4, 5].

For copy types like i32, the value is copied out. For move types like String, the ownership of the element is transferred to the caller.

remove_item

The `remove_item` function is similar to `remove`, but instead of removing an element at a specific index, it removes the first occurrence of a given value from a Vec. It searches for the value, and if found, removes it and shifts the subsequent elements left to fill the gap. Like remove, this reduces the length of the vector while maintaining its capacity.

The time complexity of remove_item is `O(n)`, where n is the number of elements in the vector. This is because it needs to search through the vector to find the first matching element, and if found, shift the remaining elements.

Consider the following example:

```
let mut v = vec![1, 2, 3, 2, 4];
let result = v.remove_item(&2);
```

Here, the first occurrence of the value 2 is removed, and the vector becomes `[1, 3, 2, 4]`. The function returns `Some(2)`, indicating that the value was successfully removed. If the value isn't found, it returns `None`.

clear

The `clear` function in a `Vec` is used to remove all elements from the vector, leaving it empty. While the vector's length is reduced to zero, its capacity remains unchanged, meaning the memory allocated for the vector is retained. This allows you to reuse the vector without triggering a reallocation if you add elements later.

The time complexity of `clear` is `O(n)`, where n is the number of elements in the vector. This is because each element is dropped, and for move types, their memory is freed as part of the operation.

Consider the following example:

```
let mut v = vec![1, 2, 3, 4, 5];
v.clear();
```

In this example, the vector `v` initially contains five elements. After calling `clear`, all elements are removed, leaving an empty vector. However, its capacity remains unchanged at 5, meaning it can still hold five elements without reallocating memory.

For both copy and move types, clear will remove all elements, but for move types like String, the ownership of each element is dropped, freeing its associated resources.

Fibonacci Example

This Fibonacci example is a great demonstration of using several core functions of `Vec` that were introduced earlier. It illustrates how to create a vector, append elements, and manage a sequence of values. In this example, we define a function `fibonacci` that generates a vector containing the first `n` Fibonacci numbers. The Fibonacci sequence is a series where each number is the sum of the two preceding ones, starting from 0 and 1. The code efficiently builds the sequence by initializing the vector with the first two values and then using a loop to append the remaining numbers to the vector. This approach showcases how to work with vectors when handling iterative, data-driven computations.

Ch09/Examples/src/bin/example01.rs

```
fn fibonacci(n: usize) -> Vec<u64> {
    match n {
        0 => vec![],
        1 => vec![0],
        _ => {
            let mut fibs = vec![0, 1];
            for i in 2..n {
                fibs.push(fibs[i - 1] + fibs[i - 2]);
            }
            fibs
        }
    }
}

fn main() {
    for i in 0..=10 {
        println!("{:?}", fibonacci(i));
    }
}
```

In this example, the function `fibonacci` generates a vector containing the first `n` Fibonacci numbers, a sequence where each number is the sum of the two preceding ones, starting from 0 and 1. The function returns a vector of Fibonacci numbers by matching on the value of `n`. If `n` is 0, it returns an empty vector. If `n` is 1, it returns a vector with a single element, 0. For values greater than 1, it starts with a vector containing the first two numbers of the sequence, `[0, 1]`. A loop then calculates the rest of the sequence by summing the two preceding numbers, appending each result to the vector.

The `main` function demonstrates how this works by generating and printing Fibonacci sequences for values of `n` ranging from 0 to 10. Each call to `fibonacci` returns a vector representing the sequence for that specific `n`, and the results are printed to the console.

`Vec` in Rust is a versatile and essential collection type, offering dynamic resizing and efficient access to elements through indexing. Its key strength lies in combining fast random access to contiguous memory with Rust's ownership and borrowing model, ensuring both performance and safety. Features like automatic memory management, amortized growth during resizing, and zero-cost abstractions make `Vec` a powerful tool for managing collections of data. With a range of methods for creating, modifying, and deleting elements, `Vec` is flexible enough to handle diverse use cases while maintaining predictable time complexity. Whether you need fast append operations, targeted element removal, or complete control over memory allocation, `Vec` is a reliable and efficient choice for handling dynamic arrays in Rust.

In the next section, we will explore `VecDeque`, a double-ended queue that allows efficient insertion and removal at both ends. Unlike Vec, which is optimized for operations at the back, `VecDeque` offers `O(1)` performance for both front and back operations, making it ideal for queue-like structures.

VecDeque

`VecDeque` (short for **double-ended queue**) in Rust is similar to a Vec but differs in how it handles adding and removing elements, particularly in terms of efficiency when working with both ends of the collection. While a Vec is optimized for fast access to elements and appending at the end, `VecDeque` provides efficient insertion and removal at both the front and the back of the collection.

In contrast to `Vec`, which has `O(1)` performance for adding elements only at the end using the push operation, `VecDeque` is designed to support `O(1)` operations for both `push_front()` and `pop_front()` (at the front) and `push_back` and `pop_back` (at the back). This makes `VecDeque` ideal for scenarios where you need to frequently add or remove elements from both ends, such as implementing queues or deques.

`VecDeque` still allows efficient `O(1)` access to elements via indexing, similar to Vec. You can access elements with indexing, like `deque[index]`, and it provides bounds checking as well as immutable or mutable references. Despite the added flexibility of working with both ends, reading elements by index remains efficient because accessing elements is a direct memory lookup.

The internal structure of `VecDeque` is implemented as a ring buffer (circular buffer), which avoids shifting elements when modifying the collection at the front. This differs from `Vec`, where inserting or removing elements near the front can lead to expensive `O(n)` shifts. The circular buffer structure ensures that `VecDeque` can efficiently manage memory when elements are inserted or removed from either end.

`VecDeque` is the right choice when you need efficient insertion and removal at both the front and back of the collection. This makes it ideal for implementing data structures like queues where operations happen at both ends. On the other hand, `Vec` is better suited when you mostly need efficient access to elements and appending at the end, as it excels in that area.

Both `Vec` and `VecDeque` allow `O(1)` access to elements via indexing, and both provide safe, efficient operations with bounds checking. They also grow dynamically and hold a contiguous block of memory, though `VecDeque` uses a circular buffer internally to support efficient front operations.

For example, you can create a `VecDeque`, add elements to both the front and back efficiently, and remove them in constant time. Consider the following code:

```
use std::collections::VecDeque;
let mut deque = VecDeque::from([1, 2, 3]);
deque.push_back(4);
deque.push_front(0);
let last = deque.pop_back();
let first = deque.pop_front();
```

In this example, `VecDeque` allows efficient operations at both ends while still maintaining fast access to elements. After adding an element to both the back and the front of the `deque` and then removing them, the deque returns to its original state.

The main drawback of `VecDeque` compared to `Vec` is that it doesn't support direct slicing due to its underlying circular buffer implementation. Since `VecDeque` allows for efficient insertion and removal from both ends, its elements aren't stored in a contiguous block of memory like `Vec`, which makes slicing impossible in the same way.

The solution to this limitation is to use the `as_slices` method. This method returns two slices that represent the front and back portions of the deque, allowing you to work with the contents in a slice-like manner, even though the data is not stored contiguously. This approach is useful when you need to access the underlying data efficiently while leveraging the benefits of `VecDeque` for double-ended operations.

`VecDeque` is a versatile collection that excels in efficiently adding and removing elements from both the front and back with `O(1)` performance, unlike Vec which is optimized for appending at the back. Its ring buffer structure prevents costly shifts when modifying the front, making it ideal for use cases like queues. While still allowing fast O(1) access via indexing, `VecDeque` is the preferred choice when operations are needed at both ends, whereas Vec is better for efficient appending and random access.

In the next section, we will explore `HashMap`, a powerful collection type in Rust that stores key-value pairs and allows for efficient lookups, insertions, and deletions. `HashMap` uses hashing to quickly locate values associated with a given key, making it ideal for scenarios where fast data retrieval is critical. We will cover how `HashMap` works, its performance characteristics, and its typical use cases in managing associations between data efficiently.

HashMap

In programming, efficiently storing and retrieving data is a fundamental requirement for many applications. One of the most versatile tools for managing data in this context is the key-value pair structure, where each unique key is associated with a specific value. In Rust, this is achieved using the `HashMap`, a widely used collection type that provides an efficient and flexible way to store, retrieve, and manage data.

A `HashMap` is an associative container that stores key-value pairs, enabling fast lookups by key. Unlike other collection types like arrays or vectors, where elements are accessed by their position, `HashMap` allows data to be accessed via unique keys. This makes it an ideal choice when you need to quickly find or update a value based on a specific identifier, such as looking up a user's profile by username or managing a cache of computed results.

Rust's `HashMap` is a hash-based collection, meaning it uses a hash function to compute an index for each key. This provides highly efficient access times for both insertions and lookups, often making it faster for these operations than other collection types like lists or trees. This is especially true for large datasets, where the ability to locate values in constant time is crucial.

Implementation

The implementation of `HashMap` is built on top of several key principles to ensure both performance and reliability. At its core, `HashMap` uses a hashing mechanism that transforms keys into hash values, which are then used to determine where the corresponding value is stored in memory. By doing this, the `HashMap` can achieve very fast average lookup, insertion, and deletion times.

To handle the possibility of hash collisions (situations where two different keys generate the same hash value), HashMap uses an internal strategy known as **open addressing** or **bucket chaining**. Open addressing is a collision resolution technique used in hash tables where, instead of storing multiple entries in a list at the same index (as in bucket chaining), the algorithm searches for the next available slot in the table according to a probing sequence (like linear probing, quadratic probing, or double hashing). All entries are stored directly in the array. In contrast, bucket chaining resolves collisions by having each bucket (array slot) store a linked list or another structure containing all key-value pairs that hash to the same index.

Another aspect of `HashMap`'s implementation is its dynamic resizing. As the number of elements in a map increases, the load factor, the ratio of stored elements to available slots, grows. Once the load factor reaches a certain threshold, the collection automatically increases its size to maintain performance. While this resizing process can be costly in the short term, it ensures long-term efficiency.

Most `HashMap` operations, like insertion, deletion, and lookup, have an average time complexity of `O(1)` due to the use of a hash function, which efficiently maps keys to indices. In the average case, accessing a value is fast because the key is directly converted to an index. However, in rare worst-case scenarios, such as when many keys collide and end up in the same bucket, the time complexity can degrade to `O(n)`, where n is the number of elements. To prevent this, `HashMap` implementations use rehashing and resizing techniques, keeping the average performance constant and efficient.

Use Cases

`HashMap` is a versatile tool with a broad range of applications across different domains. One of its most common use cases is data caching. In many applications, results of expensive computations are stored in a `HashMap` so that they can be retrieved later without recalculating.

Another frequent use case is in indexing large datasets, such as creating a directory of users based on unique identifiers (e.g., usernames or email addresses). In this scenario, a `HashMap` allows for fast lookup, update, and management of user data, making it ideal for systems where responsiveness and scalability are critical.

Lastly, `HashMap` is often used in language parsers, compilers, and interpreters, where it plays a crucial role in symbol tables, storing mappings of variable names to their respective values or memory addresses.

In summary, Rust's `HashMap` is a highly optimized, flexible tool suited for a wide range of applications. Whether it's for caching, indexing, or managing relationships between entities, `HashMap` provides developers with a reliable and efficient way to store and retrieve data based on keys.

Having established that `HashMap` is an efficient and flexible way to manage key-value pairs, we can now look at how to create and initialize one. Rust provides two main methods for starting a `HashMap`: `new` and `with_capacity`. These methods allow you to tailor the creation process based on your specific data requirements, whether you're working with an empty map or preparing for a large dataset. Understanding these options is the first step in effectively leveraging `HashMap` for various data storage and retrieval needs.

Collection Create

To start working with a `HashMap`, Rust provides two primary ways to create and initialize them: `new` and `with_capacity`. These methods allow you to create a `HashMap` tailored to your data requirements, whether you're starting with an empty map or expecting a specific number of entries. Both functions provide efficient initialization, with slight differences in memory handling depending on whether you anticipate adding a small or large number of elements. Let's explore these methods to understand when and how to use them effectively.

new

The `new` function is the simplest way to create an empty `HashMap`. This function initializes the hash map with no elements and minimal memory allocation, which means it starts with the default internal capacity. This capacity will grow dynamically as elements are added to the map. Since new doesn't pre-allocate space for future entries, it is a cost-efficient starting point for small maps or when you have no prior knowledge of how many elements will be added.

The time complexity for creating a HashMap using new is constant, `O(1)`, because it doesn't depend on the number of future elements or their operations, it simply allocates enough memory to start the map.

For example:

```
use std::collections::HashMap;
let map = HashMap::new();
```

Here, the `HashMap` is initialized without pre-allocating any significant memory, and elements can be added later. Each new element might trigger an internal resize operation, but for small datasets, this overhead is minimal.

with_capacity

`with_capacity` allows you to create a hash map with a specified capacity, pre-allocating memory for the expected number of elements. This function is particularly useful when you know the approximate size of the dataset upfront, as it avoids the overhead of multiple resizing operations during insertions. By pre-allocating memory, the hash map can handle the specified number of elements without needing to dynamically grow its internal storage. Foe example:

```
let map = HashMap::with_capacity(20);
```

In this example, the `HashMap` is created with enough space to store 20 elements, minimizing the need for future reallocation as data is inserted. This is especially advantageous for large or fixed-size datasets.

This function is best suited for cases where you can predict the number of elements that will be stored, improving performance by reducing the overhead of multiple memory allocations.

Element Create

After creating a collection, the next essential step is adding elements. In key-value collections, such as maps, adding new entries and managing existing ones is crucial. There are different methods to insert elements into a collection, each suited to specific scenarios. We'll start by looking at how you can add or replace key-value pairs, and then explore more sophisticated techniques for handling situations where you may not know if a key already exists. Let's dive into these methods for inserting and managing elements.

insert

The `insert` function in `HashMap` allows you to add a key-value pair to the map. If the key already exists, it replaces the old value with the new one and returns the old value. If the key is not present, it simply inserts the new key-value pair. This makes insert the go-to method for straightforward insertion or replacement scenarios in a hash map. For example:

```
let mut map = HashMap::new();
let previous_value = map.insert("apple", 5);
```

In this example, a new `HashMap` is created, and the key `"apple"` is inserted with the value `5`. The `insert` method returns `None` because `"apple"` was not previously in the map. If `"apple"` had existed, it would return the previous value.

For copy types, the values inserted are copied into the map. For move types, the ownership of the value is transferred to the `HashMap`.

entry.or_insert

The `entry.or_insert` method is a more sophisticated way of working with hash maps, especially when you need to handle cases where a key may or may not already exist. This method provides access to an entry for a specific key and inserts a default value if the key is absent. If the key already exists, it returns a mutable reference to the current value, allowing you to modify it without needing to replace the entire key-value pair. For example:

```
let mut map = HashMap::new();
map.entry("apple").or_insert(5);
```

In this example, if the key `"apple"` is absent, the value 5 is inserted. If the key already exists, the method returns a mutable reference to the existing value, which you can then modify directly.

The primary use case for `entry.or_insert` is when you want to ensure that a key is present in the map with a default value, avoiding unnecessary lookups or replacements. It is ideal for managing counts, accumulators, or when default initialization is required.

Element Read

After adding elements to a map, the next logical step is retrieving or interacting with that data. Reading elements from a collection is essential for accessing, verifying, or manipulating stored values based on their keys. The methods in this section allow you to retrieve values, check for the existence of keys, and even iterate through all entries in the map. We will explore various ways to access keys, values, and key-value pairs, as well as other useful functions for checking the state of the map. Let's take a closer look at these element read operations.

get

The `get` function in `HashMap` allows you to retrieve a reference to the value corresponding to a specified key. It will return an `Option<&V>`, where `V` is the value type, either `Some(&value)` if the key exists or `None` if it doesn't. For example:

```
let mut map = HashMap::new();
map.insert("one", 1);
map.insert("two", 2);
if let Some(&value) = map.get("one") {
    println!("The value is: {}", value);
} else {
    println!("Key not found");
}
```

The example creates a `HashMap`, inserts two key-value pairs, and retrieves the value for the key `"one"`. Since `"one"` exists, it prints `"The value is: 1"`.

contains_key

The `contains_key` function checks if a key exists in the map. It returns a bool: true if the key exists, false otherwise. For example:

```
let mut map = HashMap::new();
map.insert("a", 1);
println!("Contains 'a': {}", map.contains_key("a"));
```

This example initializes a HashMap and checks for the key `"a"`, printing true.

len

The len function returns the number of keys the map currently holds. The operation is `O(1)` since it's just an internal count. For example:

```
let mut map = HashMap::new();
map.insert("a", 5);
map.insert("b", 10);
println!("Length: {}", map.len());
```

This example checks the length of map, printing 2.

is_empty

The is_empty function checks if the map contains no entries, returning a bool. It's O(1) in complexity. For example:

```
let map: HashMap<i32, i32> = HashMap::new();
println!("Is empty: {}", map.is_empty());
```

It initializes an empty map, checking emptiness, producing true.

The following functions return the entire collection as an iterator. They are explained here for completeness, while a deeper exploration of iterators and their usage is covered later in chapter 11.

keys

The `keys` function returns an iterator over the references to the keys of the `HashMap`. For example:

```
for key in map.keys() {
    println!("{}", key);
}
```

Here, keys retrieve an iterator over the map's keys, printing each one in turn.

values

The `values` function returns an iterator over references to the values. For example:

```
for value in map.values() {
    println!("{}", value);
}
```

The example iterates over values, printing each one in turn.

iter

The `iter` function returns an iterator over the key-value pairs. Each iteration yields a reference to a tuple `(&K, &V)`. For example:

```
for (key, value) in map.iter() {
    println!("{}: {}", key, value);
}
```

Here the iterator walks through key-value pairs and prints them.

Element Update

Now that we've covered how to read values from a `HashMap`, let's move on to how you can modify existing elements. There are several ways to update or modify values in place within a `HashMap`, from mutating values directly to conditionally modifying them only if they exist. Below, we'll explore these methods and their use cases, including how to iterate over mutable references, apply conditional updates, and extend the `HashMap` with new key-value pairs.

entry.and_modify

The `entry.and_modify` function provides a way to modify an existing value in a `HashMap` if the key is already present. It applies a closure to the value associated with the key, allowing you to mutate it in place. If the key doesn't exist, the function does nothing, making it a safe, conditional way to update values without inserting new entries. For example:

```
let mut map = HashMap::new();
map.insert("apple", 5);
map.entry("apple").and_modify(|v| *v += 1);
```

In this example, the value associated with `"apple"` is incremented by `1`. If `"apple"` had not been present, no changes would occur, and the map would remain as it was.

extend

The `extend` function allows you to add multiple key-value pairs to a `HashMap` in one go. It takes any iterable (such as another collection) and inserts or replaces entries into the current map. If a key already exists, its value is replaced with the new one. This method is ideal for efficiently merging data from multiple sources into a single map.

The time complexity of `extend` is O(n), where n is the number of elements in the iterable being added. For each element, `extend` calls insert, making the overall operation proportional to the size of the incoming data. While this is less efficient than a single insertion, it remains optimal for batch updates. For example:

```
let mut map = HashMap::new();
map.extend([("apple", 5), ("banana", 10)]);
```

In this example, the `HashMap` is extended with two key-value pairs. If either `"apple"` or `"banana"` already existed in the map, their values would be replaced with the new ones.

values_mut

The `values_mut` function is similar to values, but it provides mutable references to the values. For example:

```
let mut map: HashMap<_, _> = [("x", 1), ("y", 2)].iter().
cloned().collect();
for value in map.values_mut() {
    *value += 10;
}
println!("{:?}", map);
```

This example exhibits mutable value iteration, incrementing each by 10.

Element Delete

After exploring how to update elements in a `HashMap`, we now turn to the methods for removing entries. `HashMap` provides a few functions to either remove individual key-value pairs or clear the entire collection. Whether you need to delete specific items based on their keys or completely reset the map while preserving its capacity, these functions offer efficient ways to manage the contents of a HashMap as data changes or needs to be refreshed. Let's dive into the `remove` and `clear` functions to understand how they work and when to use them.

remove

The `remove` function in `HashMap` allows you to delete a key-value pair from the map. If the specified key is present, both the key and its associated value are removed, and the value is returned. If the key is not present, nothing is removed, and the function returns `None`. For example:

```
let mut map = HashMap::new();
map.insert("apple", 5);
let removed = map.remove("apple");
```

In this example, the key `"apple"` and its value 5 are removed from the map. If `"apple"` hadn't existed, `remove()` would return `None`, and the map would remain unchanged.

clear

The `clear` function in `HashMap` removes all key-value pairs from the map, leaving it empty but retaining its allocated capacity. This means that while the map is cleared of all its entries, it doesn't release the memory that was previously allocated for the elements, allowing for future insertions without reallocating memory until the capacity is exceeded.

```
The time complexity of clear is O(n), where n is the number of
elements in the map. This is because clear must iterate over
the internal structure to remove each entry. For example: let
mut map = HashMap::new();
map.insert("apple", 5);
map.insert("banana", 10);
map.clear();
```

In this example, after inserting two key-value pairs, calling `clear` removes both `"apple"` and `"banana"` from the map, leaving it empty but retaining its capacity for future insertions.

The `clear` function is useful when you need to reset a `HashMap` without releasing its allocated memory, such as when reinitializing a map for reuse in a long-running program or when preparing for a new set of insertions without reallocating resources.

Example

This example demonstrates how to use a `HashMap` to count the frequency of words in a given string. The problem involves splitting the text into individual words, converting them to lowercase to ensure case-insensitive counting, and then storing each word and its corresponding frequency in the map. Using the `entry` method, the program efficiently updates the count for each word as it processes the text. The final result prints out each word along with the number of times it appears in the text. This is a common problem in text processing, and a `HashMap` provides an efficient solution.

Ch09/Examples/src/bin/example02.rs

```
use std::collections::HashMap;

fn count_word_frequencies(text: &str) -> HashMap<String, u32> {
    let mut word_count = HashMap::new();
    for word in text.split_whitespace() {
        let word = word.to_lowercase();
        let count = word_count.entry(word).or_insert(0);
        *count += 1;
    }
    word_count
}

fn main() {
    let text = "Rust is fast and memory safe and Rust is fun";
    let word_frequencies = count_word_frequencies(text);
    for (word, count) in word_frequencies {
        println!("{}: {}", word, count);
    }
}
```

In this example, the `HashMap` is used to store and count word frequencies in a string. The `entry` function is key to this solution, as it handles checking whether a word is already in the map. If the word is present, it returns a mutable reference to its count; if not, it inserts the word with a count of zero. The `or_insert` function ensures that if a word isn't found in the map, it's initialized with a value of `0`, which is then incremented. The use of `entry` and `or_insert` makes the process efficient, handling both word existence checks and updates in a single operation. After all words are processed, the map holds each word as a key and its corresponding count as the value.

In programming, the key-value structure is essential for efficiently managing data, and this is achieved using collections like `HashMap`. `HashMap` is a powerful associative container that stores key-value pairs, allowing fast access to values by their keys. This makes it ideal for scenarios like caching, indexing, and data retrieval in various applications.

The core implementation of `HashMap` involves hashing keys to quickly locate their associated values. It handles potential hash collisions using techniques like bucket chaining and dynamically adjusts its size to maintain performance as more elements are added. `HashMap` is particularly effective in large datasets, providing fast lookup, insertion, and deletion times, making it a versatile tool in many fields such as web development, compilers, and large-scale data indexing.

The text also explores the creation of `HashMap` instances using methods like new and `with_capacity`, and details various operations, including element creation, reading, updating, and deletion. It demonstrates how to efficiently add, manage, and retrieve data using insert, get, remove, and more advanced techniques like `entry.or_insert` and `entry.and_modify`.

Beyond `Vec`, `VecDeque`, and `HashMap`, Rust provides a range of other collections, including `HashSet`, `BTreeMap`, `BTreeSet`, `LinkedList`, and `BinaryHeap`. These collections will be addressed at a higher level, one by one, in the following sections.

BTreeMap, HashSet and BTreeSet

After discussing the widely used `Vec`, `VecDeque`, and `HashMap`, we now turn our attention to three additional powerful collections in Rust's standard library: `BTreeMap`, `HashSet`, and `BTreeSet`. These collections provide unique characteristics and trade-offs, making them suitable for specific scenarios where ordering or uniqueness of elements is important.

BTreeMap

`BTreeMap` is an associative container similar to `HashMap` but with one key difference: it maintains its keys in sorted order. This is achieved through a balanced B-tree data structure, which ensures that the keys are always ordered, making it ideal for situations where you need to iterate over keys in a sorted manner or perform range queries.

Operations in `BTreeMap`, such as insertions, lookups, and deletions, have a time complexity of `O(log n)`, where n is the number of elements in the map. While this is slower than the `O(1)` average complexity of HashMap, the predictability of `BTreeMap` makes it advantageous when ordering is essential.

`BTreeMap` shines in use cases where ordered data is crucial, such as:

- **Range queries**: Retrieving all key-value pairs within a specific range (e.g., all entries between two dates in a scheduling system).
- **Iterating in order**: When you need to traverse key-value pairs in ascending or descending order.

The primary advantage of `BTreeMap` is its ability to maintain order and perform efficient range queries. However, it comes at the cost of slower access times compared to `HashMap`, especially for large datasets. If you don't need ordering, `HashMap` is generally a better choice due to its faster lookups.

HashSet

`HashSet` is a collection that stores unique values. Like `HashMap`, it uses a hash-based structure for fast access, but instead of storing key-value pairs, it only stores keys. This makes `HashSet` ideal when you need to maintain a collection of distinct elements and want fast checks for membership.

The operations in a `HashSet`, including insertion, deletion, and membership checks, have an average time complexity of O(1). This efficiency is a result of its hash-based structure, allowing it to quickly determine whether an element is present in the set.

`HashSet` is useful in scenarios where uniqueness of elements is important, such as:

- **Removing duplicates**: When you need to ensure that a list of values contains no duplicates.
- **Membership testing**: When checking if an element exists in a large collection (e.g., filtering out already-seen items in a stream of data).

The major strength of `HashSet` lies in its speed for operations like membership testing and insertion, thanks to `O(1)` average complexity. However, like `HashMap`, the elements are stored without any specific order. If order is needed, a `BTreeSet` is a better option.

BTreeSet

`BTreeSet` is a sorted set, similar to `HashSet` but with the added feature of maintaining its elements in sorted order. Like `BTreeMap`, it is implemented as a balanced B-tree. This makes `BTreeSet` an excellent choice when you need uniqueness combined with the ability to iterate through elements in a specific order.

Operations in `BTreeSet`, such as insertion, deletion, and membership checks, have a time complexity of `O(log n)`, which is slower than `HashSet` but provides the guarantee of ordered elements.

`BTreeSet` is beneficial when you need a unique collection of elements that also requires sorting, such as:

- **Ordered collections**: When maintaining a set of elements that must be iterated in ascending or descending order (e.g., keeping track of unique dates or timestamps).
- **Range queries**: Like `BTreeMap`, `BTreeSet` allows you to efficiently query ranges of elements.

The primary benefit of `BTreeSet` is its combination of uniqueness and order, which is crucial in applications where the order of elements matters. However, it is slower than `HashSet` for basic operations like membership checks and insertion, due to its `O(log n)` complexity.

In summary, `BTreeMap`, `HashSet`, and `BTreeSet` each provide distinct advantages depending on your requirements for data structure operations. If you need fast, unordered lookups and uniqueness, HashSet is ideal. For ordered data with efficient range queries, `BTreeMap` and `BTreeSet` are better suited, although their operations are slower than their hash-based counterparts. The choice between these collections ultimately depends on whether order or speed is the primary concern for your application.

LinkedList and BinaryHeap

After discussing various collection types in Rust's standard library, including `Vec`, `VecDeque`, `HashMap`, `BTreeMap`, `HashSet`, and `BTreeSet`, we now turn our attention to two more specialized collections: `LinkedList` and `BinaryHeap`. These collections serve specific use cases where their unique data structures offer advantages over more common collections like vectors or hash maps.

LinkedList

`LinkedList` is a doubly linked list, where each element holds a reference to both the next and previous elements. This allows for efficient insertion and removal of elements at both ends of the list, as well as more flexible, non-contiguous memory usage compared to a vector. However, it comes with trade-offs in terms of access speed.

The primary operations in a `LinkedList`, such as inserting or removing elements at the front or back, have a time complexity of `O(1)`, making it suitable for use cases where frequent updates at either end of the collection are required. However, accessing or modifying elements by index is slow, with a time complexity of `O(n)`, as the list must be traversed element by element.

`LinkedList` is best suited for scenarios where:

- **Frequent additions/removals at both ends**: For example, implementing a queue or a deque with frequent push and pop operations at both the front and back.
- **Non-contiguous memory**: When you need a collection that won't need to reallocate large contiguous blocks of memory like Vec, especially in memory-constrained environments.

The key advantage of `LinkedList` is its O(1) performance for insertions and deletions at the front or back. However, it suffers from poor cache locality and slow access times compared to other collections like `Vec`. Therefore, it's less efficient when you need to frequently access elements at arbitrary positions.

BinaryHeap

`BinaryHeap` is a priority queue implemented as a binary heap. It stores elements in such a way that the largest (or smallest) element can be quickly accessed, making it ideal for scenarios where you need to repeatedly find and remove the maximum or minimum element.

The primary operations in a `BinaryHeap`, such as pushing an element or popping the maximum element, have a time complexity of `O(log n)`, as elements must be arranged to maintain the heap property. Accessing the top element (either the max or min) is `O(1)`, which makes `BinaryHeap` efficient for priority-based operations.

`BinaryHeap` is particularly useful when:

- **Priority-based tasks**: For example, scheduling tasks based on priority or implementing an event queue where you need to process the highest-priority task first.
- **Finding the maximum or minimum efficiently**: `BinaryHeap` ensures that finding the largest (or smallest) element is efficient, making it ideal for algorithms like Dijkstra's shortest path or heapsort.

The main strength of `BinaryHeap` is its ability to efficiently manage elements based on priority, with quick access to the largest or smallest element. However, it is not suited for use cases where you need fast access to arbitrary elements, as accessing any element other than the root requires traversal, which is slower than a sorted collection like `BTreeSet`.

Both `LinkedList` and `BinaryHeap` serve specialized roles within Rust's collection types. `LinkedList` is useful when frequent insertions and deletions at both ends of a list are necessary, but it should be avoided when random access or iteration speed is important. On the other hand, `BinaryHeap` excels in managing priority-based data, ensuring efficient access to the largest or smallest element, but is less efficient for general-purpose data storage and retrieval. Each collection has its strengths and weaknesses, and their usage depends heavily on the specific requirements of your application.

Summary

In this chapter, we explore the primary collections available in Rust's standard library, which provide efficient tools for managing dynamic sets of data. These collections are designed with a focus on performance, safety, and flexibility, making them essential for various programming tasks.

The chapter introduces several key collection types. The `Vec` is a dynamically sized array, ideal for storing elements in an ordered list where the number of items may change. Another collection is `VecDeque`, a double-ended queue that allows efficient insertion and removal at both ends. `HashMap` is a key-value data structure optimized for fast lookups using hashed keys, while `BTreeMap` offers a key-value structure with sorted keys, useful for ordered traversal and range queries.

Additionally, `HashSet` is presented as a collection for storing unique values without duplicates, providing fast lookup times through hashing. For scenarios requiring uniqueness combined with sorted order, `BTreeSet` is a suitable option, maintaining elements in a sorted order. The chapter also introduces `BinaryHeap`, a priority queue structure that allows quick access to the largest or smallest element, ideal for tasks such as scheduling or priority-based processing. Lastly, the `LinkedList` is discussed as a doubly linked list, which, while not as commonly used due to performance trade-offs, can be useful for efficient insertions or deletions from arbitrary positions in a list.

The chapter emphasizes the importance of choosing the right collection based on specific needs, performance trade-offs, memory usage, and the nature of the tasks involved. Special attention is given to `Vec` and `HashMap` as fundamental tools for managing dynamic data, while other collections are covered more broadly. By the end of the chapter, you gain a thorough understanding of how to use Rust's collections to safely and efficiently solve complex data storage and manipulation challenges.

Our next step is to explore how data flows in and out of Rust programs through input and output (I/O) operations. Just as collections help manage data internally, I/O allows your programs to communicate with the outside world, whether reading from files, capturing user input, or writing data to storage. In the following chapter, we will examine how Rust handles I/O efficiently and safely, ensuring that your applications can interact with external data sources and systems seamlessly.

Exercises

1. Write a Rust program that creates a `Vec` using the `vec![]` macro to store the first five prime numbers. Then, print the vector.
2. Create a `Vec` with 5 integer elements with value 37. Append two more elements of different values to the vector using the `push` method. Remove the last element using the `pop` method, and print the resulting vector.
3. Implement a double-ended queue (`VecDeque`) that allows adding integers to both the front and back of the queue. Add three elements to both the front and the back, then remove one element from each end. Print the final state of the `VecDeque`.

4. Create a `HashMap` that stores names of people as keys and their ages as values. Add at least five entries. Then, write a function to check if a specific name exists in the map, and if it does, print their age.

5. Use a `BTreeMap` to store the names of five students (as keys) and their scores (as values). Write a function that prints the names and scores of all students who scored above a certain threshold in order of name.

6. implement a task scheduler using `BTreeMap` where tasks have priorities (represented by integers). The map should store the priority as the key and the tasks as values. Add tasks with different priorities and print the tasks in increasing order.

7. Write a program that creates a `HashSet` of integers. Add five unique elements to the set and then attempt to insert a duplicate. Print the set to demonstrate that duplicates are not allowed.

8. Define a custom `struct` called `Book` with fields title and author. Implement the `Eq` and `Hash` traits for Book. Create a `HashMap` where the keys are `Book` structs and the values are the number of copies available. Add several entries to the map and implement a function to find the number of copies of a specific book.

9. Create a multi-set (a set that allows duplicate elements and keeps track of the number of occurrences of each element) using a `HashMap`. The keys should represent the elements, and the values should represent their occurrence count. Write functions to add elements, remove elements, and query the count of a specific element.

10. The Snake game is a classic arcade game where the player controls a growing snake. The snake moves in a chosen direction, and as it eats food, it grows longer. In this exercise, you will simulate a simplified version of the Snake game on an infinite plane. Create a `Snake` struct that tracks its body segments using a `VecDeque`. The snake can move in four directions: up, down, left, and right, using an `enum Direction`. Each body segment is a `(x, y)` coordinate on the infinite 2D plane. Implement a move function to update the snake's head and adjust its body. The function should take a `bool` to decide whether the snake grows. If growing, the tail remains; otherwise, the last segment is removed. Lastly, implement a function to print the current state of the snake.

Project: To-Do

Develop a to-do list application as a Rust library where tasks are categorized by priority. The application should allow users to:

- Add tasks with a priority level, select the most suitable collection to store the tasks in memory
- View the list of tasks sorted by priority.
- Mark tasks as completed or remove them from the list.
- Allow users to view high-priority tasks or filter tasks based on a priority range.
- Persistency is not required (tasks are stored in memory only).

Additionally, implement unit tests using Rust's built-in testing framework (`#[cfg(test)]`). The tests should verify that:

- Tasks can be added and viewed correctly.
- Tasks can be marked as completed (removed) and are no longer visible after removal.
- Users can filter tasks by high priority or by a specified priority range.

10

Input, Output

Input/Output (I/O) operations are essential components of almost every real-world application. They enable programs to interact with external environments, such as reading data from files, receiving input from users, or writing output to the console or a network.

In Rust, understanding I/O is critical for building applications that handle user input, manage files, and communicate over networks efficiently. Rust's approach to I/O is built around the language's core principles of safety and performance, ensuring that operations are handled efficiently while preventing common issues like buffer overflows or data races.

Rust provides robust support for I/O through its standard library, particularly through modules like `std::io` for basic input/output operations. These modules enable reading from and writing to streams, working with files, and performing more advanced tasks like buffering and handling errors in a type-safe manner.

This chapter aims to introduce the fundamentals of I/O in Rust, equipping you with the tools to handle common I/O tasks effectively. The chapter covers the following topics:

- Console I/O
  - Writing output with `print!` and `println!`.
  - Reading input with `stdin()` and `read_line`.
- File I/O
  - Reading files as text or binary, iterative reading with/without buffering.
  - Writing files: overwriting, appending, and buffered writing.
- Paths and Directories
  - Using `Path` and `PathBuf` for path management.
  - Creating, deleting, and iterating over directories.
- Networking
  - TCP server and client communication.
  - Handling multiple TCP requests and UDP messaging.

Let's start exploring how to handle console input and output in Rust. While it is verbose compared to other languages, Rust's approach ensures safety and control over how data is processed.

The Console

The console typically connects to the screen for output and the keyboard for input, and it is managed by the operating system through three streams: `stdin`, `stdout`, and `stderr`. Although these streams can be redirected to files by the operating system, we will focus on demonstrating console interactions by writing output to the screen and reading input from the keyboard.

Reading Input from the Console

Reading input from the console is a fundamental task, typically used when interacting with users. The standard library provides functionality to handle console input safely and efficiently through the `std::io` module. The `std::io` module includes the necessary functions and traits to read input from the console. For basic input, we use the `stdin` function along with the `read_line` method to capture user input as a string.

The `stdin` function provides access to the standard input stream (`stdin`), allowing a program to receive console input from the user, which is normally the keyboard. To read data from this stream, the `read_line` method is used. This method reads a line of input and stores it in a mutable string reference passed to it. Additionally, `read_line` returns a `Result` type, which helps manage potential I/O errors that might occur during the reading process. Errors during keyboard input are uncommon. However, since `stdin` can be redirected from a file, it becomes subject to the same types of file I/O errors that occur during file operations.

Here is an example demonstrating how to read user input from the console in Rust:

Ch10/Examples/bin/example01.rs

```
use std::fs;
use std::io;
use std::env;

fn main() -> io::Result<()> {
    let working_dir = env::current_dir()?;
    println!("Current working directory: {:?}", working_dir);

    for entry in fs::read_dir(working_dir)? {
        let entry = entry?;
        let file_name = entry.file_name();
        println!("File or dir: {:?}", file_name);
    }
```

```
    Ok(())
}
```

This example demonstrates how to interact with the user through the console, both by prompting for input and displaying output. The program starts by importing the necessary modules from the standard library, `std::io`, which provides functions for input and output, and `std::io::Write`, which is specifically needed for the `flush` method.

A mutable `String` called `input` is created to hold the data that will be entered by the user. The `print!` macro is then used to display the message “Please enter your name:”. Since the `print!` macro does not automatically flush the output buffer (i.e., send the text immediately to the console), the line `io::stdout().flush().ok()` ensures that the prompt appears on the screen before waiting for input. If the buffer isn't flushed, the output might not show up immediately.

Next, the program waits for the user's input with `io::stdin().read_line(&mut input)`. This method reads an entire line from the standard input (the console) and stores it in the mutable `input` string. The `.ok()` is called after `read_line` to ignore any potential errors that might occur while reading the input. This could be enhanced by using proper error handling, but for simplicity, it's ignored in this example. Finally, the program uses `println!` to greet the user by printing the message.

Note that the `readline` function reads an entire line, including the newline character at the end. This can interfere with correct parsing or cause other unwanted behavior. In the example, this issue is addressed by using `trim` to remove the extra newline. Additionally, the program will pause and wait for input until you press the Enter key.

Writing Output to the Console

Rust provides easy-to-use macros for writing output to the console, primarily through the `print!` and `println!` macros. These macros allow for formatted output, making it straightforward to display variables and text.

- **println!**: Outputs text followed by a newline. It is commonly used for printing formatted strings and variables, making it ideal for typical console output.
- **print!**: Outputs text without adding a newline at the end. Useful when you want to keep the cursor on the same line for further input or output.

Here's an example that demonstrates how to print a simple message with variables using the `println!` macro:

Ch10/Examples/bin/example02.rs

```
fn main() {
    let name = "Alice";
    let age = 30;
    println!("My name is {} and I am {} years old.", name,
age);
}
```

In this example, two variables, `name` and `age`, are defined. The `println!` macro is then used to print a formatted string, with the variables interpolated into the output. The curly braces `{}` act as placeholders within the string, where the values of `name` and `age` are inserted when the output is displayed.

You can also use the `print!` macro when you want to display output without automatically moving to the next line:

Ch10/Examples/bin/example03.rs

```
fn main() {
    print!("This is printed...");
    print!("and this continues op the same line.");
}
```

This will output:

```
This is printed...and this continues op the same line.
```

The placeholder syntax lets you format fields while inserting them into static text. More details on formatting options and possibilities can be found in Chapter 8, which covers strings and the topic of formatting.

Although you can access `stdout` as a stream and write directly to it, using the `println!` macro is much more convenient. It abstracts away the low-level details, making the code simpler and more concise.

In summary, Rust provides powerful and easy-to-use tools for handling both input and output through the `std::io` module and the `print!`/`println!` macros. Using these, you can build interactive applications that read from and write to the console efficiently and safely. We continue the next section with File I/O

File I/O

File I/O (Input/Output) is an essential aspect of any programming language, allowing you to read from and write to files for data storage and retrieval. In Rust, the standard library provides powerful tools for working with files in a safe and efficient manner. This section covers the basics of reading from, writing and, appending to files using Rust's standard library.

Reading from Files

The Rust standard library offers several methods for reading files, depending on your requirements:

- Reading the entire file: Load the full content of the file in one operation.
- Iterative reading without buffering: Process the file in chunks directly from the source, without using intermediate buffers.
- Iterative reading with a buffered reader: Read the file in chunks with the aid of a buffered reader for improved efficiency.

These methods are versatile and can be applied to both text and byte-based file processing. We will go through each method step by step, as each comes with its own implementation specifics to consider.

Reading a File as Text

Reading a text file in one go allows you to load the entire contents of the file into a String at once. This approach is simple and works well for small to moderately sized files that fit comfortably into memory. Rust provides the `std::fs::read_to_string` function for this purpose, which assumes that the file contains valid UTF-8 text.

This example illustrates how to read the entire contents of a file.

Ch10/Examples/bin/example04.rs

```
use std::fs;

fn main() -> std::io::Result<()> {
    let file_path = "example.txt";
    let contents = fs::read_to_string(file_path)?;
    println!("File contents:\n{}", contents);
    Ok(())
}
```

This example reads the entire contents of "`example.txt`" into a String using `std::fs::read_to_string`. The file's content is then printed to the console. If the file is missing, inaccessible, or contains invalid UTF-8, an error is returned and handled by the `?` operator.

Reading a File as Bytes

Reading a file as bytes allows you to load the entire contents of the file into a Vec<u8> at once. This method is ideal for binary files or situations where the data may not be valid UTF-8, as it reads the raw byte content without interpretation. Rust provides the std::fs::read function for this purpose.

This example demonstrates how to read an entire file as raw binary data using `std::fs::read`, which returns a `Vec<u8>` and offers greater flexibility for handling non-UTF-8 content compared to `std::fs::read_to_string`.

Ch10/Examples/bin/example05.rs

```
use std::fs;

fn main() -> std::io::Result<()> {
    let file_path = "example.txt";
    let contents = fs::read(file_path)?;
    println!("File contents (bytes): {:?}", contents);
    Ok(())
}
```

This example is similar in concept to reading a file as a string using `std::fs::read_to_string`, but with a key difference: while `read_to_string` interprets the file's contents as UTF-8 text and returns a `String`, the `std::fs::read` function reads the raw binary data of the file and returns a `Vec<u8>`.

This distinction is important for files that may not contain valid UTF-8 characters, such as binary files or those with specialized encodings. Unlike `read_to_string`, `read` does not validate or transform the content, it simply loads the exact bytes from the file, allowing you to process or interpret the data in a format that suits your needs.

Both functions are efficient for small to moderately sized files and are straightforward to use. However, if you need to process text content, `read_to_string` is more convenient as it handles UTF-8 decoding for you, while read provides more flexibility for working with binary or non-text data.

Iterative Reading

Iterative reading of a file without buffering involves reading the file in small chunks directly from the source. This approach processes data incrementally, avoiding the need to load the entire file into memory at once. While this method provides precise control over how data is handled, it is less efficient than buffered reading because each read operation involves a system call. This makes it suitable for small files or specific scenarios where you need granular control over the reading process. Iterative reading works with bytes, if you need to read text, you must convert the bytes into valid UTF-8.

Here is an example of iterative reading of text without buffering:

Ch10/Examples/bin/example06.rs

```
use std::fs::File;
use std::io::Read;

fn main() -> std::io::Result<()> {
    let mut file = File::open("example.txt")?;
    let mut buffer = [0; 16];

    loop {
        let bytes_read = file.read(&mut buffer)?;
        if bytes_read == 0 {
            break;
        }

        let text = String::from_utf8_lossy(&buffer[..
bytes_read]);
        print!("{}", text); // Output the chunk
    }

    Ok(())
}
```

This program opens a file and reads it in chunks of 16 bytes using the `read` method from the `Read` trait. Each chunk is converted into a UTF-8-compatible string using `String::from_utf8_lossy`, which gracefully handles invalid UTF-8 sequences by replacing them with a placeholder. The program continues reading and printing chunks until the end of the file is reached, indicated by the read method returning 0 bytes. This approach ensures that only a small portion of the file is in memory at any given time. However, it requires handling partial data and converting raw bytes to text manually, which adds complexity compared to buffered reading.

When the read method fills the buffer, it returns the actual number of bytes read, which might be less than the buffer's size (e.g., at the end of the file). The slice `&buffer[..bytes_read]` extracts only the portion of the buffer that was filled, avoiding the inclusion of uninitialized or leftover data.

The return type of `String::from_utf8_lossy` is `std::borrow::Cow<str>`. For now, you can think of it as a flexible type that behaves like a `&str` when the input is valid UTF-8, and like a `String` when the input contains invalid sequences that need to be replaced. We'll explore the details of this type in Chapter 12 on smart pointers.

Buffered Reading of Text

Using a buffered reader to read a text file allows you to process the file incrementally while improving performance. A buffered reader reduces the number of system calls by reading larger chunks of data into a buffer and then letting you process the data piece by piece, such as line by line. This approach is efficient and commonly used for text files, especially when handling larger files or performing repeated reads.

Here is an example of reading a text file with a buffered reader:

Ch10/Examples/bin/example07.rs

```
use std::fs::File;
use std::io::{BufReader, BufRead};

fn main() -> std::io::Result<()> {
    let file = File::open("example.txt")?;
    let reader = BufReader::new(file);

    for line in reader.lines() {
        let line = line?;
        println!("{}", line);
    }

    Ok(())
}
```

This program opens a file and wraps it in a `BufReader`, which handles buffering to optimize reading performance. The lines method provided by `BufReader` creates an iterator over the lines of the file. Each line is read as a `Result<String>`, so the program unwraps the `Result` to access the actual content. This approach automatically strips newline characters and processes the file incrementally, keeping memory usage low while maintaining performance. Buffered readers are particularly useful when reading large files or processing text data in a structured, line-by-line manner.

Buffered Reading of Bytes

Using a buffered reader to read a binary file allows you to process the file in chunks while optimizing performance. A buffered reader reduces the number of system calls by reading larger blocks of data into memory at once, making it efficient for working with binary files, especially large ones. This approach gives you precise control over how much data is read and allows for incremental processing of the file's contents.

Here is an example of reading a binary file with a buffered reader:

Ch10/Examples/bin/example08.rs

```
use std::fs::File;
use std::io::{BufReader, Read};

fn main() -> std::io::Result<()> {
    let file = File::open("example.txt")?;
    let mut reader = BufReader::new(file);
    let mut buffer = [0; 16];
    loop {
        let bytes_read = reader.read(&mut buffer)?;
        if bytes_read == 0 {
            break;
        }
        println!("Read {} bytes: {:?}", bytes_read, &buffer[..
bytes_read])
    }
    Ok(())
}
```

In this example, the program opens a binary file and wraps it in a `BufReader` to enable buffered reading. A fixed-size buffer is defined to hold chunks of data. The read method is used in a loop to read data into the buffer, and it returns the number of bytes read. If read returns zero, it indicates the end of the file, and the loop exits. Each chunk of data is then printed or processed as needed. By slicing the buffer with `&buffer[..bytes_read]`, the program ensures only the valid portion of the buffer is used.

This method is efficient for processing binary files incrementally, allowing for better memory management and performance compared to reading the entire file into memory at once. It also provides precise control over how much data is read and how it is processed.

It is important to note the presence of two buffers: one managed internally by the `BufReader` and another explicitly defined in the program, such as a 16-byte buffer. When using `BufReader`, two buffers are involved: its internal buffer and a smaller one you define, such as a 16-byte array. The internal buffer reads large chunks from the file to reduce system calls, while your code reads smaller portions from this buffer. This setup improves performance and gives you control over how data is processed without frequent direct disk access.

Writing to Files

Writing to files in Rust can be approached in various ways, depending on the purpose and method of operation. One consideration is whether the operation overwrites the file's content entirely, appends data to the existing content, or modifies a specific part of the file. Another factor is the type of data being written, such as text encoded in UTF-8 or raw binary data. The use of buffering also influences the writing process, as unbuffered writes send data directly to the file, while buffered writes optimize performance by using an in-memory buffer. These different approaches allow for flexibility in handling file-writing tasks to meet specific requirements.

We begin by exploring how to write to a new file or overwrite an existing text file, then move on to appending data to a binary file, and conclude with buffered writing for improved performance. Although Rust provides support for modifying specific parts of a file using non-sequential access techniques, such operations fall outside the scope of this book.

Writing a New Text File

Writing to a new text file or overwriting an existing one is a common file operation in Rust. This process involves creating the file if it does not exist or replacing its contents if it does. Rust provides the File::create method for this purpose, which opens the file in write mode, truncating any existing data. This approach is straightforward and is typically used when the goal is to completely replace the file's content with new data.

Here is an example of overwriting a text file:

Ch10/Examples/bin/example09.rs

```
use std::fs::File;
use std::io::Write;
```

```
fn main() -> std::io::Result<()> {
    let mut file = File::create("example_test1.txt")?;
    let text = "Writing to a file";

    file.write_fmt(format_args!("{}", text))?;
    Ok(())
}
```

In the last example, the `write_fmt` method is used to write a string directly to a file. This method, provided by the `Write` trait, accepts a `format_args!` macro, which handles formatting and conversion internally. The `format_args!` macro takes the string (or other data types) and formats it as needed, ensuring that the output is written correctly to the file without requiring explicit conversion to bytes. This approach simplifies the process by allowing strings to be written directly without worrying about their underlying representation. It is particularly useful for scenarios where you want to focus on handling text and formatted output in a clean and idiomatic way.

The code creates a new file named `example_test1.txt` using `File::create`. Errors are propagated using the `?` operator, ensuring concise and safe error handling. This approach allows for writing strings without manually converting them to bytes.

Appending a File as Binary

Appending to a binary file involves adding data to the end of an existing file without altering its current content. This operation is useful for scenarios like logging, updating datasets, or extending binary files with additional information. Rust provides the `OpenOptions` struct for this purpose, allowing you to open a file in append mode and write data directly to the end.

Here is an example of appending to a binary file:

Ch10/Examples/bin/example10.rs

```
use std::fs::OpenOptions;
use std::io::Write;

fn main() -> std::io::Result<()> {
    let mut file = OpenOptions::new()
        .append(true) // Open the file in append mode
        .create(true) // Create the file if it doesn't exist
        .open("example.bin")?;
```

```
    let data = [0xDE, 0xAD, 0xBE, 0xEF]; // Binary data to
append
    file.write_all(&data)?; // Append the data to the file

    Ok(())
}
```

In this example, the `OpenOptions::new()` builder is used to configure the file operation. The `.append(true)` option ensures that data is always added to the end of the file, while `.create(true)` creates the file if it does not already exist. The write_all method is then used to write the binary data [0xDE, 0xAD, 0xBE, 0xEF] to the file. If the file is missing or inaccessible, an error will be returned. This approach ensures that new data is seamlessly appended without modifying or overwriting the existing content.

Buffered Writing

Using a buffered writer with text allows you to write data to a file more efficiently by reducing the number of system calls. A buffered writer collects data in an in-memory buffer and writes it to the file in larger chunks, improving performance, especially for frequent or small writes. Rust provides the `BufWriter` struct for this purpose, which wraps a file handle and manages the buffering automatically.

Here is an example of using a buffered writer with text:

Ch10/Examples/bin/example11.rs

```
use std::fs::File;
use std::io::{BufWriter, Write};

fn main() -> std::io::Result<()> {
    let file = File::create("example_test2.txt")?;
    let mut writer = BufWriter::new(file);

    writer.write_all(b"This is a buffered write.\n")?;
    writer.flush()?;

    Ok(())
}
```

In this example, the `BufWriter::new` function wraps the file handle, enabling buffered writing. Text is written using the `write_all` method, which adds the data to the buffer instead of writing directly to the file. The `flush` method is called at the end to ensure that any remaining data in the buffer is written to the file. This approach is particularly beneficial when writing multiple small chunks of text, as it reduces the overhead of frequent writes and improves overall performance. Buffered writers are ideal for scenarios like logging or generating large text files incrementally.

Working with Paths and Directories

Handling paths and directories is a crucial part of many programs, particularly when working with files. Rust's standard library provides utilities for managing paths and directories in a cross-platform and efficient manner. This section introduces the key types for working with paths and shows how to create, remove, and list directories.

The Path and PathBuf Types

The standard library provides two key types for working with file paths: `std::path::Path` and `std::path::PathBuf`. `Path` is an immutable reference to a path, while `PathBuf` is an owned, mutable version of a path. These types provide platform-independent ways to manage file paths, ensuring your code works across different operating systems.

You can easily convert between paths and strings when needed. The `Path` type offers methods to convert a path to a string slice, and you can create a `Path` from a string using the `Path::new` method.

Example: Joining and Splitting Paths

Ch10/Examples/bin/example12.rs

```
use std::path::{Path, PathBuf};

fn main() {
    let path = Path::new("Ch10/Examples");
    let file_name = "example.txt";

    let full_path: PathBuf = path.join(file_name);
    println!("Full path: {:?}", full_path);

    if let Some(parent) = full_path.parent() {
        println!("Parent directory: {:?}", parent);
    }
}
```

In this example, we join a directory path with a file name to create a full path. The `join()` method is used to concatenate paths, while the `parent()` method allows us to extract the parent directory from a path.

Managing Directories

Rust's `std::fs` module provides functions to create and remove directories, as well as list the contents of a directory. These functions enable you to manage directories in a cross-platform way, making your file system interactions efficient and portable.

You can create directories using the `create_dir` or `create_dir_all` functions, where `create_dir_all` creates any necessary parent directories as well. To remove directories, you can use `remove_dir` or `remove_dir_all`, depending on whether the directory is empty or contains files.

To list the contents of a directory, you can use the `read_dir` function, which returns an iterator over the entries in the directory. Each entry provides information like the file name, type, and metadata.

Example: Iterating Over Directory Entries and Printing File Names

Ch10/Examples/bin/example13.rs

```
use std::fs;
use std::io;
use std::env;
use std::fs;
use std::io;
use std::env;

fn main() -> io::Result<()> {
    let working_dir = env::current_dir()?;
    println!("Current working directory: {:?}", working_dir);

    for entry in fs::read_dir(working_dir)? {
        let entry = entry?;
        let file_name = entry.file_name();
        println!("File or dir: {:?}", file_name);
    }

    Ok(())
}
```

This program retrieves and displays the current working directory and its contents. It uses `env::current_dir()` to get the directory path and `fs::read_dir()` to iterate over the directory's entries. Each entry's name is printed to the console. Errors are handled with the `?` operator, and the program returns `Ok(())` upon successful completion.

Overview of Path functions

The standard library provides numerous functions for working with Path. Below is an overview of these functions, organized by category.

Category	Key Functions/Methods
Creating/ Converting	`Path::new, PathBuf::from, PathBuf::new`
Querying Properties	`Path::exists, Path::is_file, Path::is_dir, Path::has_root`
Manipulating Paths	`PathBuf::push, PathBuf::pop, PathBuf::set_extension`
Accessing Components	`Path::file_name, Path::extension, Path::components, Path::iter`
Normalizing/ Cleaning	`Path::canonicalize, Path::join`
Comparing/ Matching	`Path::starts_with, Path::ends_with`
Conversions	`Path::to_str, Path::to_string_lossy, PathBuf::into_os_string`
File System Operations	`Path::read_dir, Path::metadata, Path::symlink_metadata`

Working with Metadata

In addition to reading and writing file contents, Rust allows you to retrieve file metadata using the `std::fs::Metadata` struct. This metadata includes information such as file size, permissions, and timestamps. This can be useful for inspecting the properties of files before or after performing operations on them.

You can retrieve metadata using the `metadata()` method, which returns a Metadata object that provides various file attributes. You can check if a file is read-only, determine its size, or gather other useful information.

This example illustrates how Metadata is utilized:

Ch10/Examples/bin/example14.rs

```
use std::fs::metadata;
use std::io;

fn main() -> io::Result<()> {
```

```
    let file_metadata = metadata("example.txt")?;

    if file_metadata.permissions().readonly() {
        println!("The file is read-only.");
    } else {
        println!("The file is writable.");
    }

    let file_size = file_metadata.len();
    println!("The file size is {} bytes.", file_size);

    Ok(())
}
```

In this example, the `metadata()` function retrieves the file's metadata, allowing us to check if the file is read-only using the `permissions().readonly()` method and retrieve the file size using the `len()` method.

Error Handling in I/O Operations

Error handling is a crucial aspect of working with I/O operations in Rust. Since I/O operations are inherently fallible (e.g., files may not exist, or you may not have permissions), Rust ensures that errors are handled safely and explicitly. Understanding how Rust manages I/O errors allows you to build robust programs that can gracefully handle unexpected situations.

When performing I/O operations in Rust, you often encounter errors such as "file not found" or "permission denied." These errors are common and must be handled to prevent program crashes or undefined behavior.

I/O operations can fail for several reasons, such as the file not being found, insufficient permissions, or an unexpected end-of-file (EOF). These failures return a `Result` type, which contains either the successful outcome (`Ok`) or an error (`Err`), which encapsulates details of the failure.

Example: Writing a Function That Reads from a File and Propagates Errors

Ch10/Examples/bin/example15.rs

```
use std::fs::File;
use std::io::{self, Read};

fn read_file_content(file_path: &str) -> io::Result<String> {
    let mut file = File::open(file_path)?;
    let mut contents = String::new();
    file.read_to_string(&mut contents)?;
```

```
        Ok(contents)
    }

    fn main() {
        match read_file_content("example.txt") {
            Ok(content) => println!("File content:\n{}", content),
            Err(error) => println!("Failed to read file: {}", error),
        }
    }
```

In this example, the `read_file_content` function attempts to open and read the contents of a file. The `?` operator is used to propagate any errors that occur during the file opening or reading operations. If an error occurs, it is returned immediately to the calling function (in this case, `main`), which then handles the error with a `match` statement.

In conclusion, Rust's approach to error handling is designed to ensure safety and robustness in I/O operations. By using `Result` and `Option`, you can explicitly handle potential errors, and by propagating errors with the `?` operator, you can write clean and concise error-handling code. This makes Rust's I/O operations both reliable and predictable, giving you full control over how your application responds to various failure scenarios.

Now that we have covered the console and File I/O, we proceed to the final section of this chapter: networking.

Networking

Rust's standard library provides a robust set of tools for working with networking, designed to cover fundamental needs for building reliable networked applications. It offers support for the two most widely used transport layer protocols: TCP (Transmission Control Protocol) and UDP (User Datagram Protocol). TCP is a connection-oriented protocol that ensures reliable and ordered delivery of data, making it suitable for applications like web servers or file transfers. UDP, on the other hand, is a lightweight, connectionless protocol used for scenarios where speed is prioritized over reliability, such as streaming or gaming.

The library is designed with simplicity and cross-platform compatibility in mind, abstracting low-level system-specific details while exposing essential functionality. Developers can handle server-side and client-side operations with ease, whether creating a TCP listener to accept connections or a UDP socket for sending and receiving datagrams. Additionally, the library provides utilities for managing IP addresses, socket addresses, and network configurations, making it versatile for a variety of networking tasks.

By default, Rust's networking operations in the standard library are blocking, meaning the thread pauses until the operation finishes. However, these sockets can be switched to non-blocking mode using `set_nonblocking(true)`, allowing for immediate returns if data isn't ready. The standard library doesn't include async I/O or event loops, this capability needs integration with libraries like `tokio` for custom event-driven or highly concurrent applications. While the standard library focuses on core networking primitives, it serves as an excellent foundation for building on top of, especially when combined with external asynchronous frameworks for more advanced needs.

In this section, we will explore TCP and UDP networking, focusing exclusively on blocking operations. We will begin with TCP.

TCP

TCP is a connection-oriented protocol that ensures reliable and ordered communication between two endpoints, commonly used in scenarios like web servers, APIs, and file transfers. Rust's std::net module provides the necessary tools for working with TCP, including `TcpListener` for creating servers and `TcpStream` for establishing client connections. Below is an example demonstrating a simple TCP server and client that communicate with each other.

Here is the server code:

Ch10/Examples/bin/example16.rs

```
use std::net::{TcpListener, TcpStream};
use std::io::{Read, Write};

fn handle_client(mut stream: TcpStream) -> std::io::Result<()>
{
    let mut buffer = [0; 512];
    let bytes_read = stream.read(&mut buffer)?;
    println!("Received: {}", String::from_utf8_lossy(&buffer[..
bytes_read]));
    stream.write_all(b"Hello, client!")?;
    Ok(())
}

fn main() -> std::io::Result<()> {
    let listener = TcpListener::bind("127.0.0.1:7878")?;
    println!("Server is listening on port 7878");
```

```
    for stream in listener.incoming() {
        let stream = stream?;
        handle_client(stream)?;
    }

    Ok(())
}
```

Here is the client code:

Ch10/Examples/bin/example17.rs

```
use std::net::TcpStream;
use std::io::{Read, Write};

fn main() -> std::io::Result<()> {
    let mut stream = TcpStream::connect("127.0.0.1:7878")?;
    stream.write_all(b"Hello, server!")?;

    let mut buffer = [0; 512];
    let bytes_read = stream.read(&mut buffer)?;
    println!("Server replied: {}", String::from_utf8_
lossy(&buffer[..bytes_read]));

    Ok(())
}
```

The server binds to the address `127.0.0.1:7878` and listens for incoming client connections using a `TcpListener`. When a client connects, the server accepts the connection and reads data sent by the client into a buffer. It prints the received message and sends back a response, "Hello, client!". The client establishes a connection to the server using `TcpStream::connect`, sends a message, and waits to receive the server's response, which it then prints. Together, these examples demonstrate a simple TCP communication setup where a client and server exchange messages.

To run these examples, start by launching the server first in a console, followed by the client. In an IDE, you can start the server using `cargo run --bin example16` in a console. The `--bin` flag tells Cargo to execute the specified binary file located in the bin directory. Once the server is running, you can launch the client within the IDE. Observe the output in both the client and server consoles to verify their interaction.

The previous example is intentionally simplified. In real-world scenarios, it's common to handle multiple requests over a single connection, and both requests and responses may exceed the size of the message buffer. The following example addresses these challenges, providing a more realistic implementation at the cost of added complexity. It's important to note that this example operates in a blocking mode, which is not ideal for many use cases. Additionally, the standard library handles only low-level networking operations. Depending on your needs, exploring external crates for higher-level abstractions might be a better choice.

This server code is designed to handle multiple requests over a single connection, using a newline character to indicate the end of each message. By employing a newline separator, the `BufReader` and its `read_line` function can efficiently process multiple messages without risking buffer overflow.

Ch10/Examples/bin/example18.rs

```
use std::net::{TcpListener, TcpStream};
use std::io::{BufRead, BufReader, Write};

fn handle_client(stream: TcpStream) -> std::io::Result<()> {
    let mut reader = BufReader::new(stream.try_clone()?);
    let mut stream = stream;

    loop {
        let mut message = String::new();
        let bytes_read = reader.read_line(&mut message)?;
        if bytes_read == 0 {
            println!("Client disconnected");
            break;
        }
        println!("Received: {}", message.trim());

        let response = format!("Server received -> {}\n",
message.trim());
        stream.write_all(response.as_bytes())?;
        stream.flush()?;
    }

    Ok(())
}

fn main() -> std::io::Result<()> {
    let listener = TcpListener::bind("127.0.0.1:7878")?;
    println!("Server is listening on port 7878");

    for stream in listener.incoming() {
```

```
            if let Ok(stream) = stream {
                handle_client(stream).ok();
            }
            break;
        }

        Ok(())
    }
```

This server code is a basic implementation of a TCP server that listens for incoming client connections, processes text-based messages separated by newline characters, and responds to each message. It uses the `TcpListener` to accept connections and handles communication using a `TcpStream`.

The `handle_client` function manages interaction with a single client. It starts by wrapping the `TcpStream` in a `BufReader`, which allows efficient and convenient line-based reading of messages sent by the client. A loop is used to continuously read messages from the client using the `read_line` method. Each message is appended to a String, and the function checks if the bytes_read count is zero, which indicates that the client has disconnected. If so, the loop is exited, and the connection is closed.

For every message received, the server logs it to the console and prepares a response. The response is a formatted string acknowledging the message, and it is sent back to the client using `write_all`, followed by flushing the stream to ensure the data is transmitted immediately.

The main function initializes the server by binding a `TcpListener` to the local IP address 127.0.0.1 on port 7878. It enters a loop that listens for incoming connections. For each connection, it creates a `TcpStream` and calls the `handle_client` function to manage communication with the client. The connection is handled synchronously in this version, meaning only one client is processed at a time.

The server gracefully handles client disconnection and ensures all resources are cleaned up when a client disconnects or when the server shuts down. This implementation demonstrates how to handle text-based TCP communication efficiently with Rust.

And here is the client code:

Ch10/Examples/bin/example19.rs

```
use std::io::{BufRead, BufReader, Write};
use std::net::TcpStream;
```

```
fn main() -> std::io::Result<()> {
    let mut stream = TcpStream::connect("127.0.0.1:7878")?;
    let mut reader = BufReader::new(stream.try_clone()?);

    let requests = ["Hello, server!", "Another request", "Final
message"];
    for request in &requests {
        stream.write_all(request.as_bytes())?;
        stream.write_all(b"\n")?;

        let mut response = String::new();
        reader.read_line(&mut response)?;
        println!("Server replied: {}", response.trim());
    }

    Ok(())
}
```

This client code demonstrates how to establish a TCP connection to a server, send multiple newline-delimited text messages, and receive responses from the server.

The program begins by creating a `TcpStream` object that connects to a server running on 127.0.0.1 (localhost) at port 7878. This establishes a bidirectional communication channel between the client and the server. To handle reading responses from the server efficiently, a `BufReader` is created around a cloned copy of the `TcpStream`. The cloning allows the original stream to be used for writing messages while the cloned handle is used for reading. The `try_clone` method is used to create an additional handle to the same `TcpStream`, enabling simultaneous reading and writing. This is necessary because `BufReader` takes ownership of the stream, making it unavailable for further writes. By cloning the stream, one handle can be used for writing, while the other is wrapped in `BufReader` for reading. This approach adheres to Rust's ownership rules while allowing independent operations on the same connection.

The client defines a list of requests as strings in the requests array. It iterates over each message in the array using a loop. For each message, the program sends the request to the server by writing the string to the `TcpStream` using `write_all`. It appends a newline character (\n) to mark the end of each message, ensuring the server can distinguish between separate messages.

After sending a message, the client reads the server's response using the `BufReader`. The `read_line` method reads data from the stream until it encounters a newline character, appending the response to the response string. This ensures that the client processes one complete response at a time.

The response received from the server is then trimmed of any extraneous whitespace or newline characters using the trim method and printed to the console. This process is repeated for each message in the requests array.

Finally, the program exits gracefully, and the `TcpStream` is automatically closed as it goes out of scope. This client demonstrates how to interact with a server over a TCP connection, handling multiple text-based messages and responses efficiently using `BufReader` for input and `write_all` for output.

This concludes the basics of networking with TCP. Next, let's explore UDP.

UDP

UDP, or User Datagram Protocol, is a lightweight, connectionless networking protocol that emphasizes speed and efficiency over reliability. Unlike TCP, UDP does not establish a persistent connection between a client and a server, making it ideal for scenarios where low latency is critical, and occasional data loss is acceptable, such as real-time video streaming, gaming, and broadcasting messages to multiple recipients.

In Rust, the standard library provides support for UDP networking through the `UdpSocket` type, which allows you to send and receive datagrams. This approach gives you greater control over individual messages compared to TCP's stream-oriented model. While UDP is faster and more flexible, it requires careful handling of packet ordering, loss, and retransmission if reliability is essential. Using the standard library, you can work directly with low-level UDP operations while managing these trade-offs manually.

Here's a straightforward example of working with UDP, including code for both the server and the client sides:

Ch10/Examples/bin/example20.rs

```
use std::net::UdpSocket;

fn main() -> std::io::Result<()> {
    let socket = UdpSocket::bind("127.0.0.1:7878")?;
    println!("UDP server listening on 127.0.0.1:7878");

    let mut buf = [0; 1024];
    loop {
        let (bytes_received, src) = socket.recv_from(&mut
buf)?;
        let msg = String::from_utf8_lossy(&buf[..
bytes_received]);
```

```
            println!("Received '{}' from {}", msg, src);

            let response = format!("Hello, {}!", src);
            socket.send_to(response.as_bytes(), src)?;
        }
    }
```

The server code sets up a basic UDP server that listens for messages, processes them, and responds to the sender. It begins by binding the `UdpSocket` to the address `127.0.0.1` and port `7878`, which enables the server to listen for incoming UDP packets on the specified address and port. The bind method ensures that the server is ready to receive messages, and any errors during this setup are propagated for handling.

Once the server is bound, it enters an infinite loop, continuously listening for incoming packets. Each packet is received using the `recv_from` method, which writes the packet's data into a buffer and provides information about the sender, including their IP address and port. This allows the server to identify who sent the packet.

The received data is then converted from raw bytes into a readable string using `String::from_utf8_lossy`, ensuring any invalid UTF-8 sequences are gracefully handled. The server logs the received message and the sender's address for debugging or monitoring purposes.

After processing the message, the server prepares a response. In this example, the response is a simple acknowledgment formatted as a string that includes the sender's address. The `send_to` method is used to send this response back to the sender using the address and port provided by `recv_from`.

The server runs continuously, handling each incoming message and responding accordingly. This allows it to manage multiple messages from different clients or repeated messages from the same client without interruption. The code structure ensures efficient handling of UDP communication, and errors during any part of the process are propagated upwards, allowing for appropriate handling if needed.

Ch10/Examples/bin/example21.rs

```
use std::net::UdpSocket;

fn main() -> std::io::Result<()> {
    let socket = UdpSocket::bind("127.0.0.1:0")?;
    println!("Client bound to {}", socket.local_addr()?);

    let server_address = "127.0.0.1:7878";
```

```
    let message = "Hello, server!";
    socket.send_to(message.as_bytes(), server_address)?;
    println!("Sent: {}", message);

    let mut buf = [0; 1024];
    let bytes_received = socket.recv(&mut buf)?;
    let response = String::from_utf8_lossy(&buf[..
bytes_received]);
    println!("Server replied: {}", response);

    Ok(())
}
```

This client code demonstrates how to use a UDP socket in Rust to send a message to a server and receive a response. Here's a detailed explanation:

The program starts by creating a `UdpSocket` bound to `127.0.0.1:0`. The `:0` indicates that the operating system should automatically assign an available port for the client. This ensures the client has a unique address for receiving responses from the server without requiring explicit port management. The bind function establishes the socket for communication.

The connect method associates the `UdpSocket` with the server's address (`127.0.0.1:7878`). While UDP is connectionless, this method simplifies the API by allowing subsequent send and recv operations to automatically target the specified server address and port without needing to explicitly specify the destination each time.

The client then sends a message, "Hello, server!", to the server using the send method. This method converts the message to a byte slice (`message.as_bytes()`) and transmits it to the server. Since connect was previously called, the send method knows where to direct the message.

After sending the message, the client waits for a response from the server. It does this using the `recv` method, which reads data into a buffer. The `recv` method blocks execution until a response is received, ensuring that the client waits for the server's reply.

Once data is received, the number of bytes read is stored in `bytes_received`, and the response is extracted from the buffer. The String::from_utf8_lossy method converts the raw bytes to a UTF-8 string, replacing any invalid sequences with the replacement character (�) . This ensures the output is always valid UTF-8.

Finally, the response is printed to the console, allowing the client to display the server's reply. Once all operations are complete, the program exits gracefully, and the socket is automatically closed.

This client demonstrates how to use UDP for message-based communication, simplifying the process with connect while maintaining the flexibility and lightweight nature of UDP.

Summary

This chapter provides a comprehensive overview of Input/Output (I/O) operations in Rust, emphasizing their critical role in real-world applications. I/O allows programs to interact with the external environment through tasks like reading and writing files, handling user input, and communicating over networks. Rust's approach to I/O focuses on safety and performance, leveraging the standard library's robust modules such as `std::io`, `std::fs`, and `std::net`.

The chapter begins with console I/O, explaining how to read input and write output using functions like `stdin().read_line` and macros like `print!` and `println!`. Examples demonstrate how to manage input safely and handle typical issues like flushing buffers and trimming newlines.

Next, the chapter explores file I/O, detailing methods for reading and writing files:

Reading entire files as text or binary using read_to_string and read.

Iterative reading, with or without buffering, for efficient processing of large files.

Writing files, including creating new files, overwriting content, appending binary data, and using buffered writing to optimize performance.

Path and directory management is covered, showcasing how to use `Path` and `PathBuf` to construct, query, and manipulate paths in a cross-platform manner. The chapter also explains directory creation, deletion, and iteration, supported by examples.

The final section delves into networking using Rust's standard library. It introduces the fundamentals of TCP and UDP communication, starting with simple examples and progressing to more realistic implementations that handle multiple requests and manage message buffers effectively. The TCP section demonstrates how to build a server-client model, while the UDP section highlights its lightweight, connectionless nature for scenarios prioritizing speed over reliability.

Throughout the chapter, Rust's emphasis on error handling is evident, with the Result and Option types playing a central role in ensuring robust and predictable I/O operations. Examples demonstrate how to use these tools effectively, including propagating and managing errors.

Now that you have a solid understanding of Rust's I/O capabilities, including how to interact with the console, manage files and directories, and build networked applications, it's time to explore a very different but equally powerful paradigm: functional programming. In the next chapter, we'll dive into how Rust supports functional concepts such as closures, iterators, and higher-order functions. These tools let you write concise, expressive, and often more maintainable code by focusing on what you want to achieve, rather than how to do it.

Exercises

1. Write a program that prompts the user to input their name and age, then prints a message like:

   "Hello, [name]! You are [age] years old."

2. Create a program that reads the contents of a text file and writes the reversed content to a new file.

3. Write a program that reads a text file in chunks of 16 bytes and prints each chunk to the console. Assume ASCII characters are guaranteed.

4. Create a program that reads a file line by line using a `BufReader` and counts the number of lines containing the word "Rust."

5. Write a function that attempts to read from a non-existent file and handles the error by printing a custom error message. Test the function with both an existing and a non-existent file.

6. Given a base path (e.g., /home/user/documents), append a file name (e.g., report.txt) using `PathBuf`, and print the full path and its parent directory. Observe the use of slashes.

7. Write a program to list the content of the root directory.

8. Write a program that reads metadata for a file and determines whether it is a regular file, a directory, or a symbolic link. Additionally, print the file's size in bytes.

9. Write a TCP server that receives a message from a client, counts the number of words in the message, and sends the word count back to the client. Log each message and its corresponding word count to a file.

10. Write a UDP-based program where the client reads a message from the console, sends it to the server, and the server responds with the length of the received message.

Project: User Registration System

This project is a simple command-line-based user registration and authentication system. It allows users to register with a username and password, saves their credentials securely in a file, and provides a way to log in by verifying credentials. Passwords are encrypted before being saved to ensure security.

Key Features

- User Registration:
  - The user provides a unique username and a password.
  - The system checks if the username already exists. If it does, an error message is displayed.
  - If the username is unique, the password is encrypted and both the username and encrypted password are stored in a file.
- User Login:
  - The user provides their username and password to log in.
  - The system checks if the username exists in the file.
  - If the username exists, the system verifies the password by comparing the encrypted version of the entered password with the stored encrypted password.
  - If the credentials match, the user is logged in successfully. Otherwise, an error message is displayed.
- Password Encryption:
  - Store the password as bytes, where each byte results in two hex values
- Credential Storage:
  - Credentials are stored in a file (e.g., credentials.txt) in the format:
  - username:encrypted_password
  - Each entry is stored on a new line.

Functional Requirements

- Registration:
  - Input: username (string), password (string).
  - Validation:
    - The username must be at least 3 characters long.
    - The password must be at least 8 characters long
  - Output: Success or error message.
- Login:
  - Input: username (string), password (string).
  - Validation:
    - Check if the username exists in the file.
    - Encrypt the entered password and compare it with the stored encrypted password.
  - Output: Success or error message.
- File Handling:
  - The file should be created if it doesn't already exist.
  - Read and write operations should be performed safely to avoid corruption or loss of data.
- Encryption:
  - Use a basic encryption, for example write the bytes in hex values.
  - Passwords should never be stored in plain text.

Data Flow

- Main event loop:
  - The program runs a main event loop asking the user what to do, register, login or exit the program.
- Registration:
  - User enters a username and password.
  - The system checks the file for existing usernames.
  - If the username is unique, the password is encrypted and both the username and encrypted password are appended to the file.

- Login:
    - User enters their username and password.
    - The system reads the file to check if the username exists.
    - If the username is found, the system encrypts the entered password and compares it with the stored encrypted password.
    - If they match, login is successful.

Advanced

11

Functional Programming

Functional Programming (FP) is a programming paradigm centered on pure functions, immutability, and declarative expressions, enabling robust and predictable code. Unlike imperative programming, which focuses on explicit state-changing operations, FP treats computation as the evaluation of mathematical functions, minimizing side effects and making programs easier to reason about. While Rust is primarily known as a systems programming language, it incorporates functional programming features that allow developers to write concise, expressive, and efficient code.

This chapter explores functional programming in Rust, covering key concepts such as first-class functions, higher-order functions, and closures. Readers will learn about Rust's function traits: `Fn`, `FnMut`, and `FnOnce` and how iterators enable expressive data transformations. Additionally, we will examine iterator adaptors and consuming methods, demonstrating how they facilitate composable and efficient operations. Beyond iteration, we will explore functional approaches to error handling using Option and Result, as well as techniques for implementing custom and infinite iterators. Lastly, we will discuss the performance implications of functional programming in Rust, striking a balance between expressiveness and efficiency.

This chapter will cover the following topics:

- **Key Concepts**: Foundation of functional programming and its role in Rust.
- **First-Class Functions, Higher-Order Functions, Pure Functions**: Treating functions as values and using them for composable, predictable code.
- **Closures**: Anonymous functions that capture their environment.
- **Fn, FnMut, and FnOnce**: Traits that define how closures interact with captured variables.
- **Iterators**: Lazy sequences of values that enable expressive looping.
- **Iterator Consuming Methods**: Methods like sum, collect, and for_each that process the entire iterator.
- **Iterator Adaptors**: Chainable transformations such as map, filter, and take.
- **Functional Error Handling with Option and Result**: Using combinators like map, and_then, and unwrap_or for clean error propagation.
- **Custom and Infinite Iterators**: Building your own iterator types, including those without a fixed end.

- **Performance Considerations**: Understanding the cost and benefits of functional abstractions in real-world Rust code.

By the end of this chapter, readers will gain a strong foundation in functional programming within Rust, learning to write cleaner, more maintainable code. These skills will help in leveraging Rust's functional features to build safer, more predictable applications while still taking advantage of its low-level control. In the next section, we begin by exploring the general concepts of functional programming.

Introducing Functional Programming

This introduction aims to familiarize you with the concepts of functional programming, highlight its benefits, and explore Rust's approach to integrating functional programming principles into the language.

Overview of Functional Programming Concepts

At its core, functional programming is built around several key concepts:

- **Pure Functions**: Functions that produce the same output for the same input without causing side effects, making them easier to test and reason about.
- **Immutability**: The state of variables does not change after their initialization, reducing the complexity of managing mutable state.
- **Higher-Order Functions**: Functions that accept other functions as arguments or return functions as results, enabling more abstract and reusable code.
- **Function Composition**: Combining simple functions to create more complex functionality in a modular and expressive manner.
- **Declarative Style**: Writing code that specifies *what* to do, not *how* to do it, leading to more concise and maintainable code.

Benefits of Using Functional Programming Paradigms in Rust

Rust's embrace of functional programming concepts brings several advantages:

- **Enhanced Safety**: Functional programming's reliance on immutability and pure functions aligns with Rust's ownership and borrowing model, minimizing issues like data races and unintended side effects.
- **Readability and Maintainability**: Declarative constructs such as iterators and closures allow developers to express complex logic succinctly, making the code easier to understand and maintain.

- **Concurrency**: Functional programming paradigms encourage the use of immutable data and stateless computations, simplifying concurrent programming by reducing the need for synchronization.
- **Testability and Debugging**: Pure functions are isolated and predictable, which simplifies testing and debugging.
- **Expressiveness**: Rust's functional features, like pattern matching, combinators, and algebraic data types, enable expressive solutions to complex problems.

Rust's Support

Rust provides robust support for functional programming while remaining true to its systems programming roots. Rust provides built-in support for the following features:

- **Closures**: Lightweight, anonymous functions that can capture variables from their environment.
- **Iterators**: Lazy and composable abstractions for processing collections declaratively.
- **Enums and Pattern Matching**: Algebraic data types enable expressive modelling of domain logic.
- **Combinators**: Methods like map, filter, and fold facilitate concise and declarative operations on collections.
- **Immutability by Default**: Rust enforces immutability, encouraging functional programming practices while offering controlled mutability when needed.

Rust's blend of functional and imperative paradigms, combined with its emphasis on safety and performance, makes it a versatile language for adopting functional programming techniques without compromising on low-level control. This synergy allows developers to leverage the best of both paradigms in modern software design.

Key Functional Programming Concepts in Rust

Functional programming in Rust builds on core principles like immutability and pure functions to promote safe, predictable, and expressive code. These ideas complement Rust's broader goals of safety, performance, and fine-grained control. In this chapter, we'll explore how these functional concepts are applied in Rust, examining them one by one through practical examples.

Pure Functions

A pure function is a function that:

- Always produces the same output for the same input.
- Has no side effects (e.g., modifying global state, performing I/O, or relying on external data).

Pure functions are easier to reason about, test, and debug because they operate solely on their input parameters and always produce the same output for the same input. This predictability enables techniques like memoization, where a function's results are cached based on its inputs. If a memoized version of a function consistently returns correct results from the cache, it strongly suggests that the function is pure, since its output depends only on its input and not on any external state or side effects.

Here's a simple example demonstrating a pure function in Rust:

Ch11/Examples/bin/example01.rs

```
fn add(a: i32, b: i32) -> i32 {
    a + b
}

fn main() {
    let result = add(5, 3);
    println!("Result: {}", result);
}
```

In this example, the add function is pure because it depends solely on its input arguments, a and b. It consistently produces the same output, the sum of a and b, for the same inputs. Additionally, it has no side effects, meaning it does not modify any external state or perform any input/output operations.

Immutability

Immutability refers to the inability to change a variable or data structure once it is created. In functional programming, immutability is fundamental because it ensures that data remains consistent throughout a program's execution, preventing unintended side effects and enabling safer, more predictable code.

Rust enforces immutability by default. Variables in Rust are immutable unless explicitly marked as mutable. This design choice aligns with the principles of functional programming, encouraging developers to think in terms of transformations rather than modifications.

First-Class Functions

In programming, first-class functions are functions that are treated as values. This means:

- They can be assigned to variables.
- They can be passed as arguments to other functions.
- They can be returned from functions.

Rust supports first-class functions, allowing developers to manipulate functions like any other data type. This capability is foundational for functional programming, enabling flexible and composable code.

Here is an example of assigning a function, not the return value, to a variable:

Ch11/Examples/bin/example02.rs

```
fn square(x: i32) -> i32 {
    x * x
}

fn main() {
    let func = square;
    println!("Square of 4: {}", func(4));
}
```

The `square` function is assigned to the variable `func` and invoked through the variable, demonstrating that functions can be treated as first-class values. Notice how the square function is assigned to the variable `func` without using any parameters. The function itself isn't called at this point; rather, it's bound to the new variable, which in turn can then be invoked as a function by appending parentheses.

Higher-Order Functions

Higher-order functions are functions that either take other functions as parameters or return functions as their results. These functions enhance modularity and abstraction, enabling developers to write reusable, concise, and declarative code.

Higher-order functions offer several benefits:

- They promote code reuse by abstracting common patterns, making the code more modular and versatile.

- They enhance readability by reducing boilerplate code, allowing developers to focus on the logic rather than repetitive structures.
- Higher-order functions align with functional programming paradigms, supporting a more declarative and expressive coding style.

Function as a parameter

The following example demonstrates how to define a function that takes another function as a parameter and how to invoke it:

Ch11/Examples/bin/example03.rs

```
fn apply_function<F>(value: i32, func: F) -> i32
where
    F: Fn(i32) -> i32,
{
    func(value)
}

fn double(x: i32) -> i32 {
    x * 2
}

fn main() {
    let result = apply_function(5, double);
    println!("Result: {}", result);
}
```

In this example, the `apply_function` function takes a value and a function (`func`) as parameters. The `func` function is applied to the value, and the result is returned. The double function is passed as an argument to `apply_function`, demonstrating how functions can be treated as parameters to enhance modularity and reusability. Later in the chapter, we'll take a closer look at the trait bound Fn(i32) -> i32, which represents any function or closure that takes an i32 as input and returns an i32 as output. This trait is one of Rust's function traits, used to abstract over callable types like closures and function pointers.

Function as a Return Value

Higher-order functions can also return functions as their output, enabling dynamic behavior. This capability allows the creation of specialized functions on the fly, based on runtime parameters.

For example:

Ch11/Examples/bin/example04.rs

```
fn create_multiplier(multiplier: i32) -> impl Fn(i32) -> i32 {
    move |x| x * multiplier
}

fn main() {
    let multiply_by_3 = create_multiplier(3);
    println!("3 x 5 = {}", multiply_by_3(5));
}
```

In this example, think of the closure as an anonymous function. Closures, and the move, keyword will be explained in the next section. The `create_multiplier` function takes an integer multiplier as input and returns a closure. The closure multiplies its input `x` by `multiplier` provided during the function call. When the closure is invoked later, it uses the captured multiplier value to perform its computation. This demonstrates the dynamic nature of returning functions, allowing the behavior of a function to be parameterized and reused.

Closures

Closures are a powerful and flexible feature in Rust, enabling developers to create anonymous functions that can capture variables from their environment. Closures play a crucial role in Rust's functional programming capabilities, allowing for concise and expressive code.

Understanding Closures

Closures are anonymous functions that can capture their surrounding environment. Unlike regular functions, which have a fixed signature and do not interact with the variables around them unless explicitly passed, closures can access variables from the scope in which they are defined. This makes them highly useful for scenarios requiring on-the-fly logic or customization.

Differences Between Closures and Regular Functions:

- **Environment Capturing**: Closures can capture variables from their enclosing scope, while regular functions cannot.
- **Anonymous Definition**: Closures are unnamed and can be created inline, whereas regular functions require a name and explicit declaration.
- **Flexible Type Inference**: Closures often allow Rust to infer argument and return types, reducing boilerplate code.

Example: Creating and Using Closures in Rust:

Ch11/Examples/bin/example05.rs

```
fn main() {
    let add = |x: i32, y: i32| x + y;
    println!("Sum: {}", add(5, 3));
}
```

In this example, the closure add takes two arguments and returns their sum. It is defined inline without a name and can be used just like a function

Closures and Type Inference

Rust's type inference system extends to closures, enabling concise definitions by automatically deducing the types of parameters and return values. This eliminates the need to explicitly annotate types in most cases, though type annotations can still be added for clarity or disambiguation.

Here is an example of using closures with inferred types:

Ch11/Examples/bin/example06.rs

```
fn main() {
    let multiply = |x, y| x * y;
    println!("Product: {}", multiply(4, 5));
}
```

Here, Rust infers that the parameters x and y are integers (i32) based on their usage in the closure. This simplifies the closure definition and keeps the code concise.

If required, you can explicitly specify the types:

```
let multiply = |x: i32, y: i32| -> i32 { x * y };
```

While inference often works, there are situations where specifying types is necessary, particularly when closures are used in complex contexts or generic functions.

Closures in Rust are a powerful feature, often compared to generics for their flexibility. However, one key difference between closures and generics lies in how type inference is handled when closures are used multiple times. While generics allow the use of different types in separate instances, closures with type inference require the same type to be used consistently.

Consider the following example:

Ch11/Examples/bin/example07.rs

```
fn main() {
    let closure = |x| x + 1;

    let result1 = closure(5);
    let result2 = closure(5.0);
}
```

In this example, we define a closure |x| x + 1 that takes a single argument and adds one to it. The type of the argument x is not explicitly defined; instead, Rust infers the type based on the first usage of the closure. When the closure is called with 5, Rust infers that the argument is of type i32. This works seamlessly for the first call.

However, when the closure is used a second time with 5.0, which is a f64, Rust produces a compile-time error. This happens because closures with type inference lock in the type based on their initial usage. Unlike generics, which can adapt to different types across multiple uses, closures are constrained to a single type once it is inferred.

This behavior is by design to ensure type safety and consistency. If different types were allowed within the same closure, it could lead to ambiguous or unintended behavior. To make the closure generic and accept multiple types, you would need to explicitly specify it as a generic function or use a trait object, which incurs some trade-offs in terms of flexibility and performance.

Capturing Variables in Closures

Closures in Rust can receive variables directly as parameters, allowing them to operate independently without capturing external values. However, closures can also capture variables from their surrounding scope. This flexibility makes closures a powerful tool for functional programming, callbacks, and managing deferred execution.

Closures can capture variables from their surrounding environment in three ways:

- **By Reference (Fn)**: The closure borrows variables immutably from its environment.
- **By Mutable Reference (FnMut)**: The closure mutably borrows variables, allowing them to be modified.
- **By Value (FnOnce)**: The closure takes ownership of variables, consuming them. To enable this, the `move` keyword is used.

Let's see an example of capturing variables with closures:

Ch11/Examples/bin/example08.rs

```
fn main() {
    let factor = 2;
    let multiply_by_factor = |x: i32| x * factor;
    println!("Multiply by factor: {}", multiply_by_factor(4));

    let mut count = 0;
    let mut increment = || count += 1;
    increment();
    increment();
    println!("Count: {}", count);

    let text = String::from("Hello");
    let consume_text = move || println!("{}", text);
    consume_text();
}
```

In this example:

- The closure `multiply_by_factor` captures the variable factor by reference.
- The closure `increment` captures the variable count by mutable reference, allowing it to modify the variable.
- The closure `consume_text` takes ownership of the variable text, consuming it in the process.

Note that whether a closure captures a variable by reference or mutable reference is inferred automatically based on how the variable is used inside the closure. If the closure only reads the variable, it is captured by immutable reference. If the closure modifies the variable, it is captured by mutable reference. Capturing by move, on the other hand, must be explicitly indicated using the move keyword.

Fn, FnMut, and FnOnce

In Rust, the Fn family of traits: `Fn`, `FnMut`, and `FnOnce`, represent callable objects, such as closures, functions, and types that implement these traits. These traits allow Rust to abstract over different kinds of callable entities, enabling flexibility and composability in functional programming. Each variant corresponds to a different way the callable interacts with its environment, specifically how it captures and uses variables from its enclosing scope.

Fn Trait

The `Fn` trait is used for closures or functions that do not mutate or consume the captured environment. It is the most restrictive of the three traits and is ideal for cases where only read-only access to captured variables is needed. Closures implementing Fn allow calling without modifying or consuming any variables they capture. These closures can be invoked multiple times, and the variables captured from the environment remain immutable throughout their usage.

Here is an example:

Ch11/Examples/bin/example09.rs

```
fn apply<F>(func: F, x: i32) -> i32
where
    F: Fn(i32) -> i32,
{
    func(x)
}

fn main() {
    let y = 10;
    let add_y = |x: i32| x + y;
    println!("return value: {}", apply(add_y, 5));
    println!("value of y: {}", y);
}
```

The closure `add_y` implements the `Fn` trait because it neither mutates nor consumes any captured variables. The apply function is designed to accept any callable that implements `Fn`, which makes it possible to pass `add_y` as an argument.

FnMut trait

The `FnMut` trait is used for closures or functions that mutably borrow variables from their environment. It allows the callable to modify captured variables but does not permit consuming them. Closures implementing `FnMut` can be called multiple times, with the captured variables being mutably borrowed during each invocation.

Here is an example:

Ch11/Examples/bin/example10.rs

```
fn apply_mut<F>(mut func: F, x: i32) -> i32
where
    F: FnMut(i32) -> i32,
```

```
{
    func(x)
}

fn main() {
    let mut factor = 2;
    let multiply = |x: i32| {
        factor *= 3;
        x * factor
    };

    println!("return value: {}", apply_mut(multiply, 3));
    println!("value of factor: {}", factor);
}
```

In this example, the closure `multiply` implements `FnMut` because it modifies the captured variable factor. The function `apply_mut` accepts any callable that implements `FnMut` and invokes it with mutable access to the captured variables. The behavior of multiply demonstrates how closures with `FnMut` can mutate their environment while being called repeatedly.

FnOnce trait

The `FnOnce` trait is used for closures or functions that consume the variables they capture from their environment. This means the callable takes ownership of the captured variables, and as a result, it can only be called once.

Closures implementing `FnOnce` allow invocation by moving ownership of the captured variables into their scope. Because these variables are consumed during the call, the closure cannot be reused. This trait is suitable for closures that require ownership of the data they operate on. FnOnce is explicitly specified by using the move keyword with the closure.

Here is an example:

Ch11/Examples/bin/example11.rs

```
fn apply_once<F>(func: F, x: i32) -> i32
where
    F: FnOnce(i32) -> i32,
{
    func(x)
}

fn main() {
    let factor = "5".to_string();
```

```
    let consume = move |x: i32| x * factor.parse::<i32>().
unwrap();
    println!("return value: {}", apply_once(consume, 10));
    // println!("factor: {}", factor);
}
```

In this example, the closure consume implements the `FnOnce` trait because it takes ownership of the captured variable `factor`. The function `apply_once` is designed to accept any callable implementing `FnOnce`, ensuring that it is called exactly once. After the call, the closure consume cannot be used again since it has consumed the variable factor from its environment. The `println!` statement for factor is not possible because `factor` is moved into `consume` when the closure is created, making it unavailable for further use.

Fn Hierarchy

The `Fn` traits in Rust are structured in a hierarchy where `Fn` builds on `FnMut`, and `FnMut` builds on `FnOnce`. This structure means that `Fn` functions only require immutable access to any variables they capture, while `FnMut` functions allow mutable access, and `FnOnce` functions can take ownership of captured variables.

Thanks to this hierarchy, if a program needs a function or closure that implements `FnMut`, you can also use one that implements Fn. Similarly, if an `FnOnce` is required, you can supply a function or closure that implements any of the three traits: `Fn`, `FnMut`, or `FnOnce`. This design ensures that functions or closures with more specific requirements can still be used in broader contexts, providing flexibility while maintaining clear rules for how captured variables are accessed or owned.

Iterators

Iterator is a core concept in Rust, providing a powerful and expressive way to process sequences of data. They align closely with Rust's functional programming capabilities, enabling lazy evaluation, composability, and concise data manipulation. This section explores iterators, how to create and use them, and how to adapt and chain them for complex operations.

What are Iterators?

Iterators are objects that allow you to traverse a sequence of elements, such as items in a collection, one at a time. In Rust, iterators are implemented through the Iterator trait, which defines the fundamental method next. This method retrieves the next item in the sequence or returns None when the sequence is exhausted.

Using iterators in Rust offers several advantages:

- **Laziness**: Iterators perform operations only when needed, optimizing performance for large or infinite data sets.
- **Composability**: Iterators can be combined and transformed using a rich set of methods, enabling complex data operations with minimal code.
- **Expressiveness**: Method chaining and higher-order functions make iterator-based code concise and easy to read.

Creating and Using Iterators

Rust provides built-in support for creating iterators from collections, such as arrays, vectors, and slices. The Iterator trait defines how iterators behave, with the next method serving as the primary mechanism for retrieving elements.

Here is an example of creating an iterator and using next:

Ch11/Examples/bin/example12.rs

```
fn main() {
    let numbers = vec![1, 2, 3];
    let mut iter = numbers.iter();

    println!("{:?}", iter.next());
    println!("{:?}", iter.next());
    println!("{:?}", iter.next());
    println!("{:?}", iter.next());
}
```

In this example, the `iter` object is an iterator that goes through the elements of the vector numbers. The next method is called repeatedly to retrieve each element. Once all elements have been consumed, the iterator returns `None`, signaling that it is exhausted. The next method returns an Option, with each retrieved value wrapped in a `Some`. The iterator itself manages the logic for tracking which element to return next; this behavior is separate from the collection it iterates over.

When you look more closely, `iter` returns references to the underlying values of the collection, meaning the collection itself is not consumed and remains available for further use. Alternatively, you can use `into_iter`, which takes ownership of the collection, consuming it, and produces the values directly as owned elements.

Additionally, you can use `iter_mut` to obtain mutable references, allowing you to modify the values in the underlying collection directly through the iterator.

Consuming and Adapting Iterators

Iterators can be used with methods that process the entire sequence, such as `collect`, `sum`, `product`, and `for_each`. These are known as consuming methods because they take ownership of the iterator and fully exhaust it during their execution. Importantly, the collection being iterated over is not consumed, only the iterator is. This means the original collection remains available for use afterward.

Here is an example of consuming an Iterator (not the collection):

Ch11/Examples/bin/example13.rs

```
fn main() {
    let numbers = vec![1, 2, 3, 4, 5];

    let sum: i32 = numbers.iter().sum();
    println!("Sum: {}", sum);

    numbers.iter().for_each(|x| println!("Number: {}", x));
}
```

In this example, the iterator over numbers is consumed by both `sum` and `for_each`, with each method showcasing a different approach to processing or transforming the data. Since the iterator is fully consumed by `sum`, a new iterator must be created for `for_each` to perform its operation.

Here is an overview of the consuming functions available for an iterator:

Collectors

- `collect()`: Transforms the elements of the iterator into a collection, such as a Vec, HashMap, or String.

Aggregators

- `sum()`: Computes the sum of all elements in the iterator.
- `product()`: Computes the product of all elements in the iterator.
- `count()`: Counts the number of elements in the iterator.
- `max()`: Returns the maximum element as an Option.
- `min()`: Returns the minimum element as an Option.

Searching

- `find(predicate)`: Returns the first element that satisfies the given predicate as an Option.

- `position(predicate)`: Returns the index of the first element that satisfies the predicate as an Option.
- `rposition(predicate)`: For a DoubleEndedIterator, returns the index of the first element from the end that satisfies the predicate as an Option.

Logical Operations

- `all(predicate)`: Returns true if all elements satisfy the predicate; otherwise, returns false.
- `any(predicate)`: Returns true if any element satisfies the predicate; otherwise, returns false.

Element Access

- `nth(n)`: Returns the nth element as an Option, consuming all elements up to and including the nth.
- `last()`: Returns the last element as an Option after consuming the entire iterator.

Partitioning

- `partition(predicate)`: Divides elements into two collections: one containing elements that satisfy the predicate and another with the rest.

Miscellaneous

- `fold(init, func)`: Combines all elements into a single value using an initial value and a closure.
- `reduce(func)`: Combines elements into a single value using a closure, without an initial value.
- `for_each(func)`: Applies a closure to each element of the iterator, consuming it in the process.

Chaining Iterators

Rust's iterator adaptors allow method chaining, enabling the composition of complex operations in a concise and declarative manner. Adaptors like map, filter, and take transform or filter elements without consuming the iterator immediately, thanks to laziness.

Here's an example of chaining iterator adaptors:

Ch11/Examples/bin/example14.rs

```
fn main() {
```

```
    let numbers = vec![1, 2, 3, 4, 5];

    let result: Vec<_> = numbers
        .iter()
        .map(|x| x * x)
        .filter(|x| x % 2 == 0)
        .take(2)
        .collect();

    println!("Result: {:?}", result);
}
```

In this example, the iterator adapts the original vector step by step:

1. The map adaptor transforms each element by squaring it.
2. The filter adaptor retains only even squares.
3. The take adaptor limits the output to the first two results.
4. The collect method consumes the iterator, collecting the results into a vector.

This chaining process illustrates the expressiveness and power of Rust's iterator API. Here is an overview of the adapter functions available for an iterator:

Transformation

- **map(func)**: Applies a function to each element and returns an iterator of the results.
- **filter(predicate)**: Returns an iterator with only the elements that satisfy the given predicate.
- **filter_map(func)**: Applies a function that returns an Option<T> to each element and keeps only the Some values.
- **flat_map(func)**: Maps each element to an iterator and then flattens the results into a single iterator.
- **flatten()**: Flattens an iterator of iterators into a single iterator of elements.

Access and Modification

- **take(n)**: Creates an iterator that yields only the first n elements.
- **take_while(predicate)**: Yields elements as long as the predicate evaluates to true.
- **skip(n)**: Skips the first n elements and yields the rest.
- **skip_while(predicate)**: Skips elements while the predicate evaluates to true, then yields the remaining elements.
- **step_by(n)**: Advances the iterator by n steps after each element is yielded.

Combination

- **chain(other)**: Combines two iterators into one, yielding all elements of the first, followed by all elements of the second.
- **zip(other)**: Combines two iterators into a single iterator of pairs, stopping when either iterator is exhausted.

Enumeration and Inspection

- **enumerate()**: Yields pairs of the form (index, element), where index is the position of the element in the iterator.
- **inspect(func)**: Runs a closure on each element as it is yielded, useful for debugging or logging.

Reordering

- **rev()**: Reverses the direction of a DoubleEndedIterator, iterating from back to front.
- **cycle()**: Creates an iterator that repeats the original iterator indefinitely.

Slicing and Chunking

- **windows(size)**: Creates an iterator of overlapping slices with a specified size.
- **chunks(size)**: Produces non-overlapping chunks of elements as slices.

Stateful Behavior

- **peekable()**: Creates an iterator that allows you to peek at the next element without consuming it.
- **fuse()**: Ensures the iterator returns None forever after it is exhausted.
- **by_ref()**: Borrows the iterator, enabling it to be used without consuming ownership.

Value Copying and Cloning

- **cloned()**: Creates an iterator that clones each element of the original iterator.
- **copied()**: Creates an iterator that copies each element of the original iterator.

Insertion

- **intersperse(separator)**: Inserts the specified separator between consecutive elements in the iterator.

In the next section, we will explore some of these functions and provide examples to illustrate their use. If you are accustomed to a purely declarative programming style and have not worked with functional concepts before, this approach may take some practice to become familiar and fluent.

Common Functional Techniques

Rust's iterators provide a versatile API for applying functional programming techniques to sequences of data. Methods like `map`, `filter`, `fold`, and `flat_map` allow for transformations, filtering, aggregation, and flattening, enabling concise and expressive code. In this section, we'll look at a few common functional techniques without aiming to be exhaustive.

Map and Filter

The map method transforms elements in an iterator by applying a closure to each element, returning a new iterator with the transformed results. The filter method, on the other hand, selects elements from an iterator based on a predicate, returning only those that satisfy the condition. These two are arguably among the most commonly used adapter functions for iterators.

Here is an example of mapping and filtering elements:

Ch11/Examples/bin/example15.rs

```
fn main() {
    let numbers = vec![1, 2, 3, 4, 5];

    let squares: Vec<_> = numbers.iter().map(|x| x *
x).collect();
    println!("Squares: {:?}", squares);

    let evens: Vec<_> = numbers.iter().filter(|&&x| x % 2 ==
0).collect();
    println!("Evens: {:?}", evens);
}
```

In this example, map applies a transformation to each element to produce their squares, while filter removes elements that do not satisfy the predicate (being even). The expression |&&x| x % 2 == 0 appears inside a .filter() call on an iterator produced by numbers.iter(). The method .iter() creates an iterator over references, so each item the iterator yields is of type &i32. However, the filter method itself takes a reference to each item from the iterator, which means the closure actually receives a &&i32—a reference to a reference. To work with the underlying integer value directly, the closure uses pattern matching to destructure both layers of referencing. The &&x in the closure pattern unpacks the outer reference and then the inner one, resulting in x being of type i32 inside the closure body. This allows you to apply the modulo operation directly on x without having to write explicit dereferencing logic. So, the && is not an operator here, but part of a pattern match that destructures a reference to a reference in one step.

Reduce and Fold

Reduction and folding operations aggregate elements into a single value. The fold method accumulates a result by taking an initial value and applying a closure to combine each element with the accumulated value. The reduce method performs a similar task but uses the first element as the initial value.

Here is an example of using fold to sum and multiply elements:

Ch11/Examples/bin/example16.rs

```
fn main() {
    let numbers = vec![1, 2, 3, 4];

    let sum = numbers.iter().fold(0, |acc, &x| acc + x);
    println!("Sum: {}", sum);

    let product = numbers.into_iter().reduce(|acc, x| acc * x);
    println!("Product: {:?}", product);
}
```

In this example, a vector `numbers` is created with values `[1, 2, 3, 4]`. The `fold` method is used with `numbers.iter()` to compute the sum of the elements. `iter()` yields references, so the closure destructures `&x` into `x` to perform the addition, producing a sum of 10. However, this is not strictly necessary here, omitting the `&` still works due to `deref` coercion.

Next, `numbers.into_iter()` is used with reduce to compute the product. Unlike `fold`, `reduce` uses the first two elements as the initial accumulator. It multiplies the elements step by step, resulting in a product of 24.

Flatten and Flat_map

`flatten` and `flat_map` are powerful iterator combinators that simplify the process of handling nested collections and transforming data. `flatten` is used to collapse an iterator of iterators into a single flat iterator, effectively removing one level of nesting. On the other hand, `flat_map` combines mapping and flattening in a single step, allowing you to apply a transformation that returns an iterator and seamlessly flatten the results

Flatten

Flatten takes no parameters and is simple to use, as shown in the following example.

Ch11/Examples/bin/example17.rs

```
fn main() {
    let nested = vec![vec![1, 2], vec![3, 4], vec![5]];

    let grand_total = nested
        .into_iter()
        .flatten()
        .sum::<i32>();
    println!("Grand total: {}", grand_total);
}
```

This example uses flatten to simplify summing elements from a nested vector. The code defines nested as a vector of vectors of integers. By calling `into_iter()`, the vector is consumed, and flatten merges all inner vectors into a single iterator, removing one level of nesting. The `sum::<i32>()` method then calculates the total of the flattened integers, resulting in 15. The final value is printed as `Grand total: 15`.

Flat_map

flat_map is an iterator combinator in Rust that combines mapping and flattening in a single step. It applies a function to each element of an iterator, where the function returns another iterator, and then merges all the resulting iterators into one. This removes one level of nesting, creating a flat, continuous stream of items. `flat_map` is especially useful when transforming data structures that involve nested collections, as it simplifies complex operations by eliminating the need for manual loops and additional flattening steps. It provides a concise way to perform transformations while handling nested data efficiently.

The following example expands on the previous one by doubling each item before summing, performing both the mapping and flattening operations in a single step.

Ch11/Examples/bin/example18.rs

```
fn main() {
    let nested = vec![vec![1, 2], vec![3, 4], vec![5]];

    let grand_total = nested
        .into_iter()
        .flat_map(|inner| inner.into_iter().map(|x| x * 2))
```

```
        .sum::<i32>();
    println!("Grand total: {}", grand_total);
}
```

In this updated example, `flat_map` is applied to the nested vector. For each inner vector, `flat_map` first flattens it by iterating over its elements. During this process, each element is doubled using map(|x| x * 2). This effectively performs both the mapping and flattening in a single step. Finally, the sum method calculates the total of the doubled elements and prints the result. The item in the closure is a vector, and since the closure's return type must be an iterator, a map is used inside the `flat_map`. Alternatively, you can flatten first and then apply a regular map to achieve the same result. This approach is often simpler and easier to read, as shown below:

```
let grand_total = nested
        .into_iter()
        .flatten()
        .map(|x| x * 2)
        .sum::<i32>();
```

Filter_map

Imagine you need to read a line of text from standard input or a file that contains a mix of numbers and non-parsable words. Since the number of valid numbers is unknown, and some parts of the text may not be parsable, you want to compute the sum of the numbers. This can be done elegantly using functional programming, as demonstrated below.

Ch11/Examples/bin/example19.rs

```
use std::io;

fn main() {
    println!("Enter a list of numbers separated by spaces:");
    let mut input = String::new();
    io::stdin().read_line(&mut input).ok();

    let sum: i32 = input
        .split_whitespace()
        .filter_map(|s| s.parse::<i32>().ok())
        .sum();

    println!("The sum is: {}", sum);
}
```

The `.filter_map()` function is used to transform and filter the elements of this iterator. Inside `.filter_map()`, the closure `|s| s.parse::<i32>().ok()` attempts to parse each substring into an integer. The `.parse()` method returns a Result, and `.ok()` converts a successful parse into `Some(i32)` while discarding any parsing errors by returning `None`. This ensures that only valid integers are included in the output of the iterator, effectively filtering out any non-numeric input.

The iterator now contains only valid integers. Finally, the `.sum()` method consumes this iterator and computes the sum of all the integers. By chaining these methods, the program processes the input in a lazy and composable manner, without requiring intermediate storage or explicit loops. The result is then printed as the total sum.

Custom Iterators

Rust's iterator system is not limited to built-in collections. You can create your own iterators by implementing the Iterator trait for custom types. This allows you to encapsulate logic for iterating over any data structure, giving you the flexibility to integrate iterators seamlessly into your application. Additionally, Rust supports infinite iterators, which, when used with lazy evaluation, allow efficient processing of potentially unbounded sequences.

To create a custom iterator, you implement the Iterator trait for your type. The primary requirement of the Iterator trait is to define the next method, which specifies how to retrieve the next item in the sequence. Once implemented, the iterator gains access to all the iterator adaptors and consuming methods provided by Rust.

Let's look an example of building a custom iterator for a data structure:

Ch11/Examples/bin/example20.rs

```
struct Counter {
    current: usize,
    max: usize,
}

impl Counter {
    fn new(max: usize) -> Self {
        Counter { current: 0, max }
    }
}

impl Iterator for Counter {
    type Item = usize;
```

```
    fn next(&mut self) -> Option<Self::Item> {
        if self.current < self.max {
            let result = self.current;
            self.current += 1;
            Some(result)
        } else {
            None
        }
    }
}

fn main() {
    let counter = Counter::new(5);
    for value in counter {
        println!("{}", value);
    }
}
```

In this example, the Counter struct represents a range-like sequence from 0 to max - 1. By implementing the Iterator trait, the Counter becomes a custom iterator, and you can use it with Rust's for loop or any iterator adaptor.

Infinite Iterators and Laziness

Infinite iterators are iterators that never terminate when calling their next method. Rust's iterator system, with its support for laziness, ensures that infinite iterators can be used safely by applying limiting methods like take.

Concept of Laziness in Infinite Iterators: Infinite iterators do not generate all their elements at once. Instead, they produce values only as they are consumed. This makes infinite iterators efficient and safe when combined with methods that limit or process only a finite portion of the sequence.

Here is an example of creating and using an infinite iterator:

Ch11/Examples/bin/example21.rs

```
struct Fibonacci {
    a: usize,
    b: usize,
}

impl Fibonacci {
    fn new() -> Self {
        Fibonacci { a: 0, b: 1 }
    }
```

```
}

impl Iterator for Fibonacci {
    type Item = usize;

    fn next(&mut self) -> Option<Self::Item> {
        let next_value = self.a;
        self.a = self.b;
        self.b += next_value;
        Some(next_value)
    }
}

fn main() {
    let fib = Fibonacci::new();
    let first_ten: Vec<_> = fib.take(10).collect();
    println!("First 10 Fibonacci numbers: {:?}", first_ten);
}
```

In this example, the Fibonacci struct generates an infinite sequence of Fibonacci numbers. By implementing the Iterator trait, we define how each subsequent Fibonacci number is calculated. Using the take method, we limit the infinite sequence to the first 10 numbers, demonstrating how to safely work with infinite iterators.

Custom iterators in Rust allow you to define iteration logic for any data structure, integrating seamlessly with Rust's iterator ecosystem. By implementing the Iterator trait, you can create flexible and reusable iterators that take full advantage of Rust's expressive methods and adaptors. Infinite iterators, when combined with lazy evaluation and limiting methods like take, further extend the power of Rust's iterator system, enabling efficient handling of potentially unbounded sequences.

Functional Error Handling with Iterators

Rust's iterator API integrates seamlessly with its error-handling constructs, such as Option and Result. These constructs enable functional-style error handling, allowing errors and edge cases to propagate naturally through iterator chains. Additionally, iterators can short-circuit on specific conditions using methods like find and any, making error handling concise and expressive.

Using Option and Result with Iterators

In Rust, iterators can handle Option and Result values directly, simplifying functional error handling. By chaining methods like map, filter, and collect, errors or missing values can be managed elegantly without manual branching. This approach ensures that errors are handled in a type-safe and composable way.

Let's look at an example of processing data with result-based iterators:

Ch11/Examples/bin/example22.rs

```
fn parse_numbers(input: Vec<&str>) -> Result<Vec<i32>, String>
{
    input
        .into_iter()
        .map(|s| s.parse::<i32>().map_err(|_| format!("Failed
to parse '{}'", s)))
        .collect()
}

fn main() {
    let data = vec!["42", "93", "invalid", "17"];
    match parse_numbers(data) {
        Ok(numbers) => println!("Parsed numbers: {:?}",
numbers),
        Err(err) => println!("Error: {}", err),
    }
}
```

In this example:

- The `parse_numbers` function takes a vector of strings and attempts to parse them into integers.
- If a parsing error occurs, the error message is propagated using `map_err`.
- The collect method gathers the results, returning a single Result containing either all parsed numbers or the first encountered error.

This functional approach eliminates the need for explicit loops and manual error checks, streamlining the code.

Short-Circuiting Iterators

Rust's iterators support short-circuiting methods, such as find, any, and all, which terminate iteration early when a condition is met. These methods are particularly useful for searching or validating elements in a collection without processing the entire sequence.

Here's an example of finding an element in a collection with find:

Ch11/Examples/bin/example23.rs

```
fn main() {
    let words = vec!["apple", "banana", "cherry", "date"];

    if let Some(word) = words.iter().find(|&&w| w.len() > 5) {
        println!("Found: {}", word);
    } else {
        println!("No word found with more than 5 characters.");
    }
}
```

Here:

- The find method short-circuits the iterator as soon as it locates an element satisfying the predicate (w.len() > 5).
- If no element matches, the method returns None.

Example: Validating with any:

Ch11/Examples/bin/example24.rs

```
fn main() {
    let numbers = vec![1, 2, 3, 4, 5];

    if numbers.iter().any(|&n| n > 3) {
        println!("At least one number is greater than 3.");
    } else {
        println!("No number is greater than 3.");
    }
}
```

In this example, any checks whether at least one element satisfies the condition (n > 3). The iteration stops as soon as a match is found, demonstrating efficient validation with minimal processing.

Functional error handling with iterators leverages Rust's Option and Result types to process errors and missing values concisely within iterator chains. By using short-circuiting methods like find and any, iterators can terminate early when conditions are met, ensuring efficient and expressive code. These capabilities make Rust's iterator API a powerful tool for error handling and validation.

Performance Considerations

Rust's approach to functional programming emphasizes both safety and performance, often leveraging iterators as a key component. Iterators in Rust are designed to deliver high performance through the principle of zero-cost abstractions. However, understanding how to use iterators effectively and avoiding common pitfalls is essential for writing efficient code.

Iterator Performance and Zero-Cost Abstractions

Rust's zero-cost abstraction principle ensures that using iterators incurs no additional runtime cost compared to equivalent manual loops. Iterators are compiled into highly optimized machine code, eliminating unnecessary overhead while maintaining readability and composability.

To obtain accurate timing results, the program should be run in release mode. You can do this by adding the --release flag when running or building the program. For example:

```
cargo run --release --bin example25
```

Here is an example comparing the performance of iterators and traditional loops.

Ch11/Examples/bin/example25.rs

```
use std::time::Instant;
fn main() {
    let data: Vec<i128> = (1..=1_000_000).collect();

    let start_iter = Instant::now();
    let sum_iter: i128 = data.iter().map(|x| x * 2).sum();
    let duration_iter = start_iter.elapsed();
    println!("Iterator Sum: {} in {:?}", sum_iter,
duration_iter);

    let start_loop = Instant::now();
    let mut sum_loop = 0;
    for &x in &data {
        sum_loop += x * 2;
    }
    let duration_loop = start_loop.elapsed();
    println!("Loop Sum: {} in {:?}", sum_loop, duration_loop);
}
```

Here's an explanation of the above code:

- Both the iterator and the manual loop compute the same result: the sum of all elements doubled.
- The performance of iterators roughly matches that of the manual loop because the iterator chain is optimized during compilation, eliminating unnecessary allocations or intermediate steps.
- The choice between iterators and loops often comes down to readability and expressiveness rather than performance.

Avoid a Common Pitfall

While iterators are powerful and efficient, certain patterns can inadvertently degrade performance. Understanding these pitfalls ensures that you leverage iterators optimally.

Inefficient Use of collect: Using collect unnecessarily within an iterator chain can lead to intermediate allocations, reducing the efficiency of the chain.

As with the previous example, to obtain accurate timing results, you should run the program in release mode.

Example: Avoiding Unnecessary collect:

Ch11/Examples/bin/example26.rs

```
fn main() {
    let data: Vec<i128> = (1..=1_000_000).collect();

    let start_collect = std::time::Instant::now();
    let sum_evens = data
        .iter()
        .filter(|&&x| x % 2 == 0)
        .copied()
        .collect::<Vec<i128>>()
        .iter()
        .sum::<i128>();
    let duration_collect = start_collect.elapsed();
    println!(
        "Using collect: Sum of evens is {} in {:?}",
        sum_evens, duration_collect
    );

    let start_direct = std::time::Instant::now();
    let sum_evens_direct = data.iter().filter(|&&x| x % 2 ==
0).sum::<i128>();
    let duration_direct = start_direct.elapsed();
    println!(
```

```
        "Direct sum of evens: {} in {:?}",
        sum_evens_direct, duration_direct
    );
}
```

Let's look at the explanation:

- The first approach uses collect to create an intermediate vector of even numbers before summing them, incurring the cost of allocation and copying.
- The second approach processes the data directly within the iterator chain, avoiding unnecessary intermediate steps and achieving better performance.
- While this example may be somewhat contrived, it can sometimes be tempting to collect in the middle of an iteration chain. It's important to be aware of the performance cost and aim to avoid it when possible.

Rust's iterators exemplify zero-cost abstractions, providing a high-performance alternative to traditional loops with added composability and expressiveness. While iterators are designed for efficiency, avoiding common pitfalls such as unnecessary allocations ensures optimal performance. By understanding and leveraging iterators effectively, developers can write functional and high-performance code in Rust.

Summary

This chapter introduces FP, a paradigm focused on pure functions, immutability, and declarative expressions to build reliable and predictable code. Rust, primarily a systems programming language, incorporates FP principles, offering features like closures, iterators, and pattern matching. Key FP concepts include pure functions, which consistently produce the same output for given inputs without side effects; immutability, which prevents unintended state changes; and higher-order functions, which allow functions to be passed or returned for flexible and reusable code.

The chapter explores how Rust supports FP through closures, enabling anonymous functions to capture variables; the Fn family traits (Fn, FnMut, FnOnce), which abstract different levels of environment capturing; and iterators, which facilitate lazy and composable data processing. Techniques like chaining iterator adaptors (e.g., map, filter, and fold) allow for concise and expressive transformations. Rust's iterator API also integrates error handling with types like Option and Result to manage failures in a functional style. Additionally, creating custom iterators is discussed, showcasing how Rust's powerful iterator trait can be implemented for specific needs.

The chapter emphasizes performance, highlighting Rust's zero-cost abstractions that ensure iterators are as efficient as traditional loops. Common pitfalls, such as unnecessary intermediate allocations with collect, are addressed to guide optimal usage. Practical examples, exercises, and projects are provided to reinforce understanding and application of functional programming in Rust.

In the next chapter, we explore smart pointers, a key feature in Rust for efficient and safe memory management. Covering `Box<T>`, `Rc<T>`, and `RefCell<T>`, this chapter explains how they enable heap allocation, shared ownership, and interior mutability while preserving Rust's ownership and borrowing rules. Understanding smart pointers will help readers write more efficient and flexible Rust programs.

Exercises

1. Implement a function that accepts another function as a parameter to transform a list of integers (e.g., apply a square function). Demonstrate calling this higher-order function with different transformations.
2. Create a Rust program that initializes a vector and iterates over its elements using .iter(). Use .next() to manually retrieve each element until the iterator is exhausted.
3. Write a Rust program that takes a list of integers, filters out the odd numbers, squares the remaining numbers, and collects the results into a new vector. Use iterator methods like .filter(), .map(), and .collect().
4. Write a function that takes a list of integers and returns the sum of all even numbers. Use iterator methods like filter and sum to achieve this.
5. Implement a function that parses a vector of strings into integers using .map() and .collect(). Handle parsing errors using .map_err() to provide descriptive error messages for invalid inputs.
6. Given a string of words separated by spaces, return a HashMap<String, usize> representing the frequency of each word. Use iterator methods like split_whitespace and fold.
7. Create a custom iterator for a data structure, such as a struct representing a range of numbers. Implement the Iterator trait for this struct and demonstrate iterating over it using a for loop.

8. Write a Rust program that uses .find() on a vector of strings to locate the first string longer than 5 characters. Handle the case where no such string exists by returning a custom error message.

9. Given a vector of vectors of integers, filter out all odd numbers from each inner vector and return a single flattened vector of the remaining numbers. Use flat_map, filter, and collect.

10. Given a vector of strings representing rows of comma-separated values, write a function that parses the integers from each row while skipping invalid rows. Return a vector of vectors of integers. Use filter_map, split, and collect.

Project: Practicing functional style

This project takes a different approach compared to previous chapters. As a newcomer to functional programming, gaining hands-on experience with solving problems in a functional style is crucial. This project presents a series of problems designed to be tackled using functional programming principles. Focus on solving each problem first, then review how potential errors are handled, and refactor your solutions as needed to improve error management.

1. Given a `Vec` of integers, remove all negative numbers, add 1 to each remaining number, then collect the results into a new `Vec`. This will involve chaining operations like filter, map, and collect.

2. Starting from a paragraph of text, convert it to lowercase, remove punctuation, split it on whitespace, filter out any string of length 1, and then produce a sorted list of unique words. Achieving this will require chaining methods like `to_lowercase`, `split_whitespace`, `filter`, `map`, `collect`, followed by operations to deduplicate and sort.

3. Assume you have a list of floating-point sensor readings. First, filter out invalid readings (e.g., those below 0.0 or above 100.0), round them to the nearest integer, remove duplicates, and then compute their average. This will involve chaining filter, map, collect into a `HashSet` for deduplication, and a final aggregation using fold or sum and count.

4. Given a nested data structure, such as a vector of vectors of Option<i32>, first filter out None values, flatten the structure, remove all negative numbers, scale the remaining values by a factor, and finally produce a sorted vector of unique integers. This requires a careful sequence of operations: filter_map to extract

values, flat_map to flatten, filter to remove negatives, map to scale, collect to a vector, and then deduplicate and sort.

5. Given a list of tuples representing product names and their prices (in floating-point format), filter out products with prices below a threshold, round the remaining prices to the nearest integer, and return a list of product names sorted by their rounded prices in ascending order. This will involve chaining operations like filter, map, collect, and sort_by_key.

12

Smart Pointers

Smart pointers in Rust are a powerful abstraction that extend the capabilities of regular references by providing additional functionality for managing memory and resources. Unlike basic references, which offer a non-owning view of data, smart pointers own the data they point to, enabling more advanced control over allocation, deallocation, and resource sharing. This ownership model aligns seamlessly with Rust's core principles of safety and memory management, ensuring that smart pointers enforce strict rules at compile time, preventing common bugs such as memory leaks, data races, and dangling references.

At their core, smart pointers provide more than just the ability to point to memory. They incorporate features like reference counting, interior mutability, and heap allocation, which allow developers to handle complex scenarios involving shared data or dynamically sized objects. The most fundamental smart pointer, `Box<T>`, allows data to be stored on the heap, providing heap-allocated memory with exclusive ownership. More advanced smart pointers, such as `Rc<T>` (Reference Counting) and `Arc<T>` (Atomic Reference Counting), facilitate shared ownership, making it possible for multiple parts of a program to access the same data without violating Rust's strict borrowing rules. These smart pointers help manage lifetimes automatically by tracking the number of references to the data and deallocating it when no references remain.

Another key feature of smart pointers is their ability to enable interior mutability, a design pattern in which data can be modified even when the smart pointer is immutable. This is made possible by wrappers like `RefCell<T>` and `Mutex<T>`, which allow mutable access to the underlying data while preserving Rust's borrowing guarantees. Through runtime borrow checks, these types catch violations dynamically, providing greater flexibility without sacrificing safety.

In this chapter we will cover the following smart pointers from the standard library:

- **Box<T>**: A smart pointer for heap allocation. It provides exclusive ownership of the value and ensures that the data is dropped when the Box goes out of scope.
- **Rc<T> (Reference Counted)**: Enables multiple immutable owners of the same data by using reference counting. It is used for single-threaded scenarios.

- **Arc<T> (Atomic Reference Counted)**: A thread-safe version of Rc<T>, allowing shared ownership across multiple threads. It uses atomic operations to manage reference counts.
- **Weak<T>**: A non-owning reference to data managed by Rc<T> or Arc<T>. It prevents circular references by not contributing to the reference count.
- **RefCell<T>**:Allows for interior mutability, enabling mutable access to data even when the RefCell itself is immutable. Borrow rules are enforced at runtime rather than compile time.
- **Cell<T>**:Similar to RefCell, but it allows interior mutability through copying rather than borrowing. It provides a way to replace values without returning references.
- **Mutex<T>**: Provides mutual exclusion for safe access to data across multiple threads. Only one thread can access the data at a time, blocking others until the lock is released.
- **RwLock<T>**: A read-write lock that allows multiple readers or one writer at a time. It provides more granular control over concurrent access to data.

Together, these smart pointers form a flexible and robust toolkit that empowers developers to write expressive, concurrent, and memory-safe Rust programs without sacrificing control over how data is accessed, shared, or modified.

Introducing Smart Pointers

In Rust, a smart pointer is a data structure that not only acts as a pointer to manage access to memory but also includes additional capabilities like automatic memory management, reference counting, and ownership semantics. Unlike regular pointers, smart pointers in Rust provide safety guarantees and enable more expressive ownership patterns by integrating with the Rust ownership system.

Key Features of Smart Pointers

Rust's smart pointers are built on several key features that make them essential for memory safety and resource management in modern Rust programs:

- **Ownership and Automatic Memory Management**: Smart pointers in Rust enforce the ownership model by managing who "owns" a given piece of data and ensuring that resources are cleaned up when they are no longer needed. This ensures efficient memory usage and prevents issues like memory leaks.
- **Dereferencing**: One of the most important traits implemented by smart pointers is the Deref trait, which allows smart pointers to behave like regular references.

This enables the ability to access the data they point to in the same way you would with normal references, making the use of smart pointers seamless in most situations.

- **Custom Cleanup with Drop**: Another essential feature of smart pointers is their ability to implement the Drop trait. This trait allows custom cleanup logic to be executed when the smart pointer goes out of scope, ensuring that resources are released properly. For instance, `Box<T>` will automatically free the heap memory when it is no longer in use.
- **Enhanced Features**: Beyond basic pointer functionality, smart pointers include additional features like reference counting (`Rc`, `Arc`), mutability freedom (`Cell`, `RefCell`), or thread-safe access (`Mutex`, `RwLock`). Each smart pointer is specializing in one feature
- **Composable**: Smart pointers in Rust can be combined to handle advanced use cases, such as sharing mutable data across threads. For example, you can wrap a `Mutex<T>` inside an `Arc<T>` to achieve thread-safe shared mutability, or use `Rc<RefCell<T>>` to allow multiple owners with interior mutability in single-threaded scenarios. This composability enables developers to create robust and efficient solutions tailored to their specific concurrency and ownership requirements.

Smart Pointer Traits

There are three traits related to smart pointers in Rust: `Deref`, `DerefMut`, and `Drop`. Implementing the `Deref` trait is mandatory for a struct or enum to be considered a smart pointer, while `DerefMut` and `Drop` are optional.

Deref

The Deref trait in Rust is an essential component of the language's type system, enabling custom types to behave like references. It allows seamless access to an inner value by specifying how a reference to a type can be converted into a reference to another type. This trait is integral to making smart pointers, like `Box<T>` and `Rc<T>`, feel as natural to use as regular references while retaining their additional functionality.

At its core, the `Deref` trait defines how the dereference operator `*` interacts with a custom type. When the `*` operator is applied to a value, Rust calls the `deref` method of the `Deref` trait, which must be implemented for that type. The `deref` method provides a reference to the value the type is wrapping or managing. For instance, a smart pointer that owns a heap-allocated value can implement Deref to provide access to the inner value directly, making the smart pointer act as if it were a simple reference.

In addition to explicit dereferencing with `*`, the `Deref` trait is implicitly utilized in method calls and field accesses through a mechanism known as deref coercion. When a method is called on a type that implements `Deref`, and that method is not directly defined on the type, Rust will automatically dereference the type using the `deref` method until the method is found. This behavior allows a type like `Box<T>` to seamlessly call methods on the value it contains without requiring explicit dereferencing. For example, a `Box<String>` can invoke String's `len` method directly because Rust dereferences the box to access the inner string.

Implementing the `Deref` trait involves specifying a target type, which is the type to which the custom type dereferences. This is done through an associated type, Target. The trait requires the implementation of the `deref` method, which returns a reference to the inner value. For example, a custom smart pointer wrapping a String would implement `Deref` such that the `deref` method returns a reference to the `String`.

Consider a custom smart pointer called `MySmartPointer` that wraps a value of any type. By implementing the `Deref` trait, this smart pointer can provide direct access to the wrapped value. If the inner value is a String, calling the `len` method on an instance of `MySmartPointer` automatically works because of deref coercion. The implementation of Deref enables the `MySmartPointer` to act like a reference to the `String`.

Ch12/Examples/src/bin/example01.rs

```
use std::ops::Deref;

struct MySmartPointer<T> {
    data: T,
}

impl<T> MySmartPointer<T> {
    fn new(data: T) -> Self {
        MySmartPointer { data }
    }
}

impl<T> Deref for MySmartPointer<T> {
    type Target = T;

    fn deref(&self) -> &Self::Target {
```

```
        &self.data
    }
}

fn main() {
    let my_smart_pointer =
MySmartPointer::new(String::from("Hello, Rust!"));

    println!("Length: {}", my_smart_pointer.len());
    println!("Uppercase: {}", my_smart_pointer.to_uppercase());

    println!("Value: {}", *my_smart_pointer);
}
```

This example illustrates how a custom smart pointer, `MySmartPointer`, can implement the `Deref` trait to provide seamless access to its inner value. The `MySmartPointer` struct is a generic wrapper that encapsulates any type `T` within its data field. By implementing the `Deref` trait, this custom smart pointer allows its instances to behave like references to the contained value.

The implementation of the `Deref` trait specifies the associated Target type as `T`, meaning the smart pointer dereferences to the type it wraps. The `deref` method, defined within the implementation, returns a reference to the data field. This enables direct access to the encapsulated value when the dereference operator `*` is applied. Additionally, Rust's `deref` coercion automatically uses the `deref` method to enable method calls and field accesses on the wrapped value without requiring explicit dereferencing.

In the main function, an instance of `MySmartPointer` is created to wrap a String containing `"Hello, Rust!"`. This instance demonstrates several operations made possible by the `Deref` implementation. The `len` method of `String` is called on the `MySmartPointer` instance, and `deref` coercion ensures the method is resolved correctly. Similarly, the `to_uppercase` method, which converts the string to uppercase, is invoked directly on the smart pointer. The entire structure of the `MySmartPointer` instance is printed using the `Debug` trait, which was derived for the struct. Finally, the explicit use of the `*` operator dereferences the smart pointer to access and print the raw string it contains.

This example highlights the power of the `Deref` trait in allowing custom types to integrate seamlessly with Rust's syntax and standard library. By acting as a reference to its inner value, `MySmartPointer` provides a natural and intuitive interface while maintaining the flexibility to encapsulate additional behavior or logic.

DerefMut

Building on the understanding of the `Deref` trait, the `DerefMut` trait adds another layer of functionality by enabling mutable dereferencing. While Deref allows read-only access to the inner value of a custom type, `DerefMut` enables write access, letting you modify the inner value directly through the smart pointer. This trait is essential for custom types that need to support mutable access to their wrapped data, offering an interface similar to Rust's mutable references (`&mut T`).

At its core, `DerefMut` defines how the mutable dereference operator `*` interacts with a custom type in a mutable context. Just like Deref, the `DerefMut` trait must be implemented for the type, and its `deref_mut` method must return a mutable reference (`&mut`) to the inner value. When the `*` operator is applied in a mutable context, Rust invokes the `deref_mut` method, providing direct write access to the encapsulated data.

One of the most powerful features of `DerefMut` is its integration with Rust's coercion rules, known as mutable deref coercion. Similar to deref coercion with `Deref`, mutable deref coercion allows methods requiring a mutable reference (`&mut T`) to be called on types implementing `DerefMut`, even if those types are not actual references. This ensures a seamless user experience, as the smart pointer behaves like a mutable reference when needed.

To illustrate, consider a custom smart pointer called `MySmartPointer` that wraps a mutable value of any type. By implementing both `Deref` and `DerefMut`, this smart pointer can provide both read and write access to its inner value. When mutable deref coercion is applied, methods that require a `&mut` reference to the inner value can be called directly on the smart pointer without explicit dereferencing.

You can extend the previous example by implementing the `DerefMut` trait for `MySmartPointer` using the following code snippet.

```
impl<T> DerefMut for MySmartPointer<T> {
    fn deref_mut(&mut self) -> &mut Self::Target {
        &mut self.data
    }
}
```

While `DerefMut` enhances the flexibility of smart pointers, it also introduces additional responsibilities. Mutable access to the inner value must respect Rust's borrowing rules, ensuring that only one mutable reference exists at a time. Improper management of mutable references can lead to runtime errors or undefined behavior.

However, Rust's compile-time checks prevent most issues, ensuring safe and predictable behavior.

The combination of `Deref` and `DerefMut` allows custom types to fully integrate into Rust's reference model. Together, they provide an intuitive and powerful mechanism for creating smart pointers that behave like regular references while encapsulating additional logic, such as resource management or ownership semantics. With these traits, custom types can seamlessly support both read and write access, making them versatile tools for advanced Rust programming.

Drop

The `Drop` trait in Rust is a fundamental part of the language's memory management system, designed to provide custom cleanup logic when a value goes out of scope. It enables developers to define how resources, such as memory, files, or network connections, should be cleaned up or released when they are no longer needed. This trait is automatically invoked by Rust's ownership model, ensuring that resources are cleaned up predictably and safely.

At its core, the Drop trait allows you to specify a destructor for a type. A destructor is a special method called automatically when an instance of the type goes out of scope. In Rust, the destructor is the drop method, which you implement by defining the Drop trait for your type. This method provides a clean-up mechanism for releasing resources that cannot be managed by Rust's default memory handling, such as closing file handles or deallocating external resources.

How the Drop Trait Works

When a value goes out of scope in Rust, the `Drop` trait's drop method is automatically called. This process happens regardless of whether the value is part of a simple local variable, a field within a struct, or a member of a container like a vector. The drop method is executed in a deterministic order, starting with the most nested scopes and moving outward. For structs, Rust ensures that the fields of the struct are dropped in the order they are declared, following the custom drop logic if defined.

The drop method cannot be explicitly called. If you need to force a value to be dropped earlier than it would naturally, you can use the std::mem::drop function. This function explicitly deallocates the value and calls the destructor at that point, giving you more control over resource cleanup.

Implementing the Drop Trait

To implement the Drop trait, you define a drop method for your type. This method typically includes logic to release resources or perform other cleanup tasks. For example, if your type wraps a resource like a file handle, the drop method could ensure the file is properly closed when the wrapper goes out of scope.

Here is an example that demonstrates the use of the Drop trait:

Ch12/Examples/src/bin/example02.rs

```
struct Resource {
    name: String,
}

impl Drop for Resource {
    fn drop(&mut self) {
        println!("Cleaning up resource: {}", self.name);
    }
}

fn main() {
    let _res1 = Resource { name: String::from("File1") };
    let _res2 = Resource { name: String::from("Database
Connection") };
    println!("Resources created");
}
```

In this example, the Resource struct represents a generic resource that has a name field. When an instance of Resource goes out of scope, the drop method is automatically invoked, and the message indicating the cleanup of the resource is printed. When the program is run, the drop calls for res1 and res2 occur at the end of the main function, in reverse order of their creation.

Key Use Cases of Drop

The `Drop` trait serves several practical purposes, making it indispensable for managing resources effectively. Some common scenarios where implementing the `Drop` trait proves beneficial include:

- **Resource Management**: The `Drop` trait is essential for managing resources that are not automatically cleaned up by Rust's ownership model. Examples include closing file handles, freeing network sockets, and deallocating memory allocated through external libraries.
- **Custom Data Structures**: When implementing custom data structures like linked lists, trees, or graphs, the `Drop` trait ensures that all nodes or elements are properly deallocated, preventing memory leaks.

- **RAII Pattern**: The Drop trait enables the RAII (Resource Acquisition Is Initialization) pattern in Rust, where resource cleanup is tied to the lifetime of objects.

Limitations and Best Practices

The Drop trait comes with some limitations and requires careful use:

- **Deterministic Cleanup**: Rust ensures that destructors are run deterministically when values go out of scope. However, for cyclic references created with types like `Rc`, cleanup may require manual intervention using `Weak` references to prevent memory leaks.
- **No Explicit Calls**: The drop method cannot be called explicitly. Use `std::mem::drop` for immediate cleanup if necessary.
- **Panic Safety**: If a destructor panics during cleanup, it can cause a double panic if other destructors are running. Avoid panicking in drop methods.

By using the `Drop` trait effectively, Rust developers can create robust and efficient programs that manage resources predictably, ensuring safety and reliability even in complex scenarios.

Standard Library smart pointers

Box<T>

`Box<T>` is one of the simplest and most fundamental smart pointers in Rust. It provides a way to allocate data on the heap while maintaining ownership on the stack. This is particularly useful in Rust's memory management system, where data is usually allocated on the stack for performance reasons, but certain scenarios demand heap allocation, such as for recursive data structures or large objects.

Key Characteristics of Box<T>

- **Heap Allocation**: The primary purpose of `Box<T>` is to allocate data on the heap. This allows for dynamic memory allocation, which is essential when dealing with large or recursive data structures.
- **Dereferencing**: `Box<T>` implements the Deref trait, which allows you to access the value inside the `Box<T>` as if it were a regular reference. This means that you can dereference the Box<T> using the operator, just like with a reference (&T).
- **Automatic Memory Management**: When a `Box<T>` goes out of scope, Rust automatically deallocates the heap memory it points to. This is managed by the `Drop` trait, ensuring that memory leaks are avoided.

- **Immutable and Mutable Access**: You can have both immutable and mutable access to the value inside the `Box<T>`. By default, you can borrow the inner value immutably, but with `Box<T>` itself declared mutable, you can also borrow it mutably.

How Box<T> Works

When you create a `Box<T>`, Rust allocates memory on the heap for the value `T`, stores the value in that memory, and returns a `Box<T>` smart pointer that points to the memory.

Here's a simplified explanation of what happens: When Box::new(value) is called, the value is allocated on the heap. The `Box<T>` then manages a pointer to the heap memory where the value is stored, and this pointer itself is stored on the stack. To access the value stored on the heap, the Deref trait is used, enabling you to dereference the `Box<T>`.

Here is an example:

Ch12/Examples/src/bin/example03.rs

```
fn main() {
    let b = Box::new(5);
    println!("b = {}", b);
}
```

The variable `b` is stored on the stack and contains a pointer to the integer `5`. The integer `5` itself is stored on the heap. When `b` goes out of scope at the end of `main`, Rust will automatically call the `drop` function for `Box<T>`, which deallocates the heap memory used by the integer.

Use Cases of Box<T>

Recursive Data Structures

One of the most common use cases for `Box<T>` is managing recursive data structures like trees, linked lists, and graphs. Rust requires that the size of all types be known at compile time, but recursive data types do not have a fixed size. `Box<T>` allows us to circumvent this limitation by placing recursive elements on the heap.

Here's an example of using `Box<T>` to create a simple linked list:

Ch12/Examples/src/bin/example04.rs

```
enum List {
    Cons(i32, Box<List>),
    Nil,
}

use List::{Cons, Nil};

fn main() {
    let list = Cons(10, Box::new(Cons(20, Box::new(Cons(30,
Box::new(Nil))))));

    let second_payload = match list {
        Cons(_, next) => match next {
            Cons(payload, _) => payload,
            _ => 0,
        },
        _ => 0,
    };

    println!("the second payload is: {}", second_payload);
}
```

This code defines a linked list structure using a `Cons` variant to hold a value and a reference to the next element in the list, and a `Nil` variant to represent the end of the list. The term cons is derived from "construct" and refers to the operation of creating a new list node by combining a value with an existing list. Each time a new value is added to the list, a new `Cons` node is created that stores the value and points to the rest of the list. This way, the list is built by recursively chaining nodes together, with each node holding a value and a reference to the next. Inside the main function, a linked list is created with the values 10, 20, and 30. The program then extracts the value of the second element in the list using pattern matching.

The match statement first checks if the list is a `Cons` variant. If it is, the next element is extracted from the Box pointer using dereferencing. The next level of match checks if this extracted value is also a Cons variant. If so, the payload of the second element is assigned to the variable `second_payload`. If the list structure does not match this expected pattern at any stage, a default value of 0 is assigned to `second_payload`. Finally, the program prints the value of `second_payload`. This approach ensures safe traversal of the linked list structure without causing runtime errors.

Large Data on the Heap

When dealing with large data that would exceed the size of the stack, `Box<T>` allows you to allocate that data on the heap, where there is much more space. This prevents stack overflow errors in scenarios where you need to store large objects.

Here is an example of a large struct put on the heap:

Ch12/Examples/src/bin/example05.rs

```
struct LargeStruct {
    data: [u8; 1_000_000],
}

fn main() {
    let large = Box::new(LargeStruct {
        data: [0; 1_000_000],
    });

    println!("LargeStruct is on the heap, but the pointer is on
the stack.");
    println!("The struct contains {} elements", large.data.
len());
}
```

In this example, the large array of one million bytes is allocated on the heap using `Box<T>`, with only the pointer residing on the stack. This approach avoids problems associated with limited stack space. However, it is important to note that this example will only work correctly when run in release mode using `cargo run –release –bin example05`. In debug mode, the array is initially created on the stack before being moved to the heap, which can result in a stack overflow.

Dynamic Dispatch (Trait Objects)

`Box<T>` can be used for dynamic dispatch, which allows you to work with trait objects (types that implement a certain trait) at runtime. This is achieved by storing a trait object in a `Box<dyn Trait>`.

This example demonstrates the use of a trait object in combination with `Box<T>`:

Ch12/Examples/src/bin/example06.rs

```
trait Animal {
    fn speak(&self);
}
```

```
struct Dog;

impl Animal for Dog {
    fn speak(&self) {
        println!("Woof!");
    }
}

fn main() {
    let dog: Box<dyn Animal> = Box::new(Dog);
    dog.speak();
}
```

Here, `Box<dyn Animal>` allows for dynamic dispatch at runtime. The actual type (in this case, `Dog`) is determined at runtime, and the appropriate method (`speak`) is called.

Limitations of Box<T>

While `Box<T>` is very useful, it does have some limitations:

- **Single Ownership**: `Box<T>` only supports exclusive ownership of the data. If you need multiple owners, consider using `Rc<T>` or `Arc<T>`.
- **No Shared Mutability**: If you need shared mutable access, you'll need to combine `Box<T>` with other tools like `RefCell<T>`, `Mutex<T>`, or `RwLock<T>`.

This concludes the first smart pointer in the next section we are going to look at `Rc<T>`

Rc<T>

`Rc<T>` stands for a Reference Counting smart pointer in Rust. It is a smart pointer that enables shared ownership of a value in a single-threaded environment. Unlike `Box<T>`, which provides exclusive ownership, `Rc<T>` allows multiple parts of your program to access the same data by keeping track of how many owners exist. It achieves this by maintaining a reference count, ensuring that the data is only deallocated when the last reference to it goes out of scope.

Key Characteristics of Rc<T>

These are the key characteristics of a RC:

- **Shared Ownership**: Unlike `Box<T>`, which enforces single ownership, `Rc<T>` allows multiple parts of the program to share ownership of the same value.

- **Immutability**: By default, `Rc<T>` only allows shared, immutable access to the value it holds. If you need to mutate the data, you need to combine `Rc<T>` with interior mutability (e.g., using `RefCell<T>`).
- **Reference Counting**: Every time you clone an `Rc<T>`, the reference count increases. This allows multiple owners to coexist, and the value will only be dropped when the last owner goes out of scope.
- **Single-threaded Only**: `Rc<T>` is not thread-safe. It is designed for use in single-threaded environments where shared, immutable ownership is needed. For multi-threaded contexts, you would use `Arc<T>` (Atomic Reference Counting).

How Rc<T> Works

`Rc<T>` internally holds a pointer to the data on the heap, which is the value shared across multiple references. Additionally, it maintains a reference count, stored on the heap alongside the data, to track the number of `Rc<T>` instances pointing to the same value. Each time an `Rc<T>` is cloned, the reference count is incremented, and when an `Rc<T>` is dropped, the count is decremented. Once the count reaches zero, both the value and the reference count are deallocated.

Here is a simple example:

Ch12/Examples/src/bin/example07.rs

```
use std::rc::Rc;

fn main() {
    let rc1 = Rc::new(5);
    println!("Reference count: {}", Rc::strong_count(&rc1));

    let _rc2 = Rc::clone(&rc1);
    println!("Reference count: {}", Rc::strong_count(&rc1));

    {
        let _rc3 = Rc::clone(&rc1);
        println!("Reference count: {}",
Rc::strong_count(&rc1));
    }

    println!("Reference count after rc3 is out of scope: {}",
Rc::strong_count(&rc1));
}
```

This example demonstrates how the Rc (reference counting) smart pointer in Rust is used to manage shared ownership of data.

The program starts by creating a reference-counted smart pointer named rc1, wrapping the value 5, using Rc::new. At this point, rc1 is the sole owner of the value, so the reference count is 1. This count is printed using the Rc::strong_count function.

Next, the program creates another reference, _rc2, by cloning rc1 using Rc::clone. Instead of duplicating the data on the heap, this action increments the reference count to reflect that there are now two references to the same value. The updated reference count, now 2, is printed.

Then, within a nested scope, a third reference _rc3 is created by cloning rc1 again. This further increases the reference count to 3, indicating three active owners of the value. The reference count at this point is printed.

When the nested scope ends, _rc3 goes out of scope and is dropped. This decrements the reference count back to 2, as only rc1 and _rc2 remain. The program prints the updated reference count to show the effect of _rc3 being dropped.

Finally, the program ends, and both rc1 and _rc2 are dropped, reducing the reference count to 0. At this point, Rust automatically deallocates the shared value (5) and the reference count itself. This cleanup is managed implicitly by Rust's ownership and memory management system.

This example clearly illustrates how Rc allows multiple ownership of a value while keeping track of the references, ensuring the value is deallocated only when the last owner is dropped.

Cloning an Rc<T>

It's important to understand that cloning an Rc<T> does not duplicate the data on the heap. Instead, cloning creates another pointer to the same data and increments the reference count.

Cloning an Rc<T> is a lightweight operation since it only increments the reference count and creates another reference to the existing data. The actual value isn't duplicated.

Use Case for Rc<T>

Rc<T> is designed for shared ownership in a single-threaded context, enabling multiple parts of a program to safely own the same data. It is particularly useful in two key scenarios:

The primary use case for Rc<T> is when multiple parts of a program need to share ownership of immutable data. Instead of duplicating the data for each owner, Rc<T>

provides a way to reference the same data, ensuring memory efficiency while allowing read-only access to all owners. This is especially beneficial when working with immutable data structures shared across different components of a program.

Another common use case is recursive data structures, such as graphs or trees, where nodes may share ownership of other nodes. Rust's ownership system normally prevents multiple ownership of data, but Rc<T> overcomes this limitation by allowing safe, shared ownership of nodes. This is crucial in structures like cyclic graphs, where nodes can reference one another without causing ownership conflicts.

Limitations of Rc<T>

Despite its usefulness, Rc<T> has some important limitations:

- **Not thread-safe**. It cannot be used in multi-threaded contexts because its reference counting is not atomic. If multiple threads attempt to update the reference count simultaneously, it could lead to race conditions. For thread-safe shared ownership, Rust provides Arc<T> (Atomic Reference Counting), which is safe to share across threads.
- **No mutable access:** to its inner value. It only provides shared, immutable access. If you need to mutate the data while sharing ownership, you need to combine Rc<T> with a type that allows interior mutability, such as RefCell<T>.
- **No Cyclic References Prevention**: Rc<T> does not handle cyclic references, which can lead to memory leaks if two Rc<T> instances reference each other. In such cases, the reference count will never reach zero, preventing the memory from being deallocated.

To enable safe shared ownership across threads, Rust provides Arc<T>, a thread-safe alternative to Rc<T> that uses atomic reference counting, this is the focus of the next section.

Arc<T>

After understanding how Rc<T> works as a reference-counted smart pointer for single-threaded environments, we now turn to Arc<T>, which stands for Atomic Reference Counting. Arc<T> is designed to provide shared ownership of data in multi-threaded contexts. It is essentially the thread-safe counterpart of Rc<T> and allows for safe, concurrent access to shared data across multiple threads.

Just like `Rc<T>`, `Arc<T>` allows multiple owners to share ownership of the same data, but it uses atomic operations to manage the reference count, making it safe to use across threads.

Key Characteristics of Arc<T>

- **Thread-Safe Shared Ownership**: `Arc<T>` allows multiple threads to safely share ownership of a value without causing data races or invalid memory access. It uses atomic reference counting, which guarantees that the reference count is updated correctly even when accessed from different threads simultaneously.
- **Immutable Data**: Like `Rc<T>`, `Arc<T>` only allows immutable access to the data by default. If you need shared, mutable access to the data, you need to combine `Arc<T>` with types like `Mutex<T>` or `RwLock<T>`.
- **Atomic Reference Counting**: Each time an `Arc<T>` is cloned, the reference count is atomically incremented. When one clone is dropped, the count is atomically decremented. When the count reaches zero, the data is deallocated.
- **Cheap Cloning**: Cloning an `Arc<T>` is a lightweight operation since it only increments the atomic reference count. The underlying data itself is not duplicated.

How Arc<T> Works

Like `Rc<T>`, `Arc<T>` holds a pointer to the data on the heap, which is shared by all the references, and an atomic reference count, which is also stored on the heap and tracks how many `Arc<T>` instances are pointing to the same data. Every time you clone an `Arc<T>`, it increments the reference count using atomic operations. When an `Arc<T>` is dropped, the reference count is decremented atomically. Once the reference count reaches zero, the data and the reference count are both deallocated.

Here is an example using an `Arc<T>` to share data for reading across multiple threads:

Ch12/Examples/src/bin/example08.rs

```
use std::sync::Arc;
use std::thread;

fn main() {
    let shared_value = Arc::new(42);

    let clone1 = shared_value.clone();
    let clone2 = shared_value.clone();

    let handle1 = thread::spawn(move || {
        println!("Thread 1: {}", clone1);
```

```
    });

    let handle2 = thread::spawn(move || {
        println!("Thread 2: {}", clone2);
    });

    handle1.join().unwrap();
    handle2.join().unwrap();

    println!("Reference count after threads: {}",
Arc::strong_count(&shared_value));
}
```

In this example, an `Arc` is created to wrap a value, in this case, the integer `42`. Two clones of the `Arc` are made using shared_value.clone(), one for each thread. Each clone increases the reference count of the Arc, ensuring that the value remains valid as long as any thread holds a reference to it.

Next, two threads are spawned using `thread::spawn`. Each thread receives one of the cloned `Arc` instances, and they both print the value contained in the `Arc`. The move keyword ensures that the clones are moved into the closure executed by the threads.

After starting the threads, the join method is called on each thread handle to ensure that the main thread waits for both threads to finish executing. Finally, the program prints the reference count of the `Arc` after the threads complete, showing that all references are accounted for and demonstrating how `Arc` manages reference counting across threads.

Use Case for Arc<T>

The main use case for `Arc<T>` in Rust is to enable shared ownership of immutable data across multiple threads in a thread-safe manner. In concurrent programming, it is common to have data that needs to be read by multiple threads without duplication, and `Arc<T>` facilitates this by wrapping the data and managing its lifetime through atomic reference counting. Each thread can clone the `Arc<T>` to obtain its own reference, and the internal atomic counter ensures that the memory is deallocated only when all references are dropped. This makes `Arc<T>` particularly useful in scenarios such as parallel processing, where immutable data needs to be shared between worker threads, or in multi-threaded server applications, where configuration data or state must be accessible concurrently.

Limitations of Arc<T>

- **Immutable Sharing Only**: `Arc<T>` allows multiple threads to share a single value, but the shared value itself is immutable. To modify the shared data, you need additional synchronization mechanisms like `Mutex` or `RwLock`, which can add complexity and overhead.
- **Reference Count Overhead**: Every clone of an `Arc<T>` increases the reference count, and each drop decreases it. This involves atomic operations, which can be slower than non-atomic operations, especially in scenarios with frequent cloning and dropping.
- **Single Ownership of Mutability**: `Arc<T>` does not allow mutable access to its content. If you need mutable access across threads, you must use `Arc<Mutex<T>>` or similar wrappers, which can introduce runtime locking and potential contention issues.
- **No Cyclic References Prevention**: `Arc<T>` does not handle cyclic references, which can lead to memory leaks if two `Arc<T>` instances reference each other. In such cases, the reference count will never reach zero, preventing the memory from being deallocated.
- **Performance Impact**: The atomic operations required to manage reference counting can have a performance impact, particularly in scenarios with high contention or frequent operations on the `Arc`.

Next, we'll look at Weak<T>, which helps prevent memory leaks caused by cyclic references.

Weak<T>

After learning about `Rc<T>` and `Arc<T>` and how they provide shared ownership of data using reference counting, we now turn to `Weak<T>`, a specialized form of reference that is closely related to both `Rc<T>` and `Arc<T>`. `Weak<T>` helps address a key limitation of reference-counted smart pointers: reference cycles.

When multiple `Rc<T>` or `Arc<T>` pointers refer to each other in a cycle, they can create a memory leak because the reference count of each pointer will never drop to zero, preventing the data from being deallocated. `Weak<T>` solves this problem by allowing non-owning references to data managed by `Rc<T>` or `Arc<T>`. These non-owning references don't increment the reference count, breaking the cycle and allowing the data to be cleaned up when all owning references are dropped.

Key Characteristics of Weak<T>

- **Non-Owning Reference**: Weak<T> references do not increment the reference count of the data, which means that they do not participate in the ownership model. As a result, Weak<T> references cannot keep the data alive on their own.
- **Preventing Memory Leaks**: By using Weak<T>, you can prevent cyclic reference problems that would otherwise lead to memory leaks. Since Weak<T> does not affect the reference count, it does not create a cycle, allowing memory to be freed when the last strong (Rc<T> or Arc<T>) reference is dropped.
- **Upgrading to Rc<T> or Arc<T>**: Before accessing the data, you need to "upgrade" the Weak<T> pointer to a strong reference (Rc<T> or Arc<T>). This upgrade ensures that the data is still valid (i.e., it hasn't been deallocated yet). If the data is still alive, the upgrade succeeds; otherwise, it returns None.

How Weak<T> Works

In Rust, Weak<T> maintains a weak reference count alongside the strong reference count managed by Rc<T> and Arc<T>. The weak reference count tracks how many Weak<T> pointers exist but does not contribute to keeping the actual data alive. Once the strong reference count drops to zero, the data is deallocated, even if weak references still exist. However, the allocation that holds the control block, containing both reference counts and other internal metadata, remains alive as long as any Weak<T> pointers exist. This allows operations like Weak::upgrade() to safely determine whether the data is still available without risking a dangling pointer.

Accessing the data inside a Weak<T> cannot be done directly. Instead, you must "upgrade" the Weak<T> to a strong reference (Rc<T> or Arc<T>) using the upgrade() method. The upgrade succeeds if the strong reference count is greater than zero, meaning the data is still alive. If the data has been deallocated, the method will return None.

Here's an example for clarification:

Ch12/Examples/src/bin/example09.rs

```
use std::rc::{Rc, Weak};

fn main() {
    let strong_rc = Rc::new(5);
    let weak_rc: Weak<i32> = Rc::downgrade(&strong_rc);
    println!("Strong count: {}", Rc::strong_count(&strong_rc));
    println!("Weak count: {}", Rc::weak_count(&strong_rc));
```

```
    if let Some(upgraded) = weak_rc.upgrade() {
        println!("Upgraded value: {}", upgraded);
    } else {
        println!("Value has been dropped");
    }

    drop(strong_rc);

    if let Some(upgraded) = weak_rc.upgrade() {
        println!("Upgraded value: {}", upgraded);
    } else {
        println!("Value has been dropped");
    }
}
```

This example demonstrates the interaction between `Rc` and `Weak` in Rust. First, a strong reference is created using `Rc::new` to wrap the value `5`. A `Weak<i32>` pointer is then created from the strong reference using `Rc::downgrade`. The program displays the initial strong and weak reference counts associated with the `Rc` value, showing that the Weak pointer is tracked independently.

The Weak pointer is then "upgraded" to a strong reference using the upgrade method. If the data is still valid (i.e., at least one strong reference exists), upgrade returns an `Option` containing a new `Rc` instance. The value wrapped by the `Rc` is printed in this case.

The strong reference (strong_rc) is then explicitly dropped using drop. This action reduces the strong reference count to zero and deallocates the data. After the drop, the program attempts to upgrade the Weak pointer again. Since the data is no longer valid, upgrade returns `None`, and the program prints a message indicating that the value has been dropped.

This example highlights how Weak pointers allow non-owning references that do not prevent the underlying data from being deallocated when all strong references are dropped. It also demonstrates the need to check the result of upgrade to determine whether the data is still valid.

Use Case for Weak<T>

The most common use case for `Weak<T>` is in cyclic data structures, where two or more nodes refer to each other. If all references are strong (`Rc<T>` or `Arc<T>`), the reference count will never drop to zero, creating a reference cycle and a memory leak. Using `Weak<T>` for non-essential, non-owning references breaks this cycle, allowing the memory to be freed when appropriate.

Limitations of Weak<T>

Here are the limitations of `Weak<T>` in Rust:

- **No guarantee of valid data**: A `Weak<T>` reference does not keep the data alive. If all owning references (`Rc<T>` or `Arc<T>`) are dropped, the value is deallocated, and the `Weak<T>` reference becomes invalid. Upgrading a `Weak<T>` to a strong reference may fail, returning None if the value no longer exists.
- **Cannot directly access data**: Unlike `Rc<T>` or `Arc<T>`, a `Weak<T>` reference cannot be dereferenced directly. You must first upgrade it to a strong reference using the upgrade method, adding an extra step and potential failure point.
- **Limited use cases**: `Weak<T>` is primarily designed to prevent reference cycles in data structures like graphs or trees. Outside these scenarios, its utility is limited compared to strong references.
- **No borrow checking guarantees**: `Weak<T>` does not integrate with Rust's compile-time borrow checker. Instead, it relies on runtime checks to ensure the reference is valid, which is less safe than standard borrowing mechanisms.
- **Increased complexity**: Code that uses `Weak<T>` requires additional logic to handle cases where the value has been deallocated, complicating implementation.
- **Slight runtime overhead**: Managing `Weak<T>` references adds runtime overhead, such as atomic operations for `Arc<T>` or internal bookkeeping for `Rc<T>`.

After exploring shared ownership, we now shift our focus to interior mutability with `Cell<T>`.

Cell<T>

`Cell<T>` is a smart pointer in Rust that provides interior mutability, allowing you to modify the value stored inside a struct even when the struct itself is not mutable. This concept is particularly useful when you need to mutate data while maintaining immutability on the outside. `Cell<T>` is one of Rust's mechanisms to achieve interior mutability alongside `RefCell<T>`, though they work differently and serve different purposes.

The key difference between `Cell<T>` and `RefCell<T>` is that `Cell<T>` works by value-based access (copying the value in and out of the cell), whereas `RefCell<T>` provides reference-based borrowing with runtime checks. `Cell<T>` is particularly useful for types that implement the `Copy` trait, making it ideal for handling primitive types like integers, booleans, and other small, copyable data.

Key Characteristics of Cell<T>

- **Copy Semantics**: If the type T implements the Copy trait (e.g., integers, booleans, or small data structures), Cell<T> allows you to get and set the value inside the Cell without needing mutable references. This is useful for primitive types and types that can be easily duplicated.
- **No Borrowing**: Unlike RefCell<T>, Cell<T> doesn't provide any borrowing mechanism. You can't get a reference to the value inside the cell, but instead, you copy or replace the value.
- **Interior Mutability**: The primary feature of Cell<T> is its ability to enable interior mutability. This allows you to mutate the data inside even when the Cell is part of an immutable structure.

How Cell<T> Works

Cell<T> works by storing a value directly without exposing references to the value it contains. This design ensures that the borrowing rules of Rust are bypassed in a controlled manner, allowing interior mutability. Instead of allowing direct reference-based access, Cell<T> provides methods like get and set to interact with the stored value.

The get() method allows you to copy the value stored inside the Cell<T>, but this only works for types that implement the Copy trait. By copying the value rather than borrowing it, Cell<T> avoids the need for mutable references.

The set(value) method enables you to replace the existing value inside the Cell<T> with a new one. This process involves moving the new value into the cell, which overwrites the previous value without requiring mutable references to the cell itself.

This functionality makes Cell<T> particularly useful for scenarios where you need to update values in a way that circumvents Rust's borrowing restrictions, while still maintaining safety guarantees.

Here's a simple example to demonstrate how Cell<T> works:

Ch12/Examples/src/bin/example10.rs

```
use std::cell::Cell;

fn main() {
    let cell = Cell::new(5);
    println!("Initial value: {}", cell.get());
```

```
    cell.set(10);
    println!("Updated value: {}", cell.get());
}
```

This example demonstrates the use of `Cell<T>` to enable interior mutability in Rust. The `Cell<T>` is created with an initial value of `5` using the `Cell::new` method. Unlike regular variables, `Cell<T>` allows you to mutate its contents even if the Cell itself is not declared as mutable.

The initial value stored in the cell is accessed using the get method, which retrieves a copy of the value since Cell does not expose references to the internal data. The program then uses the set method to update the value stored in the cell to `10`. This action replaces the old value with the new one, demonstrating how Cell enables controlled mutability.

Finally, the updated value is retrieved again using the get method, and the new value is printed. This example highlights how `Cell<T>` allows safe mutation of the internal value without requiring mutable references to the Cell itself, which is particularly useful in scenarios where the borrowing rules of Rust would otherwise prevent such mutations.

Use Case for Cell<T>

Rust enforces that you cannot mutate data through an immutable reference. However, sometimes you need to mutate internal state while maintaining the outward immutability of a struct. This is where `Cell<T>` helps. An intriguing example is a struct where the majority of its fields remain immutable, but a single field is mutable, allowing you the flexibility to manage both immutable and mutable data within the same struct.

As sown in the following example:

Ch12/Examples/src/bin/example11.rs

```
use std::cell::Cell;

struct Point {
    x: Cell<i32>,
    y: i32,
}

fn main() {
    let point = Point {
        x: Cell::new(10),
        y: 20,
```

```
    };

    point.x.set(15);
    println!("Updated x: {}", point.x.get());
    println!("y: {}", point.y);
}
```

In this example, the `Point` struct is immutable, but because `x` is wrapped in a `Cell`, we can mutate it without needing a mutable reference to the entire struct. It's not possible to mutate `y`.

Limitations of Cell<T>

Here are the limitations of Cell<T> in Rust:

- **Limited to Copy Types**: `Cell<T>` can only work with types that implement the `Copy` trait, as it relies on copying values in and out of the cell. This excludes complex types like `Vec` or custom structs without the `Copy` trait.
- **No References to Inner Data**: `Cell<T>` does not allow references to the value it holds. You can only interact with the data through methods like get (to copy the value) or set (to replace it).
- **Not Thread-Safe**: `Cell<T>` is not Sync, which means it cannot be safely shared between threads. For thread-safe interior mutability, `Mutex<T>` or `RwLock<T>` should be used instead.
- **Limited Mutability**: While `Cell<T>` allows value mutation, it does not support borrowing or mutating complex inner structures. For example, you cannot partially modify a field in a struct stored inside a Cell.
- **No Borrowing Rules Enforcement**: Since `Cell<T>` bypasses Rust's usual borrowing rules, it requires careful usage to avoid logical bugs, as it does not provide the compile-time guarantees of typical borrowing.

These limitations make `Cell<T>` best suited for specific use cases involving simple, copyable types.

RefCell<T>

After discussing how `Cell<T>` enables interior mutability for types that implement the `Copy` trait, allowing value-based access to mutate data, we now turn to `RefCell<T>`, a more flexible tool for interior mutability. Unlike `Cell<T>`, which works best with small, copyable types, `RefCell<T>` allows for mutable borrowing of non-`Copy` types at runtime. This makes it an essential tool when you need to mutate data through immutable references, particularly with more complex or heap-allocated types.

`RefCell<T>` is a crucial part of Rust's interior mutability pattern and enables mutation of data while still respecting Rust's borrowing rules, but with checks enforced at runtime rather than compile-time.

Key Characteristics of RefCell<T>

- `Reference-Based Mutation`: Unlike `Cell<T>`, which relies on value-based access, `RefCell<T>` allows for true borrowing of references, both immutable and mutable.
- `Runtime Borrow Checking`: While regular references in Rust are checked at compile-time, `RefCell<T>` checks borrowing rules at runtime. This allows more flexibility but adds runtime overhead.
- `Non-Copy Types`: `RefCell<T>` is particularly useful when dealing with non-Copy types (e.g., `String`, `Vec`, or user-defined structs), where you need to mutate the data but still ensure safety through Rust's borrowing rules.

How RefCell<T> Works

`RefCell<T>` operates by tracking the borrow state using an internal counter. This counter monitors how many immutable references (`&T`) and mutable references (`&mut T`) are currently active. The borrowing rules enforced by `RefCell<T>` allow multiple immutable borrows through the `borrow()` method, but only one mutable borrow is permitted at a time using the `borrow_mut()` method. A mutable borrow cannot coexist with any active immutable borrows. If these rules are violated at runtime, such as attempting to create a mutable borrow while immutable borrows are still active, the program will panic. This ensures interior mutability is safe while providing flexibility for runtime borrowing.

Here's an example of basic usage of `RefCell<T>`:

Ch12/Examples/src/bin/example12.rs

```
use std::cell::RefCell;

fn main() {
    let data = RefCell::new(5);

    {
        let value = data.borrow();
        println!("Immutable borrow: {}", value);
    }
```

```
    {
        let mut value_mut = data.borrow_mut();
        value_mut += 10;
    }

    println!("New value after mutation: {}", data.borrow());
}
```

This example demonstrates how `RefCell<T>` enables interior mutability by enforcing borrowing rules at runtime. A RefCell is created to wrap the value `5`, allowing mutable and immutable borrows of the contained value, even when the RefCell itself is not mutable.

The program begins by creating an immutable borrow using the borrow method. This immutable borrow retrieves the value stored inside the RefCell, and the value is printed. Since this borrow is enclosed in its own block, it goes out of scope at the end of the block, and the borrow is dropped.

Next, a mutable borrow is created using the `borrow_mut` method, which allows modification of the value inside the RefCell. The mutable borrow is used to increment the value by `10`. This mutable borrow is also enclosed in its own block, ensuring it is dropped as soon as the block ends.

Finally, a new immutable borrow is created using borrow to retrieve and print the updated value. At this point, there are no active borrows, so the program executes without runtime errors.

This example highlights how RefCell dynamically enforces Rust's borrowing rules, ensuring safe access to mutable and immutable borrows at runtime while still allowing interior mutability. The use of explicit scoping ensures that the borrowing rules are adhered to, preventing conflicts between immutable and mutable borrows. The output of the program demonstrates the successful mutation and retrieval of the value.

Note that in this case, the scope of the variable determines overlapping borrows, rather than the lifetime of the reference, which is defined as the period from its creation to its last use.

Use Cases for RefCell<T>

`RefCell<T>` is particularly useful in situations where mutable access to data is required within an otherwise immutable data structure. It enables interior mutability by allowing modifications to fields that are part of immutable objects. This is especially valuable when working with non-Copy types, where value-based access, as in

`Cell<T>`, is not feasible. Additionally, `RefCell<T>` ensures that borrow checking is performed dynamically at runtime rather than at compile time, providing flexibility in scenarios where compile-time rules would otherwise impose limitations.

For example, in a situation where you need to mutate a field within an immutable struct, `RefCell<T>` allows this behavior by wrapping the field and dynamically managing its borrow state. This makes it ideal for cases where internal mutability is necessary while maintaining the overall immutability of the structure. By adhering to runtime borrowing rules, `RefCell<T>` prevents simultaneous mutable and immutable borrows, ensuring safe access even in complex use cases.

Ch12/Examples/src/bin/example13.rs

```
use std::cell::RefCell;

struct Logger {
    messages: RefCell<Vec<String>>,
}

impl Logger {
    fn log(&self, message: String) {
        self.messages.borrow_mut().push(message);
    }

    fn show_logs(&self) {
        for msg in self.messages.borrow().iter() {
            println!("{}", msg);
        }
    }
}

fn main() {
    let logger = Logger {
        messages: RefCell::new(Vec::new()),
    };

    logger.log("First message".to_string());
    logger.log("Second message".to_string());

    logger.show_logs();
}
```

This example demonstrates an immutable struct that holds a `RefCell<Vec<String>>`, allowing internal mutability through an immutable reference to the struct.

Limitations of RefCell<T>

Here are some limitations of a `RefCell<T>` in Rust:

- **Runtime Borrow Checking**: Unlike regular references, which enforce borrowing rules at compile time, `RefCell<T>` performs borrow checking at runtime. Violations, such as simultaneous mutable and immutable borrows, result in a runtime panic rather than a compile-time error.
- **Single-threaded Use**: `RefCell<T>` is not thread-safe and cannot be shared between threads. For thread-safe interior mutability, you need to use synchronization primitives like `Mutex<T>` or `RwLock<T>`.
- **Increased Complexity**: Using `RefCell<T>` adds complexity to your code because it introduces runtime checks and requires careful management of borrows to avoid panics.
- **Performance Overhead**: Each borrow involves incrementing or decrementing an internal counter to track borrowing state, which incurs slight runtime overhead compared to regular references.

These limitations make `RefCell<T>` powerful but best suited for specific scenarios where compile-time borrow checking is too restrictive, and interior mutability is essential.

Finally, we'll cover the two smart pointers in the standard library that provide locking mechanisms for safe concurrent access.

Mutex<T>

In Rust, `Mutex<T>` is a synchronization primitive used to provide mutual exclusion for shared, mutable data in a multi-threaded environment. It allows only one thread to access the data inside the Mutex at a time, preventing data races by ensuring safe, serialized access to shared resources.

When working in multi-threaded environments, race conditions can occur if multiple threads attempt to modify shared data simultaneously. `Mutex<T>` helps avoid these race conditions by allowing a single thread to "lock" the data, ensuring exclusive access. Once the thread finishes its operation, the lock is released so that other threads can access the data.

Key Characteristics of Mutex<T>

Here are some limitations of a Mutex`<T>` in Rust:

- **Exclusive Access**: Only one thread can hold the lock on the data at a time. Other threads must wait until the lock is released.

- **Locking and Unlocking**: When a thread locks a Mutex<T>, it gains exclusive access to the data. The lock is automatically released when the guard (a special object representing the lock) goes out of scope.
- **Thread-Safe Interior Mutability**: Mutex<T> allows mutation of data across multiple threads by providing a safe, controlled way to access the data. Even if the Mutex itself is immutable, you can mutate the data inside it once a lock is acquired.
- **Automatic Lock Release**: Rust ensures that the lock for a Mutex<T> is automatically released when the guard goes out of scope. This design guarantees that the lock is properly released without requiring explicit actions from the programmer, preventing potential issues from forgetting to release the lock.

How Mutex<T> Works

`Mutex<T>` works by wrapping a value of type `T` and managing access to it through a locking mechanism. To access the value inside the `Mutex<T>`, a thread must acquire a lock using the lock() method. This method returns a guard object, which represents ownership of the lock. The guard acts as a proxy to the data, allowing the thread holding it to access and modify the value. The lock is automatically released when the guard is dropped, typically when it goes out of scope. If another thread attempts to acquire the lock while it is already held, the second thread will block and wait until the lock is released.

Here's a simple example demonstrating the use of `Mutex<T>`:

Ch12/Examples/src/bin/example14.rs

```
use std::sync::Mutex;

fn main() {
    let m = Mutex::new(17);
    {
        let mut num = m.lock().unwrap();
        num += 1;
    }

    println!("Updated value: {:?}", m.lock().unwrap());
}
```

This example demonstrates the use of a `Mutex<T>` to safely manage mutable access to a shared value in Rust. First, a Mutex is created using `Mutex::new`, which wraps the initial value `17`. This Mutex ensures that access to the value is controlled through locking.

Within a block, the program locks the Mutex using the lock() method, which provides access to the inner value through a MutexGuard. The `unwrap()` method is called to handle any potential errors that might occur if the lock is poisoned (for example, if another thread panics while holding the lock). The returned MutexGuard allows mutable access to the value inside the Mutex. The program modifies the value by dereferencing the guard and incrementing it by `1`.

When the block ends, the MutexGuard goes out of scope, and the lock on the Mutex is automatically released. This ensures that other threads, or subsequent operations in the current thread, can access the Mutex.

Finally, the program locks the Mutex again to retrieve the updated value. The `println!` macro is used to print the value, which now reflects the increment operation, showing `18`. This demonstrates how the Mutex effectively manages safe access to mutable shared data, ensuring correctness even in concurrent scenarios.

Use Case for Mutex<T>

`Mutex<T>` is typically used in scenarios where multiple threads need to mutate shared data safely. It is particularly useful for protecting shared resources such as counters, configuration data, or caches in concurrent applications. For example, when multiple threads increment a shared counter, a `Mutex<T>` ensures that only one thread can modify the counter at a time, preventing race conditions. Similarly, when maintaining a shared cache that can be updated or read by multiple threads, `Mutex<T>` allows exclusive access during updates while still enabling safe concurrent use. By providing thread-safe interior mutability, `Mutex<T>` makes it possible to share ownership of mutable data across threads while adhering to Rust's safety guarantees.

Limitations of Mutex<T>

Here are some limitations of a `Mutex<T>` in Rust:

- **Lock Contention**: Performance can decrease when multiple threads compete for access to the same Mutex.
- **Synchronization Overhead**: Acquiring and releasing a lock introduces additional runtime cost compared to non-synchronized access.
- **Deadlocks**: Deadlocks may occur if multiple Mutexes are locked in an inconsistent order across threads.
- **Poisoning**: If a thread panics while holding a Mutex, the lock becomes "poisoned," requiring extra logic to handle recovery.

- **Granularity**: The entire wrapped data is locked, even if only a portion needs modification, leading to inefficiencies with large structures.
- **Fairness**: High-contention scenarios lack fairness guarantees, potentially leading to starvation for some threads.

RwLock<T>

After learning about `Mutex<T>`, which ensures mutual exclusion by allowing only one thread to access data at a time, we now turn to `RwLock<T>` (short for Read-Write Lock). While `Mutex<T>` allows only exclusive access for one thread, `RwLock<T>` allows multiple readers or one writer at any given time, making it more flexible in scenarios where read-heavy operations are frequent but write operations are less common.

`RwLock<T>` is ideal when you need to allow multiple readers to access shared data concurrently while ensuring that only one writer can modify the data at a time. It is often used in performance-sensitive applications where data is read more frequently than it is modified.

Key Characteristics of RwLock<T>

Here are the characteristics of a `RwLock<T>` in Rust:

- **Multiple Readers, One Writer**: `RwLock<T>` allows for concurrent reading by multiple threads and ensures exclusive access for writing by one thread at a time.
- **Interior Mutability**: Like `Mutex<T>`, `RwLock<T>` follows the interior mutability pattern, allowing you to mutate shared data even when the `RwLock<T>` itself is immutable. However, it ensures that only one writer can modify the data at a time, while multiple readers can access it concurrently.
- **Blocking and Waiting**: When a thread requests a write lock while readers are holding read locks, the write lock request will block until all read locks are released. Similarly, if a write lock is held, any request for read or write access will block until the writer releases the lock.
- **Automatic Lock Release**: Rust ensures that the lock for a `RwLock<T>` is automatically released when the guard goes out of scope. This design guarantees that the lock is properly released without requiring explicit actions from the programmer, preventing potential issues from forgetting to release the lock.

How RwLock<T> Works

`RwLock<T>` manages two types of locks: a read lock and a write lock. The read lock, accessed through the `read()` method, acquires a shared lock, allowing multiple threads to read the data at the same time. The write lock, accessed through the `write()` method, acquires an exclusive lock, permitting only one thread to modify the data while preventing any other access. When a read lock is requested while other threads are already reading, it is granted immediately. However, if a write lock is requested while read locks are active, it will block until all readers have released their locks. Similarly, when a read lock is requested while a write lock is held, it must wait until the writer releases the lock.

Here's an example demonstrating basic usage of `RwLock<T>`:

Ch12/Examples/src/bin/example15.rs

```
use std::sync::RwLock;

fn main() {
    let lock = RwLock::new(17);

    {
        let r1 = lock.read().unwrap();
        let r2 = lock.read().unwrap();
        println!("Read lock 1: {}", r1);
        println!("Read lock 2: {}", r2);
    }

    {
        let mut w = lock.write().unwrap();
        w += 1;
        println!("Write lock: {}", w);
    }

    println!("Updated value: {}", lock.read().unwrap());
}
```

In this example, an `RwLock` is created to wrap the value 5. The RwLock allows for both shared read access and exclusive write access to the data it manages, depending on how the lock is acquired.

In the first block, two read locks are acquired using the `read()` method. The method returns a shared lock, allowing multiple threads, or in this case, multiple scopes in the same thread, to read the data concurrently. The values of the read locks (`r1` and `r2`) are printed to demonstrate that they both have access to the shared value. Once the block ends, the read locks go out of scope, releasing their hold on the `RwLock`.

In the second block, a write lock is acquired using the `write()` method. This method grants exclusive access to the data, preventing any other read or write locks from being acquired until the write lock is released. The value inside the `RwLock` is modified by incrementing it by 1. The updated value is printed to confirm the modification. When the block ends, the write lock is released as it goes out of scope.

Finally, outside of both blocks, a new read lock is acquired, and the updated value inside the `RwLock` is read and printed. This shows the final state of the data after the modification made by the write lock. The `RwLock` ensures that the data was accessed safely and correctly throughout the program, maintaining thread safety even though no actual threads were used in this example.

Use Cases for RwLock<T>

`RwLock<T>` is particularly useful in scenarios where the data is mostly read and only occasionally modified. It allows multiple readers to access the data concurrently, improving performance in read-heavy workloads.

Limitations of RwLock<T>

`RwLock` suffer from the same limitations as `Mutex<T>`

Combining Smart Pointers

Combining multiple smart pointers in Rust is common, especially when different aspects of memory management, mutability, and thread safety are required simultaneously. Below are some typical examples and use cases where multiple smart pointers are combined to achieve specific goals, such as thread-safe, mutable, or shared ownership of data.

Shared State, Partially Mutable

In Rust, when managing shared ownership of data where certain fields require controlled mutability and the data type implements the `Copy` trait, the combination of `Rc` and `Cell` is a more efficient choice. `Rc` enables multiple owners of the data in a single-threaded context, while `Cell` provides interior mutability through value-based updates without borrowing. This approach is particularly well-suited for lightweight, copyable data types like integers, where the need for runtime borrowing checks can be avoided. By using `Rc` with `Cell`, developers can achieve safe and efficient shared ownership with mutable state while adhering to Rust's safety guarantees.

For example:

Ch12/Examples/src/bin/example16.rs

```
use std::rc::Rc;
use std::cell::Cell;

struct SharedState {
    immutable_field: String,
    mutable_field: Cell<u32>,
}

fn main() {
    let shared_state = Rc::new(SharedState {
        immutable_field: String::from("Shared State"),
        mutable_field: Cell::new(42),
    });

    let owner1 = Rc::clone(&shared_state);
    let owner2 = Rc::clone(&shared_state);

    println!("Owner1: Immutable: {}, Mutable: {}", owner1.
immutable_field, owner1.mutable_field.get());

    owner2.mutable_field.set(84);
    println!("Owner2 updated the mutable field.");

    println!("Owner1: Immutable: {}, Mutable: {}", owner1.
immutable_field, owner1.mutable_field.get());
    println!("Owner2: Immutable: {}, Mutable: {}", owner2.
immutable_field, owner2.mutable_field.get());
}
```

This code demonstrates the use of `Rc` and `Cell` to manage shared ownership of a structure with both immutable and mutable fields in a single-threaded context. The `SharedState` struct contains two fields: an immutable String and a mutable u32 wrapped in a Cell. The Cell enables interior mutability, allowing updates to `mutable_field` even when the `SharedState` instance is shared and otherwise immutable.

The program begins by creating a `SharedState` instance wrapped in an `Rc`. This allows multiple owners to share the same data. Two owners, owner1 and owner2, are created by cloning the `Rc`. Both owners have access to the same `SharedState`.

Initially, the values of the fields are printed through `owner1`, showing the immutable field and the initial value of the mutable field. The mutable field is then updated to a new value (84) through `owner2` using the set method of `Cell`. This update affects the shared SharedState instance, as both owners point to the same underlying data.

Finally, the program prints the values of the fields again through both owner1 and owner2. Both show the updated value of mutable_field, demonstrating how the Cell allowed mutation of shared state while maintaining the immutability of the overall structure. immutable_field remains unchanged throughout, ensuring the integrity of data not meant to be altered.

Shared Concurrent Mutable State

In scenarios where managing a thread-safe shared collection is required, particularly when there are frequent readers but only occasional writers, the combination of Arc<RwLock<T>> provides an effective solution. This setup enables multiple threads to access the data concurrently for reading while ensuring that write access is limited to a single thread at any given time, maintaining both safety and efficiency in multi-threaded environments.

For example:

Ch12/Examples/src/bin/example17.rs

```
use std::sync::{Arc, RwLock};
use std::thread;

fn main() {
    let shared_data = Arc::new(RwLock::new(vec![1, 2, 3]));
    let mut handles = vec![];

    for i in 0..3 {
        let shared_data = Arc::clone(&shared_data);
        let handle = thread::spawn(move || {
            let mut data = shared_data.write().unwrap();
            data.push(i);
        });
        handles.push(handle);
    }

    for handle in handles {
        handle.join().unwrap();
    }

    println!("Data: {:?}", shared_data.read().unwrap());
}
```

In this program, an `Arc<RwLock<Vec<i32>>>` is used to manage a shared vector across multiple threads in a thread-safe manner. The `Arc` ensures shared ownership of the `RwLock` across threads, while the `RwLock` provides synchronized access to the vector, allowing only one writer or multiple readers at a time.

Initially, the vector `[1, 2, 3]` is wrapped inside an `RwLock` and then further wrapped in an `Arc` to enable safe sharing. A loop iterates three times, and in each iteration, the `Arc` containing the shared data is cloned and passed to a new thread. Within each thread, the write method of the `RwLock` is called to acquire a write lock on the vector, ensuring exclusive access. The thread then appends its loop index to the vector, demonstrating a mutation of the shared data.

After all threads complete their work, the join method is called on each thread handle to ensure that the main thread waits for their execution to finish. Finally, the program acquires a read lock on the `RwLock` using the read method and prints the updated vector, which now includes the values appended by each thread. This ensures that the shared data remains safe and consistent throughout the concurrent modifications.

Summary

Smart pointers in Rust extend the functionality of standard references by combining memory management capabilities with additional features, such as automatic cleanup and resource sharing. They adhere to Rust's principles of ownership and borrowing, ensuring safety, performance, and memory correctness. Unlike standard references, smart pointers manage the lifetime of the data they point to, often owning the data and cleaning it up when no longer needed.

Smart pointers in Rust offer a variety of types, each serving specific purposes. `Box<T>` provides exclusive ownership of a value stored on the heap, making it particularly suitable for recursive data structures and large objects. `Rc<T>` enables multiple ownership of immutable data in single-threaded contexts through reference counting. For multi-threaded environments, `Arc<T>` serves as a thread-safe version of `Rc<T>`, facilitating shared ownership. `RefCell<T>` allows interior mutability with runtime-checked borrowing rules, while `Cell<T>` provides value-based interior mutability for types that implement the Copy trait. In scenarios requiring exclusive access in multi-threaded contexts, `Mutex<T>` ensures safe access to shared data. Similarly, `RwLock<T>` provides a mechanism for allowing multiple readers or a single writer at any given time. To address the problem of reference cycles, `Weak<T>` serves as a non-owning reference to data managed by `Rc<T>` or `Arc<T>`.

Rust's smart pointers rely on key traits for their functionality. The `Deref` and `DerefMut` traits enable smart pointers to behave like standard references, providing seamless access to their inner values. The Drop trait allows custom cleanup logic to execute automatically when a smart pointer goes out of scope. Additionally, interior mutability is a significant feature, permitting mutation of data even through immutable references, as supported by `RefCell<T>` and `Mutex<T>`.

Smart pointers find applications in various scenarios. Box<T> is widely used for dynamic memory management, particularly for allocating data on the heap. Shared ownership scenarios benefit from `Rc<T>` and `Arc<T>`, with the latter adding thread safety. Interior mutability, a core feature of `RefCell<T>` and `Cell<T>`, enables modifying data while preserving external immutability. In multi-threaded environments, `Mutex<T>` and `RwLock<T>` play crucial roles in ensuring safe access to shared data and enabling concurrency.

In addition to standard library types, custom smart pointers can be designed to encapsulate data, provide specialized behavior, and manage resources such as file handles or network connections. Implementing `Deref` and `Drop` allows these custom types to integrate seamlessly with Rust's ownership and borrowing model.

Smart pointers offer robust memory safety, efficient resource management, and flexibility for handling shared and mutable data. However, they come with runtime overhead, potential for deadlocks (e.g., with `Mutex<T>`), and complexity in managing reference cycles, requiring careful design and usage.

In the next chapter, we will build on these concepts by exploring Rust's approach to concurrency. You'll learn how threads, message passing, and synchronization primitives work together to enable safe, data-race-free parallelism in multi-threaded applications.

Exercises

1. Write a program that creates a large struct containing an array of integers. Allocate this struct on the heap using `Box<T>` and print the size of the array as well as the size of the `Box<T>`.

2. Define a recursive linked list using an `enum List`, where the `enum` has two variants: `Nil`, representing the end of the list, and `Cons`, which contains a tuple as its payload with a value and a Box<List>. Implement a function to traverse the list and print its elements.

3. Write a program where multiple owners share a single read-only string using `Rc<T>`. Clone the `Rc<T>` and print the reference count before and after cloning.
4. Implement a parent-child relationship in a tree-like structure where the parent holds strong references (`Rc<T>`) to its children, and the children hold weak references (`Weak<T>`) to their parent. Print the parent's value starting from one of its children
5. Create a program where multiple owners modify shared state using `Rc<Cell<T>>`. Implement a counter that can be updated by different owners, and print its value after each update.
6. Create a multi-threaded program where multiple threads increment a shared value using `Arc<Mutex<T>>`. Each thread should acquire the lock, double the value, and release the lock. Initialize the value on 1.
7. Write a program where multiple threads read a shared value using `Arc<RwLock<T>>`. Occasionally, one thread updates the value while ensuring no readers are accessing it.
8. Construct a simple directed graph using `Rc<RefCell<T>>` for nodes and edges. Implement methods to add nodes, create edges, and display the graph structure
9. Create a struct containing immutable fields and a mutable field wrapped in `Cell<T>`. Write a method to update the mutable field while keeping the struct immutable and print the values before and after mutation.
10. Write a program that intentionally causes a borrowing conflict by creating both mutable and immutable borrows of a `RefCell<T>` simultaneously.

Project: Linked List

Project Description: Linked List in Rust with Smart Pointers

This project focuses on creating a fully functional linked list in Rust, utilizing the language's smart pointers for memory management. The implementation will leverage `Box<T>` for heap allocation, `Rc<T>` for shared ownership, and `RefCell<T>` for interior mutability, enabling efficient and safe data management. The linked list will feature a head pointer to track the start of the list and a current pointer for traversal and operations. A complete set of CRUD (Create, Read, Update, Delete) operations will be implemented, offering flexible interaction with the data structure.

Objectives

The primary goal is to develop a robust linked list, either singly or doubly linked, that efficiently uses Rust's smart pointers to manage memory and references. The project will include features for adding, removing, updating, and accessing nodes within the list. Special attention will be given to maintaining adherence to Rust's ownership and borrowing rules, ensuring memory safety throughout the implementation. The linked list will also include mechanisms for traversal and dynamic size management.

Core Features and Requirements

The linked list will support the fundamental CRUD operations, enabling practical use and manipulation:

1. **Create**: Nodes can be added at the head, the tail, or any specified position within the list.
2. **Read**: The structure will allow traversal to retrieve all values or access a specific node by position or value.
3. **Update**: Nodes can be updated by modifying their value, either by position or directly by value reference, maintaining structural integrity.
4. **Delete**: Removal of nodes will be supported at the head, tail, or any given position, with automated memory cleanup handled via Rust's Drop trait and smart pointers.

Advanced Features

Beyond basic CRUD functionality, the project will include features to enhance usability and performance:

- **Traversal**: A current pointer will facilitate navigation, enabling forward and backward movement (if implementing a doubly linked list) or resetting to the head.
- **Dynamic Size Management**: The size of the list will be dynamically tracked, with methods provided to retrieve this information.
- **Error Handling**: Meaningful error messages will be returned for invalid operations, such as accessing or updating nodes at non-existent positions.
- **Doubly Linked List Support**: As an optional enhancement, the list can include support for backward traversal, with each node containing references to both its predecessor and successor.

Methods and Functionality

The linked list will include the following operations:

- Adding nodes to the head, tail, or a specific position.
- Retrieving a node's value or traversing the entire list to collect all values.
- Modifying the value of a node at a given position.
- Removing nodes while preserving the list's integrity.
- Helper methods, such as traversing to a specific position or clearing all nodes, will be implemented to simplify interaction with the structure.

13

Concurrency

Concurrency is a cornerstone of modern software development, enabling programs to perform multiple tasks simultaneously. From responsive user interfaces to high-performance servers, the ability to manage multiple threads of execution efficiently and safely is essential in a world where applications must handle increasingly complex workloads. However, with the power of concurrency comes the responsibility of managing shared resources, avoiding data races, and ensuring the correctness of programs under parallel execution.

Rust stands out in the concurrency landscape by offering a unique approach that balances performance, safety, and ease of use. Unlike many other programming languages, Rust guarantees memory safety and eliminates data races at compile time without sacrificing low-level control. This is achieved through its innovative ownership model, strict borrowing rules, and rich type system, which work together to ensure that concurrent code is both efficient and robust.

In traditional programming paradigms, concurrency often introduces challenges like thread synchronization, race conditions, and resource deadlocks. These problems stem from unrestricted access to shared memory and a lack of guarantees about how data is accessed and modified. Rust addresses these issues head-on by enforcing rules that prevent threads from causing undefined behavior through conflicting access patterns. The result is a programming model where developers can write concurrent code with confidence, knowing that many potential pitfalls have been eliminated before the program even runs.

This chapter will cover the following topics:

- **Thread creation and management**: Learn how to spawn and control threads using Rust's standard library, including handling thread lifetimes and joining threads safely.
- **Shared state with Arc<T>**: Understand how to share data across threads using atomic reference counting combined with mutual exclusion for safe interior mutability.
- **Message passing with channels**: Use channels to communicate between threads without sharing memory, following the principle of "shared-nothing" concurrency.
- **Synchronization using Barrier**: Coordinate multiple threads to reach a synchronization point before continuing, useful in structured parallel tasks.

- **Concurrency traits**: `Send` and `Sync`: Learn how Rust's type system enforces thread safety through the Send and Sync traits, and how they relate to data movement and access across threads.
- **Deadlock prevention**: Discover strategies to design concurrent code that avoids deadlocks, such as consistent locking order and minimizing lock scope.

By the end of this chapter, you will understand the fundamental principles of concurrency in Rust and how its type system and ownership model help avoid common pitfalls in multi-threaded programming.

The Concurrency Landscape

OS Threading versus Green Threading

Concurrency and parallelism are critical aspects of modern programming, with threads serving as a fundamental unit to achieve these goals. Threads allow programs to perform multiple tasks simultaneously or handle operations that would otherwise block progress. Two primary threading models exist: Operating System (OS) threads and green threads. While their purposes align, the way they operate and their ideal use cases differ significantly.

Operating System threads, or OS threads, are managed directly by the operating system's kernel. The kernel handles all aspects of thread management, including scheduling, context switching, and maintaining thread states such as running, waiting, or terminated. These threads are tightly integrated into the operating system, enabling them to leverage multiple CPU cores for true parallelism on multi-core systems. However, this power comes at a cost. OS threads are heavyweight due to the involvement of the kernel in their creation, destruction, and scheduling. Context switching between OS threads is also expensive, as it involves saving and restoring the state of each thread. Despite these overheads, OS threads excel in scenarios requiring compute-intensive tasks or true parallel execution, such as server backends, real-time systems, and large-scale simulations.

In contrast, green threads are managed entirely at the application level by a language runtime or a library, bypassing the operating system's kernel. These lightweight threads are implemented in user space, making them significantly cheaper to create and manage compared to OS threads. Green threads typically rely on cooperative scheduling, where the threads themselves determine when to yield control to others. This approach avoids the kernel's involvement and reduces overhead but introduces some limitations. Green threads are often restricted to a single OS thread, meaning they cannot achieve true parallelism. Additionally, if a green thread makes a blocking system call, it may halt all other green threads running on the same OS thread, potentially affecting performance. Despite these challenges, green threads shine in workloads with a high degree of I/O-bound tasks, such as web servers or event-driven programming, where tasks spend much of their time waiting for external events.

The choice between OS threads and green threads depends on the nature of the workload. For tasks requiring true parallelism, low-level hardware control, or direct interaction with system APIs, OS threads are the ideal choice. Conversely, for workloads with a high degree of concurrency, particularly I/O-bound operations with many lightweight tasks, green threads offer a more efficient solution.

Understanding the mechanics and trade-offs of OS threads and green threads is essential for building efficient and scalable concurrent applications. By selecting the appropriate model based on the requirements of the workload, developers can leverage the strengths of each approach to achieve optimal performance and maintainability.

Introducing Tokio

While this book focuses on operating system (OS) threading, it's important to acknowledge Rust's ecosystem for managing concurrency using green threading, specifically through Tokio, one of Rust's most popular asynchronous runtime libraries. Tokio provides a highly efficient and lightweight framework for handling hundreds of thousands of concurrent tasks. It achieves this by implementing green thread tasks managed in user space rather than by the operating system. These green threads are particularly well-suited for workloads that are I/O-bound, such as web servers, network communication, or asynchronous file operations.

Tokio uses a model where lightweight tasks, called futures, are scheduled onto a small number of OS threads. This design allows Tokio to balance the benefits of green threading, low overhead and high concurrency, with the ability to leverage OS threading for parallelism. By multiplexing many tasks onto a few threads, Tokio ensures efficient utilization of system resources while abstracting away much of the complexity of manual thread management.

Despite these differences in implementation, many of the synchronization mechanisms used in OS threading, such as Mutex, RwLock, and channels, are conceptually similar in green-threading environments. For instance, a Mutex in Tokio is designed to work with asynchronous tasks, but its purpose, to ensure mutual exclusion, is the same as in OS-threaded systems. Similarly, channels in asynchronous programming provide a way for tasks to communicate, mirroring the role they play in OS-threaded models.

However, it's important to note that this chapter is dedicated to OS threading, focusing on how Rust's standard library facilitates multi-threaded programming. While the synchronization mechanisms and communication patterns discussed here often parallel those in green-threading environments, the underlying execution model differs significantly. For developers aiming to explore green threading in Rust, Tokio serves as an excellent next step, offering tools for building scalable and highly concurrent applications.

Threads in Rust

Threads are the foundation of concurrency in many programming languages, and Rust is no exception. In Rust, threads are provided by the standard library through the `std::thread` module, which allows developers to create and manage multiple threads of execution within a program. Rust's threading model is built on the principles of safety, performance, and low-level control, ensuring that developers can write concurrent code with confidence and without compromising reliability.

Safety Guarantees

Rust provides strong safety guarantees for concurrency, ensuring that programs are free of data races, memory corruption, and other common pitfalls associated with multithreaded programming. These guarantees are enforced at compile time through Rust's ownership system, borrowing rules, and type system. Here's an explanation of how these features work together to ensure safety in concurrent programs:

- **Ownership Model**: Rust's ownership system guarantees that each piece of data has a single owner at any point in time. In concurrent programming, when data is moved between threads using the `move` keyword, ownership is transferred explicitly and tracked at compile time. This strict model ensures that resources are properly deallocated when they go out of scope, even across thread boundaries, preventing memory leaks without the need for a garbage collector.
- **Borrowing Rules**: Rust's strict borrowing rules ensure that mutable references (`&mut`) are exclusive, meaning only one mutable reference to a piece of data can exist at a time. Similarly, multiple immutable references (`&`) are allowed, but they cannot coexist with mutable references. These rules prevent situations where one thread modifies data while another thread is reading it, avoiding race conditions.

- **Send and Sync Traits**: Rust uses the Send and Sync traits to control how data can be shared between threads: Send indicates that a type can safely be transferred between threads. Most types in Rust are Send by default, but types like `Rc<T>` (reference-counted pointers) are not, because they cannot be safely shared between threads without additional safeguards. Sync indicates that a type can be safely accessed from multiple threads concurrently. Types like `Arc<T>` (atomic reference-counted pointers) are Sync because they use internal mechanisms to ensure thread safety.
- **Fearless Concurrency**: Rust's design allows you to write concurrent programs without worrying about undefined behavior or subtle bugs. For example, Rust prevents access to data from multiple threads unless the data is either immutable or explicitly synchronized using thread-safe types like `Mutex<T>`, `RwLock<T>`, or Atomic types.
- **Compile-Time Guarantees**: Low-level concurrency-related issues, such as improper data sharing or invalid references, are caught at compile time rather than at runtime. This approach ensures that the program is free of common concurrency errors before it is even executed.
- **Thread-Safe Abstractions**: Rust provides high-level abstractions for common concurrency patterns, such as channels for message passing and synchronization primitives like `Mutex<T>` and `RwLock<T>`. These abstractions are designed to be safe and ergonomic while ensuring the programmer retains control over performance-critical decisions.

By combining these features, Rust provides a concurrency model that is both powerful and safe, allowing developers to write highly efficient multithreaded programs without sacrificing correctness or safety. This design is often referred to as "fearless concurrency," as it removes the typical risks associated with concurrent programming by leveraging the language's strict compile-time checks and robust type system.

Creating Threads

In Rust, creating a thread is straightforward using the `std::thread` module. A thread allows a program to perform multiple tasks concurrently by running a separate flow of execution. Here's a minimal example:

Ch13/Examples/src/bin/example01.rs

```
use std::thread;
use std::time::Duration;
```

```
fn main() {
    let handle = thread::spawn(|| {
        for i in 1..=5 {
            println!("Hello from the thread! Count: {}", i);
            thread::sleep(Duration::from_millis(500));
        }
    });

    for i in 1..=5 {
        println!("Hello from the main thread! Count: {}", i);
        thread::sleep(Duration::from_millis(500));
    }

    handle.join().unwrap();
}
```

In this example, the `thread::spawn` function creates a new thread and runs the code inside the closure passed to it. The spawned thread prints messages with counts from 1 to 5. Simultaneously, the main thread continues its execution, printing its own set of messages.

The `join` method is called on the thread handle to ensure that the main thread waits for the spawned thread to complete before exiting. Without join, the program could terminate before the spawned thread finishes execution. This basic example demonstrates concurrency, where two threads run independently but may interleave their outputs based on the scheduler.

Joining Threads

In Rust, the join method plays a crucial role in managing threads by waiting for a spawned thread to complete its execution. When a thread is created using `thread::spawn`, it runs independently of the thread that initiated it. This independence means that without a mechanism like join, the main thread or any calling thread might continue executing and potentially terminate the program before the spawned thread has finished its work.

The primary purpose of join is to synchronize threads, ensuring that the calling thread pauses until the spawned thread has completed its task. This is particularly important for maintaining order and predictability in concurrent programs. By using join, you can ensure that all threads complete their work before the program exits, preventing premature termination and resource leakage. Threads consume system-level resources, and without proper synchronization, these resources might be left in an inconsistent or wasteful state.

When join is invoked on a thread, it blocks the caller until the associated thread completes. The method is part of the `JoinHandle` type, which is returned by `thread::spawn`. Once join is called, the calling thread waits for the spawned thread to finish executing its closure. This mechanism not only ensures that all threads complete their work but also allows the main thread to handle any errors or panics that might occur in the spawned thread.

The join method returns a Result type, where a successful execution of the spawned thread is represented by `Ok(())`. If the spawned thread panics during its execution, join returns an Err variant containing details about the panic. This provides a structured way to handle errors, making it possible to log, inspect, or recover from failures in the spawned thread.

By integrating join into a program, developers can create robust and predictable concurrency patterns. It ensures that all threads terminate gracefully and provides mechanisms for error detection and handling. This makes join a fundamental tool for working with threads in Rust, where safety and correctness are core principles.

Thread Parameters

A thread can only perform meaningful tasks if it knows what work it needs to carry out. In Rust, the task itself is defined by a closure, but this closure doesn't directly accept parameters when passed to `thread::spawn`. The only way to provide information to the closure is by capturing variables from its surrounding environment.

While mechanisms like channels or shared memory can also be used to communicate with the thread, the closure still needs access to these objects, whether it's the pointer to the shared memory or the components required for setting up a channel.

To make this process seamless, we can extend the functionality of the closure by leveraging its ability to capture variables from the environment. By parametrizing the closure in this way, we enable it to carry the information it needs to execute its task effectively.

When passing information to a thread in Rust, the data must be owned by the thread. This requirement stems from Rust's ownership and concurrency safety guarantees. Threads can run independently and potentially outlive the scope in which they were created. If a thread were allowed to access borrowed data, that data could become invalid if the original scope ends before the thread completes, leading to undefined behavior. Rust's ownership rules ensure that such situations are avoided.

Ownership allows the thread to take full control of the data, ensuring its validity for the entire lifetime of the thread. When you use the move keyword to capture variables in the closure passed to `thread::spawn`, ownership of those variables is transferred to the thread. This means the thread now "owns" the data, and no other part of the program can modify or drop it while the thread is still running.

For example, if you want to pass a String to a thread, the thread must take ownership of the String. This guarantees that the thread has exclusive access to it and prevents data races or dangling references. Rust enforces these rules at compile time, ensuring safe concurrency by design.

Here is a minimal example:

Ch13/Examples/src/bin/example02.rs

```
use std::thread;

fn main() {
    let data = String::from("Hello from captured
environment!");

    let handle = thread::spawn(move || {
        println!("{}", data);
    });

    handle.join().unwrap();
}
```

First, the String variable data is declared in the main thread, initialized with the text "Hello from captured environment!". This data variable resides in the scope of the main function. Next, a new thread is spawned using thread::spawn. A closure is passed to the spawn function to define the task that the new thread will execute. Within the closure, data is accessed and printed.

To enable the thread to access data, the move keyword is used in the closure. This transfers ownership of the data variable from the main thread to the thread being spawned. The move keyword is critical because threads can run asynchronously and potentially outlive their parent scopes. By transferring ownership, Rust ensures that data remains valid for the duration of the spawned thread's execution.

Once the thread has been started, the join method is called on the thread handle. This causes the main thread to wait for the spawned thread to finish its work before continuing. The unwrap ensures that any errors during the thread's execution, such as a panic, are surfaced and dealt with immediately.

Thread Return Values

Imagine you're managing a factory where workers build custom parts. Each worker performs a task and hands you the finished product when they're done. However, to stay organized, you track which worker is responsible for which part so you can collect everything efficiently. In Rust, threads function much like these workers. Each thread can execute a task and return a result, which you can retrieve using the JoinHandle mechanism provided by the standard library.

Consider a scenario where you need to calculate the square of several numbers. Each thread can take a number, compute its square, and return the result. Here's an example to illustrate:

Ch13/Examples/src/bin/example03.rs

```
use std::thread;

fn main() {
    let numbers = vec![2, 4, 6, 8, 10];

    let handles: Vec<_> = numbers
        .into_iter()
        .map(|num| {
            thread::spawn(move || {
                println!("Calculating square of {}", num);
                num * num
            })
        })
        .collect();

    let results: Vec<_> = handles
        .into_iter()
        .map(|handle| handle.join().unwrap())
        .collect();

    println!("Squares: {:?}", results);
}
```

In this program, a vector of numbers is created as input for the threads. For each number, a new thread is spawned using thread::spawn. The closure inside spawn takes ownership of its number, calculates the square, and returns the result. The JoinHandle returned by spawn acts as a reference to the thread and its eventual result. Each handle is stored in a vector to keep track of all threads.

After all the threads are spawned, the main thread retrieves the results by iterating over the JoinHandle vector. The join method on each handle blocks execution until the corresponding thread finishes its task. Once the thread completes, its result is extracted and stored in a new vector. Finally, the program outputs all the computed squares.

This example highlights how Rust's ownership model ensures safety and clarity. The move keyword explicitly transfers ownership of the number to the thread, ensuring that no other thread or part of the program can access it simultaneously. This prevents data races and guarantees correctness. Additionally, the join method ensures that all threads complete their work before their results are accessed, providing predictable execution.

Returning values from threads in Rust is a natural extension of its safe concurrency model. The JoinHandle abstraction allows threads to not only perform tasks independently but also communicate their results back to the main thread. This mechanism integrates seamlessly with Rust's type system, ensuring correctness and eliminating many common pitfalls of multithreaded programming. By using threads effectively, you can write concurrent applications that are both powerful and safe, with Rust's guarantees providing the confidence to focus on solving the problem at hand.

Shared State and Synchronization

In the world of concurrent programming, threads often need to access shared data. Managing shared state safely and efficiently is one of the key challenges of multithreaded development. Without careful synchronization, threads can inadvertently cause data races, inconsistent state, or even program crashes. Rust tackles these challenges by combining its ownership model with synchronization primitives, ensuring that shared state is both safe and well-defined at compile time.

This section delves into the tools Rust provides for shared state management and synchronization, each tailored to specific needs in concurrent programming. It begins with `Arc<T>`, Rust's atomic reference-counted smart pointer, which allows threads to share ownership of data. By ensuring that shared data is properly managed and deallocated only when no threads are using it, `Arc<T>` forms the foundation for sharing immutable or read-only state across threads.

Building on this, the section explores `Mutex<T>`, a fundamental synchronization primitive for ensuring mutually exclusive access to shared data. With a `Mutex<T>`, you can safely mutate shared state, knowing that only one thread can access it at a time. The combination of `Arc<T>` and `Mutex<T>` further enables thread-safe shared mutable state, offering a powerful pattern for managing complex interactions between threads.

As powerful as synchronization primitives are, they can also introduce risks, such as deadlocks, where threads become stuck waiting for each other to release locks. This section provides guidance on deadlock prevention, equipping you with best practices to write robust and deadlock-free concurrent code.

Through practical examples and explanations, this section prepares you to handle shared state and synchronization with confidence, whether you're building high-performance servers, real-time systems, or other multithreaded applications.

Arc<Mutex<T>>

Imagine a concert venue with a limited number of tickets. Multiple ticket booths sell tickets simultaneously, but to avoid overselling, they must coordinate their updates to the available ticket count. This scenario requires a combination of shared ownership and safe mutability.

In Rust, you achieve this by combining `Arc<T>` and `Mutex<T>`. The `Arc<T>` provides shared ownership of the ticket count, while the `Mutex<T>` ensures that updates are made safely, one thread at a time.

Here's an example where multiple threads increment a shared counter:

Ch13/Examples/src/bin/example04.rs

```
use std::sync::{Arc, Mutex};
use std::thread;

fn main() {
    let counter = Arc::new(Mutex::new(0));
    let mut handles = vec![];

    for _ in 0..10 {
        let counter = Arc::clone(&counter);
        let handle = thread::spawn(move || {
            let mut num = counter.lock().unwrap();
            *num += 1;
        });
        handles.push(handle);
    }

    for handle in handles {
        handle.join().unwrap();
    }

    println!("Final counter value: {}", *counter.lock().
unwrap());
}
```

In this program, the shared counter is wrapped in `Arc<T>` and `Mutex<T>`. Each thread increments the counter by locking the mutex, performing the update, and releasing the lock. The `Arc::clone` method ensures that all threads share the same counter, while the mutex guarantees that updates happen one at a time. The final value of the counter reflects the total number of increments performed.

This combination of `Arc<T>` and `Mutex<T>` is a common pattern in Rust for managing shared mutable state. It provides both safety and flexibility, making it ideal for scenarios that require threads to collaborate on shared tasks.

Deadlock Prevention

Imagine a busy intersection where cars from all directions are trying to pass simultaneously. If every car insists on moving first, none can proceed, causing a traffic jam. This deadlock scenario mirrors a common problem in concurrent programming when multiple threads lock resources in a conflicting order.

In Rust, deadlocks can occur if threads attempt to acquire multiple locks in an inconsistent order. For example, if one thread locks A and then B while another locks B and then A, both threads may end up waiting indefinitely for each other to release their locks.

Here's an example that avoids deadlock by enforcing a consistent lock acquisition order:

Ch13/Examples/src/bin/example05.rs

```
use std::sync::{Arc, Mutex};
use std::thread;

fn main() {
    let resource1 = Arc::new(Mutex::new(()));
    let resource2 = Arc::new(Mutex::new(()));

    let r1 = Arc::clone(&resource1);
    let r2 = Arc::clone(&resource2);

    let handle1 = thread::spawn(move || {
        let _lock1 = r1.lock().unwrap();
        let _lock2 = r2.lock().unwrap();
        println!("Thread 1 acquired both locks");
    });

    let r1 = Arc::clone(&resource1);
    let r2 = Arc::clone(&resource2);
```

```
    let handle2 = thread::spawn(move || {
        let _lock1 = r1.lock().unwrap();
        let _lock2 = r2.lock().unwrap();
        println!("Thread 2 acquired both locks");
    });

    handle1.join().unwrap();
    handle2.join().unwrap();
}
```

In this program, both threads lock resources in the same order, preventing deadlock. By establishing a consistent order of lock acquisition, the program ensures that no thread blocks another indefinitely.

Avoiding deadlock requires careful design, including consistent lock ordering and minimizing the scope of locks. Rust's tools, like `Mutex<T>`, provide the foundation, but understanding and applying best practices is key to writing robust, deadlock-free concurrent code.

Arc<RwLock<T>>

Imagine a shared library database where multiple visitors want to read the catalog at the same time, but occasionally a librarian needs to update the catalog with new entries. To maintain order, readers are allowed to access the catalog simultaneously, but when the librarian updates it, all reading must pause until the update is complete. This scenario highlights the need for managing shared state that supports both concurrent reading and exclusive writing.

In Rust, this kind of access pattern is efficiently managed using a combination of `Arc<T>` and `RwLock<T>`. The `Arc<T>` enables shared ownership of the catalog across threads, while the `RwLock<T>` provides a mechanism for safe, synchronized access. `RwLock<T>` allows multiple readers to access the data simultaneously, but it enforces that only one writer can modify the data at any given time.

Here's an example where multiple threads read from a shared vector, and occasionally one thread writes to it:

Ch13/Examples/src/bin/example06.rs

```
use std::sync::{Arc, RwLock};
use std::thread;

fn main() {
    let catalog = Arc::new(RwLock::new(vec![1, 2, 3]));
```

```
    let mut handles = vec![];

    // Readers
    for _ in 0..5 {
        let catalog = Arc::clone(&catalog);
        let handle = thread::spawn(move || {
            let read_lock = catalog.read().unwrap();
            println!("Thread {:?} read: {:?}",
thread::current().id(), *read_lock);
        });
        handles.push(handle);
    }

    // Writer
    let catalog_writer = Arc::clone(&catalog);
    let writer = thread::spawn(move || {
        let mut write_lock = catalog_writer.write().unwrap();
        write_lock.push(4);
        println!("Thread {:?} wrote to the catalog.",
thread::current().id());
    });

    handles.push(writer);

    for handle in handles {
        handle.join().unwrap();
    }

    println!("Final catalog: {:?}", *catalog.read().unwrap());
}
```

In this example, the catalog is a vector shared among multiple threads and wrapped in both `Arc<T>` and `RwLock<T>`. Threads that need to read the catalog acquire a read lock using `RwLock::read`, allowing them to access the data concurrently. Meanwhile, the writer thread acquires a write lock using `RwLock::write`, which temporarily blocks readers and ensures exclusive access to the data for updates. The `Arc::clone` method ensures that all threads share the same catalog, and the RwLock coordinates the access to prevent data races.

This combination of `Arc<T>` and `RwLock<T>` is particularly powerful for scenarios where read operations vastly outnumber write operations. It maximizes performance by allowing multiple readers to access data concurrently while maintaining safety for the occasional write. With `Arc<RwLock<T>>`, Rust provides an ergonomic and efficient way to manage shared state that requires both high concurrency and controlled mutability.

Channels

Imagine a factory floor where workers at different stations complete tasks and pass their results to a central manager for further processing. Each worker might specialize in a specific task, but the final assembly requires the manager to collect input from all of them in an organized way. In programming, this type of workflow is achieved through message passing, where threads communicate by sending data to one another.

Rust provides powerful tools for message passing using channels, available through the `std::sync::mpsc` module. A channel consists of a sender and a receiver: the sender is used by threads to send messages, while the receiver collects those messages in the order they arrive. Channels in Rust are designed to be thread-safe, ensuring that messages are transferred reliably between threads without requiring shared memory.

Using Channels for Message Passing

Consider a scenario where you want multiple workers (threads) to send updates to a manager thread. Channels make this straightforward. Rust's `std::sync::mpsc` supports two main models: single-producer, single-consumer (SPSC) and multiple-producer, single-consumer (MPSC). While SPSC involves one sender and one receiver, the more commonly used MPSC allows multiple senders to share a single receiver, enabling greater flexibility in multithreaded applications.

Creating and Using Channels

Here's how you might create a basic channel for communication between threads:

Ch13/Examples/src/bin/example07.rs

```
use std::sync::mpsc;
use std::thread;

fn main() {
    let (tx, rx) = mpsc::channel();

    let handle = thread::spawn(move || {
        tx.send("Hello from the thread!").unwrap();
    });

    let message = rx.recv().unwrap();
    println!("Main thread received: {}", message);

    handle.join().unwrap();
```

```
}
```

In this example, the `mpsc::channel` function creates a channel with a transmitter (`tx`) and a receiver (`rx`). The transmitter is sent into the spawned thread, where it sends a message. The receiver in the main thread then retrieves the message using `recv`, which blocks until a message is available. Finally, the program outputs the received message and ensures the spawned thread completes by calling join.

Handling Channel Errors

Channels, like any communication mechanism, can encounter errors. For instance, if a sender tries to send data after the receiver has been dropped, a `SendError` occurs. Similarly, if a receiver attempts to retrieve data when the sender is no longer active and the channel is empty, a `RecvError` is raised.

Here's an example illustrating error handling in channels:

Ch13/Examples/src/bin/example08.rs

```
use std::sync::mpsc;

fn main() {
    let (tx, rx) = mpsc::channel::<i32>();

    drop(tx);

    match rx.recv() {
        Ok(msg) => println!("Received: {}", msg),
        Err(e) => println!("Error receiving message: {}", e),
    }
}
```

This program explicitly drops the transmitter before receiving, simulating a situation where no messages are available. The receiver handles this gracefully by checking the `Result` returned by `recv`.

Cloning Senders for Multiple Producers

For more complex scenarios, you can clone the sender to allow multiple threads to send messages to the same receiver. This is particularly useful when managing multiple producers sending data to a single consumer.

Here's an example:

Ch13/Examples/src/bin/example09.rs

```
use std::sync::mpsc;
use std::thread;

fn main() {
    let (tx, rx) = mpsc::channel();
    let mut handles = vec![];

    for i in 1..=5 {
        let tx = tx.clone();
        let handle = thread::spawn(move || {
            tx.send(format!("Message from thread {}", i)).
unwrap();
        });
        handles.push(handle);
    }

    for handle in handles {
        handle.join().unwrap();
    }

    for received in rx {
        println!("Received: {}", received);
    }
}
```

This example spawns multiple threads, each of which sends a message using a cloned transmitter. The main thread collects and processes all messages using the receiver. Cloning the sender allows seamless communication from multiple threads to a single receiver, with all messages arriving in the order they were sent.

Channels in Rust provide a safe and effective way to communicate between threads. By leveraging the `std::sync::mpsc` module, you can implement various patterns, from single-producer to multiple-producer message passing. With robust error handling and support for cloning senders, channels enable efficient and flexible thread communication. Whether you're coordinating tasks in a factory-like setup or managing complex workflows, channels are a cornerstone of Rust's concurrency model.

Barrier

Imagine a team of runners preparing to start a relay race. Each runner must wait at the starting line until all their teammates are ready before the race can begin. If even one runner isn't prepared, the race cannot start. This concept of coordination among multiple participants is central to Rust's `std::sync::Barrier`, a synchronization primitive that ensures multiple threads reach a common point before proceeding further.

A Barrier in Rust allows threads to synchronize at a designated point in their execution. It is initialized with a count, representing the number of threads that must wait at the barrier before any of them can proceed. Once all threads have reached the barrier, they are released simultaneously, allowing coordinated progress.

Here's an example of using Barrier to synchronize a group of threads:

Ch13/Examples/src/bin/example10.rs

```
use std::sync::{Arc, Barrier};
use std::thread;

fn main() {
    let num_threads = 5;
    let barrier = Arc::new(Barrier::new(num_threads));
    let mut handles = vec![];

    for i in 0..num_threads {
        let barrier_clone = Arc::clone(&barrier);
        let handle = thread::spawn(move || {
            println!("Thread {}: Performing initial work...",
i);
            // Simulate some work before the barrier
            std::thread::sleep(std::time::Duration::from_
millis(100 * i as u64));

            println!("Thread {}: Waiting at the barrier.", i);
            barrier_clone.wait(); // Synchronize here
            println!("Thread {}: Proceeding after the barrier.",
i);
        });
        handles.push(handle);
    }

    for handle in handles {
        handle.join().unwrap();
    }
}
```

In this example, the Barrier is created with a count equal to the number of threads (`num_threads`). Each thread performs some initial work, simulating different preparation times by sleeping for a unique duration. After completing their initial tasks, the threads wait at the barrier by calling the wait method. The Barrier ensures that none of the threads proceed until all have reached this synchronization point.

Once the last thread calls wait, the barrier releases all waiting threads simultaneously, allowing them to continue execution. This ensures that all threads remain synchronized, progressing in unison beyond the barrier.

The Arc is used to share ownership of the barrier across threads, as Barrier itself does not implement the Send or Sync traits directly. By wrapping it in an Arc, we ensure thread-safe shared ownership.

The `std::sync::Barrier` is a powerful tool for scenarios where threads need to reach a common synchronization point before proceeding. It is particularly useful in parallel processing tasks that require coordination, such as simulations, phased computations, or distributed algorithms. By ensuring that all threads reach a specific point before continuing, the Barrier guarantees consistent and predictable thread coordination, making it an essential synchronization primitive in Rust's concurrency toolbox.

Traits for Concurrency

Rust's concurrency model is built around strict safety guarantees, and several traits play a critical role in enabling safe and predictable concurrent programming. These traits, provided by the standard library, ensure that data can be shared or transferred between threads without causing data races or undefined behavior.

Send

The Send trait indicates that a type can be transferred (moved) safely between threads. If a type implements Send, it means that ownership of values of that type can be passed from one thread to another.

Automatically implemented: Most types in Rust are automatically marked as `Send` if all their components are Send. For example, `i32` and `String` are `Send` because their underlying components are thread-safe.

Not Send by default: Some types, like `Rc<T>` (reference-counted smart pointer), are not Send because they are not thread-safe. These types are typically replaced with their thread-safe counterparts, like `Arc<T>` (atomic reference counting).

For example:

Ch13/Examples/src/bin/example11.rs

```
use std::thread;

fn main() {
    let data = String::from("Hello, threads!");

    // String implements Send, so it can be moved into a thread.
    let handle = thread::spawn(move || {
        println!("{}", data);
    });

    handle.join().unwrap();
}
```

Sync

The `Sync` trait indicates that a type can be safely shared between threads through references. If a type is Sync, it means that a reference to the type can be accessed by multiple threads simultaneously.

Automatically implemented: Types composed entirely of Sync types are automatically Sync. For instance, `&i32` (a shared reference to an integer) is `Sync` because `i32` is immutable and inherently thread-safe.

Not Sync by default: Types like `Cell<T>` and `RefCell<T>` are not `Sync` because their internal mutability model is not thread-safe without additional synchronization.

For example:

Ch13/Examples/src/bin/example12.rs

```
use std::sync::Arc;
use std::thread;

fn main() {
    let data = Arc::new(String::from("Hello, threads!"));

    let mut handles = vec![];
    for _ in 0..5 {
        let data = Arc::clone(&data);

        // Arc<T> is Sync, so it can be shared between threads
safely.
        let handle = thread::spawn(move || {
            println!("{}", data);
        });
```

```
        handles.push(handle);
    }

    for handle in handles {
        handle.join().unwrap();
    }
}
```

How These Traits Work Together

The Send and Sync traits are the cornerstones of Rust's concurrency guarantees. At compile time, Rust enforces these traits to ensure that data used across threads is either immutable, thread-safe, or properly synchronized.

Using Send for Ownership Transfer:

- When you move data into a thread (e.g., using `std::thread::spawn`), the compiler ensures that the data is `Send`.
- Types like `Arc<T>` and `Mutex<T>` implement `Send`, allowing shared ownership or synchronization of data across threads.

Using Sync for Shared References:

- When multiple threads need to access shared data, the compiler ensures that the data is Sync if accessed via shared references.
- For example, `Arc<T>` is `Sync` when `T` is `Sync`, enabling multiple threads to share access to the same value safely.

The Send and Sync traits form the foundation of Rust's concurrency safety. By ensuring that only types meeting these constraints can be shared or transferred between threads, Rust eliminates common issues like data races and undefined behavior at compile time. This enables developers to write concurrent programs that are both safe and efficient, with minimal runtime overhead.

Summary

Concurrency is essential in modern software development, allowing applications to execute multiple tasks simultaneously. It underpins responsive user interfaces, high-performance servers, and scalable systems. Rust excels in concurrency by ensuring memory safety, eliminating data races, and providing robust compile-time checks through its ownership model, borrowing rules, and type system.

The chapter explores fundamental concurrency concepts and their implementation in Rust. It begins with thread creation and management, demonstrating how Rust's `std::thread` module provides tools for safe and efficient multi-threading. It introduces synchronization primitives like `Arc<T>`, `Mutex<T>`, and `RwLock<T>` for managing shared state, ensuring threads can safely access or mutate data. Deadlock prevention techniques are covered to help developers write reliable, conflict-free code.

Message passing is presented as an alternative to shared state, using Rust's channels (`std::sync::mpsc`) to enable thread communication. The chapter highlights advanced synchronization tools like Barrier for thread coordination and explains how traits like `Send` and `Sync` ensure thread safety.

By combining practical examples and detailed explanations, this chapter provides a comprehensive guide to leveraging Rust's concurrency model, empowering developers to build efficient, robust, and safe concurrent applications.

Having seen how Rust's ownership and type system enforce safety in concurrent contexts, in the next chapter we turn to another core concept that ensures memory safety: lifetimes, Rust's way of tracking how long references remain valid and preventing dangling pointers at compile time.

Exercises

1. Write a program that spawns a new thread to print "Executing the thread...!" and ensure the main thread waits for it to complete using join.
2. Create a program where a thread calculates the square of a number. Pass the number to the thread using a closure and print the result in the main thread.
3. Use `Arc<T>` to share a read-only vector between multiple threads. Each thread should print the vector's elements.
4. Implement a counter that is incremented by multiple threads. Use `Arc<Mutex<T>>` to ensure the counter is updated safely and print the final count in the main thread.
5. Write a program that simulates a shared library catalog. Use `Arc<RwLock<T>>` to allow multiple threads to read the catalog simultaneously, while a single thread can update it by adding a new book.

6. Design a program where two threads need to lock two resources. Introduce an intentional deadlock first, and then modify the program to prevent the deadlock by enforcing consistent lock acquisition order.
7. Create a producer-consumer program where one thread produces a series of numbers and sends them to another thread via a channel. The consumer thread should print the received numbers.
8. Extend the previous exercise to have multiple producer threads, each sending a unique range of numbers to a single consumer thread. Use `mpsc::Sender` cloning for this purpose.
9. Simulate a team of workers that all start a task simultaneously after preparing their individual setups. Use `std::sync::Barrier` to ensure all threads wait until they are ready before starting the task.
10. Simulate multiple player threads, each performing actions like reading the leaderboard or submitting a new score. Use `Arc<RwLock<HashMap<String, u32>>>` to represent the shared leaderboard. Some threads will read and display the current top scores, while others will update the leaderboard with new scores.

Project: Parallel Merge Sort

The goal of this project is to implement a parallel version of the merge sort algorithm using Rust.

Requirements

1. **Sequential Merge Sort Implementation**: Start with a baseline sequential implementation of merge sort.
2. **Parallel Merge Sort**:
   - Divide the array into subarrays and sort them in parallel using multiple threads.
   - Merge the sorted subarrays concurrently.
3. **Use Rust's Concurrency Tools**:
   - Use `std::thread` for manual thread management

Detailed Steps

1. **Setup and Sequential Merge Sort**:
   - Implement a standard merge sort algorithm.
   - Test it on an array of integers to ensure correctness.

2. **Divide the Problem**:
   - Divide the array into smaller parts recursively.
   - Each division should handle a subset of the array concurrently.
3. **Parallelism with std::thread**:
   - Spawn threads to sort the left and right halves of the array concurrently.
   - Join the threads and merge the sorted halves.
4. **Error Handling**:
   - Ensure proper thread management to avoid panics or deadlocks.
   - Handle edge cases like empty arrays or arrays with a single element.

Further Reading

- The Rust Async Book
- Tokio: Rust's most popular asynchronous runtime, including topics on green threads, futures, and task scheduling.
- Rayon: A data-parallelism library for easily parallelizing computations over collections.
- Crossbeam: A powerful library for concurrent programming that extends Rust's standard library with tools like scoped threads and lock-free data structures.

14

Lifetimes

In Rust, lifetimes are one of the core mechanisms that enforce memory safety without relying on garbage collection. They ensure that references are valid for as long as they are needed while preventing them from outliving the data they point to. While Rust's borrow checker automatically handles most lifetime scenarios through its lifetime elision rules, there are cases where explicit lifetime annotations are necessary to provide clarity and enable complex reference relationships.

This chapter dives deep into the concepts and practical applications of lifetimes, including the rules and patterns for managing references in functions, structs, and other scenarios. It explores how lifetimes enable safe borrowing and how to manage lifetime bounds to avoid dangling references or overly constrained code. You'll learn how to design functions and structs that gracefully handle references, use lifetimes in ways that balance flexibility and safety.

We will also examine when and why explicit lifetime annotations are needed, how lifetimes are inferred, and the distinctions between lifetimes like 'static and scoped lifetimes. Through examples and explanations, this chapter aims to demystify lifetimes, making them an intuitive tool rather than a challenging hurdle.

Topics covered in this chapter:

- **Introduction to Lifetimes**: Understand the concept of lifetimes in Rust, which ensure that references remain valid and prevent dangling pointers at compile time.
- **Functions with Lifetimes**: Learn how to annotate function signatures with lifetime parameters to express how the lifetimes of input and output references relate.
- **Lifetime Elision Rules**: Explore Rust's built-in rules that infer lifetimes in simple cases, reducing the need for explicit annotations in function definitions.
- **Static Lifetimes**: Discover the 'static lifetime, which represents data that lives for the entire duration of the program, commonly used for global constants and string literals.
- **Structs with Lifetimes**: See how to define structs that hold references, requiring explicit lifetime annotations to ensure those references stay valid.
- **Best Practices for Managing Lifetimes**: Gain insight into practical techniques for designing code that minimizes lifetime complexity while maintaining safety and clarity.

By the end of this chapter, you'll understand how lifetimes work, when to use them, and how to design efficient and safe Rust code using this feature.

Introduction

In a previous chapter, we introduced the concept of scoping, which defines the visibility and accessibility of variables within specific blocks or regions of code. Scoping determines when a variable is created and destroyed during a program's execution, tied to the structural boundaries of the program.

Building on that understanding, lifetimes take this idea a step further. While scoping focuses on the syntactical rules governing a variable's lifecycle within a block, lifetimes deal with the relationships between references and the data they point to, ensuring that borrowed data is not accessed beyond its validity. Lifetimes enforce these guarantees at compile time, providing a safety mechanism that extends beyond the immediate scope of the reference, often spanning function boundaries or other areas of program flow. A reference's lifetime begins when it is created and extends through its last use. The Rust compiler uses this lifetime to ensure that references do not overlap in invalid ways and that the referenced value remains valid for the entire duration. These rules are enforced by the borrow checker, as discussed in the chapter on ownership and borrowing. In this chapter, however, we focus on how to manually work with lifetimes, rather than how the borrow checker enforces them.

By distinguishing lifetimes from scoping, we see how Rust's ownership model not only manages memory allocation and deallocation but also ensures memory safety through precise control over references and their valid duration. This layer of abstraction ensures that references are always tied to valid data, avoiding issues such as dangling references or unsafe memory access.

Functions with Lifetimes

One common scenario that requires careful lifetime management is when returning references from functions. Since a function cannot return a reference to a value that doesn't outlive the function itself, Rust enforces strict rules on lifetimes to avoid returning invalid references. The most common and safest way to return a reference is to borrow an existing reference from a function parameter, ensuring the output reference's validity is tied to the input reference's lifetime.

In this section, we'll explore how lifetimes affect functions that return references, examine common pitfalls, and learn how to use lifetime annotations to explicitly define relationships between input and output references. Through examples, we'll see how Rust's borrow checker ensures safety and how to apply lifetime bounds when needed.

Returning a Reference

In Rust, references allow us to borrow data without taking ownership. When working with functions that return references, managing lifetimes becomes crucial to ensure memory safety. Lifetimes explicitly define the scope during which a reference is valid, and they prevent dangling references at compile time. A key concept here is that when you return a reference from a function, the safest and most common scenario is to accept a reference as a parameter and return that same reference. This ensures that the returned reference's validity is tied to the input reference's lifetime.

Imagine we want a function to return a reference to a value. Rust requires that we explicitly define the relationship between the lifetimes of the input and output references. The function must borrow data, and its output reference must live as long as (or shorter than) the borrowed input.

Here is an example that demonstrates the concept of returning references by borrowing an input, specifically using a function that splits a book title into individual words and returns references to these words.

Ch14/Examples/bin/example01.rs

```
fn get_words_from_title(title: &str) -> Vec<&str> {
    title.split_whitespace().collect()
}

fn main() {
    let book_title = String::from("Learning Rust");
    let words = get_words_from_title(&book_title);
    for word in words {
        println!("{}", word);
    }
}
```

In this example, the `get_words_from_title` function takes a reference to a string slice (`&str`) and returns a vector of string slices (`Vec<&str>`). It uses the `split_whitespace` method to split the input string into words, collecting the results into a vector.

In main, a String called `book_title` is created with the value "Learning Rust". The function is called with a reference to this string, and the resulting vector contains references to the words in the title. A for loop iterates over the vector, printing each word.

This approach avoids creating new strings, as the vector contains references to parts of the original string. Rust's borrow checker ensures these references remain valid as long as the original string (`book_title`) exists, maintaining memory safety and efficiency.

When returning a reference, the function must have some data to reference. If a reference is not passed in as a parameter, the function would have to create a reference to some data it owns. However, this would result in a dangling reference when the function ends and its local stack frame is destroyed. For example:

```
// This will not compile
fn invalid_reference() -> &String {
    let value = String::from("Hello");
    &value
}
```

Here, value is dropped as soon as the function ends, leaving the returned reference pointing to invalid memory. Rust prevents this at compile time.

Passing a parameter by ownership creates the same problem because the parameter is consumed and will be destroyed once the function completes its execution. As a result, the data will no longer be available after the function finishes.

When a function returns a reference, it is essential that the reference points to data that outlives the function's scope. This is why functions that return references typically take references as parameters. By explicitly managing lifetimes, Rust guarantees memory safety and prevents dangling references at compile time.

Lifetime Bounds

In the following example, we define a function that returns the part of a string that comes after a specified prefix. The prefix is removed from `text`, and the function accepts two parameters: the string to be searched (`text`) and the prefix (`prefix`).

```
// This will not compile
fn substring_after(text: &str, prefix: &str) -> &str {
    text.split_once(prefix).map(|(_, rest)| rest).unwrap_or("")
}
```

When compiling, the following error is thrown:

```
error[E0106]: missing lifetime specifier
```

This error occurs because the compiler doesn't know whether the returned reference is borrowed from `text` or `prefix`. The suggested fix introduces a named lifetime parameter `'a` to indicate that the returned reference is tied to both input references. Although the suggested fix may not always be the best solution, it's often a good starting point. If the program compiles, you can proceed. If not, further adjustments may be needed.

A complete working example is as follows:

Ch14/Examples/bin/example02.rs

```
fn substring_after<'a>(text: &'a str, prefix: &'a str) -> &'a
str {
    text.split_once(prefix).map(|(_, rest)| rest).unwrap_or("")
}

fn main() {
    println!("{}", substring_after("Learning Rust", " "));
}
```

Here, we added a lifetime bound 'a, which tells the compiler that the return value could be based on either text or prefix. In this simple example, this is perfectly valid because both references live long enough.

However, this approach is not always correct. In the following example, we intentionally use the same function in a way that causes a compile-time error:

Ch14/Examples/bin/example03.rs

```
// This will not compile
fn substring_after<'a>(text: &'a str, prefix: &'a str) -> &'a
str {
    text.split_once(prefix).map(|(_, rest)| rest).unwrap_or("")
}

fn main() {
    let result;
    let text = String::from("Learning Rust");
    {
        let prefix = String::from(" ");
        result = substring_after(&text, &prefix);
    }
```

```
    println!("{}", result);
}
```

Here, the function specifies that the return value can be based on either text or prefix. However, in the main function, prefix falls out of scope before result is used. This creates a dangling reference and leads to a lifetime error.

To fix this, we can adjust the function's signature to clarify that the return value is only based on text:

Ch14/Examples/bin/example04.rs

```
fn substring_after<'a>(text: &'a str, prefix: &str) -> &'a str {
    text.split_once(prefix).map(|(_, rest)| rest).unwrap_or("")
}

fn main() {
    let result;
    let text = String::from("Learning Rust");
    {
        let prefix = String::from(" ");
        result = substring_after(&text, &prefix);
    }
    println!("{}", result);
}
```

By removing the lifetime bound on prefix, we inform the compiler that the return value depends solely on text. As a result, result is only tied to the lifetime of text, avoiding any issues when prefix goes out of scope.

In summary, lifetime bounds in function signatures inform the compiler about which references the return value depends on. This ensures safe memory management and prevents dangling references. When applying lifetime bounds, carefully analyse the relationships between input references and the returned reference to avoid unnecessary or incorrect constraints. The compiler is not able to do this analysis for you.

Lifetime Elision

Lifetime elision rules are a set of guidelines used by the Rust compiler to infer lifetimes in function signatures when explicit annotations are omitted. These rules reduce code verbosity while maintaining memory safety. However, when lifetimes cannot be inferred unambiguously, the compiler generates an error and requires explicit annotations to resolve the ambiguity.

The rules for lifetime elision are as follows:

1. Each elided lifetime in an input position becomes a distinct lifetime parameter.
2. If there is exactly one input lifetime parameter (elided or not), that lifetime is assigned to all elided output lifetimes.
3. If there are multiple input lifetime positions, but one of them is &self or &mut self, the lifetime of self is assigned to all elided output lifetimes.
4. If none of these rules apply, it is an error to elide an output lifetime.

To illustrate how these rules work, consider the following examples:

Rule 1: Each Elided Input Lifetime Becomes a Distinct Parameter

For a function with two input references:

```
fn test(a: &str, b: &str) -> &str {}
```

Applying Rule 1, the compiler transforms this into:

```
fn test<'a, 'b>(a: &'a str, b: &'b str) -> &str {}
```

Here, the input references are assigned distinct lifetime parameters, ‘a and ‘b. However, since Rule 2 and Rule 3 do not apply (no single input lifetime or self), the code will not compile because the compiler cannot determine which input reference the output should depend on.

Rule 2: Single Input Lifetime is Assigned to All Outputs

For a function with one input reference:

```
fn test(a: &str) -> &str {}
```

Applying Rule 1 transforms this into:

```
fn test<'a>(a: &'a str) -> &str {}
```

Then, applying Rule 2, the compiler assigns the single input lifetime ‘a to the output:

```
fn test<'a>(a: &'a str) -> &'a str {}
```

This is a successful application of elision, and the code compiles.

Rule 3: self Lifetime is Assigned to the Output

For a method on a struct:

```
fn test(&self, a: &str) -> &str {}
```

Applying Rule 1 transforms this into:

```
fn test<'a, 'b>(&'a self, a: &'b str) -> &str {}
```

Rule 2 does not apply because there are multiple input lifetimes. However, Rule 3 applies because self is an input. The compiler assigns the lifetime of self to the output:

```
fn test<'a, 'b>(&'a self, a: &'b str) -> &'a str {}
```

This is a successful application of elision, and the code compiles.

By applying these rules systematically, Rust ensures that simple cases can omit explicit lifetime annotations while preserving clarity and safety in more complex scenarios.

Static lifetimes

The `'static` lifetime is different from a "normal" lifetime. A normal lifetime in Rust refers to the time during which a reference remains valid within a specific scope, depending on the program's flow and ownership rules. The `'static` lifetime, however, represents the longest possible lifetime in Rust: it means the referenced data is valid for the entire duration of the program.

When you specify a `'static` lifetime, you are telling the Rust compiler that only data that lives for the entire program is allowed in that reference or context. This is stricter than other lifetimes because `'static` references cannot be tied to temporary or scoped data.

For example:

- A `'static` lifetime applies to string literals like "Hello, world!" because they are embedded in the program's binary and are valid for as long as the program runs.
- It can also apply to data that is explicitly managed to live forever, such as heap-allocated data leaked with `Box::leak`.

`'static` Lifetime Different From Normal Lifetimes in these ways:

- **Scope Duration**: `'static` ensures that the data lives for the program's lifetime, whereas normal lifetimes depend on local scopes, function boundaries, or block structures.

- **Safety Enforcement**: When you annotate something with `'static`, you restrict the data that can be referenced there to only data guaranteed to exist for the entire program. This ensures safety but also limits flexibility.

Example of a function accepting only `'static` references:

Ch14/Examples/bin/example05.rs

```
fn print_static(data: &'static str) {
    println!("{}", data);
}

fn main() {
    let long_lived_data = "I live forever!";
    print_static(long_lived_data);

    let temporary_string = String::from("Temporary data");
    // print_static(&temporary_string); // This will not
compile.
}
```

Here, `print_static` only accepts references to data with `'static` lifetimes. The compiler rejects the `temporary_string` because it doesn't have a `'static` lifetime (it's scoped to main).

You should use 'static lifetime for the following case:

Restrict references: You use `'static` when you explicitly want to enforce that only data valid for the program's entire runtime can be referenced.

Global constants: `'static` is inherent in constant or immutable global data.

Thread-safe data sharing: For example, `'static` is often needed in multi-threaded contexts where references must outlive the current thread.

When you annotate something with `'static`, you are effectively saying, "Compiler, I want only references to data that is guaranteed to exist for the entire program to be allowed here." This ensures that temporary or short-lived data cannot accidentally be used in places requiring a `'static` lifetime, preventing dangling references.

Think of `'static` as a constraint on the lifetimes. While normal lifetimes provide flexibility to tie references to shorter-lived data, `'static` is the ultimate "safety net" that ensures the referenced data is available at all times during program execution.

Structs with Lifetimes

Lifetimes in structs are essential when a struct contains references to data owned elsewhere. Since references have lifetimes that depend on the scope of the data they point to, the Rust compiler needs explicit lifetime annotations in the struct to ensure the references remain valid while the struct exists. Lifetimes in structs are required to prevent dangling references and enforce memory safety. For example, if a struct holds references to strings or other variables, lifetimes tell the compiler how long those references are guaranteed to live in relation to the struct itself. This is especially critical when designing reusable or complex data structures that work with borrowed data.

One Lifetime Parameter on a Struct

Here's a minimal example demonstrating the need for lifetimes in structs:

Ch14/Examples/bin/example06.rs

```
struct Borrowed<'a> {
    data: &'a str,
}

fn main() {
    let text = String::from("Hello, Rust!");
    let borrowed = Borrowed { data: &text };

    println!("{}", borrowed.data);
}
```

In this example, we define a struct called Borrowed that contains a reference to a string slice (`&str`). The lifetime annotation `'a` in the struct definition ensures that any instance of Borrowed cannot outlive the data it references. In the main function, we create a String called text and then create an instance of Borrowed that holds a reference to text. When we access the data through the Borrowed instance, the reference is still valid because text exists within the same scope.

The need for the lifetime annotation arises because the struct does not own the data it references; it only borrows it. Rust's ownership model requires the compiler to verify that the data being referenced will not be dropped while the struct is still using it. The lifetime annotation `'a` explicitly ties the validity of the reference within the struct to the lifetime of the data being referenced. This ensures that when text is dropped at the end of the main function, the reference in the Borrowed instance also becomes invalid, maintaining memory safety.

Without the lifetime annotation, the compiler would not know how long the reference inside the struct is valid. This lack of clarity would lead to a compilation error because the compiler could not guarantee that the reference would not outlive the data it points to. By explicitly annotating the lifetime, you provide the compiler with the necessary information to enforce these guarantees, ensuring that your code is safe and free from dangling references.

More Lifetime Parameters on a Struct

A situation that often arises is when the references within the struct have different lifetimes. In such cases, we can use separate lifetime parameters to clearly communicate the missing relationship to the compiler.

Consider the following example where we define a Message struct that holds two references, from and to. These references may have distinct lifetimes, and to properly encapsulate this in the struct definition, we use two lifetime annotations 'a and 'b.

Ch14/Examples/bin/example07.rs

```
struct Message<'a, 'b> {
    from: &'a String,
    to: &'b String,
}

fn main() {
    let from_unpacked;
    let to_unpacked;
    let message: Message;

    {
        let from = &String::from("world");
        {
            let to = &String::from("hello");
            {
                message = Message { from, to };

                from_unpacked = message.from;
                to_unpacked = message.to;
            }
            println!("{to_unpacked}");
        }
        println!("{from_unpacked}");
```

```
    }
}
```

In this example, the Message struct is designed to hold references to String values. The references from and to are created in different nested scopes, meaning they have distinct lifetimes. Let's break this example down to understand why different lifetime annotations are necessary and how the struct works:

- **The Struct Definition**: The Message struct has two fields: `from` and `to`. Each field has a separate lifetime parameter, `'a` and `'b`. These lifetimes represent the valid duration of the references held by the fields. By using separate lifetimes, we allow `from` and `to` to have independent lifetimes.
- **Nesting Scopes**: In the `main` function, the references `from` and `to` are created in nested blocks. The `from` reference is valid in a broader scope, while `to` exists in a narrower, inner scope. Without separate lifetime annotations, the compiler would attempt to enforce a single lifetime for both references, which would be incompatible with their actual lifetimes.
- **Creating the Struct**: Inside the innermost block, the `Message` struct is initialized with the `from` and `to` references. The compiler verifies that the lifetimes of `from` and `to` conform to the constraints of `'a` and `'b` in the struct definition. Here, `'a` is assigned the lifetime of `from`, and `'b` is assigned the lifetime of `to`.
- **Extracting References**: The `from` and `to` fields of the `Message` struct are unpacked into `from_unpacked` and `to_unpacked`, respectively. These variables inherit the lifetimes of the original references, ensuring that they remain valid only within their respective scopes.
- **Printing References**: The `to_unpacked` reference is printed before the scope of to ends, and the `from_unpacked` reference is printed before the scope of from ends. This ensures that neither reference outlives the data it points to, maintaining Rust's strict memory safety guarantees.

If the Message struct were defined with a single lifetime parameter (e.g., `Message<'a>`), the compiler would enforce that both from and to share the same lifetime. This would not work in our example because from and to are created in different scopes, and their lifetimes do not overlap entirely. By using separate lifetimes (`'a` and `'b`), we explicitly tell the compiler that the two references may have different validities, allowing the struct to accommodate such cases.

When working with lifetimes in structs, the compiler uses the annotations to track how long each reference is valid. It ensures that any operation involving these references adheres to the lifetimes specified. In our example, the compiler verifies that:

- The from and to references in the Message struct are valid when assigned.
- The extracted references from_unpacked and to_unpacked do not outlive their respective data.

By explicitly specifying lifetimes, we provide the compiler with the necessary information to safely manage references, even in complex scenarios with nested scopes or differing lifetimes. This example highlights how Rust's lifetime system enables precise and safe memory management, preventing common bugs like dangling references.

Best Practices

Using lifetimes in Rust can feel challenging at first, but following best practices ensures safe and maintainable code while making the most of Rust's memory safety features. Here are some best practices for working with lifetimes:

Start Simple: Avoid Lifetimes Until Necessary

When writing functions or designing structs, avoid adding explicit lifetimes unless the compiler demands it. Rust's lifetime elision rules often handle most cases automatically, especially for simple function signatures.

For example:

Ch14/Examples/bin/example08.rs

```
fn first_word(s: &str) -> &str {
    s.split_whitespace().next().unwrap()
}
```

In this case, explicit lifetimes are unnecessary because the elision rules infer them.

Use Explicit Lifetimes When References Have Ambiguity

If a function has multiple input references or a mix of references and output, explicitly annotate lifetimes to clarify relationships. This helps both the compiler and other developers understand how references are related.

For example:

Ch14/Examples/bin/example09.rs

```
fn longest<'a>(x: &'a str, y: &'a str) -> &'a str {
    if x.len() > y.len() {
```

```
        x
    } else {
        y
    }
}
```

Here, the lifetime 'a specifies that the return value is tied to the same lifetime as the inputs.

Use Separate Lifetimes When References Are Independent

When references in a struct or function are unrelated, use different lifetimes to avoid unnecessary constraints. This provides flexibility and avoids overly strict borrow checking.

For example:

Ch14/Examples/bin/example10.rs

```
struct Message<'a, 'b> {
    sender: &'a str,
    receiver: &'b str,
}
```

Separate lifetimes 'a and 'b ensure that the sender and receiver references can originate from different scopes.

Tie Lifetimes to Self in Methods When Appropriate

In methods where the output is based on the struct's internal references, tie the output lifetime to the lifetime of &self. This is a common pattern for borrowing struct data.

Example:

Ch14/Examples/bin/example11.rs

```
struct Config<'a> {
    key: &'a str,
}

impl<'a> Config<'a> {
    fn get_key(&self) -> &'a str {
        self.key
    }
}
```

Minimize Lifetimes on Structs Where Possible

Adding lifetimes to structs can propagate complexity throughout your codebase. If a struct doesn't need lifetimes (e.g., when working with owned data), avoid them by using String or Vec<T> instead of &str or &[T].

Example:

```
struct OwnedMessage {
    sender: String,
    receiver: String,
}
```

This avoids requiring lifetime annotations when using the struct, simplifying its usage.

Avoid Over-Constraining Lifetimes

Be mindful not to over-constrain lifetimes in function signatures or structs. For example, using the same lifetime for unrelated references can make code less flexible and harder to use.

Bad Example:

```
fn unrelated<'a>(x: &'a str, y: &'a str) -> &'a str {
    x // Forces x and y to share the same lifetime
unnecessarily
}
```

Use static Lifetime Sparingly

Avoid assigning the 'static lifetime unless the data truly has a 'static lifetime (e.g., string literals or globally leaked data). Misusing 'static can lead to unintentional memory leaks or overly restrictive APIs.

Iterate with Compiler Feedback

Rust's compiler provides detailed suggestions when lifetime issues arise. Follow its feedback iteratively, and let the compiler guide you to add or adjust lifetimes. This approach often leads to clearer and safer code.

Summary

This chapter delves into the concept of lifetimes in Rust, a mechanism that ensures memory safety by tying references to the lifespan of the data they point to. This eliminates issues such as dangling references while allowing flexible borrowing. Although Rust's compiler automatically infers lifetimes in most scenarios through its elision rules, certain complex cases demand explicit lifetime annotations to clarify relationships between references.

The chapter explores various topics related to lifetimes, including how they work in functions and structs, the rules governing their inference, and their practical application in designing safe and efficient code. It highlights lifetime elision rules, which reduce the need for explicit annotations, and explains when explicit lifetimes are necessary. Static lifetimes are discussed as a special case, indicating data that persists for the program's entire duration. Additionally, the chapter examines how lifetimes can be applied in structs to manage references to external data, ensuring safety and preventing errors.

Practical examples illustrate the use of lifetimes in functions and structs, demonstrating how to manage borrowing and avoid constraints that could limit flexibility. The chapter emphasizes best practices, such as minimizing lifetime annotations where possible, tying lifetimes to self in methods, and using separate lifetimes for independent references. It also introduces techniques like combining lifetimes with smart pointers or ownership to simplify lifetime management.

By the end, readers will have a comprehensive understanding of lifetimes, enabling them to confidently design safe, efficient, and flexible code in Rust. The chapter provides exercises and a project to reinforce these concepts, offering hands-on experience with the practical application of lifetimes.

In the final chapter, we'll introduce *unsafe Rust*, explaining what it is, when it's used, and why it's sometimes necessary for low-level systems programming.

Exercises

1. Write a function that takes a reference to a string slice and returns the first word from the string. Ensure that the function includes appropriate lifetime annotations.
2. Define a struct that contains a single reference to a string slice. Write a function to create an instance of this struct and ensure the reference lifetime matches the data it points to.

3. Modify the substring_after example to use String instead of &str as input and return a substring as a reference. Compare the behavior with the original version.
4. Create a function that accepts two references to string slices and returns the longer one. Explicitly annotate the lifetimes of the references and explain why the annotations are needed.
5. Implement a struct that holds references to two different string slices with independent lifetimes. Add methods to retrieve each reference and test their validity with nested scopes.
6. Write a method for a struct that takes &self and a reference to a string slice, and returns a reference to the string slice with the lifetime tied to the struct. Test it with different scopes in the main function.
7. Modify a function that uses lifetime elision rules to include explicit lifetime annotations. Compare the behavior of the function before and after adding the annotations.
8. Create a struct that uses a 'static lifetime reference. Demonstrate its usage with string literals and explain why the 'static lifetime is appropriate in this context.
9. Write a function that takes multiple references, each with distinct lifetimes, and performs operations that depend on those references. Show how lifetimes are enforced at compile time.
10. Design an example where lifetimes in a struct must align with the nested scopes of the references it contains. Use this example to demonstrate why multiple lifetime parameters are necessary for such scenarios.

Project: String Slicer

Implement a StringSlicer struct that holds a reference to a string slice (&str). This struct will provide methods to extract substrings either by using a specified delimiter or by specifying start and end indices. The extracted substrings must maintain references tied to the original string to ensure proper lifetime management. Additionally, the implementation will include test cases to verify the correctness of substring extraction and enforce Rust's strict borrowing rules, ensuring that the returned references remain valid throughout their intended usage.

15

Unsafe Code

Rust is renowned for its strong safety guarantees, achieved through its ownership model, borrowing rules, and strict type system. These features ensure that common programming errors, such as null pointer dereferencing, buffer overflows, and data races, are eliminated at compile time. However, there are scenarios where adhering to these safety rules becomes restrictive, particularly in low-level systems programming or performance-critical tasks. In such cases, Rust provides an escape hatch: unsafe code.

This chapter serves as a first introduction to unsafe Rust. It is intended to help you understand what unsafe code is, why it exists, and what it enables, but it is by no means a practical guide on how to write or structure unsafe code in production.

Unsafe code allows developers to bypass Rust's compile-time safety checks and access features that are otherwise restricted. This includes dereferencing raw pointers, calling unsafe functions, accessing mutable static variables, and working with unsafe traits. While unsafe code is powerful, it comes with the caveat that the programmer, not the compiler, is now responsible for ensuring memory safety.

The need for unsafe code arises in situations where high performance, low-level hardware interactions, or interfacing with external libraries written in other languages (like C) are critical. For instance, operating systems, device drivers, and embedded systems often require direct manipulation of memory or hardware, which cannot always be expressed within Rust's safe abstractions.

Using unsafe code effectively involves balancing safety and performance. Unsafe code should only be used when it is absolutely necessary and when the safety guarantees can be upheld manually. Ideally, unsafe operations are encapsulated within well-defined, small sections of code, and safe abstractions are built around them to minimize the risk of introducing bugs. This balance is crucial in systems programming, where performance is paramount, but reliability and correctness cannot be compromised.

In this chapter we will cover:

- **Unsafe Code**: A special Rust construct that lets you bypass certain compiler safety checks when absolutely necessary.
- **Calling Unsafe Functions or Methods**: Functions marked as unsafe must be invoked inside unsafe blocks to signal potential risks.

- **Implementing Unsafe Traits**: Traits that have safety requirements which the compiler can't enforce, so it's up to the implementer to ensure correctness.
- **Raw Pointers**: Pointers like `*const T` and `*mut T` that can point anywhere in memory and are not subject to Rust's borrowing and ownership rules.
- **Global Variables**: Mutable global state can lead to data races, so accessing mutable static variables requires unsafe blocks.

Unsafe code gives you controlled access to operations outside Rust's usual safety checks, but with that power comes responsibility. In the rest of this chapter, we'll explore how to use unsafe features correctly and when their use is appropriate.

What is Unsafe Code?

In Rust, unsafe code refers to sections of code that bypass the language's strict safety guarantees. While Rust's safe abstractions ensure that common errors like null pointer dereferencing, data races, and buffer overflows are prevented at compile time, unsafe code gives developers the ability to opt out of these protections. This opt-out mechanism is necessary for certain low-level operations, but it shifts the responsibility for ensuring safety from the compiler to the programmer.

Definition of Unsafe Code in Rust

Unsafe code in Rust allows you to perform operations that the compiler cannot guarantee are safe. These include dereferencing raw pointers, modifying mutable static variables, calling unsafe functions (like those interacting with foreign code or low-level APIs), and implementing unsafe traits. The key distinction between safe Rust and unsafe Rust is that safe Rust guarantees memory safety, while unsafe Rust merely assumes it.

For example, in safe Rust, dereferencing a reference is always valid because the compiler enforces strict borrowing rules. However, in unsafe Rust, you can work with raw pointers, which do not have these guarantees. While this flexibility is powerful, it also introduces risks, as the programmer must manually uphold the safety guarantees that Rust would typically enforce.

Unsafe Blocks and Unsafe Functions

The unsafe keyword in Rust is used to mark sections of code where unsafe operations are performed. It acts as a signal to the programmer and compiler that extra caution is needed. Unsafe code must be enclosed in either an unsafe block or an unsafe function, depending on the scope and nature of the operations.

An unsafe block is a scoped region of code where unsafe operations are allowed. It is used when unsafe code is limited to a specific part of a larger function.

For example:

Ch15/Examples/bin/example01.rs

```
fn main() {
    let raw_pointer: *const i32 = &10;

    unsafe {
        println!("Value at raw pointer: {}", *raw_pointer);
    }
}
```

In this example, the `raw_pointer` is a raw pointer, and dereferencing it is an unsafe operation. The `unsafe` block ensures that the potentially dangerous operation is explicitly marked.

An `unsafe` function is a function that performs unsafe operations or calls other `unsafe` functions. The entire function is marked as `unsafe`, indicating that the caller must ensure all safety guarantees are met.

For example:

Ch15/Examples/bin/example02.rs

```
unsafe fn unsafe_function() {
    println!("This is an unsafe function");
}

fn main() {
    unsafe {
        unsafe_function();
    }
}
```

Here, the `unsafe_function` is defined as unsafe, and calling it requires an `unsafe` block. This ensures that any `unsafe` function cannot be called accidentally or without the programmer explicitly acknowledging the risks.

By design, the `unsafe` keyword does not make the entire program unsafe; it merely signals that within a specific scope, Rust's usual safety checks are not enforced. Proper use of `unsafe` blocks and functions enables developers to handle low-level tasks effectively while minimizing risks by keeping `unsafe` operations contained and well-documented.

Safe Abstractions

While unsafe Rust allows bypassing the compiler's strict safety guarantees, it is crucial to limit its use and contain unsafe operations within safe abstractions. A safe abstraction is a wrapper around unsafe code that ensures all safety invariants are upheld while exposing a clean, safe API to users. This prevents undefined behavior and makes working with low-level features safer and more ergonomic.

The goal of a safe abstraction is to hide the unsafe details from users while guaranteeing memory safety and soundness. To achieve this, safe abstractions must:

- **Enforce Validity Invariants**: Ensuring that operations like memory access and pointer arithmetic are always valid.
- **Minimize the Surface of Unsafe Code**: Containing unsafe within a small, well-audited section of code.
- **Provide a Safe Interface**: Exposing only methods that prevent incorrect usage.

The following example demonstrates a safe abstraction for manual memory management, encapsulating raw pointer manipulation within a struct called `SafeBuffer`. This ensures safe reads and writes to a manually allocated memory region.

Ch15/Examples/bin/example03.rs

```
struct SafeBuffer {
    ptr: *mut u8,
    size: usize,
}

impl SafeBuffer {
    fn new(size: usize) -> Self {
        let ptr = unsafe {
std::alloc::alloc(std::alloc::Layout::array::<u8>(size).
unwrap())
        };
        if ptr.is_null() {
            panic!("Memory allocation failed");
        }
        Self { ptr, size }
    }

    fn get(&self, index: usize) -> u8 {
        assert!(index < self.size, "Index out of bounds");
```

```
        unsafe { *self.ptr.add(index) }
    }

    fn set(&mut self, index: usize, value: u8) {
        assert!(index < self.size, "Index out of bounds");
        unsafe { *self.ptr.add(index) = value; }
    }
}

impl Drop for SafeBuffer {
    fn drop(&mut self) {
        unsafe { std::alloc::dealloc(self.ptr,
std::alloc::Layout::array::<u8>(self.size).unwrap()) };
    }
}

fn main() {
    let mut buffer = SafeBuffer::new(10);
    buffer.set(0, 42);
    let value = buffer.get(0);
    println!("Value at index 0: {}", value);
}
```

The `SafeBuffer` abstraction enables manual memory management while eliminating the risks associated with direct raw pointer manipulation. It achieves safety by encapsulating memory allocation within the `new()` method, preventing uninitialized access. Every access operation, whether retrieving or modifying data, includes bounds checking to ensure valid memory access. Additionally, memory deallocation is handled automatically through the implementation of the Drop trait, preventing memory leaks. The use of unsafe code is confined to a few well-defined methods, while the public API remains entirely safe, allowing users to interact with the abstraction without exposing themselves to potential memory errors.

Encapsulating unsafe operations within a safe API ensures that users do not need to manually verify safety guarantees. Instead, they can rely on Rust's type system and the well-defined interface to enforce correctness. This approach provides the best of both worlds, low-level control with high-level safety, making Rust a powerful choice for systems programming.

In the next section, we explore the powerful capabilities that unsafe Rust provides, demonstrating each with small examples.

The Unsafe Super Powers

In Rust, unsafe superpowers refer to the capabilities granted when working within unsafe code. These are operations that the Rust compiler cannot guarantee as safe at compile time but are sometimes necessary for low-level programming, interfacing with hardware, or working with performance-critical systems.

Here are the main unsafe superpowers in Rust:

Dereferencing Raw Pointers

In Rust, a raw pointer is a type of pointer that is not subject to the usual ownership, borrowing, or lifetime checks enforced by the compiler. Raw pointers come in two forms:

- ***const T**: a raw pointer to read-only data
- ***mut T**: a raw pointer to mutable data

Unlike references (`&T and &mut T`), raw pointers can be null, unaligned, or dangling, and Rust does not prevent you from creating or using them in unsafe ways. Because of this, raw pointers can only be dereferenced inside an unsafe block, where the programmer is responsible for ensuring that the pointer is valid and that any aliasing or memory safety rules are upheld.

Raw pointers are typically used when interfacing with C code, working with low-level memory, or implementing safe abstractions that need to bypass some of Rust's restrictions internally.

For example:

Ch15/Examples/bin/example04.rs

```
fn main() {
    let x = 42;
    let raw_pointer: *const i32 = &x;

    unsafe {
        println!("Value at raw pointer: {}", *raw_pointer);
    }
}
```

Risk: Dereferencing raw pointers can lead to undefined behavior if the pointer is invalid, dangling, or misaligned.

Calling Unsafe Functions or Methods

In Rust, a function or method is marked unsafe when its correct usage cannot be guaranteed by the compiler. This means the compiler assumes the caller will uphold the required safety invariants manually. You can only call such functions from within an unsafe block, which serves as an explicit signal that you're taking responsibility for upholding safety guarantees.

Unsafe functions are common in scenarios where Rust cannot statically verify memory safety, such as:

- **Low-level system operations**: Functions that manipulate raw memory, access hardware registers, or perform system calls often require unsafe because they can easily lead to undefined behavior if misused.
- **FFI (Foreign Function Interface)**: When calling into code written in another language, such as C, Rust cannot check that the external function behaves safely. Any FFI function must be declared unsafe because the compiler cannot analyze the foreign code.
- **Custom unsafe abstractions**: Sometimes, you may write a function that internally uses unsafe code and requires the caller to meet certain conditions (like alignment, initialization, or aliasing guarantees). In this case, you mark the function itself as unsafe to enforce that the caller must understand and honor those conditions.

For example:

Ch15/Examples/bin/example05.rs

```
unsafe fn dangerous_function() {
    println!("Performing an unsafe operation!");
}

fn main() {
    unsafe {
        dangerous_function();
    }
}
```

Risk: Unsafe functions must be explicitly marked and carefully implemented to ensure safety. It's the caller's responsibility to use them correctly.

Accessing or Modifying Mutable Static Variables

Static variables in Rust have a 'static lifetime and are shared across the entire program.

- **Immutable statics**: Immutable static variables are safe and can be accessed from any part of the program without restrictions, as they cannot be modified.
- **Mutable statics (static mut)**: Mutable static variables, declared with `static mut`, are unsafe by design. Since they are shared across all threads and accessible globally, modifying them can lead to data races, which Rust's safe code normally prevents. Because the compiler cannot enforce exclusive access or prevent concurrent modifications, any access (read or write) to a static mut variable must occur within an unsafe block.

For example:

Ch15/Examples/bin/example06.rs

```
static mut COUNTER: i32 = 0;

fn main() {
    unsafe {
        COUNTER += 1;
        println!("Counter: {}", COUNTER);
    }
}
```

Risk: Accessing or modifying static mut variables can lead to undefined behavior if multiple threads modify them simultaneously without proper synchronization.

Implementing Unsafe Traits

Some traits are marked as unsafe because implementing them incorrectly could violate memory safety or other invariants. For example, the Send and Sync traits are unsafe if implemented manually, as they control thread-safety guarantees.

This code defines and uses an unsafe trait, but does not require an unsafe block to call the method:

Ch15/Examples/bin/example07.rs

```
struct MyStruct;

unsafe trait DangerousTrait {
    fn dangerous_method(&self);
```

```
}

unsafe impl DangerousTrait for MyStruct {
    fn dangerous_method(&self) {
        println!("inside dangerous_method");
    }
}

fn main() {
    let my_struct = MyStruct;
    my_struct.dangerous_method();
}
```

This code defines an unsafe trait and implements it for a struct. The trait itself is marked as unsafe, which means that implementing it carries certain requirements the compiler cannot check, it's up to the implementer to ensure those requirements are met. However, the method within the trait is not marked as unsafe, so calling it doesn't require an unsafe block. Even though the trait is unsafe, the method behaves like any regular method from the caller's perspective. The only point where the unsafe keyword is required is during the implementation, where the compiler expects you to declare that you're aware of and responsible for any safety invariants the trait assumes. Once implemented, as long as the method itself is safe, it can be used in normal, safe Rust code.

Risk: The correctness of unsafe trait implementations depends entirely on the implementer, and incorrect implementations can break Rust's safety guarantees.

Accessing Union Fields

In Rust, a union is a low-level data structure that allows different fields to occupy the same memory space, much like a union in C. This means that all the fields in a union start at the same memory address, and writing to one field overwrites the data in the others.

Unions are used when you need to work with different data types stored in the same memory location, usually to:

- Interact with C code via FFI (Foreign Function Interface)
- Save memory by reusing space across fields
- Implement low-level abstractions like bit manipulation or raw data interpretation

For example:

Ch15/Examples/bin/example08.rs

```
union MyUnion {
    int: i32,
    float: f32,
}

fn main() {
    let u = MyUnion { int: 10 };

    unsafe {
        println!("Union value: {}", u.float);
    }
}
```

Risk: Accessing the wrong field or using improper alignment can result in undefined behavior.

Bypassing Lifetime and Borrowing Rules

Unsafe code can bypass Rust's lifetime and borrowing checks, allowing you to create references that the compiler would normally reject. For example, you can create a reference with a fake lifetime or cast raw pointers into references.

For example:

Ch15/Examples/bin/example09.rs

```
fn main() {
    let mut x = 42;
    let raw_pointer: *mut i32 = &mut x;

    unsafe {
        let reference: &i32 = &*raw_pointer; // Bypassing
borrow checker
        println!("{}", reference);
    }
}
```

Risk: It's up to the programmer to ensure the reference is valid for its intended use, as the compiler cannot verify it.

Performing Inline Assembly

Rust allows inline assembly with the asm! macro in unsafe blocks, which is useful for low-level hardware interactions and performance optimizations. This feature gives you full control over CPU instructions.

For example:

Ch15/Examples/bin/example10.rs

```
use std::arch::asm;

fn main() {
    unsafe {
        asm!("nop"); // Perform a no-operation instruction
    }
}
```

Risk: Inline assembly can lead to unpredictable results if used incorrectly, as the compiler cannot analyze or optimize it.

The following sections provide a detailed examination of selected capabilities introduced earlier.

Raw Pointers

Raw pointers in Rust come in two forms: `*const T`, which is an immutable pointer to some value of type `T`, and `*mut T`, which is a mutable pointer to `T`. Unlike Rust's references (`&T` and `&mut T`), raw pointers do not enforce borrowing rules, lifetimes, or automatic validity checks. This means they can be null, dangling, or point to unaligned memory, issues that are impossible with safe Rust references.

The primary reason Rust includes raw pointers is to enable interaction with low-level systems where strict safety checks would be impractical. In cases such as working with C code via Foreign Function Interface (FFI), implementing unsafe abstractions such as memory allocators, or achieving performance optimizations by bypassing certain safety checks, raw pointers provide essential capabilities. Despite their power, raw pointers should be used with caution and only within unsafe blocks, as they circumvent Rust's usual guarantees and place the responsibility of correctness on the developer.

By understanding when and how to use raw pointers effectively, you gain the ability to write high-performance and low-level Rust code while minimizing risks.

The following sections will explore raw pointer operations, their interaction with unsafe code, and best practices to ensure they are used responsibly.

Creating and Using Raw Pointers

Raw pointers provide direct memory access, bypassing Rust's usual borrowing and ownership rules. They are a powerful tool for low-level programming, but using them requires care, as Rust does not guarantee their safety. This section explores how to create raw pointers, convert between raw pointers and references, handle null and dangling pointers, and safely read and write through raw pointers.

Creating Raw Pointers from References

Raw pointers can be created from references. When creating a raw pointer, Rust does not enforce lifetime checks or aliasing rules, meaning multiple raw pointers can exist simultaneously, even if they point to mutable data.

Ch15/Examples/bin/example11.rs

```
fn main() {
    let mut x = 42;
    let raw_const: *const i32 = &x;
    let raw_mut: *mut i32 = &mut x;

    unsafe {
        *raw_mut += 1;
        println!("raw_mut: {}", *raw_mut);
        println!("raw_const: {}", *raw_const);
    }
}
```

In this code, we start by declaring a mutable variable `x` with the value `42`. We then create two raw pointers to it: `raw_const`, a `*const i32` pointing to `x`, and `raw_mut`, a `*mut i32` created from a mutable reference to `x`. Because these are raw pointers, Rust allows both to coexist without triggering its usual borrowing checks.

Within the unsafe block, we increment the value pointed to by `raw_mut` and then print both the value through `raw_mut` and the value through `raw_const`. Since both pointers reference the same memory, they reflect the same updated value.

This works because raw pointers are not checked by Rust's borrow checker, allowing you to bypass the usual rule that prevents having a mutable and an immutable reference to the same variable at the same time.

Creating References from Raw Pointers

To use raw pointers in a meaningful way, they must be converted back into references. Since dereferencing a raw pointer is an unsafe operation, it must occur within an unsafe block.

For example:

Ch15/Examples/bin/example12.rs

```
fn main() {
    let mut value = 10;
    let ptr: *mut i32 = &mut value;

    let r = unsafe {
        *ptr = 20;
        &mut *ptr
    };

    *r += 1;
    println!("value: {}", r);
}
```

This example is converting a raw pointer back into a normal reference. The program starts with a mutable variable value, from which a raw mutable pointer `ptr` is created. Inside the unsafe block, the raw pointer is first used to update the value to `20`. Then, it is converted back into a mutable reference using `&mut *ptr`. This reconstructed reference, stored in `r`, is now a regular Rust reference and can be used safely outside the unsafe block. The final line increments the value through `r` and prints the result. This pattern, temporarily dropping into raw pointer territory and then safely re-entering Rust's reference system, is a common and powerful use of unsafe.

Null Pointers and Dangling Pointers

Unlike Rust references, raw pointers can be null or dangling. A null pointer explicitly points to nothing and is commonly used in FFI to indicate the absence of a value.

In the following example, `null_ptr` is explicitly initialized to a null pointer and then checked to confirm that it is indeed null:

Ch15/Examples/bin/example13.rs

```
fn main() {
    let null_ptr: *const i32 = std::ptr::null();
```

```
    println!("{}", null_ptr.is_null());
}
```

A dangling pointer, on the other hand, points to invalid or deallocated memory. This can happen if a raw pointer is created to a stack variable that goes out of scope or if it points to heap memory that has been freed.

The following example illustrates a dangling pointer, though its effects typically become apparent only when the program is run in release mode.

Ch15/Examples/bin/example14.rs

```
fn main() {
    let raw_dangling: *const i32;
    {
        let x = 10;
        raw_dangling = &x;
        unsafe {
            println!("raw_dangling: {:?}", *raw_dangling);
        }
    }

    // polute the stack
    let y1 = 100;

    unsafe {
        println!("raw_dangling: {:?}", *raw_dangling);
    }

    // prevent optimization
    println!("y1: {}", y1);
}
```

Dereferencing a null or dangling pointer results in undefined behavior, making it critical to track pointer validity manually.

Dereferencing Raw Pointers Safely

To safely dereference a raw pointer, you must manually ensure that:

- The pointer is non-null.
- The pointer is properly aligned.
- The memory the pointer refers to is initialized and valid.
- There are no concurrent mutable accesses to the same memory.

A common technique to check for null before dereferencing a raw pointer is using is_null().

Ch15/Examples/bin/example15.rs

```
fn main() {
    let raw: * const i32 = std::ptr::null();

    unsafe {
        if !raw.is_null() {
            println!("{}", *raw);
        } else {
            println!("Pointer is null, cannot dereference.");
        }
    }
}
```

For non-null pointers, you must ensure the data remains valid throughout the pointer's lifetime. Using an invalid pointer can cause segmentation faults or data corruption.

Avoiding Undefined Behavior

Undefined behavior (UB) refers to actions that Rust's memory model does not define, leading to unpredictable results. The following operations with raw pointers can trigger UB:

Dereferencing a null or dangling pointer: If a pointer does not point to valid memory, dereferencing it causes a crash or silent memory corruption.

Reading uninitialized memory: If a pointer refers to memory that has not been initialized, accessing it can lead to arbitrary values being read.

Violating aliasing rules: Rust enforces strict aliasing rules to ensure memory safety and enable compiler optimizations. If a raw pointer is used to perform mutable access while another reference (mutable or immutable) to the same memory exists, the behavior is undefined. This rule applies even in single-threaded applications, because the compiler relies on these aliasing guarantees when generating optimized code.

Global Variables

In Rust, global variables are declared using the static or const keywords. However, unlike many other languages, Rust enforces strict rules around global variables to ensure memory safety and concurrency correctness. Since global variables persist for the entire program's execution, improper use can lead to data races, undefined behavior, or unexpected side effects in multi-threaded environments.

Declaring Global Variables with const and static

Rust provides two ways to declare global variables:

const (Immutable, Compile-Time Constant)

- Evaluated at compile time
- No memory allocation at runtime
- Does not allow mutation
- Thread-safe by default
- Substituted directly into the code during compilation

Ch15/Examples/bin/example16.rs

```
const MAX_USERS: u32 = 1000;

fn main() {
    println!("Max users allowed: {}", MAX_USERS);
}
```

Since `const` variables are inlined wherever they are used, they do not behave like true global variables but rather as **compile-time constants**.

static (Global, Runtime Allocated, Possibly Mutable)

- Exists in memory for the program's lifetime
- Not inlined by the compiler
- Can be immutable (static) or mutable (static mut)
- Requires unsafe for mutation

Ch15/Examples/bin/example17.rs

```
static WELCOME_MESSAGE: &str = "Welcome to Rust!";

fn main() {
```

```
    println!("{}", WELCOME_MESSAGE);
}
```

This static variable is a true global, allocated once and shared across the entire program.

Mutable Global Variables with static mut

If a global variable needs to be mutable, Rust requires marking it as static mut. However, modifying a static mut variable is inherently unsafe, as it can lead to data races if accessed from multiple threads.

Ch15/Examples/bin/example18.rs

```
static mut COUNTER: i32 = 0;

fn main() {
    unsafe {
        COUNTER += 1;
        let value = COUNTER;
        println!("Counter: {}", value);
    }
}
```

This example demonstrates how to work with a `static mut` variable in Rust. The `COUNTER` variable is declared as a mutable static, meaning it exists for the entire duration of the program and can be accessed from anywhere. However, because mutable statics are not inherently safe to access, especially in multithreaded contexts, Rust requires all reads and writes to them to occur inside an unsafe block.

In the main function, the unsafe block allows us to increment the `COUNTER` by one and then read its value into a local variable. Instead of printing `COUNTER` directly, the code assigns its value to value and prints that. This avoids taking a reference to `COUNTER`, which would trigger a compiler warning, since creating a shared reference to a static mut is discouraged even in single-threaded code. By copying the value into a local variable, we avoid that issue while still demonstrating how to mutate and read from a mutable static variable.

Summary

This chapter explores Rust's unsafe code feature, which serves as a deliberate escape hatch from the language's strict compile-time safety guarantees. Rust's ownership model, borrowing rules, and type system are designed to eliminate entire classes of errors, such as null pointer dereferencing, buffer overflows, and data races. These checks are enforced by the compiler and ensure that safe Rust code upholds strong memory safety guarantees. However, in certain scenarios, such as low-level systems programming, interfacing with C code, or writing performance-critical abstractions, these rules can become restrictive or impractical. For such cases, Rust provides the unsafe keyword, allowing developers to bypass the usual protections and access features that are otherwise off-limits.

Unsafe code enables operations like dereferencing raw pointers, calling unsafe functions, accessing mutable static variables, implementing unsafe traits, and interacting with unions or inline assembly. These capabilities, often referred to as "unsafe superpowers," are necessary for tasks such as manual memory management, writing device drivers, or building custom memory allocators. However, the moment you enter unsafe code, the compiler stops checking that your code is memory safe. The responsibility now falls entirely on you, the programmer, to uphold Rust's guarantees manually.

Despite its name, unsafe Rust does not mean the code is inherently dangerous or broken, it simply means that the compiler cannot verify it for you. When used with care, unsafe code can be a tool to unlock performance and control without sacrificing the integrity of a program. The best practice is to isolate unsafe operations in small, well-audited sections and wrap them in safe abstractions. These abstractions provide a public interface that guarantees memory safety, while internally relying on unsafe operations to accomplish tasks that safe Rust cannot express directly.

This chapter demonstrates how to write and reason about unsafe code effectively. It explains how to use unsafe blocks and functions to clearly delineate the boundaries where safety checks are relaxed. It shows how raw pointers differ from references, and how they can be created, dereferenced, and converted back into safe references when appropriate. It highlights the risks of null and dangling pointers, and the importance of manual checks for validity, alignment, and aliasing. It also discusses how global variables behave in Rust, particularly when declared as mutable statics, and why accessing them requires unsafe blocks.

Finally, the chapter emphasizes the principle that unsafe code should serve safe code. By encapsulating low-level operations in rigorously tested, well-documented

APIs, developers can safely unlock the full power of Rust's systems programming capabilities while preserving the reliability and correctness that define the language.

Exercises

1. Create a program that declares an integer variable, then creates a raw pointer (`*const i32`) pointing to that variable. Use an unsafe block to print the value by dereferencing the pointer.

2. Extend the previous exercise by creating a mutable raw pointer (`*mut i32`) that allows modifying the integer's value. Modify the value using an unsafe block and print both the original and modified values.

3. Write a program that creates a null pointer using `std::ptr::null()`, then checks if the pointer is null before attempting to dereference it. Print an appropriate message instead of dereferencing the null pointer.

4. Create a function that accepts a reference to an integer and returns a raw pointer to it. Then, in main, call this function and use an unsafe block to dereference and print the value.

5. Implement a struct that contains a raw pointer to an integer and provides a safe API for getting and setting the value while ensuring safety using proper checks inside the functions.

6. Write an unsafe function that accepts a raw pointer to an integer and modifies the value. Call this function from main within an unsafe block and verify the result.

7. Create a struct that acts as a simple smart pointer for managing a heap-allocated integer. Implement a `Drop` trait for it to ensure that the allocated memory is properly freed when the struct goes out of scope.

8. Create a union that can store either a `u32` or an `f32`. Write a value to one field and read it back from the other, then explain what happens and why. Use an unsafe block to access the union field.

9. Define a safe wrapper around a raw pointer to an integer. The wrapper should expose get and set methods that check for null before accessing the value. Ensure that the pointer is valid during its use, and include a method to explicitly free the memory. Demonstrate usage in main.

10. Create a function that takes a raw pointer to a byte buffer (`*mut u8`) and its length. Inside the function, fill the buffer with a repeating pattern (e.g., `0xAA`). Use unsafe code to write to the buffer, and demonstrate calling the function from main using a manually allocated array.

Epilogue

Writing this book has been a journey into the core of Rust—a language that challenges you to think clearly about memory, correctness, and design. We've explored its unique guarantees around safety and performance, and how its strict model enables you to build fast, predictable systems with clarity and control.

For those coming from C++, many of Rust's ideas will feel both familiar and refreshingly strict. Concepts like RAII and zero-cost abstractions reappear, but are reinforced by a type system that enforces correctness by construction. The borrow checker, lifetimes, and move semantics may have felt demanding at first, but they exist to help you write code that is safe by default, not by discipline.

Throughout the chapters, the goal has not only been to explain how Rust works, but to expose the reasoning behind its design. You now have the foundation to write idiomatic Rust, to understand the difference between safe and unsafe code, and to approach concurrency, memory management, and performance without sacrificing reliability.

That journey doesn't stop here. Rust continues to grow, and so will your understanding. To support your ongoing learning—and to gather your feedback—we've created a companion website at www.rustexpertisecenter.com. There you'll find errata, and updates as the ecosystem evolves. Just as importantly, you'll find a way to reach out. Your feedback—corrections, suggestions, or questions—is not only welcome, but crucial. It helps make the material clearer and more accurate for future readers.

Rust isn't just a new language. It's a new mindset. It teaches precision, rewards thoughtful design, and opens doors to systems programming with fewer regrets and more confidence.

Thank you for reading. Now it's your turn—go build something that lasts.

Freek

Bibliography

1. **The Rust Programming Language** — The official book introducing all core Rust concepts. https://doc.rust-lang.org/book/
2. **Rust by Example** — A collection of runnable examples that complement the official book. https://doc.rust-lang.org/rust-by-example/
3. **Standard Library Documentation** — Reference for all modules in the standard library. https://doc.rust-lang.org/std/
4. **Cargo Book** — Official guide to Rust's build and dependency manager. https://doc.rust-lang.org/cargo/
5. **Learning Rust (GitHub curated list)** — Community-contributed learning paths. https://github.com/ctjhoa/rust-learning
6. **Collection Types** — Overview of Vec, HashMap, and others. https://doc.rust-lang.org/std/collections/
7. **Iterators in Rust** — How iterators work, and how to chain them effectively. https://doc.rust-lang.org/book/ch13-02-iterators.html
8. **Testing Rust Applications** — From unit testing to test organization. https://doc.rust-lang.org/book/ch11-00-testing.html
9. **Fearless Concurrency with Rust** — Overview of threads, channels, Arc, and Mutex. https://doc.rust-lang.org/book/ch16-00-concurrency.html
10. **Programming Rust (2nd Edition)** — Systems-level book exploring memory safety and performance. Jim Blandy, Jason Orendorff, Leonora Tindall
11. **Understanding Ownership and Smart Pointers** — Patterns and idioms in Rust. https://rust-unofficial.github.io/patterns/idioms/deref.html
12. **Learning Rust With Entirely Too Many Linked Lists** — Advanced ownership/lifetimes example. https://rust-unofficial.github.io/too-many-lists/
13. **ChatGPT (OpenAI)** — Used for interactive assistance, explanation of concepts, and code generation support during manuscript development. https://chat.openai.com

14. **The Hitchhiker's Guide to the Galaxy (Douglas Adams)** — The origin of *Don't Panic!* — an attitude every Rust developer may appreciate when facing ownership errors.

[https://en.wikipedia.org/wiki/The_Hitchhiker%27s_Guide_to_the_Galaxy](https://en.wikipedia.org/wiki/The_Hitchhiker's_Guide_to_the_Galaxy)

Further Reading

1. **Error Handling with anyhow and thiserror** — Crate documentation on docs.rs https://docs.rs/anyhow https://docs.rs/thiserror
2. **Serde for Serialization** — Read/write data structures to JSON and other formats. https://serde.rs
3. **Rust Async and Tokio** — Official site and documentation for the Tokio async runtime. https://tokio.rs/
4. **Rayon for Parallelism** — Crate for data-parallel collection processing. https://crates.io/crates/rayon
5. **Rust CLI Development with Clap** — Command-line argument parsing. https://docs.rs/clap
6. **Regex Crate** — Regular expression matching for text processing. https://docs.rs/regex
7. **Rustonomicon** — Unsafe Rust, memory layout, lifetimes, and raw pointers. https://doc.rust-lang.org/nomicon/

Community

1. **Rust Users Forum** — Official forum for Rust questions and community topics. https://users.rust-lang.org/
2. **Stack Overflow (Rust Tag)** — Community Q&A for Rust implementation problems. https://stackoverflow.com/questions/tagged/rust
3. **Reddit r/rust** — Discussions, announcements, and learning resources. https://www.reddit.com/r/rust/

Reference works

1. **Rust Reference** — Formal and complete reference for the Rust language. https://doc.rust-lang.org/reference/
2. **Crates.io** — Registry of open-source Rust libraries (crates). https://crates.io

Index

www.ingramcontent.com/pod-product-compliance
Ingram Content Group UK Ltd.
Pitfield, Milton Keynes, MK11 3LW, UK
UKHW051118290926
15471UKWH00010B/1743

9 789083 574806